VILLAGES IN INDONESIA

Map 1. Location of Village Communities

KOENTJARANINGRAT

VILLAGES
IN
INDONESIA

EQUINOX
PUBLISHING
JAKARTA   KUALA LUMPUR

EQUINOX PUBLISHING (ASIA) PTE LTD
No 3. Shenton Way
#10-05 Shenton House
Singapore 068805

www.EquinoxPublishing.com

Villages In Indonesia
by Koentjaraningrat

ISBN 979-3780-51-7

First Equinox Edition 2007

Preface

Within the territorial confines of the Indonesian nation live people representing a wide variety of ethnic groups. Although a growing number of her people are moving to urban centers, the village continues to be the home of the great majority of Indonesia's 105 million citizens. But, just as there is ethnic diversity among her people, wide variety is also exhibited among her villages.

Up to the present time, it has been difficult to assess the true range of diversity in Indonesian villages because of a lack of up-to-date, comparable descriptive studies. Such village studies as exist are mostly written in Dutch and are scattered in numerous ethnographies, *adat* law monographs, or as separately published articles which are becoming obsolete or difficult to obtain. This lack of modern village studies was generally felt to constitute a major gap in the literature on contemporary Indonesia. The idea of filling this gap by the publication of a collection of contemporary descriptive studies of Indonesian villages was first broached to colleagues in 1961 during the informal sessions at the Tenth Pacific Science Congress in Honolulu, and afterwards at the Annual Meeting of the American Anthropological Association in Philadelphia. The suggestion received a favorable response, and during the following months I developed an outline for the book and began to solicit articles. Originally, fourteen Indonesian, American, and Dutch specialists, all with relatively recent field experience, were invited to participate in the project. All fourteen accepted the invitation, although four later withdrew. Two additional scholars joined the project in 1963, bringing the number of villages covered to thirteen. The long process of preparing the manuscript for the publisher was completed in June 1964.

In comparison with the prewar published literature on Indonesian villages, the data presented in the chapters of this book are relatively recent. Rarak is studied between 1954 and 1956, Soba between 1959 and 1961, Telang between 1963 and 1964, Kutagamber between 1961 and 1962, Allang between 1960 and 1961, while Muremarēw was visited by the author in the middle of the year 1959. The description of Bontoramba applies to the years prior to the outbreak of World War II, but the author has revisited the village in 1948 and 1949. The other villages, Tihingan, Tjelapar, Kaliredjo, and Situradja are studied by the authors respectively between 1957 and 1958, between 1958 and 1959, between 1956 and 1957, and between 1956 and 1957; while the data from Djagakarsa and Taram refer to the situation in 1960.

The descriptions of the thirteen villages are arranged according to the type of subsistence system upon which the economy of each is based. The villages of Rarak, Soba, Telang, Kutagamber, and Allang, described in Chapters II–VI, are all associated with a swidden agricultural subsistence economy. A primitive West Irian community of sago gatherers is described in Chapter VII. The villages of Bontoramba, Tihingan, Tjelapar, Kaliredjo, Situradja, Djagakarsa, and *negeri* Taram, covered in Chapters VIII–XIV, are associated with sedentary agricultural economies. It should be mentioned that Djagakarsa, a community of fruit gardeners located near a large metropolitan city, represents a special type of village.

The collection of village surveys presented in this book is designed not only to illustrate the range of Indonesia's ethnic diversity, but also to provide greater understanding of the social phenomena and processes that form an integral part of the contemporary Indonesian village. It is hoped that these studies will stimulate future research in this field, especially in the formulation and testing of hypotheses concerning the general nature of the social system characteristic of the Indonesian village.

Like the editor, the majority of the contributors are anthropologists. Representatives of other disciplines are Harsja Bachtiar, primarily a sociologist; Kampto Utomo, an agronomist; and Hendrik T. Chabot, an authority on *adat* law. Although the individual contributions reflect the particular interests of their respective authors, certain general anthropological topics have been covered by each author in order to facilitate comparison among the various studies.

In the treatment of orthography, it has been impossible to adopt consistent spellings for certain terms that recur in different sections because each writer has followed the local usage or pronunciation of his respective area. The term for an Islamic marriage contract, for example, is pronounced *nika* in Rarak, *nikka* in Bontoramba, and *nikah* in *negeri* Taram. Indonesian geographical names have been used (e.g., Kalimantan for Borneo, Irian for New Guinea), but the standard international terms and orthography have been retained for Java.

The funds required for translating certain chapters, typing the manuscript, and preparing the maps and charts were granted by the Ministry of National Research of the Republic of Indonesia. I wish to express my sincere gratitude to His Excellency Professor Dr. Soedjono D. Poesponegoro, the Minister of National Research, for his support of my project.

I also wish to express my appreciation to all the persons who have assisted in bringing this volume to completion. In particular, I wish to acknowledge my indebtedness to Alfred B. Hudson and Judith M. Hudson, who have carefully checked the English of the chapters that were translated or written by non-English-speaking authors, and who have made numerous useful suggestions for improvement of the whole manuscript. Finally, a special word of thanks is due to Professor George McT. Kahin of Cornell University for the special interest he has demonstrated in the publication of this symposium.

KOENTJARANINGRAT

University of Indonesia
January 1966

Contents

ix

List of Maps

Villages in Indonesia

Chapter I

A Survey of Social Studies on Rural Indonesia

KOENTJARANINGRAT
UNIVERSITY OF INDONESIA

1. The Earliest Accounts of Rural Indonesia

Since time immemorial, the attention of the outside world must have been drawn toward Indonesian villages and village life, when first Indonesian native rulers and later European colonial governments tried to understand and control village social forces. Today, however, we can only obtain a few insights into the nature of this relationship through the records left by western Europeans of their contacts with the Indonesian rural population. The earliest records come from travelers and sailors, from explorers, from missionaries, from translators of the Bible, and from civil servants of the colonial administration.

The travelers, whose contact with the populations of the coastal villages was usually quite brief, consequently wrote very sketchy accounts of Indonesian coastal peoples that mainly stressed peculiar or ridiculous elements. Such is, for example, the information on several places in Sumatra, Nusa Tenggara (Lesser Sunda Islands), and Maluku (Moluccas) that is recorded in the *Suma Oriental*, an account from 1512 of travels from Malaya to China by way of Indonesia, written by a Portuguese merchant, Tomé Pires (A. Cortesão 1944, I, 135–228; II, 230–289), or also the descriptions from 1521 of the coastal populations on Alor, Timor, and several other islands in East Indonesia, recorded in the diary of Antonio Pigafetta, one of the officers on the ship of Juan de Elcano; Elcano succeeded Captain Fernao Magelhães after the latter's death in Matan, the Philippines, on the famous round-the-world journey (Le Roux 1928).

Explorers, who were very often geographers, botanists, or zoologists by training, generally also had only very brief contacts with the populations of the villages they passed through on their expeditions. Many did not seem particularly interested in things they encountered on their way (Sirks 1915), or were attracted only by peculiar cultural phenomena, as, for example, cannibalism among the Batak (Burton 1855, Friedmann 1871). To several explorers of Indonesia, however, we are indebted for their early descriptions of the rural populations. A Swiss botanist, H. Zollinger, who explored several areas in South Sumatra, Java, South Sulawesi (Celebes), and in particular several islands of Nusa Tenggara in 1847, has given much valuable information on the cultures of these islands, which he included in his chapter on the fauna (1850). The British explorer H. O. Forbes, who traveled through the eastern islands of Indonesia (Forbes 1885), even wrote ethnographic accounts of the inhabitants of the Tanimbar Islands (1884) and Timor (1884a). Another explorer, C. B. H. von Rosenberg, in his reports of explorations to West and Central Sumatra, North Sulawesi, Maluku, and the Geelvink Bay in West Irian (New Guinea) around the year 1870, included much information on the people whom he met on his travels (Rosenberg 1878). Similarly, C. Schwaner, who explored the headwaters of the Barito River in Central Kalimantan (Borneo) during the years 1843–1847, gave brief descriptions on the village populations along the rivers in his two-volume book (1853–1854); L. M. d'Albertis, an ornithologist who spent several months exploring the northwest coast areas of Geelvink Bay, also included some data on the population in his report (1881). M. Krieger, a German doctor who explored the area of Humboldt Bay on the north coast of West Irian, even gave quite extensive details on the village life of the population (1899).

One scientific expedition, the Sumatra Expeditie, deserves our special attention. Consisting of twenty-three members, including specialists from various disciplines such as geographers, biologists, zoologists, and linguists, this expedition was planned and organized by P. J. Veth, at the time professor of Geography and Ethnology at the University of Leiden. Its two field teams explored Central Sumatra during the years 1877–1879 (Hasselt 1885). The nine-volume report called *Midden Sumatra* (1881–1892), edited by Veth, also included a wealth of information on the native populations of the areas visited by the expedition.

The next group, the missionaries, very often experienced longer and more intensive contact with the rural population, but their descriptions of rural cultures too often included subjective evaluations of the cultural elements described. An example of such a report is S. E. Harthoorn's article on Javanese Moslems (1857), which contrasted the miserable existence of the Javanese Moslems with that of the Javanese Christians, and also C. Hupe's description of the religious practices of the inland population of Kalimantan (1846), which organized the descriptive data according to the Christian concepts of *godsdienst* (religion) and *bijgeloof* (superstition). Many similar articles were published in the missionary journal *Mededeelingen van Wege het Nederlandsche Zendelinggenootschap*, which started in 1857. Some early missionary reports, however, are more valuable than the ones already mentioned. M. Teffer's brief description of a shamanistic ritual in Boana (Maluku) is one example (1860); P. N. Wilken's article on the rural population of the Minahasa, North Sulawesi (1863), among whom he had worked as a missionary, is also a very useful early source on the area. Similar in nature are: N. Graafland's elaborate two-volume account of his travels among the Minahasa to check on the Christian schools there (1867–1869); C. Poensen's very valuable early descriptions of Javanese folklore, including systems of numerology and curing (1864–1865), on naming ceremonies (1870), on *wajang* (shadow puppet) plays (1872–1873), on housebuilding and architecture (1875), on clothing (1876–1877), and several others. Finally B. Hagen's general description on the Batak religion (1892), although only based on data of one particular group, in the Karo region, is, in addition to G. K. Niemann's article (1870), one of the first sources of information on the area.

Dutch translators of the Bible who worked in Indonesia were usually linguists who had received intensive training at the University of Leiden, an institution with an outstanding reputation as the center for the study of Oriental languages during the eighteenth century (Nat 1929). Attempts by missionaries to translate the Bible into Malay started as early as the seventeenth century with the Dutch—A. C. Ruyl in 1629, M. Leydekker in 1692—and about thirty years later with the Swiss G. H. Werndly (Boetzelaer van Asperen en Dubbeldam 1941). Several of the Bible translators did excellent pioneering work in the study of various Indonesian languages and folk cultures. During the second half of the eighteenth century, the Bible translator B. F. Matthes not only made the earliest studies on the Macassarese and Buginese languages of South Sulawesi but also wrote many reports on the cultures of these ethnic groups (see Kennedy 1955, II, 325, 338–339, 344). Similarly, H. N. van der Tuuk

4 · Villages in Indonesia

made excellent pioneering studies in the Toba Batak villages of North Sumatra, at approximately the same time as Matthes (see Kennedy 1955, I, 162).

The most important group of people who have written about rural Indonesia were members of administrative branches of the colonial governments. In addition to long intensive contact with the rural population, they were supposed to be informed about the social problems in their respective areas.

The officials of the oldest colonial authority in Indonesia, namely the Dutch East India Company (V.O.C.), did not leave many valuable records to document their concern with or comprehension of the social problems of the Indonesian population.

The British officials were more productive. Among them, W. Marsden paid attention to the rural population of Sumatra and wrote descriptions of the ethnic groups of "Menangcabau, Malays, Achenese, Battas, Rejangs, Lampoons," which are published in his book *The History of Sumatra* (1783). The greatest part of this book, however, concentrates on the Redjang, the rural population of Bengkulu, where Marsden worked as a civil servant during the period when this part of South Sumatra was still a British colony.[1] Only a small part treats comparatively briefly the other Sumatran ethnic groups, information which Marsden usually obtained from secondary sources (Wink 1924).[2] Sir Thomas Stamford Raffles, head of the British colonial government during British rule between 1811 and 1816, also devoted special attention to the Indonesian rural population, in particular that of Java, in order to introduce a new system of land revenue, the land-rent system. For that reason, Raffles appointed a commission, consisting of four officials under the chairmanship of Colin Mackenzie, to investigate the various land tenure systems in Java. Early in 1812, the members of the commission started their work by traveling individually through the rural areas of Java to inter-

[1] For W. Marsden's life and career, see his autobiography (1838).
[2] On the Redjang, Marsden presented material on the physical characteristics of the people, on clothing, on implements and technology, on houses and traditional architecture, on food, on production and subsistence economics, on social organization, on *adat* law and *adat* norms, and on ritual and beliefs; on the Minangkabau, by contrast, he only discussed several peculiars about the Sultan of Minangkabau; on the Batak he used only two pages to talk about cannibalism; while the section on Atjeh is mainly an account of the region's history.

view local administrative officials. The magnitude of the project, the difficulties in communication which forced the researchers to confine their investigations to those villages which were easily accessible, the language difficulties in dealing with the interviewees, and the superficial methods of investigation did not produce a very insightful view of the social institutions of rural Java (Bastin 1954).

Most of the Dutch civil servants following the period of British control were relatively unsophisticated concerning the social institutions of rural Indonesia, due to their insufficient training. However, the quality of the Dutch colonial civil servant seems to have improved considerably after the establishment of training courses for colonial administrators in 1842, a program which became an academy in 1864 and finally a department of the University of Leiden in 1891. An important part of the curriculum was devoted to courses on Indonesian cultures and languages, *Indologie* (see Hoëvell 1849; Pijnappel 1859, 1863, 1868; Snouck Hurgronje 1924; Leur 1932; Boeke 1938). Numerous valuable articles on various aspects of rural social life in Indonesia, written by administrative officials during their service in their respective areas, appeared in the journal of the colonial civil service, the *Tijdschrift voor Nederlandsch Indië*, or in another important journal, *Tijdschrift voor Indische Taal-, Land- en Volkenkunde*, published by the Bataviaasch Genootschap van Kunsten en Wetenschappen, an important scientific association established in 1778 in Djakarta. Several writings of government officials were also published as separate monographs: the description of Mandailing Batak *adat* law (1846)[3] and the report of the exploration of the island of Buru in Maluku (1858), which give much information on the customs of the population, by T. J. Willer, a civil servant with long experience in North Sumatra, Riau, West Kalimantan, East Java, and Maluku; several works of L. T. Mayer, a civil servant who became a serious student of Javanese language and culture (1893, 1894, 1897, 1898).[4] Descriptions of various elements and aspects of cultures of Gorontalo in North Sulawesi, Biliton, Timor, and Ambon were published by J. G. F. Riedel, a Dutch civil

---

[3] Willer published a general description in English of the Mandailing Batak of the early eighteenth century in the *Journal of the Indian Archipelago and Eastern Asia* (1849, 366–378), edited by a British government official in Singapore, J. R. Logan.

[4] Mayers' early textbooks of Javanese language that are not included in Kennedy's bibliography are: *Javaansch-Hollandsche Samenspraken* (1894b) and *Javaansche Legenden en Sagen* (1894a).

servant with thirty years of experience (between 1853 and 1883), either as articles in journals or as books (see Kennedy 1955, I, 232, 236; II, 326, 330, 355, 366, 376–378, 382, 582, 583, 591, 602, 612, 624, 656). One of the books, *De Sluik- en Kroesharige Rassen Tusschen Selebes en Papua* (1886), a comprehensive account of the peoples occupying the islands between Sulawesi and Irian, brought Riedel international renown among European anthropologists. Finally, the writings of G. A. Wilken, a civil servant who also became an anthropologist of international fame, will be discussed separately in the next section.

2. George Alexander Wilken

George Alexander Wilken was the son of P. N. Wilken, the missionary in North Sulawesi mentioned previously. He began his career in 1869 as a civil servant for the Dutch colonial government in Buru (Maluku), Gorontalo and Ratahan (North Sulawesi), Sipirok and Mandailing (North Sumatra). During his career as a civil servant, he wrote early descriptive articles discussing land tenure and naming rituals among the Minahasa (Wilken 1873, 1875), a short ethnography of the island Buru in Maluku (1875a), and also theoretical articles like those on the evolution of marriage and the family (1880, 1881). In this last article Wilken outlined Bachofen's evolutionary stages of promiscuity, matriarchate, patriarchate, and parental family, using a wealth of illustrative material taken mainly from Indonesia.[5] After his appointment as lecturer at the academy for civil servants in 1883, his *honoris causa* doctorate in 1884, and his appointment as professor of *land- en volkenkunde van Nederlandsch-Indië* (ethnology of Indonesia) in 1885, he devoted his life entirely to ethnology (see Kindern 1892).

Wilken's subsequent work was mainly theoretical in nature and concentrated on the extensive ethnographic material of the Indonesian cultural area. Occasionally he referred to comparative material in ethnographies treating groups in other parts of the world, like the Bisaja (Bisaya) and Tagala (Tagalok), Fiji, Shoshoni, Abipon, Arawak; much material on the classical cultures of Greece and Rome and the Semitic peoples from West Asia was introduced through quoting such scholars as Robertson Smith. Wilken formulated theories on numerous cultural

[5] Wilken later seems to have abandoned the concept of promiscuity as the earliest stage in the evolution of the human family (cf. Wilken 1886, 150, footnote 35).

and social phenomena, for instance on teknonymy (1875); on the essence of the bride price, which he thought initially to be nothing more than a means of reconciliation between the groom and the bride's family following an elopement, a frequent occurrence during the evolutionary change between the matriarchate and patriarchate stages (1880, 662, 655–659, 662–664); on exogamy (1880, 614–617); on property and inheritance in relation to marriage and the family (1883, 1883a); on the custom of levirate (1883); on animism in Indonesia (1884, 1885); on the meaning of totemism (1885, 991–1000); on circumcision rituals in Indonesia (1885a); on marriage by elopement (1886); on the counting of days among the people of Malayo-Polynesia (1886a); on the material culture of northwest Irian (1887); on *adat* law (1888); on the emergence and diffusion of matriarchate in Sumatra (1888a); on tooth mutilation in Indonesia (1888b); on the couvade in Indonesia (1889); on marriage rituals and wedding ceremonies in Indonesia (1889a); on the worship of skulls in Indonesia (1889b); on the problem of incest (1890); on marriage and inheritance in South Sumatra (1891); on child marriage (1891a); and on offertory rituals (1891b).

These cultural and social phenomena were usually connected in one way or another with Wilken's basic theory of the evolution of the family. His view of animism is based on Tylor's concepts, but on the other hand, his concept of totemism, which, according to him, was originally the belief in the sacredness of animal species in which ancestors' spirits had been reincarnated, considerably influenced Tylor's own view on the subject (cf. Tylor 1899, 146–148). Finally, Wilken's views on customary law in Indonesia are often considered the basis for the development of several concepts of Indonesian *adat* law (Vollenhoven 1928, 101–102). Consequently, Wilken's articles on *adat* law have been collected in a single volume, *Opstellen over Adatrecht* (1926), in addition to the four-volume *De Verspreide Geschriften* (1912).

3. Intensification of Exploration and Field Work after Wilken

Few of Wilken's students became anthropologists or ethnologists in the formal sense of the word. An important scholar with an international reputation like S. R. Steinmetz is often classified as a sociologist, but he did not concentrate exclusively on Indonesian studies and much of his work did not attract the attention of specialists on Indonesia.[6] Many of the explorations and the field-work projects carried out very intensively in the period after Wilken were usually also performed by nonprofessionals.

One of the travelers who had visited Indonesia on several world tours as ship's doctor was Adolf Bastian. The result of this visit was the five-volume *Indonesien; oder die Inseln des Malayischen Archipel* (1884–1894), an extensive but unsystematic conglomeration of his notes.

Intensive exploration of several areas of Indonesia during the late nineteenth and early twentieth centuries was sometimes carried out by medical doctors but more usually by geographers or biologists. Two famous explorers, P. Sarasin and F. Sarasin, traveled extensively in North and Central Sulawesi, between the years 1893 and 1896 and also between 1902 and 1903, and included much information on the population of the area in their report (1905). An expedition to investigate Central Sumatra in 1906, led by a German explorer, A. Maass, published an extensive two-volume report, also including considerable information on the population of Kuantan, Gunung Sahilan, and Kampar Kiri (Maass 1910–1912). Another expedition to Sumatra, Java, and Nusa Tenggara led by the geographer J. Elbert and sponsored by the Frankfurter Vereins für Geographie und Statistik produced a book on the physical features of the islands that also included some information on the rural populations of Bali, Lombok, Sumbawa, Salayer, Flores, Wetar, Muna, and Buton (Elbert, 1911–1912). Very important also was the exploration of Central Kalimantan sponsored by the Maatschappij tot Bevordering van het Natuurkundig Onderzoek der Nederlandsche Koloniën. Three expeditions in 1893, 1896, and 1898 under the leadership of a medical doctor, A. W. Nieuwenhuis, finally succeeded in crossing Kalimantan, starting from Pontianak, on the west coast, journeying up the Kapuas River to its headwaters, crossing the Central Kalimantan jungle to the headwaters of the Mahakam, and then going downstream to Samarinda on the east coast (Nieuwenhuis 1898, 1900). Much data on the ethnic groups inhabiting the area of the Kapuas and the Mahakam rivers like the Ulu-Air, the Kajan Mandalam, the Bahau Mahakam, and the Apo Kajan, were

[6] Some information on S. R. Steinmetz's contribution to anthropology is included in A. J. Köbben's article, originally published in the Dutch journal *Mensch en Maatschappij*, afterward in the *Journal of the Royal Anthropological Institute*, and recently in F. W. Moore's volume on cross-cultural methodology (1961, 175–192).

included in the two-volume reports of the second (1900) and third (1904–1907) expeditions. Nieuwenhuis himself became a professional anthropologist who published many articles, especially in the *Internationales Archiv für Ethnographie*, and was appointed as professor in anthropology at the University of Leiden in 1904.

The same institute that sponsored Nieuwenhuis' expeditions was also very active in West Irian, especially after an article appeared by a member of the Dutch parliament (Colijn 1907, 7), suggesting more intensive exploration and research in the colonies, which might lead to more effective exploitation. A series of almost 140 expeditions, sponsored by the above-mentioned institute and also by many other associations or corporations, as, for instance, Mijnbouw Maatschappij Nederlandsch Nieuw Guinea, were carried out between the years 1900 and 1914. Most of those expeditions are listed in Le Roux's handbook on West Irian (1935, I, 32–35, 64–74).

The later missionaries were also intensive explorers of the Indonesian rural populations. Many had more or less detailed training in Indonesian languages and ethnology and thus were more able than their earlier colleagues to investigate the cultures of the rural populations. Among those in the period after Wilken who have, beside their missionary work, written valuable early ethnographic information (mainly on religious practices of various ethnic groups in their respective areas) are: J. L. van der Toorn, who wrote on the kinship system of the Minangkabau, including an early list of the kin terms (1881), and on animism in the area (1890), as well as several articles on the Minangkabau language; F. Grabowsky, who published several articles, usually in the journal *Internationales Archiv für Ethnographie*, on the religion of the Ulu Ngadju in southeast Kalimantan (1888, 1889, 1889a, 1892); J. H. Meerwaldt, who wrote on Toba Batak culture, among other articles a peculiar one on survivals of matriarchate (1892), and also articles and a book on the Toba Batak language; G. L. Bink, who produced the earliest accounts of the inhabitants of the Humboldt Bay, West Irian (1897, 1902); J. H. Neumann, author of numerous books and articles on the Karo Batak (see Kennedy 1955, I, 156–157); F. and J. Warneck, who did the same on the Toba Batak (see Kennedy 1955, I, 170–171); M. C. Schadee, who wrote on the religion of several ethnic groups in Kalimantan (1903–1908); J. Woensdregt, who produced a great deal on the Tobadak of Central Sulawesi (see Kennedy 1955, II, 356); and A. Hueting, who has written much on the inhabitants of Tobelo, northern Maluku (see Kennedy 1955,

II, 653–654). More recent missionary ethnographers are: P. Drabbe, who has written many articles on the Jamdena of East Tanimbar, South Maluku, and an important ethnography on the same ethnic group (1940); P. Middelkoop, who until quite recently was one of the few specialists on Timor (cf. Kennedy 1955, II, 590); H. Geurtjens, the specialist on the Tanimbar and Kai islands of South Maluku (see Kennedy 1955, II, 623, 625–626) and Southwest Irian (Geurtjens 1921, 1926, 1928, 1933); and Wilhelm Schmidt's students, P. Arndt, J. A. J. Verheijen, and B. A. G. Vroklage, who were looking for traces of high gods or collecting material for the construction of *Kulturkreise* and *Kulturschichten*, respectively, among the Ngadha and the Sikka of Central Flores (Arndt 1929–1931, 1932, 1936–1937, 1939), the inhabitants of Adonare and Solor, north of Flores (Arndt 1951), the Dongo near Bima, East Sumbawa (Arndt 1952), the Manggarai of West Flores (Verheijen 1951), and various other ethnic groups in East Indonesia (Vroklage 1936, 1949). Apart from these missionary ethnographers, one field worker deserves our specific attention: A. C. Kruyt.

Kruyt began his missionary work in Gorontalo, North Sulawesi, but his main area was Central Sulawesi, where he worked intensively among the Bare'e and among the Western Toradja. It is on these ethnic groups that he has written his main works: the three-volume ethnography on the Bare'e, in cooperation with the linguist N. Adriani (Adriani and Kruyt 1912–1914), the four volumes on the Western Toradja (Kruyt 1938), and approximately one hundred other articles published in various journals (see Kennedy 1955, I, 32–33, 153, 247–248; II, 325, 329, 350–354, 357, 359, 362, 363, 366, 374–375, 577, 585, 589). Afterwards Kruyt also visited several other places in Indonesia—for instance, Rote, Sumba, and Timor in Nusa Tenggara, the Mentawai Islands west of Sumatra, and East Sulawesi (Kruyt 1921, 1921a, 1924)—and wrote ethnographies on the rural populations of the above-mentioned places (1921b, 1922, 1923, 1923a, 1930). In addition, he wrote numerous other articles on various elements of these cultures and also several theoretical ones.[7]

According to his critics, the tremendous number of articles Kruyt wrote included only pure descriptive data, which were reported in an unprofessional way, without any framework or integrating scheme. This made his ethnographies "meer feitenopsommingen dan functioneele studies" (more factual summaries than functional studies; Fischer 1948–1949, 484). In a later stage of his work, he seems to have made

[7] Information about A. C. Kruyt and his works are included in an article by M. C. Capelle (1951) and in H. T. Fischer's obituary (1948–1949).

extensive use of the *Notes and Queries on Anthropology*, which indeed
improved his ethnographic descriptions after 1920. Kruyt's intensive
factual knowledge of several Toradja cultures and extensive comprehension of comparative material from other parts of rural Indonesia provided
a basis for the development of some theoretical concepts. Very important,
for example, was his concept of animism, which he explained as a religious
complex based on belief in an impersonal supernatural essence, or *zielestof*,
present in the environment of man. He called the religious complex based
on belief in more personal spiritual beings *spiritisme* (1906). Kruyt's
concept of *zielestof* influenced several field workers, including the previously mentioned missionary J. Warneck, who considered the Batak
religious concept *tondi* as *Seelenstoff* (Warneck 1909); and the ethnolo-
gist E. Camerling, who, in making a study of ancestor worship among
various ethnic groups on the Southeast Asian mainland and in Indonesia
(1928), still used Kruyt's concept long after its modification. Kruyt
himself altered his concept after a critique of his book on animism appeared, written by G. P. Rouffaer (1907), and shifted to the concept
of pre-animism (see Kruyt 1918–1920) to explain the background of
such cultural phenomena in Central Sulawesi as the magical aspect of
the sales price (1923b), magical knots, and the practice of the *Hocker-
bestattung*, burial in the sitting position (1937).

Among translators of the Bible, special mention must be made of
Kruyt's contemporary, N. Adriani, a philologist and linguist who spent
recurrent periods between 1895 and 1919 among the rural population
of Central Sulawesi to make an intensive study of the Bare'e language
under the sponsorship of the Nederlandsch Bijbelgenootschap. Besides a
grammar, a dictionary, and texts, he also wrote numerous articles on
Bare'e cultural and social life that were later republished in three volumes,
Verzamelde Geschriften (1932).

Intensive exploration of many places in Indonesia was also undertaken
by members of the Dutch colonial civil administration. Especially in
the interior of West Irian, several have done important ethnographic
work. Others have gathered valuable information about disappearing customs of the Indonesian rural population, like M. Joustra, who wrote
numerous books on the Karo, Toba, and other Batak customs and languages of the early twentieth century and who has also written a comprehensive book on the Minangkabau people (see Kennedy 1955, I,
151–152, 176). Most civil administrators contributed valuable data on
various aspects of the folk culture and society of the rural populations
in their respective areas, while several have written ethnographies which

until recently have been the only comprehensive sources for particular areas. A great deal of this material has become obsolete, but it still proves valuable as a starting point for modern social studies. G. D. Willinck's large ethnography of the Minangkabau, for example (1909), although written on the basis of obsolete concepts, is still a rich source to which recent social studies often must return;[8] E. E. W. G. Schröder's voluminous description of the culture and language of Nias, west of Sumatra, is still the only comprehensive source on the island's population (1917); while Snouck Hurgronje's work on Atjeh and Gajo needs special attention.

C. Snouck Hurgronje was a scholar in Semitic and Arabic philology and an experienced student of the Islamic religion and its institutions. He started his Indonesian career in 1889 as adviser for Islamic affairs to the Dutch colonial government. In 1891–1892 he conducted research on the Atjehnese in North Sumatra from a distance, by extensively interviewing a stratified sample of informants coming from the rural areas to Kutaradja, the capital of Atjeh (1893–1894, I, 11–16). His research, which mainly concentrated on the problem of Islamic influences on the social, political, and religious systems of the Atjehnese people, could not be conducted by visiting Atjehnese villages, because it seemed to be too dangerous for Dutchmen to leave the towns or cities during the Atjeh War. The result was, however, the important two-volume ethnography (1893–1894). After his appointment as professor in Arabic at the University of Leiden, Snouck Hurgronje continued his interest in Indonesian Islam and Islamic law. Consequently he is also considered as one of the pioneers for Indonesian *adat* law studies (see Vollenhoven 1928, 106–110). His total work, apart from his two volume description of Mecca (1888–1889), consists of the seven volume *Verspreide Geschriften*.

4. Government Commissions to Survey the Social Conditions in Rural Indonesia

Apart from the members of the Dutch civil service, who carried out research in their respective areas individually, the Dutch colonial

[8] The book received a favorable review by F. C. Hekmeyer (1909) but very sharp criticism by professional social scientists like F. D. E. van Ossenbruggen (1911a) and P. E. de Josselin de Jong (1951, 15–17).

government several times sponsored extensive surveys concerning social institutions at the village level, with methods of investigation similar to the Mackenzie land-tenure survey already mentioned.

In 1867, for example, an official commission consisting of three residents (administrative officials subordinate to the governor) was appointed to investigate twenty-nine previously defined problems in rural Java and Madura concerning patterns of individual property, communal property, and the relationship between the two systems. According to the instructions, the three investigators were to travel over most of Java to interview local officials, even including the village heads of at least two villages per district, within a period of approximately nine to twelve months. They were guided by an extensive list of leading questions, which covered fifty-five printed folio pages (see Eindrésumé 1876, ix–lxiv). The investigators, however, managed to complete their gigantic task and submitted a preliminary report to their superiors in 1870. The final report was completed in three stages and published as *Eindrésumé* (Eindrésumé 1876, 1880; Bergsma 1896). Taking into consideration the extensive methods of investigation upon which the survey was based, the results could only have been superficial; yet, the three-volume final report does include a large amount of early data on systems and patterns of land tenure and land property in Java and Madura which can still be considered valuable as points of departure for modern social studies.

In 1888, a similar survey to investigate recruitment systems and customs of corvée labor was carried out by a team appointed by the colonial government, under the leadership of F. Fokkens. The final report, which was published as a one-volume *Eindrésumé* (Fokkens 1903), includes much information on systems of labor recruitment in village communities of Java and Madura and, if used critically, is still very useful as an early source on the subject.

In accordance with the initiation of the new "ethical policy" at the beginning of the twentieth century, the colonial government needed information on the causes of the diminishing welfare of the Indonesian rural population. An official commission to carry out a gigantic investigation on the low living standards of the village populations of Java and Madura, called the Commissie van Onderzoek naar de Mindere Welvaart der Inlandsche Bevolking (Commission for the Investigation of the Diminishing Welfare of the Indonesian Population), was inaugurated in 1902. The investigation was carried out by 594 research workers, consisting of social scientists and members of the civil administration in the various local areas of Java and Madura. The first two years were spent in completing the research design and producing an extensive list of 533 questions to guide the field workers (see Does 1948, 259–265). The tremendous volume of material accumulated during the next twelve years of extensive research included information on many aspects of the economic and social life of Javanese village communities, such as fishery, poultry farming, animal husbandry, communications, agriculture, trade, cottage industries, irrigation, law, social control and police, village economics, basic personality traits, child marriage, criminality, prostitution, gambling, food and diet, housing, hygiene, savings, and capital formation. The reports were published periodically between 1905 and 1920 and in all filled thirty volumes. The material included in these volumes, however, is very poorly organized and thus difficult to use. In addition, it has often proved unreliable, due to the superficial and extensive methods used during the investigations. No student of Javanese village life, however, can ever neglect the thirty-volume report of this commission.

5. *The Various Branches of* Indologie *in Relation to Anthropology*

At the end of the nineteenth century and the beginning of the twentieth, *Indologie*, or Indonesian studies, very rapidly developed into a number of specializations. The study of Indonesian languages was developed by philologists and historians; the study of Indonesian Islam, by specialists in Islamic history who usually also had basic training in philology. The study of village communities, which in many other countries often became the responsibility of social anthropologists, was carried out in Indonesia by a number of social scientists with differing backgrounds. The study of Indonesian folklore was usually handled by philologists; the study of customary law and the description of village community social organization was carried out by *adat* law scholars with basic training in law or by civil servants; the study of rural economics, local agriculture, and demography was done primarily by agronomists, economists, or civil servants. As G. J. Held, the Dutch anthropologist, has correctly described the situation, anthropology in Indonesia became "a science of leftovers" (1953, 868).

The different kinds of Dutch scholars paid very little attention to the work that had been done in Indonesia by non-Dutch anthropologists in the period between the two world wars; such anthropological activity never became fully integrated into Dutch *Indologie*. The articles of the German geographer and ethnographer, M. Moszkowski, reporting his travels and research in the Rokan and Siak areas of Central and East Sumatra in 1907 (see Kennedy 1955, I, 209), are not frequently quoted by Dutch specialists in Indonesian studies. His description on the population of the Mamberamo area in West Irian (1911), however, received much more attention from Dutch West Irian specialists. The work of W. Kaudern, a Swedish museum anthropologist who, during the three years from 1917 to 1920, had done field work in Central Sulawesi and written a number of articles on games, dances, musical instruments, art objects and art motifs, megalithic remains, fishing equipment, and migrations of the various ethnic groups inhabiting Central Sulawesi (1925–1944), stands very much on its own. J. Belo's articles on various aspects of Balinese rural life (see Kennedy 1955, II, 560–561) did not receive much attention from Dutch Indologists, nor did the work on Bali of the Mexican anthropologist, M. Covarrubias (see Kennedy 1955, II, 561–562), although his book (1938) became popular among laymen. M. Mead's and G. Bateson's approach to Balinese personality[9] in the village Bajung Gdé was largely unknown to the majority of the Dutch social scientists in the period around 1935, as was C. Du Bois's study of the personality of the Atimelang villagers on the island of Alor in East Indonesia (1944).[10] The work of the German anthropologists A. E. Jensen, H. Niggemeyer, and J. Röder, who explored the island of Ceram in Maluku (Jensen and Niggemeyer 1939, Jensen 1948, Röder 1948), and who also visited Kapaur, on West Irian's west coast, under the sponsorship of the Frobenius Forschungsinstitut für Kulturmorphologie (Röder 1940), also remained largely unnoticed.

The work of two non-Dutch anthropologists, however, did receive some attention. E. M. Loeb, an American anthropologist who has written articles on Mentawai and Sumatra (1928, 1929, 1929a, 1933, 1933–1934),

[9] For references to G. Bateson and M. Mead's work, see Kennedy 1955, II, 560, 565.
[10] Studies on the relation of culture and personality, however, have been made in Indonesia by Dutch anthropologists, e.g., by the previously mentioned A. W. Nieuwenhuis, based on the methods of product analysis and thematic analysis (1913), by clinical psychologists like C. F. Engelhard (1923) and P. van Schilfgaarde (1925), and by A. Kits van Heyningen, who applied several psychological tests to a sample of teachers and pupils in Langsa, Atjeh (1925).

has been criticized by H. T. Fischer for his careless use of the concept of cross-cousin marriage in his theory about the diffusion of a "Dravidian-Australian kinship system" (Fischer 1936). The numerous books and articles of P. Wirz, a German anthropologist, on the Sentani Lake area of northern West Irian, on the Swart Valley in the central highland of West Irian, on the Marindanim area of southern West Irian, on southeast Kalimantan, on Nias, and the Mentawai Islands west of Sumatra (1924, 1925, 1926, 1928–1929, 1929, 1929a, 1929–1930, 1931, 1950), were frequently quoted.

Generally, however, we may say that, for almost three decades at the beginning of the twentieth century, anthropology as practiced both by Dutch and by non-Dutch anthropologists failed to find an important place among the various specializations which constituted Indonesian social studies. Quite different was the case with *adat* law studies.

6. *The Study of* Adat *Law in Indonesia*[11]

The Dutch had recognized, even in the early period of the Dutch East India Company, the existence of particular systems of indigenous customary law quite different from their own legal system, but they had not paid attention to them. In the early days of colonial administration, the Dutch had not felt the need to deal with the social problems of the Indonesian rural population, as they ruled Indonesia only through indigenous states or local princedoms. Even when, throughout the nineteenth and early twentieth centuries, several parts of Indonesia came under the closer control of the Dutch colonial government, attention toward and deeper understanding of these various systems of customary law did not develop immediately. A general fallacy which prevailed initially, even among some scholars and Indonesian specialists like L. W. C. van den Berg (1892, 1897), was the notion that local legal systems could be studied through their law books or through Hindu and Moslem religious legal codes. The quite different aspects of *adat* law which manifest themselves in the actual social life of rural Indonesia were consequently to be considered only as *afwijkingen*, or deviations, from the legal rules included in the indigenous Hindu or Moslem law codes.

---

[11] An excellent account of the development of *adat* law studies in Indonesia was written by C. van Vollenhoven (1928), and this book was initially reviewed by B. ter Haar (1929).

Certain officials in the administrative service, particularly those who were in close contact with the rural populations in their respective administrative areas, such as the aforementioned J. G. F. Riedel, J. H. F. Sollewijn Gelpke in Java, P. J. Kooreman in the Kerintji Highlands of West Sumatra, F. A. Liefrinck on Bali, and several others, never had such misconceptions. However, even though such scholars as G. A. Wilken, with great influence among Indonesian specialists, did not adhere to the fallacy either, it was not until the critical writings of C. Snouck Hurgronje and C. van Vollenhoven that the phenomena of *adat* law became generally recognized among Indonesian scholars as a subject to be studied with particular methods of investigation and analysis.

Snouck Hurgronje's comprehensive knowledge of Indonesian Islam made him conscious that Indonesian *adat* law was not just Moslem law with deviations but also contained many additional elements, with great variations as one moved from one Indonesian locality to another. He developed the concept that *adat* law indicates that part of a community's customs that have legal consequences, and thus he initiated the term "*adat* law" (1893–1894, I, 16, 357, 386; II, 354). Such an understanding of *adat* law consequently necessitated an extensive and comprehensive knowledge of both customs and social systems of the varied ethnic groups in Indonesia.

The lack of knowledge about the variety of Indonesian cultures in Indonesia was recognized and regretted by a broader circle of lawyers at the beginning of the twentieth century.[12] It was C. van Vollenhoven, however, who designed the framework for comparative studies of the diverse local customs in Indonesia. This scholar struggled to gain recognition for the phenomena of Indonesian *adat* law both among specialists on Indonesia and among key persons of the Dutch colonial government. He made further detailed criticisms of misconceptions about *adat* law (1909, 1919) and fought against attempts to unify or displace *adat* law with Western law. A large part of his work, however, was devoted to the accumulation of data on local customs and social systems throughout Indonesia. In order to have a framework into which this large amount of data could be classified and handled comprehensively, he designed

[12] In an article suggesting the possibilities of a legal system for Chinese in Indonesia, C. W. van Heeckeren, a lawyer, made the remark: "Het is te betreuren dat . . . niet . . . eene ernstige studie van de zeden en gewoonten der Inlanders van de rechters wordt gevorderd." (1901, 40).

the nineteen *adatrechtskringen*, or *adat* law areas (see Haar 1948, 5–10),[13] which were actually based on classification systems proposed by specialists in Malayo-Polynesian linguistics (Vollenhoven 1933).[14] Vollenhoven also directed the collection of factual data on decisions of judges from rural communities which were found in the previously published reports of travelers, explorers, missionaries, administrative officials, or anthropologists, as well as those from local official archives. From 1910 on, these pieces of information were published in a periodical called *Adatrecht-bundel* and thus were made easily accessible to all students of Indonesia. Another collection of data was published serially in ten volumes, the *Pandecten van het Adatrecht*, which includes selections from the literature on ethnological jurisprudence organized according to the particular categories of *adat* law that also were initially devised by Vollenhoven. His greatest achievement, a result of more than thirty years of work, was the comprehensive three-volume standard work on Indonesian *adat* law (1906–1933), a real magnum opus, which he himself modestly called *Legger* (register).

Another pioneer in the study of *adat* law also demands our special attention, F. D. E. van Ossenbruggen. His main role in the development of *adat* law studies was in achieving a deeper understanding of the institutional setting and the world view which form the background for legal activities in rural communities in Indonesia. This lawyer had long experience in the Dutch colonial service before he assumed the position of

[13] Hoebel and Schiller, in their introduction to the translation of ter Haar's textbook on Indonesian *adat* law, have incorrectly associated Vollenhoven's *adat* law areas with the culture areas of the American anthropologists (Haar 1948, 6). Although the purpose might be the same, i.e., to classify a large number of cultural elements from a great variety of diverse cultures, the way in which Vollenhoven's framework was constructed was quite different from the way in which C. Wissler and other American anthropologists established their culture areas (see Koentjaraningrat, 1958).

[14] Further intensive research done in particular areas by Vollenhoven's students has of course suggested changes in the rather rough classification system of their teacher. J. W. de Stoppelaar, for instance, working on the *adat* law system of Blambangan, East Java, considered it legitimate to split Vollenhoven's *adatrechtskring Middel- en Oost-Java met Madoera* into two separate *adat* law areas (1927, 115–132); similarly, G. Kuperus suggested the separation of Sumbawan *adat* law from the *adat* law area of Bali and Lombok (1937); while J. J. Dormeier attempted to establish a much sharper delineation of *adat* law areas of the Toradja, South Sulawesi, and in the Ternate archipelago (1947).

lecturer at the training school for indigenous administrative officers in Magelang (Central Java). Among his numerous articles on practical issues concerning Indonesian law and the administration of justice, five attempted to explain the world view of the Indonesian peoples who practiced *adat* law. One was an explanation of the Javanese system of village confederations called *mantjapat*, in which five or nine villages unite for certain cooperative purposes. In this study Ossenbruggen applied a concept developed by E. Durkheim and M. Mauss in their famous article (1901–1902) in which they suggested that the primitive mind often uses the divisions of its society as the categorical framework into which it classifies its universe. The confederations of five villages and the social division into five sections are thus an ancient and very basic social structure in Java, as five and nine are extremely important numbers in Javanese culture, and conceptual schemes based on categories of five or nine are frequent in the Javanese way of thinking (Ossenbruggen, 1918). Two other articles were the result of an extensive study on rituals and magical practices in Indonesia to prevent smallpox which Ossenbruggen analyzed by using the concept of preanimism (1911, 1916).[15] Another article summarized his ideas on the Indonesian religio-magical mentality which constitutes the background of *adat* law (1926), while still another applied his concepts on the social institutions and kinship system of the Toba Batak (1935).

The pioneers in the study of Indonesian *adat* law, Vollenhoven in particular, created an atmosphere conducive to research; they initiated the active collection of material on local Indonesian cultures among specialists in *Indologie*, administrative officials, and lawyers who were working in Indonesia. As most of the works which resulted from these extensive research activities are listed in ter Haar's textbook (1948, 237–248), I will only mention briefly those I consider to be of particular interest. Among the studies which attempt to give a comprehensive description of the *adat* law system of a community or group of communities within a single *adat* law area, V. E. Korn's description of Bali (1924), J. C. Vergouwen's description of the Toba Batak (1933), Soepomo's description of West Java (1933), and Djojodigoeno and Tirtawinata's description of the central part of Java (1940) certainly rank highest. J. Mallinckrodt's ambitious description of the *adat* law of Borneo (1928) has often proved

---

[15] Ossenbruggen used the concept of preanimism as developed in particular by A. Vierkandt in his *Naturvölker und Kulturvölker* (1898) or his later articles, e.g., "Die Anfänge der Religion und Zauberei" (1907).

inaccurate, in that material from several local areas in South Kalimantan are mixed together and generalized for the whole of Kalimantan, while the single concept of the Indonesian religio-magical mind is overused to explain many legal phenomena in Kalimantan. Others, as for example, F. D. Holleman's description of the *adat* law of Ambon (1923), J. W. van Royen's description of land and water laws in the Palembang area of South Sumatra (1927), W. Hoven's description of kinship and inheritance in the Pasemah Highlands of South Sumatra (1927), T. Nieuwenhuyzen's description of the *adat* law of Lombok (1932), and Hazairin's description of the *adat* law of the Redjang in West Sumatra (1936), still must be valued as the only sources of information on areas in Indonesia where comprehensive ethnographic descriptions are lacking.

The topical *adat* law studies which have drawn data from the whole of Indonesia, using Vollenhoven's nineteen *adatrechtskringen* as a framework for comparative analysis, however, do not belong to the most outstanding *adat* law studies. The majority of these studies are publications of doctoral (LL.D.) dissertations. Some, however, as for example B. ter Haar's study on the *adat* procedure in Indonesian *adat* law (1915) and A. M. P. A. Scheltema's study on sharecropping systems in Indonesia (1931), are quite good; the studies on the Indonesian village community of L. Adam (1924) and of W. P. van Dam (1937) remain important references for further studies of Indonesian village communities; Soebroto's study of the mortgaging of rice fields in Indonesia (1925) adds to the understanding of the problem of land tenure in Inonesia; but works like S. R. Boomgaard's study on the legal status of women under Indonesian *adat* law (1926) or Soekanto's study on property rights of cultivated plants (1933), as well as several others, are rather poor products of Indonesian *adat* law studies.

Finally, another important figure in the development of Indonesian *adat* law studies must be discussed more fully—B. ter Haar, professor of *adat* law at the law school in Djakarta before World War II. In addition to his numerous works on problems of *adat* law policy and the administration of justice, one of his interests was the delineation of *adat* law. Even since Snouck Hurgronje, *adat* law scholars, aware of the fact that the *adat* law of a given community is part of its customs and social system, had never seriously examined what indicates (*kenbron*) the exact borderline between customary rules on the one hand and *adat* law rules on the other. Ter Haar's attention to this aspect seems to have been derived from a problem of field-work methodology. How can the investigator in the field who wants to collect the rules of *adat* law distinguish those rules that belong to the realm of *adat* law from those that are just customs, mores, or folkways? Ter Haar suggested that the observation and recording of judicial decisions in village courts would provide the best method to obtain information on living *adat* law in its natural environment. In an important work (1937), he concluded that *adat* law is primarily manifested in the judicial decisions of the community's legal authorities, "de beslissingen van de gezagdragende functionarissen der groep (hoofden, rechters, volksvergaderingen, grond-voogden, godsdienst- en dorpsbeambten)" (the decisions of the group's recognized officials [chiefs, judges, popular assemblies, trustees of land use, religious and village functionaries]; Haar 1937, 4). After the comments on ter Haar's conclusion by F. D. Holleman (1938), J. H. A. Logemann's discussion of Holleman's comments (1938), the comments of the anthropologist J. P. B. de Josselin de Jong (1948), and L. Pospisil's brilliant analysis of customary law among the Kapauku of the Wissel Lakes area, West Irian (1958), we now know that ter Haar's delineation of *adat* law is insufficient and that the attribute of authority is only one among several which make up the concept of customary law. Just before his death in 1939, ter Haar delivered an important lecture (published posthumously in 1941) in which he suggested the way in which Indonesian judges who had received formal education could change and modernize the primitive mentality which forms the background for Indonesian *adat* law.

7. The Study of Rural Economics

In certain circles some concern with the poverty of the Indonesian rural population, apparent after the colonial government's introduction of the ethical policy, initiated the intensive study of rural economics, beginning approximately in the period before World War I. The people who were engaged in these studies were specialists in *Indologie*, agronomists, and economists. These scholars tried to develop a particular approach toward the economic problems of rural Indonesia which gave rise to a new discipline in Dutch universities called *tropisch-koloniale staathuis-houdkunde*, or tropical-colonial economics.

A Dutch specialist in *Indologie* and economy, with long experience as a civil servant in Indonesia, J. H. Boeke, emphasized the individual character of Indonesian rural society, where custom and tropical environment have produced social and economic needs fundamentally different from those of Western society (see Boeke 1910, 6–14). In a great number of writings, of which his doctoral dissertation (1910), his inaugural address (1930), and a much later book (1953) are the most important, Boeke developed a conception of the separate position of Indonesian economics in the framework of economy and methodology. This position was brought about by at least six elements: (1) the lack of mobility in factors of production and among the agrarian masses, (2) the great gap between rural and urban society, (3) the simultaneous existence of cash and barter economies, (4) the disturbance of village autonomy and economy through central government interference, (5) the lack of mechanized production, and (6) the contrast between producers' and consumers' economy. According to Boeke, these factors made Western economic concepts and theories inapplicable to economic processes in Indonesia. He extended his concept with the idea that the particular character of Indonesian economics is not limited only to tropical colonial societies but generally to societies which he called "dualistic" and which can be compared with societies recently called "underdeveloped." In studying such societies, economists must use a different conceptual and methodological framework. However, Boeke had little to suggest in terms of positive approaches, except for stating that any industrialization or agricultural improvement should be small-scale and must represent a "slow process" through "village reconstruction" and that the disintegration of the Oriental backward village community has to be prevented (Boeke 1952).

Several economists, G. Gonggrijp (1919) for one, basically agreed with Boeke's viewpoint. Others, however, like J. van Gelderen (1927), E. P. Wellenstein (1930), and the Indonesian economist Aboetari (1932, 103–142), denied the validity of Boeke's concepts and attempted to demonstrate that the apparently large gap between the economics of a modern Western society and of a dualistic society was only temporary in nature, or merely a matter of degree. These economists believed that Western economic theory was applicable to Indonesian society.

In his works after World War II, Boeke does not seem to have changed his views very much, and recent criticisms, in particular from non-Dutch scholars, are basically similar to the earlier ones. The anthropologist R. Firth feels that the problem in Boeke's theories "seems due to a . . . failure to distinguish . . . between the basic theory and the application of that theory to a particular type of economic system" (Firth 1946, 26). In his elaborate criticism of Boeke's three most recent works, B. Higgins states that Boeke has too often referred to obsolete theoretical economic concepts and that Boeke's picture of the strong contrast between the economy of a Western and an Eastern community seems to have been based too exclusively on data from Holland on the one hand and Indonesia on the other (Higgins 1955, 65, note 34). Higgins has also demonstrated that Western economic theory can be a useful tool for the analysis of economic problems in underdeveloped areas, suggesting more positive approaches toward problems of economic development than Boeke's "back-to-the-village policy" (1954). Recent Indonesian economists are of the same opinion (Sadli 1957).

8. *The Ancient Social Structure of Rural Indonesia*

The study of the ancient social structure of rural Indonesia was initiated by a Dutch specialist on Javanese literature, W. H. Rassers. Stimulated by Ossenbruggen's explanation of the original meaning of the Javanese *mantjapat* village confederations, Rassers attempted to analyze the principal motif of the Javanese Pandji epics in his dissertation, *De Pandji-roman* (1922). The two opposing parties in the epics consist of mythical figures symbolic of the various phases of the moon and the sun. Pandji's party symbolizes the waning moon and the sun; the opposition, the waxing moon.[16] Applying the Durkheim-Mauss-Ossenbruggen concept of the system of primitive classification previously discussed, Rassers deduced the existence of an ancient Javanese social structure based on a moiety division. These two parts of ancient Javanese society had been used by the primitive Javanese mind as basic categories for classifying the universe, including such concepts as the waxing moon, waning moon, sun, and so on. These moieties were further subdivided

[16] Rassers actually relied on a study by W. Schmidt about the diffusion of mythical stories symbolizing the sun or moon in southwest Oceania. Mythical stories of the moon are known among the inhabitants of Nias, the Bataks, and among several ethnic groups in Kalimantan and Melanesia, while stories of the sun are known mainly among the ethnic groups in Nusa Tenggara, Maluku, and Polynesia. Schmidt concluded that the moon stories originated from Asia and diffused over the Southeast Asian archipelago, while the sun stories diffused from the east, both culture complexes meeting each other and forming *Kulturschichten* in Sulawesi (Schmidt 1910).

into four groups, each of which was associated with a totem symbol. The social solidarity between the moieties, the subdivisions, and the clans was maintained by periodic totemistic ceremonies, of which initiation was the most important. These totemistic ceremonies were held in a sacred clan house which was taboo for women and children. Ancient Javanese social structure is, according to Rassers, reflected in Javanese mythology—in stories connected with agriculture (1925), stories with Buddhist backgrounds (1926), stories of the *wajang* or shadow play (1925, 1931)—as well as in decorative art, such as the ornamental design of batik and the kris, the Javanese sacred weapon (1940).

Rassers' ideas received much criticism, primarily from philologists but also from anthropologists like W. Schmidt (1929); K. A. H. Hidding, a specialist on Sundanese literature (1929, 95–101, 103–104; 1931, 1935); T. Pigeaud, a specialist on Javanese language and folklore (1927, 345; 1938, 360–363); H. B. Sarkar, an Indian philologist (1934); R. N. Poerbatjaraka, a specialist on old Javanese philology (1938, 180); W. F. Stutterheim, a specialist on Indonesian archaeology (1925, *Textband*, 81–82) and several others.

On the other hand, Rassers' ideas were developed by the anthropologist J. P. B. de Josselin de Jong. This anthropologist has, referring also to Malinowski's concept of the function of mythology in society (see Malinowski 1948, 72–124), suggested Rassers' method as a tool to analyze other mythological complexes in other parts of Indonesia, in order to get at the "structurele kern der oud-Indonesische beschavingsvormen" (the "structural core of ancient Indonesian cultural manifestations," J. P. B. de Josselin de Jong 1935, 6). According to him, the Indonesian archipelago, with its great diversity of cultures all based on a similar substratum, will provide the student of culture an excellent *ethnologisch studieveld*, or area of study, where he can attempt to analyze the basic social structure that forms the core of all the cultures in the area. In his inaugural address (1935), Josselin de Jong suggested several components of ancient Indonesian social structure. Beside those elements already mentioned by Rassers as parts of the Javanese ancient social structure, i.e., a moiety system with four or more subdivisions or clans, forming the basic categories for a primitive classification system, and a totemistic initiation complex with sacred men's houses taboo for women and children, Josselin de Jong also suggested the widespread occurrence in Indonesia of the system of asymmetrical connubium, which automatically implies the preference for marriage with the mother's brother's daughter.

The whole system of moieties with subdivisions is reflected in a mythological complex which often included the occurrence of a deity with dualistic characteristics, like the divine trickster. The latter element had been developed and discussed earlier by Josselin de Jong (1929).

Many of Josselin de Jong's students indeed have attempted to reconstruct the social structure of several Indonesian regions through the analysis of local mythology. J. P. Duyvendak, for example, studied the social structure of ancient secret societies in West Ceram, Maluku (1926), H. J. Friedericy studied the class structure of the Macassarese and Buginese of South Sulawesi (1933), F. A. E. van Wouden did a comparative study of the social structure of eastern Nusa Tenggara (1935), Koes Sardjono studied Javanese rural mythology and folklore of the shepherd's boy (1947), P. E. de Josselin de Jong studied the social structure of the Minangkabau and Negri Sembilan (1951), and R. E. Downs studied the religion of the Toradja of Central Sulawesi (1956) through A. C. Kruyt and N. Adriani's material.

Most of these, which were library studies, succeeded in abstracting some elements of what was supposed to represent ancient Indonesian social structure. Other similar studies were done in the field by individuals in addition to their regular work, such as the government official C. Nooteboom's study of East Sumba (1940), and the missionary H. Schärer's study of Ngadju religion in Central Kalimantan (1946). There were also intensive anthropological field studies, such as M. M. Nicolspeyer's study of Alor (1940), conducted in the village Atimelang at approximately the same period when C. Du Bois did her field work. G. J. Held's study of the Waropen of West Irian (1947) was done mainly in the village Nubuai on the east coast of Geelvink Bay. N. J. C. Geise's study of the Badui of Banten, West Java (1952), was carried out by visiting the fringe villages of the Badui; F. A. E. van Wouden's study of double descent in the West Sumba (1956), by field work in the villages of the Kodi area.

Indonesian social studies in the period before World War II seem to have emphasized the ancient and static aspects of Indonesian cultures, thus leaving little room for the study of the social and psychological processes of acculturation or for investigations into the principles and theory of culture change. The *adat* law scholars, who had to deal with ever-changing customs in their jurisdiction, have indeed, like Snouck Hurgronje (1893–1894, I, 9–10) and van Vollenhoven (1906–1933, III, 309), always been aware of the phenomena of culture change. Except

for ter Haar (1941), however, they never paid explicit attention to the
problem. Other studies of culture change, like those included in the volume called the *Effect of Western Influences on Native Civilisations in
the Malay Archipelago* edited by B. J. O. Schrieke (1929), were mainly
descriptive and historical in approach. The great attention paid by rural
economists to the static aspects of the Indonesian village community and
the particular emphasis by Josselin de Jong and several of his students
on the study of ancient social structures also gave little opportunity for
the study of acculturation in rural Indonesia.

9. The Study of Rural Indonesia after World War II

In the early period immediately following World War II, during
the Indonesian revolution, not much social research was carried out. Several studies were actually continuations of prewar projects or plans, such
as the study of the German anthropologist H. Kähler on several places
in the Riau Islands of East Sumatra (1960); the study of an *adat* law
scholar, H. T. Chabot, of the villages of Borongloë, South Sulawesi,
in recurrent periods during 1948 and 1949, which produced a Ph.D.
dissertation on *adat* law (1950); the previously mentioned village studies
of the anthropologist F. A. E. van Wouden in Kodi, West Sumba; and
G. J. Held's study of the social structure of Dompu and Bima, East
Sumbawa. As there were no Dutch civil administrators in the local areas
of Indonesia, research on Indonesian *adat* law almost reached a standstill
for nearly one decade.

Since 1950, however, Dutch social research has increased tremendously
in West Irian. A summary of social studies in West Irian *adat* law studies
and anthropology in particular, presented as a paper at the Ninth Pacific
Science Congress by J. V. de Bruyn (1958), shows growing research
activities in the fields of the social sciences. Social and cultural studies
in the villages have been carried out by local administrative officials and
missionaries as well as by professional anthropologists. Besides *adat*
law studies, a great majority of the research was carried out with anthropological methods or focused on anthropological problems. The results
of some of the research activities have already been published as doctoral
theses, separate monographs, or numerous articles in various scientific
journals concerning West Irian. Much, however, is still in mimeographed
or typed form, awaiting publication (see Bruyn 1958, 27–33).

Reflecting the attention paid by the United States of America to

Southeast Asia after World War II, American social scientists, among them several anthropologists, began research in various parts of rural Indonesia. A team of social scientists from the Center of International Studies of the Massachusetts Institute of Technology, including social anthropologists like C. Geertz, studied the rural area around Paré or "Modjokuto" in East Java between 1952 and 1954.[17] An anthropologist from Yale University, P. R. Goethals, studied village communities in West Sumbawa, approximately at the same time as G. J. Held from the University of Indonesia studied village communities in East Sumbawa, between 1954 and 1956. Another anthropologist from Yale, L. Pospisil, studied customary law among the Kapauku in the Kamu Valley of the Wissel Lakes area, West Irian, while the missionary M. Bromley did ethnographic as well as linguistic work in the Baliem valley of the central highland of West Irian. Subsequently several other American social scientists have studied the rural areas of North Sumatra, West Java, Lombok, West Timor, and Ambon. The results of these research activities have only been partly published in journals like the *Far Eastern Quarterly* (Jay 1956); *Economic Development and Cultural Change* (C. Geertz 1956) or others (C. Geertz 1959–1960); *American Anthropologist* (C. Geertz 1957, 1959; Pospisil 1958a; Bruner 1961); *Nieuw Guinea Studien* (Bromley 1960); and as separate publications of Yale University (Pospisil 1958, Cunningham 1958; Skinner 1959), Cornell University (Goethals 1961), and the Free Press of Glencoe, (C. Geertz 1960, H. Geertz 1961, Dewey 1962).

Besides American social scientists, some attention to the Indonesian field has also come from social scientists of other nationalities. The Swedish anthropologist J. E. Elmberg has worked in Ajamaru area in West Irian (1955); the German anthropologist F. W. Funke has traveled through Indonesia, worked in South Sumatra, and published an extensive report (1959)[18] and a two-volume ethnography on the *orang* Abung of Lampung, South Sumatra (1958–1961); a British social anthropologist, R. Needham, has worked and published on Sumba (1956, 1957, 1957a) and on the Punan of Kalimantan (1954, 1954a, 1954b, 1955); and the British anthropologist L. H. Palmier has worked in two Javanese rural towns to study social stratification (1960). Until recently, several foreign social scientists have still been working in Indonesia, among whom several are concentrating on rural problems. As for recent research activities

---

[17] The director of the team was R. Hendon.
[18] This report was unfavorably reviewed by W. F. Wertheim.

in West Irian, information about these can be obtained through the bulletins of the International Committee on Urgent Anthropological Research in New Guinea.

For several years after the Indonesian revolution, which ended in 1949, no Indonesian social scientists were available for research work. Most were occupied by important positions and were too much engaged in administration, politics, or other work.[19] However, there were retired Indonesian senior civil administrators who wrote down the knowledge about village communities that they had accumulated during their long periods of service. These books are highly unsystematic and uncritical compilations of factual material about various aspects of village life (e.g., Raka 1955), which are only valuable as sources of raw material for further research. One book written by Soetardjo Kartohadikoesoemo (1953), however, is much more systematic and sophisticated in arrangement.

Beginning with 1955, Indonesian universities started to initiate research. In 1956, Gadjah Mada University began a survey concerning land tenure, land rights, agricultural affairs, and so forth throughout the rural areas of Java, using quantitative methods, with the official distribution of a very extensive questionnaire through the *pamong pradja* or administrative service. This research, known as Angket Agraria, did not bring about favorable results. The manner in which district or subdistrict heads went through the many questions of the questionnaires, at large meetings with village heads of their respective areas, produced many biased answers. When the responses were returned, piles of sheets containing these responses accumulated in the office of the project leader, while nobody really knew what to do about them.

Another social study of village communities was conducted by the University of Indonesia between 1954 and 1956. Large questionnaires, including questions on systems of village administration and leadership, social change, processes of community development, community initiative, and demography, were used to gather data in twenty-three villages throughout Java. The field workers were students who went into the villages without research experience, except for some basic instructions from the project leaders. Here, too, responses piled up, and the only results of this very extensive field survey were a few short articles

[19] G. J. Held's statement in the *International Directory of Anthropological Institutions* that "most scientific work in Indonesia is done by Europeans" (Thomas, Pikelis; 1953, 25), was thus correct for the early period of the Indonesian Republic, prior to 1955.

(Widjojo Nitisastro and Ismaël 1959, Widjojo Nitisastro 1956) and a short general report (Ismaël 1960).

Meanwhile, the school of agronomy at the University of Indonesia also showed interest in rural community life. Several comparative studies of transmigration villages in Lampung, South Sumatra, and of villages in North Central Java resulted in doctoral dissertations (e.g., Kampto Utomo 1957, Bachtiar Rifai 1958). The Institute of Social Research and *Adat* Law Studies of Gadjah Mada University in Jogjakarta has also been active in research on village communities within the framework of field training for students in public administration. Several good reports by these field workers have been published in the journal of the Institute, *Sosiografi Indonesia;* or have been used as dissertations for M.A. degrees at the University of Gadjah Mada or elsewhere (e.g., Soedjito Sastrodi-hardjo 1959).

Recently, there has been a great increase in social research in general, and village studies in particular, approached from the viewpoint of various scientific disciplines and sponsored or carried out by Indonesian universi-ties, research institutes, or government departments. As far as I know, not much has as yet been published (except, for example, Selosoemardjan 1962, 1963; Slamet 1963). Extensive reports on social studies carried out by Indonesian social scientists, as, for instance, Selosoemardjan's book on *Social Changes in Jogjakarta* (1962a), are still very recent and rare.

Chapter II

Rarak: A Swidden Village
of West Sumbawa[1]

PETER R. GOETHALS
UNIVERSITY OF NORTH CAROLINA

1. Sumbawa Island and Its Peoples

Sumbawa, the third large island lying due east of Java, forms a major land link in Indonesia's Nusa Tenggara chain. Separated from Lombok and Flores only by narrow straits, it parallels the equator along its total length of almost 275 kilometers. Together with its fringing islands, Sumbawa measures about 13,300 square kilometers, an area larger than that of Bali and Lombok combined and roughly three quarters that of Flores.

Sumbawa's landscape is dominated by extensive rolling uplands, eroded foothills, volcanic ridges, and ancient crater walls. Closely flanking the island's entire southern coastline is a chain of extinct volcanic peaks that drop precipitously into the Indian Ocean. By contrast the north

[1] The field work upon which most of this paper is based was conducted during three visits (totaling seventeen months) to West Sumbawa between March 1954 and April 1956. I am indebted to the Ford Foundation for the grant which made this research possible; for its generous help with special problems I am further indebted to the Institute of Linguistic and Cultural Research of the University of Indonesia. I must thank collectively the many scholars and government officials in Indonesia whose individual help and encouragement was essential to my work. However, the statements in this paper are exclusively my own responsibility and do not necessarily represent the opinions of any of the individuals or institutions assisting me. Where I write here in the present tense the "ethnographic present" should be understood but with reference to the time period of my research on Sumbawa.

coast is broken by a series of shallow drainage basins and coastal plains from which most of the island's permanent rivers empty into the Flores Sea. Two large bays, Teluk Saleh and Teluk Bima, deeply indent the northern coastline and give access to the interior lowlands of central and eastern Sumbawa. Teluk Saleh, the larger of the two bays, thrusts some fifty miles southeastward, almost bisecting Sumbawa at the Saleh isthmus, long the ethnic boundary between the Sumbawan- and Biman-speaking peoples of the island. To the north, Teluk Saleh is bounded by a wide peninsula, which rises symmetrically to form the jagged 2,820-meter peak of Mount Tambora. One of the archipelago's loftiest volcanoes, the now-quiescent Tambora towers some 915 meters above any other point along Sumbawa's mountainous profile.

In its climate, fauna, and flora, Sumbawa reveals affinities with both Asia and Australia. The island's position between eight and nine degrees south of the equator ensures a tropical climate marked by little variation in daily temperatures; its proximity to the Australian land mass accounts for an annual rainfall distribution sharply divided between wet (west monsoon, or *barat*) and dry (east monsoon, or *balét*)[2] seasons of roughly equal length. Although situated east of Wallace's line, Sumbawa shares its limited variety of animal life largely with the more westerly islands of Indonesia.

Providing the natural habitats for this wildlife are Sumbawa's three broadly defined zones: woodland, savannah, and a zone of mixed cultivated flora.[3] The woodland zone covers about one-third of the island at altitudes generally above 1,100 meters, acts as the natural dry-season reservoir for the island's river systems, and embraces a rich variety of

[2] The orthography of the Sumbawan terms given in this paper follows Indonesian spelling conventions with generally similar phonetic values for consonants. However, the eight vowel phonemes of *basa* Semawa (Sumbawan) as spoken in the town and hill area close to Sumbawa Besar are given as follows:

	(unrounded) - - - - - - - (rounded)		
	front	*central*	*back*
high	i		u
mid	é	e	o
	è		
low		a	ò

[3] For an extended description of these zones, see Kuperus, 1937, Chapters II and IV, the work on which this outline is based. For background data on Sumbawa, see the titles listed in Kennedy's bibliography (1955, II, 572–575).

both deciduous and nondeciduous trees. The areas of the second, or savannah, vegetation zone range from sea level to 1,200 meters in altitude and support many types of flora. These are combined variously into grassland sectors, patches of tangled scrub, and copses of secondary forest distributed widely throughout the island. Conspicuous in many savannah areas are such drought-resistant flora as spiny bush, acacia, thorn bamboo, and several kinds of cactus, all attesting to the Australian climatic influence in Sumbawa's rainfall calendar. Yet today these same savannah areas support a substantial part of the island's human population, for this is the primary zone of shifting field (swidden) cultivation of dry rice. Accordingly, the cycles of land tillage and fallowing practiced by Sumbawan swidden farmers here have caused the spread of special types of secondary growth across the savannah. The most widespread is the tough, thorny bush known locally as *sang mamong* (*Lantarna camara* L.) which is found throughout western Sumbawa outside the woodlands. By choking out less resilient secondary flora, the wiry fire-resistant *sang* has today become the dominant form of ground cover surrounding the savannah-zone settlements of Sumbawa's upland swidden farmers.

The island's third vegetational zone comprises permanently irrigated riceland and its contiguous orchard, garden, and settlement areas. In western Sumbawa these lands lie almost entirely below 90 meters in elevation and within the river basins along the north and west coasts. Their location is thus both coastal and marginal with respect to the woodland and savannah zones; their irrigation capacity has allowed them to develop as the main centers of the western peninsula's village population. The domestic flora of this zone include a wide variety of economically important plants and trees. While the staple crop here is rice, many types of field vegetables, legumes, and certain root crops are also raised, together with sugar cane and cotton. Tree crops include coconuts, many types of banana, figs, *mangga*, several types of citrus fruits, and *nangka* (*Artocarpus integrifolia* L.). Kapok trees and both *aren* and *lontar* palms are also of economic importance to the villagers of this zone. The most familiar animal life here is the domesticated livestock raised either for draft purposes or food: horses, water buffaloes, goats, chickens, and ducks. Dogs, too, are common village animals, but because they are *nadjés*, or unclean, in Moslem Sumbawa, they are seldom well cared for.

At present Sumbawa is inhabited by well over 400,000 people, who are divided into three coordinate administrative divisions and represent two major language groups.[4] Census data from 1951 established the island's total population at 382,164 distributed as follows both by area and administrative division:

Eastern Sumbawa: That portion of Sumbawa island east of the Saleh isthmus from a point about 118° 15′ east longitude and including the Tambora peninsula and eastern offshore islands (principally Sangeang) and sometimes designated merely as "Bima." It consists of two administrative areas, Daerah Swatantra Tingkat II Bima and Daerah Swatantra Tingkat II Dompu, with a total population of 247,664 people.

Western Sumbawa: That portion of Sumbawa island west of the Saleh isthmus from a point about 118° 15′ east longitude and including the western offshore islands (principally Mojo) and often designated merely as "Sumbawa." It consists of one administrative area, Daerah Swatantra Tingkat II Sumbawa, with a total population of 134,500 people.

The island's three administrative divisions (the three *swatantra* units listed) are generally coextensive in area with, respectively, the former sultanates of Bima, Dompu, and Sumbawa. In 1958, however, with the establishment of the new province of Nusa Tenggara Barat to embrace the populations of the islands of Lombok and Sumbawa, the present administrative designations were adopted.

Culturally, Sumbawa's population may be most readily divided into the Biman and Sumbawan language communities. The inhabitants of eastern Sumbawa, as just defined, speak *basa* Bima, or Biman; those of the more sparsely populated western peninsula speak *basa* Semawa, or Sumbawan. While these two languages share a common Indonesian ancestry within the Malayo-Polynesian language family, they differ sharply in their phonology, lexicon, and grammar. Both languages are further split into a number of regionally diverse dialects: the Taliwang dialect of *basa* Semawa, for example, can prove to be virtually unintelligible to the citizen of Sumbawa Besar. Similarly, the speech of the non-Moslem

[4] In its ten-volume series entitled *Republik Indonesia* (covering events until 1953 but with no listed date of publication), the Ministry of Information, Djakarta, quotes (in the volume entitled *Propinsi Sunda Ketjil*, p. 132) "the last census" (no date cited) of Sumbawa as having shown 460,000 inhabitants of the island distributed as follows:

Swapradja Sumbawa: 160,000
Swapradja Dompu: 50,000
Swapradja Bima: 250,000

Donggo highlander in eastern Sumbawa remains as a strikingly divergent dialect of Biman. Moreover, the dialects spoken along Sumbawa's entire northern coastline differ considerably from those of the interior mountains —evidence of the historically protracted and still continuing coastal immigration of people from Sulawesi, Kalimantan, Java, Bali, and Lombok.

2. *Rarak Village and Its Subsistence Cycle*

Situated on a broad ridge 275 meters above sea level, a cluster of about eighty wooden houses and rice barns makes up Rarak's main settlement. In Malay style, each building stands on wooden pilings; in typically Sumbawan fashion, the entire compact settlement is enclosed by broken sections of a low stick fence. Well worn footpaths converge from every direction on the settlement, linking it with the community's half-dozen outlying *keban* (homesteads) and with neighboring communities several miles distant. The typical Rarak homestead is located no more than one and a half kilometers from the main settlement and consists of a fenced cluster of from four to seven buildings and garden land, where a few Rarak families live permanently to cultivate fruit trees, sugar cane, and root crops. Although dwelling outside the main settlement, these homestead families live within the village community's land tract and are regarded as full citizens of Rarak. Signifying their common membership is the one community structure of the main settlement which the homestead inevitably lacks: the *mesigét* or mosque. In this square tile-roofed building, all the villagers of Rarak gather periodically as members both of a common community and a single *djuma'at*, or religious congregation.

Such bonds of community are reinforced by the preoccupation of all villagers with the problems of subsistence rice farming. Since the nearest river estuary allowing permanently irrigated rice fields lies fifteen kilometers distant, the Rarak farmer must raise his annual paddy on upland fields watered only by the west monsoon (*barat*) rains. This he does each year by clearing and planting one or more fallow stretches of hillside within the thirteen square kilometers of savannah zone upland surrounding Rarak's main settlement and traditionally subject to its disposal.[5] This pattern of shifting field, or swidden, agriculture in 1955

[5] This figure is purely my own estimate and is not based on any kind of survey, official or otherwise. No villager in 1955 could estimate the total land area of Rarak's tract, although many of the older men could describe very clearly the natural features of the tract's boundary.

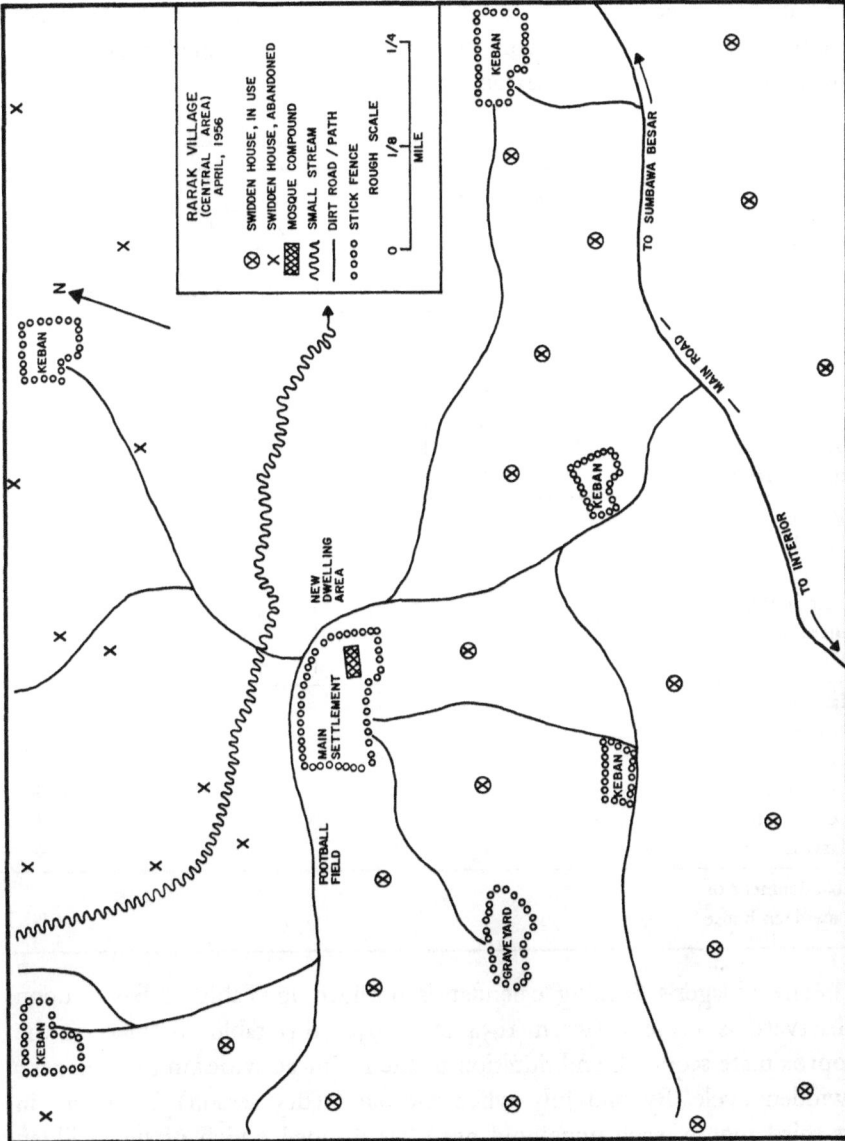

RARAK VILLAGE
(CENTRAL AREA)
APRIL, 1956

⊗ SWIDDEN HOUSE, IN USE
✕ SWIDDEN HOUSE, ABANDONED
▨ MOSQUE COMPOUND
∿∿∿ SMALL STREAM
— DIRT ROAD / PATH
ooo STICK FENCE

ROUGH SCALE

0   1/8   1/4
MILE

N

NEW DWELLING AREA

MAIN SETTLEMENT

FOOTBALL FIELD

GRAVEYARD

KEBAN

TO SUMBAWA BESAR

MAIN ROAD

TO INTERIOR

Map II. Settlement Pattern of Rarak

fed a Rarak population of over 450 people. It requires that the typical village household (a man, his wife, and their unmarried children) divide the year about equally, living in two separate domiciles, the one a permanent house located in the main settlement (or homestead), the other a temporary house located on the swidden and occupied only during the months of the growing season.

Table 1. Calendar of swidden activities at Rarak

Seasons:						‑ ‑ ‑ ‑ ‑ ‑ ‑‑*balét:* dry‑ ‑ ‑ ‑ ‑ ‑					‑.‑.‑.‑.‑.‑.‑.‑*barat:* wet‑.‑.‑.‑.‑.‑	
Months:	Jun.	Jul.	Aug.	Sep.	Oct.	Nov.	Dec.	Jan.	Feb.	Mar.	Apr.	May
Cutting & clearing			+	+								
Drying			+	+	+							
Burning				+	+							
Fencing				+	+							
Housebuilding					+	+						
House transfer					+	+						
Planting:												
paddy						+	+					
maize						+	+					
catch crops						+	+	+	+			
Guarding						+	+	+	+	+	+	+
Weeding							+	+	+	+		
Harvesting:												
maize									+			
unripe paddy										+	+	
ripe paddy											+	+
catch crops	+	+										+
Harvest storage	+											+
Abandonment of												
swidden house	+											+

The villager's farming calendar is outlined in Table 1. Based upon observations made between 1954 and 1956, this table summarizes the approximate sequence and duration of the major activities in the villager's swidden cycle. By mid-July when the *balét* (dry season) is already in its third month, each household head has decided which of his swidden parcels he will clear and plant for the coming rainy season. Whichever one he chooses, he will ordinarily plan to farm it as one unit in a cluster of contiguous swiddens enclosed by a common fence, whose owners cooperate in many of the growing-season chores. He will decide precisely when to begin clearing his land by taking into consideration many factors, including the swidden's degree of slope and exposure, the time it has already fallowed and, accordingly, the density of the brush and tree cover that must be cleared before burning. He may also be influenced by the weather predictions of experienced older men in the village, by horoscope auguries of favorable starting dates, or merely by the press of such important dry-season activities as a trading trip or his daughter's marriage ceremony. Nevertheless, usually by mid-August he has at least begun the arduous task of swidden clearing.

Having felled the swidden brush and tree cover, the villager allows September's intense *balét* sun to parch it dry for ten days or more. Then, shortly before the early west monsoon (*barat*) showers of mid-October, he fires the withered brush and tree limbs and, in less than two hours, has transformed his swidden into naked, charred hillside. If the swidden burns clean, this constitutes one of the best possible omens of a subsequently good harvest. Yet the very tendency for the villager to regard this as an omen reflects his uncertainty in judging the whims of the seasonal change. Planting cannot begin until the regular rains of the west monsoon strike, usually by mid-November. However, if the rains arrive unexpectedly early, the swiddens may be either insufficiently dried or not yet burned. On the other hand, if the rains are delayed even by a week or ten days, a recently burned swidden may already be choked with the rapidly growing young weeds and *sang* brush that will stifle much of any subsequent crop. Either eventuality can cripple or destroy a swidden's yield even before its seeds are planted. Therefore, in the final weeks of the *balét* the timing of swidden burning always involves calculated risk: although the cleanly burned swidden may be an already accomplished fact, the onset of the *barat* rains can still betray the expectations of the most seasoned village farmer.

The three weeks after mid-October will usually bring rain squalls and sharp thunderstorms marking the transition to the *barat*. By this time the villager is usually engaged in the simultaneous tasks of fencing his swidden and making it livable. Working with his neighbors from the same swidden cluster, he devotes several days to building a sturdy pile fence to protect the common swidden area from animal incursions. He must also lash together the frame for the cramped, one-room swidden house that he will occupy with his family to guard the swidden during the growing season. This he constructs from an assortment of poles and small timber saved from his earlier swidden-clearing activity. Meanwhile, his wife and older children are busy transferring, by foot or on horseback, the household property and supplies from the homestead to the small swidden house. In November, when the nightly rains have steadied and the time for planting is at hand, each villager has moved his entire household to the swidden and left his permanent home in the main settlement or homestead locked and vacant until the following June.

The planting phase begins with November's soaking *barat* rains and may extend for two or three weeks, until the villager's main crops have been sown. Paddy planting throughout the community generally commences only after the *lebè*, Rarak's mosque head and most experienced diviner, has announced the critically auspicious planting date, has implored Allah's blessing upon the new crops, and has then initiated planting on his own swidden with the help of fellow villagers in a day-long dibble planting party. Maize and rapidly maturing (90 to 100 days) types of paddy are usually planted together as soon as possible to provide some insurance against the annual semifamine period between January and March. Slower-maturing types of paddy and catch crops are individually planted later, according to each villager's work assistance, the rainfall pattern over his particular hillside, and his attention to horoscope auguries. Catch crops (beans, squash, many types of greens, peppers, tobacco, tomatoes, eggplant) are either sown directly or transplanted from small nurseries onto individual swiddens as late as March and then may well be harvested during the cool dry months of the early *balét*. However, in terms of Rarak's basic food crop—the approximately thirty types of hill paddy known and used in the village—planting has usually been completed by mid-December.

To the average villager, the growing season is the most grueling period of the year. Because of the varied, relentless threats to his crops, he can seldom rest from a steady vigil over his swidden. Fire-resistant weeds and hardy new *sang* shoots rapidly reinfest his planted hillside; by neglecting to weed his swidden even during the first month after planting, the villager forfeits much of his future paddy harvest. Whether as freshly dibbled seed, small green seedlings, or mature heads of grain, his paddy is at all stages subject to the attack of many kinds of highland birds. In March, as it begins to mature, the new grain attracts marauding gray monkeys from the high *sang* brush and woodlands along the swidden perimeters. Voracious ant colonies, plagues of field mice, and paddy borers add to the dangers. Against such hungry pests, thrown stones, slings, crude snares, and scarecrows provide only partial defense. Despite their neck clappers, itinerant livestock (horses, *karbau*, goats) owned by the villagers themselves often break unnoticed through swidden fences. Other marauders attack at night as well: vicious wild pigs can root stealthily under the stoutest fences and lay waste to large planted areas. Depredations by deer are less frequent, although, unlike pigs, they are eagerly killed for their meat whenever possible. The only weapons available against these larger wild animals are dogs, spears, clubs, and an occasional trap. In 1956 the villagers lacked effective firearms entirely.

Basic to the villager's simple defenses is the continual guard he must maintain. A twenty-four-hour vigil is often essential even for the least exposed of swidden sites. This means long, sleepless nights for the man of the family and sometimes for his wife and sons as well. Periodic nocturnal sallies become the rule. Armed with torch and spear, the villager prowls his swidden fence along a circuit of small fires near guard platforms where he can warm himself or catch a brief nap. Sometimes he arranges with a neighbor to share the vigil, but, even so, he is lucky to catch more than a couple of hours consecutive sleep.

As the *barat* months wear on, weather and health give new cause for worry. Unusually heavy rains can quickly wash out an entire hillside of swidden paddy. Prolonged cloudy skies can disastrously delay ripening and cause the paddy to rot on its stalks. Already by early December, food supplies have fallen perilously low in many households, and the "knobby knees" and empty bellies of the *barat* are again familiar. To the anxious villager, such conditions magnify every small deviation in the weather pattern or threat to his swidden. Fatigue, anxiety, and increasing malnutrition are aggravated by sleeping in damp, rickety swidden huts under only light cover. Illnesses such as pleurisy, pneumonia, arthritis, and active tuberculosis spread; malaria, augmented by the *barat* mosquitoes, invades every household. The meager, protein-deficient diet of boiled weeds and plain rice adds a faint tinge of red to the hair of village children, a symptom of kwashiorkor. As debilitation increases, sociability and neighborly cooperation give way to inertia, drowsiness, and resignation. Many villagers await the harvest in desperate anticipation.

By mid-March the *barat* rains over Rarak have begun to slacken, and patches of the villagers' 90-to-100-day paddy are ready to harvest. Three weeks before this the village *lebè* has ceremonially "bathed the stomach" of the community's first "pregnant" paddy; at least for many older villagers he has thereby safeguarded the final development and "birth" of the new rice.[6] In April the *barat* rains dwindle further, and warm, clear days rapidly ripen all but the slowest varieties of paddy. While poorer villagers have often begun in February to subsist on their semiripe or early paddy, most wait to harvest their crop in April and May. With the ripening of each hillside, local parties of high-spirited men, women, and children begin the long-anticipated work of cutting, bunching, and tying the bundles of sweet new paddy. Senior village officials and wealthy men meet to plan the timing of their individually sponsored, community-wide festivals of the period. Organized as day-long harvesting parties on the host's swidden, these are among Rarak's major annual social events. Attracting villagers of all ages, both from Rarak and from many neighboring communities, they are occasions of marked geniality, abundant good food, competitive display (drumming, *pantun* recital, *pentjak*), and, for the young people, covert romantic encounter. While the bulk of Rarak's paddy crop is actually harvested by innumerable smaller work groups of family or swidden neighbors, the exuberant display of these ten or twelve community festivals not only legitimates the social position of individual village leaders but also dramatizes the villager's annual feeling of physical relief from the privations of the *barat* and his renewed optimism for the future.

After harvest, a few chores remain before the villager abandons his swidden for the year. His paddy is allowed to dry for about ten days on a raised swidden platform; then, usually with the help of a half-day working party of male relatives and friends, he binds his paddy into the larger bundles suitable for storage. If the paddy must be transported from an especially distant swidden (usually by horseback or carrying pole), if he has certain catch crops (such as tomatoes or tobacco) to be harvested shortly, or if his main house or rice barn needs repairs, he may be delayed in returning to the main settlement. However, after first moving his paddy and ceremonially laying it "to rest" either in a village rice barn or the loft of his main house, he will usually shift his household back by mid-June. Now and again during the dry season he will return to the swidden to collect such crops as beans, gourds, cucumbers, and squash that continue to fruit on the vines around his abandoned swidden house.

[6] Further details of the paddy planting ritual are given in Goethals (1960, 94–196). Apparently, these rituals have either never been well established in upland Sumbawa or are today rapidly disappearing.

During the cool, dry weeks from early June through mid-August, relatively few villagers earn extra income from outside activities; house-building or the preparations for wedding feasts, major preoccupations of this period, demand considerable time from many hands. Activities such as deer hunting, river shrimp fishing, and honey collecting are frequently productive to the villager, both by enriching his diet and as recreation, yet the products are only occasionally traded beyond the village. But by cutting and transporting upland timber for sale in the lowlands or by working as hired paddy harvesters in neighboring communities (1956 payment: one paddy bundle for each day's work), a handful of younger village men are able to supplement their income considerably. Rarak's recognized craftsmen in 1956 numbered four carpenters and three smiths, all but one of whom (who was too old to work) earned their extra income mainly during this period. The two leading carpenters were also *sanro* (shamans) who specialized in house construction and received their payment either in paddy or promises of assistance (figured in working days) in that year's swidden clearing. A third carpenter, new to the village, made furniture in return for cash or paddy. The three village smiths, who usually open their forges in July and August to make parang and brush-knife blades, were, like the carpenters, later compensated by their customers with swidden-clearing assistance. Cash earnings were perhaps most familiar to the two energetic village women who traded two or three days weekly with the town market some twelve miles distant. Accumulating small surpluses of rice, eggs, fruit, tobacco, and vegetables from fellow housewives, they supplied at small profit in return such necessities as fish, cigarettes, kerosene, coconut oil, needles, and cloth.

About a dozen village farmers working homestead land command yet an additional source of income. Like most villagers, they hold locally recognized, mostly inherited usufruct title to between five and eight parcels of swidden land of varying size and quality scattered throughout the community land tract. Yet they also possess government registered title (dating mainly from 1930 to 1938) to the permanently cultivated, taxed plots of land near the main settlement where their main houses are located.[7] With the sugar cane, citrus fruits, bananas, cassava, betel,

---

[7] These homestead plots, together with a number of garden land plots lying close to the central Rarak settlement, comprise some 90 hectares of the entire village land tract. They are the only parcels within the Rarak tract which the government has surveyed, mapped, and given by title deed

and other products of these fenced homesteads, or *keban*, they can usually supplement considerably their annual swidden resources. Brown sugar pressed from the sugar cane of two such farmers is a constantly profitable item of trade.

Rarak's tract of rolling upland remains today the village's most basic resource, even though its traditional boundaries, so clearly known to the older Rarak citizens, were still unmapped in 1956. While land rights within this tract may be inherited or even loaned between villagers, they had not begun to be sold or rented, either within the community or to outsiders, yet the increasing shortage of land resources was being felt at Rarak as in neighboring communities: disputes over land between men of these upland villages with common traditional boundaries were increasing. With the rapid decline of soil fertility, larger swaths must be cut each year along the upland hillsides to keep pace with diminishing swidden yields. At the same time, the cycle of burning-planting-fallowing on each parcel gradually accelerates (in 1955 being, on the average, four to five years for each parcel), and eventually Rarak, like adjacent villages, tends to spill its excess population beyond its traditional boundaries. Thus Rarak, settled originally by pioneers migrating up from the lowlands over a hundred years ago, has already attained and passed through its "golden age" of land usage. Thirty years ago, according to senior villagers, one could still plant one bundle of seed paddy dibbled into the timber area north of the village, and the harvest would be roughly one hundredfold. About 1930, the government closed large sections of Sumbawa's uplands to swidden farming. Since then, Rarak's traditional tract has gradually been worked more rapidly; ever more of the big wood within it has been felled and the land forced to feed more and more mouths on increasingly meager—albeit more frequent—paddy harvests. On top of this, the villagers now face growing encroachment from lowland villages, as land-hungry neighbors are driven to seek swidden land in the uplands because of even more rapid expansion of their own villages. The prospects of an increase in all these land pressures was a matter of considerable worry to many village men in 1956.

---

to registered owners. Before 1942 a larger proportion of these plots was occupied with housing and was worked more steadily as garden area than today. In 1955 about 70 per cent of these plots had reverted entirely to swidden land, and these were being cultivated for hill paddy once every four or five years.

3. *The Organization of Work*

In Rarak there are no special terms in use, either to designate the several cooperative work groupings locally recognized or the working roles and agreements involved in each. An artificial but useful vocabulary includes the following terms: (1) initiator: a village man or woman who enlists the assistance of other villagers in accomplishing his or her work project; (2) assistant: a villager who helps the initiator with his or her project; (3) participant: a villager belonging to a well-defined (i.e., all members mutually known), temporary grouping that pools its participants' labor to accomplish the same, or a similar, job for each participant in turn during a short time period; (4) host participant: a participant who acts as an informal director and host to other participants in his work grouping when they are working specifically on his premises or portion of the project; (5) payment: overt and contractual compensation in the form of money (*rupiah*) or paddy for a specific amount of work performed; (6) informal reward: tacit compensation for assistance, usually given in the form of an outstandingly good meal at noontime or a day of work assistance but not explicitly agreed upon between the initiator and an assistant.

The three types of cooperative group labor to which these terms apply are as follows:

Nulong. This term, meaning literally "assisting," applies to a number of well-defined tasks (see Table 2). Any task handled under a *nulong* arrangement is essentially contractual in nature and involves a clear understanding between the initiator and each assistant (of whom there may be almost any number, depending upon the task). The explicit nature of the contract is matched by the definite payment involved: in 1956 the unit of time generally contracted for was a full day's work (7 to 8 hours); for this amount of labor either a *gutés* (bundle) of paddy or cash in the amount between 2½ and 3 *rupiah* were generally acceptable payments. Usually, but not inevitably, payment also included a meal at noontime, especially if the assistant concerned had traveled from another village area to do the day's work. This type of working arrangement is most usual between any villager and men or women from other villages, regardless of any type of kinship tie linking them. In the *nulong* category, each unit of labor is bought and paid for and no further obligations are generally thought to remain between the parties after completion of the job.

Saléng tulong. This term literally means "assisting one another." The activities to which it may be applied are shown in Table 2. None of these is explicitly contractual in nature, although the initiator may enlist either a few specially invited assistants or a large number who respond to a widely publicized invitation issued to the community at large. As with the *nulong* arrangement, the unit of labor is the day's work or a part thereof and the appropriate reward for either consists of a heavy midday meal (including meat, rice, vegetables, and often cigarettes or cheroots in addition). Subsidiary, informal rewards are considered to be the camaraderie of the occasion and the leisurely pace of the work involved. If the initiator seeks assistants from outside the village, he will usually invite them specially for the occasion and then may attend with a few friends or primary relatives. On the other hand, if the work occasion is to be of any real size (fifteen people or more), the initiator will normally expect many of his fellow villagers to attend voluntarily without specific invitation. Only if he intends to keep the gathering relatively restricted will he issue personal invitations by word of mouth among friends and relatives. Workers who contribute their energies to this type of labor are rewarded in specific fashion with the midday meal but are not contractually paid as if they worked under a *nulong* arrangement.

Basiru. The meaning of this term differs little from that of *saléng tulong;* literally it denotes "to give mutual aid." Nevertheless its implication is considerably different, and *basiru* activities are generally more common. All such activities are of a contractual nature, since *basiru* groupings are usually formed to carry out a common task for each participant and are clearly defined in size. Accordingly, every participant in a *basiru* task both knows that his contribution will be exactly matched in kind by the eventual return and can determine from knowledge of the group's size what expenditure and what benefits he will incur through participation. The unit of *basiru* assistance is usually the day or half day of work devoted to a common task (swidden clearing, harvesting, etc.; for complete summary see Table 2) and clear reciprocity is expected. The villager finds *basiru* groupings advantageous for the following reasons: (1) he can accomplish certain of his own tasks quickly when time is limited, such as swidden burning; (2) he may be enabled to share the use of certain tools owned by his neighbors; (3) he is not obliged to work alone. On *basiru* projects, participants either supply their own midday meals or agree in advance that these will be consistently provided by each host participant in turn. If, for any reason, an individual within a *basiru* grouping must default on his participation, he is then obliged either to supply a substitute worker or to reimburse the group for the defaulted period. Any substitution must be made with a worker appropriate to the task: an adult woman, for example, would be an adequate substitute for her husband at a *mataq siru,* or harvest work party; she would not, however, be an acceptable substitute for him in the man's role of swidden clearing. Payment for default, on the other hand, is usually made in kind:

a *gutés* of paddy must be paid to the group for each day's work defaulted from a *basiru* grouping. In 1956 it was also said that, if necessary, payment might also be made in cash at the rate of 3 *rupiah* per working day. Few villagers, however, seemed to consider this the normal method of *basiru* reimbursement.

Table 2. Work projects classified by type of working group, Rarak

Work projects for men	*nulong*	*saléng tulong*	*basiru*
Swidden clearing			+
Swidden burning			+
Fencing			+
Swidden house construction			+
Hunting			+
Cutting timber	+	+	+
Smithing			+
House construction (main settlement and homestead)		+	+
Paddy tying and bundling		+	+
Work projects for men and women	*nulong*	*saléng tulong*	*basiru*
Fishing			+
Planting		+	+
Harvesting	+	+	+
Work projects for women	*nulong*	*saléng tulong*	*basiru*
Paddy threshing			+
Food preparation for feasts and weddings		+	+

4. Transition and Marriage in the Villager's Life Cycle

At childbirth, a Rarak mother is usually delivered by one of the several village women known from their combined medical and ritual skills as competent midwives. In 1955 Rarak's two leading midwives were also *njai* (wife of a *hukom* official) of the *lebè* and the *pengulu*, the two paramount *hukom* officials and each a *sanro* in his own right. Those women bearing their first children usually come under the care of one of these *njai* midwives some two months before delivery, at the time of the *biso tian sowai*, or washing of the pregnant woman's stomach. This takes place at the seventh month of pregnancy, when the expectant mother accompanies a *njai* to the river and is there ritually bathed and massaged with special lotions. This is done expressly to ensure an easy delivery and is generally followed on the same day by a small feast to which the husband invites family members and a member of the *hukom* to recite prayers. At the time of childbirth, the *njai* (or any other village midwife if delivering a woman's second or subsequent child) is often assisted by the woman's mother, her half-grown daughter, or occasionally even by her own husband. Except for a few prayers by an invited *hukom* member, most villagers hold no special ceremony for the delivery of their children. However, traditional payment is usually made for the midwife's services in the form of cloth, cooked food, or old coins.

Some village women nurse their children for up to three years before weaning. During the nursing period a woman may, if of robust health, also agree to suckle the baby of a relative, friend, or neighbor who is unable to suckle her own child. This practice, however long its duration, establishes a quasi-sibling relationship between all children suckled by a single woman; any such "milk siblings" of the opposite sex can never be allowed to marry. Following the Moslem law of the village, such a relationship is deemed incestuous, even if such "siblings" are otherwise unrelated or raised completely separately. Not even the relationship between a couple's natural and adopted children (*anak ènèng*), usually much more siblinglike in nature, seems as stringently circumscribed in any one respect as this tie between "milk siblings."

At birth, each child receives an informal nickname from its parents. This may be nonsensical in nature but also may mark the child's character, his physical peculiarities, or even his resemblance to a familiar animal. The formal, permanent name, usually Koranic in origin, is chosen according to criteria of assonance and horoscope and is officially bestowed at the child's naming ceremony (*kèkaq*). This naming feast ideally requires the sacrifice of an uncastrated male goat for the child to ride upon when making his (or her) eventual spirit journey to heaven; it may occur any time in the life cycle up to the time of marriage. Some villagers feel that prior to the *kèkaq* a child's permanent name should be kept secret between the parents and the *sanro* who helped select it. Often the timing of the *kèkaq* depends upon the child's health, as name changing is felt to be one of the most effective ways of altering a child's disposition to illness. Hence, a child who is sickly from birth may undergo his *kèkaq* within his first or second year—although not before the end of his mother's forty-four-day period of sexual abstinence after childbirth. If the child continues sickly, further name changings may be directed by its parents or by a specialist such as the *lebè* or another *sanro*. However, these are more specifically therapeutic in nature than the *kèkaq* itself, are not elaborately celebrated, and are not regarded as being additional *kèkaq* ceremonies. For the child whose health is generally good, the *kèkaq* ceremony is less urgent and may be celebrated at the time of another life-cycle feast (including marriage), when the parents can more easily afford the cost of the sacrificial animal. The *kèkaq* may also be held on one of the large feast days of the Moslem calendar; on Hari Raja Hadji (Idhul Adha), however, when a water buffalo is ceremonially slaughtered for the entire village religious community, *kèkaq* sacrifices for individual children are forbidden. Furthermore, whenever a person undergoes the *kèkaq*, he or she is—unlike the guests at the feast—forbidden to eat any of the meat of the sacrificial animal.

Between the first months of life and the time of marriage, village children may undergo several other rites of passage. On an auspicious date between their third and sixth months, baby girls experience the ear-piercing and hair-cutting ceremony. This is usually done for several girls at one time, a female specialist (*tukang tamang*) conducts the operation, and the accompanying feast is seldom elaborate. By contrast, young boys frequently receive their first haircut without any accompanying ceremony and today no longer undergo the operation of toothfiling within their first six years. However, at the age of about seven years, as he begins to wear clothing regularly, each boy must be circumcised (*sunat*). This is generally carried out for several boys at once, is marked by a substantial feast given jointly or individually by the families involved, and requires the reading of the Serakal by an invited *hukom* member. Village girls may also be circumcised (in superficial fashion) at roughly the same age, but this rite is neither as regularly nor as elaborately conducted as for boys. Circumcision is generally a dry-season occurrence and at Rarak must be entrusted to the hands of male and female specialists (*tukang sunat*) from lowland villages. These specialists are paid for their services because there are no Rarak resident *sanro* or *hukom* members trained to carry out the operation. The one remaining rite which some village youngsters experience before marriage is the demonstration of Koran reading prowess (*mengadji*), but this is restricted generally to wealthier or especially devout villagers anxious to demonstrate by means of a well-attended feast (usually with the *lebè* presiding) the abilities of their teen-age sons in recitation of the scriptures.

As elsewhere in Indonesia, a first marriage is usually sealed by a pair of ceremonies: the *nika*, or Moslem marriage contract, and the *pe-*

ngantan, or *adat* ceremony. At Rarak the *nika* usually precedes the *adat* ceremony, often by as much as a week or more. Nevertheless, even after the bride's *wali* (guardian) has signed the *nika* contract on her behalf with the groom, the marriage cannot properly be consummated or the couple allowed to live together until after completion of the *adat* ceremony. Preparations for the *pengantan* feast are elaborate, usually require the expenditure of substantial resources of cash and paddy by the immediate families of both bride and groom, and frequently lead to the most lavish single feast of the villager's life cycle. Yet partly because there is no prevalent pattern of bride-price payment in Rarak and, accordingly, the transactions of marriage must always be carefully negotiated and haggled over,[8] the period of a village marriage is generally one of considerable tension between the families concerned. This is true despite the explicitly stated desirability and frequent occurrence of marriage between closely related cognates.

At Rarak, first-cousin marriage is preferred. Among the attributes of the ideal spouse is his or her status as a first cousin. Locally it is often said that marriage with a first cousin is "profitable" or "fortunate," and, more specifically, that the negotiations for the marriage of such cousins are facilitated by the siblingship of the connecting parents. However, among a person's first cousins there is no single preferred type: parallel and cross cousins are stated to be equally desirable as potential spouses. In 1955 the twenty-two first-cousin marriages at Rarak were divided between thirteen parallel- and nine cross-cousin unions. The distribution of all types of cousin marriages in the village was as follows:

Between full first cousins: 22 cases (26 per cent)
Between full second cousins: 25 cases (30 per cent)
Between full third cousins: 21 cases (25 per cent)
Between unrelated villagers: 16 cases (19 per cent)

As these data suggest, the individual's more distantly related cousins also fall within the range of more eligible potential spouses. If a villager is unable to marry a first cousin, the next most desirable candidate is either his (or her) second or third cousin. As with first cousins, there is no explicit preference for either a patrilateral or matrilateral type, and the sex of the connecting cognates is irrelevant. The outer limits of this circle of preferred, marriageable cognates is generally bounded by one's third cousins. While few villagers are able actually to trace

[8] For some detail on the history of Rarak marriage negotiations and their present *adat*, see Goethals (1959).

the genealogical identity of all their third cousins, virtually no villager regards his more distant cousins either as "related" or as lying within the circle of preferred marriageable cognates.

Many villagers view this marriage circle in terms of a definite developmental perspective. In 1955 a familiar marriage maxim, referring to the maintenance of bilateral ties over time, was, "To the third, return to the stem." Here "third" refers to the third degree of cousinship, and the maxim establishes the ideal pattern that all those having common ancestors in the last four generations (a common great-great-great grandparent or less remote ancestor) should re-establish marriage links with one another before their children pass beyond the third degree of cousinship or become "unrelated" fourth cousins. Such reweaving of affinal ties, or "return to the stem," does not and cannot mean that all people must give top priority to marrying a third cousin. Rather it means that sibling *sets* that have come to stand in a simple (neither otherwise related nor related as double third cousins) third-cousin relationship must ideally act to renew their connections through intermarriage. Specifically, this involves only one member of each sibling set concerned and therefore no more than a single marriage linking the two cousin sets of siblings.

The marriage data cited indicate that approximately one of every four village unions represents such a pair of third cousins reaffiliating with the "stem" from maximally attenuated cognatic positions. Unions between first, second, and third cousins comprised 81 per cent of all marriages represented in Rarak in 1955. The first- and second-cousin categories were each slightly more favored (26 per cent and 30 per cent) than was that of third cousin (25 per cent) and appear to be somewhat more important in delineating the actual cognatic circle of preferred spouse candidates. Nevertheless, marriage among the first three degrees of cousin, as compared with those among unrelated people, indicates that the conception of "stem" expressed in the Rarak marriage maxim is of functional significance in channeling the selection of a spouse. Not only do the villagers envisage a collateral circle of cognates within which one should marry, but at least to some extent the descent from a common ancestor is felt to obligate the members of this circle to re-establish marriage links between their respective sibling sets before cognatic ties become too far attenuated.

Rarak marriages between all degrees of cousins and unrelated individuals tended strongly in 1955 to be contracted either within the village itself or within the nearby upland villages of Rarak's own "circle" (see part 5, following). The details on these marriages are given elsewhere (Goethals 1960) but cannot be elaborated here.

The final rite of the villager's life cycle occurs just after his death when his body is laid to rest in the small village burial ground not far from the village mosque. At Rarak the funeral rites and the periodic recitation of prayers after the funeral are typically Islamic and Indonesian; some variation occurs according to the prestige of the deceased, and the most scrupulous observance of the post-funeral prayer sessions tends to mark the death of a village *adat* or *hukom* official. However, except in the case of young children who have not yet attained religious maturity, a funeral rite must include at least the recitation of the *teleként* and usually also prayers at the deceased's home following burial. A member of the *hukom* group generally officiates both at the graveside and at the deceased's home. It is also the *hukom* leaders (*lebè, pengulu, rura*) or their wives—depending upon the sex of the deceased—who are impervious to the miscellaneous dangers of handling the deceased's body and who prepare it for burial. The funeral rite and the burial of a villager always takes place within twenty-four hours of his death and usually considerably sooner.

5. *Structure and Horizon in Village Society*

Throughout west Sumbawa a rural villager can usually be fully identified through joint reference to his or her village or residence and family membership. Family of origin is sometimes designated by a formal patronym, i.e., Abdul bin Abdullah, Sulasia binte Seleiman. Sometimes, instead, family of procreation is emphasized by adding directly the name of a person's spouse, i.e., Sulasia-Karim. However, despite the occasional patrilineal bias in name reference, social structure throughout the area is organized entirely upon a bilateral principle. This allows Rarak's social system to be delineated according to the nine structural features utilized by Murdock (1960, 14) in his recent typology of bilateral social organization. These are as follows:

(1) The small domestic unit is prominent at Rarak. As indicated in the previous discussion of Rarak's subsistence calendar, the community's most common residential and subsistence unit is the household, a domestic group that shifts its residence twice a year while maintaining a stable membership. Of Rarak's (August) 1955 total of 91 households, 80 (comprising 401 villagers) were of this shifting, stable membership

type; 58 of these 80 households, in turn, represented nuclear, monogamous families. Thus, 298 villagers, or about 67 per cent of Rarak's total 1955 population, lived throughout the year in domestic units (households) made up of nuclear family groups. The other 22 shifting households of stable membership (comprising 4 genealogical types and totaling 103 villagers) most frequently included a surviving parent (widow, widower, or divorcee) living either with unmarried dependent children or with one married child plus that child's spouse and the couple's dependent children. The 43 remaining village inhabitants were divided between two other household types (shifting residence with splitting membership; stable residence with stable membership) which included three genealogical types between them (Goethals 1960, 188–190).

(2) There are no extended families at Rarak. Not a single extended family or household organization embracing "two or more married siblings in its senior generation" (Murdock 1960, 4) was revealed in a 1955 census of the community (Goethals 1960, 186 ff).

(3) A bilateral kindred, defined as a "category of cognates, a set of persons who have in common the characteristic that they are all related cognatically to the same person" (Freeman 1961, 202), is of sociological importance to each individual and his siblings at Rarak. Such kindreds, centered maximally upon a sibling group, are not terminologically recognized in the village; they cannot and do not form discrete groups in village society nor are they corporate in any sense. However, from time to time action groupings recruited from each villager's cognates (and therefore kindred based) take part in such activities as the rites of passage (at birth, circumcision, marriage, name changing or *kèkaq*, and death), working parties, and hunting groupings. Yet because, on the one hand, no villager is ever able to recruit all his known cognates for any of these occasions and because, on the other hand, some affines and friends are inevitably included in each of them, the Rarak kindred per se cannot be regarded as a sociological group. Rather his kindred provides the Rarak villager (and his siblings) with a category of cognates, many of whom may live in other villages and some of whom may be relied upon for interest and assistance at certain times. Sociologically, therefore, it is important only as the personal kinship category from which occasional action or interest groupings are very largely recruited (Freeman 1961, 202).

(4) There are no descent groups at Rarak. Descent groups such as ambilineal ramages, if construed to be "the precise functional equivalents

of lineages" (Murdock 1960, 11) cannot from present evidence be discerned at Rarak. Nevertheless, the village pattern of cousin marriage (see foregoing part 4) suggests some local awareness of group affiliation based upon common descent.

(5) The rule of residence is neolocal at Rarak. Even when one partner to a marriage is of non-Rarak origin, a marriage usually precipitates the establishment of a new household within two months of the wedding ceremony. While there may be an initial post-wedding period when the groom lives with his wife in her parents' home, the pattern thereafter is clearly one of neolocal residence.

(6) and (7) Marriage with first and second cousins is allowed at Rarak (for details see part 4).

(8) The Rarak kinship terminology for cousins is formally of the "Eskimo" type. While a villager may—and often does—extend the sibling terms of kinship to his familiar cousins, Sumbawan kinship terminology distinguishes Ego's true siblings from other cognates of his own generation.

(9) Avuncular kinship terminology is of the lineal type. At Rarak this means not only that the parents' siblings are terminologically distinguished from parents but also that they are grouped, both in reference and address, by their age relative to the connecting parent. These same terms are also widely extended to other people who, while not cognatically linked to the speaker, are nevertheless established members of his parental generation and may be bracketed as either senior or junior in age to a parent. Such usage not only emphasizes the classificatory nature of Rarak kinship and its stress on relative age but also indicates a more pervasive sociological effect: the proper assignment of each individual to his or her own generation level. In effect, it means that each villager becomes permanently affiliated with a particular generational group having members not only in his own village but (with the occasional aid of semifictitious kinship ties) also among his friends and associates in distant communities as well. Generational difference is further reinforced by the prevalence of teknonymy: by this pattern a villager is constantly reminded of his exact generational level and this, in turn, does much to pattern the interpersonal etiquette between all villagers. Many characteristically Indonesian tokens of respect and deference, for example, must be shown in the speech and behavior directed toward a person of one's parental or grandparental generation.

These nine structural features establish the close resemblance of

Rarak's social system to that of several neighboring Indonesian peoples.[9] They further show that beyond the limits of his nuclear family the villager belongs to no clearly bounded subsociety, such as a matrilineage or patrilineage, structured by the ties of consanguinity. Nevertheless, it is largely through recognition of widespread ties of generation and cognatic kinship that each Rarak villager gains familiarity with other Sumbawans from the discernible, but fluidly defined, circle of neighboring communities. These five settlements are scattered within a radius of about eight kilometers and, while smaller in size, share Rarak's economy, social structure, pattern of religious leadership, and the lack of aristocratic tradition. By frequent visits to relatives and friends among these families in those settlements, every Rarak citizen develops a personal social network of regional scope which supplements the more routine social ties within his home community. In terms of this more extended social participation, each villager becomes aware of another dimension to his social identity: membership in a regional society characterized by a common "horizon" of sentiment and subculture.

Historically the villagers of Rarak's circle have looked to the coastal belt both for their trade goods and for leadership in government. In addition to their resident Chinese and Arab shopkeepers, Sumbawa's lowland towns and hamlets have long housed the aristocratic families of the officials in the Sultan of Sumbawa's prerevolutionary government. Among these were the *demong*, or district officers, who in 1956 still acted as the paternal intermediate links in authority between the village headmen and the post-1950 government of western Sumbawa. Yet as he figuratively looks up to the lowlands, the villager looks down on the people from Sumbawa's remote hinterlands, the uncouth mountaineers whom he often sees passing by Rarak en route to lowland markets to sell their horse loads of woven mats and baskets. Their dialect is barely intelligible, their clothing often in rags, and, had not their distant village produced several well-known *hadji*, their identity in Rarak as bona fide Sumbawans would be tenuous indeed.

To the villager of the Rarak circle, then, the more important members of his greater society reside in the lowlands. Yet his upland background separates him from these neighbors, even from those among them whom he numbers as kinsmen. While seldom aware that his own district (*kedemongan*) boundary links Rarak with several lowland villages, he

[9] For a convenient summary of the data on several of these groups, see Murdock (1960).

is inevitably aware of the social boundary separating him from all low-landers. Among his more educated, urbane, and prosperous lowland neigh-bors, this boundary tends to block his social acceptance by fixing him with a regional identity—one primarily as a swidden farmer and a poor man. Many lowlanders have cousins living in the Rarak circle, but only an especially congenial tie can usually bridge the social gulf between them. The lowlander often regards even his cousins of the uplands as rough-hewn, somewhat superstitious, but fairly dependable people; they are neither the hinterland rustics of the distant interior nor yet sophisticated in the refinements of lowland *adat*. At times he can feel only condescen-sion for their clothing, dialect, or ignorance of the scriptures. Yet, while realizing that such uplanders lack resident aristocrats to exemplify the finest of interpersonal etiquette, he cannot overlook such differences. Only with misgivings would he consent to his daughter's marrying a man from Rarak or its circle.

On the other hand, a Rarak man is seldom reluctant to marry a low-lander if the opportunity arises. If such a woman stands to inherit wet paddy land, house property, or livestock, her eligibility usually attracts attention well beyond her own village. For men of the Rarak circle, the lowland paddy area holds promise of a far more settled and less precarious existence than the upland swiddens. Personal industry, luck, and opportune kinship connections may all play a part in such a man's overcoming the barrier of locale, winning a lowland wife, and establish-ing himself and his household in the lowlands. However, this remains the exception, and Rarak marriages are mostly contracted within the village or in the closely adjacent communities of its circle. Among Rarak's married couples in 1955, only about fifteen involved spouses of lowland origins; without exception these were men.

Rarak's pattern of religious ritual and leadership typifies another as-pect of the regional horizon. Throughout the year, whether living on swidden or in the main settlement, most Rarak households participate not only in the ceremonial of the Islamic calendar but also in that of the agricultural cycle. In both these cycles, Rarak's mosque officials headed by the *lebè* act as the key ritual experts. Daily prayers and Friday mosque services provide these men with their most regular responsibilities, and, during the *barat*'s period of dispersed living, the weekly mosque gatherings become especially important in maintaining village social cohe-sion. Less frequent, but of equal importance, is their direction of the community-wide observances of Puasa, Lebaran, Idhul Adha, Maulud, and lesser Islamic feast occasions. Yet, by contrast to the lowlands, where religious leadership by mosque officials tends to be restricted to their formal Koranic duties, the skills of the same officials at Rarak are equally essential to the efficacy of village agricultural ritual. At times such as first paddy planting, ritual washing of the new paddy crop (see section 2), and the opening of the harvest period, the village *lebè* and other *hukom* officials are expected to establish the timing and mode of auspicious observance. In turn, each household head reciprocates through his annual payment of *djakat*, a tithe he pays (in the form of paddy) to his community religious leaders in fulfillment of one of the primary obligations of Islam.

A concern with yet more remote religious leadership and interests also shapes the regional horizon. While Rarak's leaders are usually adequate to administering the Islamic domestic law of the community, all villagers are also cognizant of the higher religious jurisdiction represented by such figures as western Sumbawa's *imam, kadi,* and *pengulu,* all of whom live in the lowland capital town. Appearance before these paramount judicial figures has been the experience of only about half a dozen older village men, participants in those rare village conflicts over divorce or inheritance that have required jurisdiction at the highest level. Yet because their cases are locally remembered in detail, they provide the entire Rarak circle a vicarious but vivid contact with the outermost circle of religious authority. Similarly vicarious is the local pattern of "fulfilling" the religious obligation of the *hadj,* or pilgrimage to Mecca. Whereas in 1956 no villager of the Rarak circle had yet become a bona fide *hadji,* a number of older men in each of the villages were quietly confident of having shared in the merit of pilgrimages made in earlier years by more affluent lowland men. This they had achieved through the widespread Sumbawan practice of sending money or gifts with such pilgrims to be bestowed on designated, worthy recipients in the Holy City. Among lowland villagers, by contrast, the individual's familiarity with higher religious officialdom and his likelihood of personally achieving the *hadj* were, in 1956, far greater.

These several features of regional subculture can suggest how villagers of the Rarak circle tend to feel themselves collectively distinct within their greater society. While many Sumbawans like, as a matter of course, to point out the distinctiveness of their individual village traditions and *adat,* it seems that spouse selection and ritual leadership represent fields of Sumbawan *adat* that, as concomitants of interregional differences in subsistence economy, show clear subcultural patterning. Such *adat* differences, realized very largely through the ties of his upland regional society, make the villager of the Rarak circle aware of an important segment of his own subcultural tradition.

6. *Authority and Leadership*

Formal civil and religious authority at Rarak[10] rests in the hands of two separate hierarchies of male village leaders. In civil affairs (*adat*) the deputy head (*wakil kepala*), known before 1952 as the *kepala kampung*, acts as the paramount leader. Guidance in matters of religious law and belief (*hukom*) falls under the jurisdiction of the mosque staff (*isi mesigét*) headed by the village *lebè*. These two paramount village leaders, assisted by their subordinates and in frequent consultation with Rarak's responsible older men, are explicitly accorded the villager's trust when he needs either counsel or representation. In Rarak and in neighboring upland villages there have never been resident Sumbawan aristocratic families: all villagers are commoners, and claim to local leadership has therefore never rested upon inherited rank as such. While the ascribed statuses of generational seniority and of formal office command automatic respect, the constant face-to-face contact of village life usually ensures that a village leader of any following, whether or not he is appointed to formal *adat* or *hukom* office, has already developed special and even charismatic qualities.

Of the two hierarchies, the *adat* group has traditionally been the smaller, the *hukom* group or *isi mesigét* the larger. In 1956 Rarak's deputy head was assisted by a foreman (*mandur*), an unpaid helper who acted occasionally as a messenger, and by a *malar*, or "inspector of village lands." The *malar* held his job in title only; his hypothetical responsibilities of periodically inspecting, measuring, and reporting upon the conditions of village crop land were, in fact, never performed, and he received no compensation for such "services." A fourth member of Rarak's *adat* group was the deputy assistant (*wakil kepala gabungan*), a man who acted exclusively as the personal messenger for the village union headman in his supra-village administrative role (see below). As head of the second, or *hukom*, hierarchy, the *lebè* has seven appointed assistants: a *pengulu*, a *rura*, a *mudom*, two *ketip*, and two *marbat*. By virtue of their juniority,

[10] A considerably more extended discussion of this general topic can be found in Goethals (1961).

the two *ketip* and *marbat* (aged twenty-five and thirty-five years) are charged with the routine administration of the mosque. For the *ketip*, these duties principally involve conducting the Friday noon prayer service and reading its *chotbah* (sermon); for the *marbat*, the main duties comprise cleaning the mosque building, filling its ablution water containers, and beating its *bedok* (drum) calls to prayer each day.

During the turbulent years since 1940, traditional qualifications for formal leadership at Rarak have been steadily changing. No longer, for example, is the village *adat* head necessarily conspicuous for his dominant personality, his agility in the traditional modes of debate or physical combat, his strong hand in averting village violence, or his halting literacy restricted to Arabic texts. Rarak's deputy head of 1955 might appear—as he certainly did to some older villagers—almost incompetent by contrast: a quiet, tactful man, he seemed almost inarticulate and conciliatory in village meetings; physically aggressive only on the soccer field, he relied on persuasion to keep village peace; minimally competent in the national language and its Roman orthography, he was increasingly burdened with administrative paper work dictated from outside the village. No longer were his journeys to the lowland capital undertaken largely in the capacity of village "defender" against the royal demands of the Sultan's court; in 1955, his trips took him instead to political rallies and educated him in regional or national politics and the affairs of new governmental agencies whose powers were already apparent within the village. Nevertheless, he still resembled the traditional *adat* head in being above thirty-five years of age before he assumed formal office and in representing a family line which not only had given Rarak previous leaders but had also bequeathed to him considerable wealth in choice land parcels. Furthermore, his wife numbered other former *adat* or *hukom* leaders among her own immediate ancestors; thereby their marriage symbolized the continued close alliance of descent, wealth, and public leadership. Finally, the longer he continued to hold office responsibly, the more consistently he was locally rumored to possess special powers. Like successful leaders of an earlier period he was, in fact, showing abilities as a *sanro* (shaman), one who had proved his specialty in guarding Rarak's soccer players from enemy magic (*sihér*) when playing in neighboring villages.

Qualifications for top *hukom* leadership remain somewhat more traditional. To be picked for *hukom* membership, a villager must have a basic knowledge of the scriptures, especially the Koran, and be able to recite and chant the Arabic of these texts. He begins to develop this

ability between the ages of six and ten years as he studies to *mengadji*
(recite) under the guidance of a parent, a village elder, or an even more
recognized authority such as a *hadji*. Much of this training is built upon
rote memorizing, and few villagers achieve either real comprehension
or adequate pronunciation of the Arabic. The village youth fortunate
enough to *mengadji* for a period under a lowland *hadji* or *ulama* and
develop a superior grasp of the scriptures is, upon his return to Rarak,
especially likely to assume office as a *hukom* member. He may be appointed a *ketip* or *marbat* while still in his twenties and, if responsible,
like the successful *adat* leader will then begin to exhibit yet new qualities
of leadership as he continues. While wealth and family background also
play a part in his eventual attainment of high *hukom* office, his knowledge
of and commitment to Islamic doctrine is basic to any influence he will
have. But this identification tends to carry him further: often it either
bestows or enhances an aptitude in magical activities. Such a villager
may then come to be described as *barkat*, or blessed with unique powers
that validate his leadership potential yet more fully. Each of Rarak's
leading *hukom* members (*lebé*, *pengulu*, *rura*) was described in 1955
by fellow villagers as *barkat*. Two of the junior members of the *hukom*
hierarchy were also then felt to be showing signs of the same condition.

   In 1955, then, the formal authority of each senior *adat* and *hukom*
leader was reinforced by certain, individually distinct powers as a *sanro*.
The *adat* head protected village soccer players. The *rura* exercised healing
powers as a masseur and leech. The *pengulu*, second only to the *lebè*
in *hukom* seniority, was known for his ability to cure and protect hunting
dogs; more importantly, he was also charged with periodically purifying
and blessing the village territory against spirits of disease and misfortune.
The *lebè*, Rarak's oldest and most influential single leader, was pre-emi-
nent as a carpenter *sanro*, specializing in the intricate techniques and
ritual of successful house and mosque construction. Because of his related
knowledge of natural signs and long experience in horoscopy, villagers
tended to seek his advise as a diviner in many other matters as well.
Even the *mudom*—to many villagers, a man of dubious competence as
a *hukom* official—was known for some magical powers, even though
these were sometimes suspected as being antisocial in nature.

   While representing nominally separate fields of authority, Rarak's
adat and *hukom* leaders usually cooperate closely in the administration
of all village affairs. Because the basic duty of the *adat* head (other
than the annual collection of taxes) is to keep peace in the village, he

will inevitably be called whenever a matter of *hukom* must be decided. Most threats to village peace are, in fact, *hukom* issues: divorce, adultery, inheritance disputes, runaway marriage, illegitimacy. Matters such as theft (of clothing or livestock) or bodily assault, which may be regarded as *adat* offenses, occur far less frequently. Yet these, too, will normally be considered jointly by *adat* and *hukom* leaders, often in consultation with village elders. After assembling to hear the complaints of all parties, their collective decision will settle most village conflicts. If their counsel or warnings go unheeded, the *lebè* and *adat* head will refer the case to the *demong*, or district officer, on his monthly routine visit to the village. As the appointed representative of the regional government, the *demong* is charged with supervising election of village officials in his district, collecting tax money, and personally arbitrating all unresolved village-level disputes. In 1955–56 the half-dozen Rarak cases put before the *demong* were settled finally—by his affirming in all but one instance the previous decisions by village leaders. Described by village elders as "acting like a father here," the *demong* is still widely idealized in traditional terms: he is a man of knowledge and rank who is articulate and discreet, able to check dissension with a firm hand and, if necessary, administer punishment on the spot.

Selection of Rarak's two paramount leaders is controlled largely by the villagers themselves. In 1955 the traditional pattern persisted whereby a caucus of male household heads, usually convened by the *demong*, chooses every new *adat* head or *lebè*. After the *demong*'s confirmation, each leader then holds office either for life, until voluntary retirement, or until such time as discontent with his performance prompts the *demong* to intervene and call for the selection of a successor. On taking office, each leader is entitled to appoint and discharge his own assistants; generally this is done in consultation with Rarak's influential elder men. While he controls more appointments than does the *adat* head, the *lebè*'s choices for *hukom* office are also relatively more restricted by their need of qualifying experience and scriptural proficiency. This means that the *lebè* himself has normally already served for many years either as *ketip* or *pengulu* (never only as *marbat*) to establish his eligibility for paramount *hukom* office. Similarly, his own appointments will very largely predetermine the identity of his successor.

Those community resources which provide Rarak's officials with remuneration for their services derive, as previously mentioned, from the third primary obligation of Islam: that of *zakat*, or alms-giving. *Djakat*, the Indonesian and Sumbawan rendition of the term, has locally come to mean the religious tithe annually required from each devout Moslem of the religious community. At Rarak the tithe applies only to the villager's staple commodity—his paddy harvest—and is paid in kind principally to the religious personnel of the mosque (i.e., *isi mesigét*) and to dependent relatives and elders within the community. Before Allah a community member is excused from *djakat* payment only if he possesses just enough paddy "income" to support himself and his family but nothing more.

The details of how the *djakat* at Rarak is collected and distributed are given elsewhere (Goethals 1961, 68–74). Although traditionally the *djakat* "fund" at Rarak has been used to help support the community leaders and to supply some relief to the older or poorer citizens of the community, it is of interest to note that a new and very untraditional type of leader had, by 1955, achieved enough acceptance among the people of Rarak to be included as a regular recipient of the village *djakat*. This leader was the village union head (*kepala gabungan*), a man who resided in Rarak holding an office that had been established a scant four years previously and whose social role, degree of local authority, and source of salary appear to have been left largely or completely undefined by the government which arranged his election. Like other villages throughout western Sumbawa, Rarak in 1951 had been grouped administratively with two or three other closely contiguous villages of the same district into an artificial new unit, the "village union" (*gabungan*). Under the guide of their *demong*, the people of Rarak had then voted with their fellow *gabungan* members for a man to assume the new headmanship—a man whose duties were vaguely supposed to be halfway between those of village headman and *demong*. Only gradually had this man, who had chosen Rarak to be the administrative village of its *gabungan*, achieved enough prestige with the villagers by 1955 to be allowed a portion of the *djakat* for his services.

The extent of the villager's comprehension of the new national political processes felt increasingly in Rarak since 1950 may be glimpsed in terms of the village campaign leading to the 1955 elections. Knowledge of the issues, the parties, and the candidates for office was at best limited. Political currency consisted rather of party labels, a few slogans, and established rumors as to the local meaning of each. The choice posed in the village was among the Masjumi, the Nationalist, and the Nahdatul Ulama parties. A month before the village voting began, gossip increasingly centered on who had just switched his support to which party. The focal points around which these allegiances shifted were three personalities: the *lebè*, who staunchly supported the Masjumi; the village union head, who headed the small NU contingent; and a younger man of lowland origins (not a member of either the *adat* or *hukom* hierarchies), who led the Nationalist faction. The *demong* was rumored to belong to the NU because it was further rumored to be the party of the *swapradja* head (now the *swatantra* head), the former Sultan of Sumbawa. The *lebè* and most of the *hukom* group justified their support of the Masjumi by identifying it as the party of the *imam*—the top religious official—of western Sumbawa. Opponents of the Masjumi faction claimed that, if the Masjumi candidate won, Indonesia would become a Moslem state and all women would then be barred from voting. According to the few younger men in the village who could frame an opinion, the NU was basically a liberal party which was "like the Nationalists." On these grounds, many of the village's avowed Nationalist supporters hoped that the village union head and the *demong* would at the last minute throw their weight behind the Nationalist candidate, while maintaining an NU affiliation as a *pro forma* symbol of religious propriety and devotion befitting their station. As it turned out, the village union head did switch his support to the Nationalists, while the *demong* ended up by backing the town candidate of the Partai Serikat Islam Indonesia (Islamic Association Party of Indonesia). These maneuvers were aimed primarily at weakening the strong and conservative local Masjumi group.

Nevertheless, the villagers voted well over 60 per cent for the Masjumi candidate. The village elders joined the leaders in the religious hierarchy in support of Masjumi, and together they carried with them a majority of the other household heads and their wives. The Nationalist supporters were concentrated among younger heads but included prominent members of the *adat* group as well. Those who had been torn between identification with the town-oriented Nationalists, on the one hand, and with the elderly illiterate backers of the Masjumi, on the other, apparently provided the NU with its small local vote. Thus party allegiances in the village developed as a close reflection of traditional personal loyalties, with those to the established village-level leaders taking precedence over more distant or newly established ties.

Such election alignments gave particularly dramatic indication of the closed corporate community structure which persisted in 1955 at Rarak (Goethals 1961, 105–108). Still predisposed by their marginal economic location and essentially traditional technology to subsistence level production, the villagers tended also to define their community in terms of their political-religious system as a whole. Rarak's twin interlocking hierarchies of leaders were not only legitimated by corporate community patterns of "conspicuous consumption" but also supported by typically strong informal mechanisms of social control. Yet even at this time the village's marginal economy and conservative patterns of sociopolitical self-sufficiency were already being reshaped by new ideas propagated from the administrative nexus of regional and national government in the lowland town sixteen kilometers distant. Prospects for further modification of its corporate structure depend fundamentally upon the improvement of the villager's economy from his current meager subsistence level. Development of a higher standard of living can only parallel further spread of education and literacy into western Sumbawa's impoverished uplands. As in many other parts of Indonesia, this education at the village level poses perhaps the paramount challenge to the new national government.

Chapter III

Soba: An Atoni Village of West Timor[1]

CLARK E. CUNNINGHAM
YALE UNIVERSITY

1. The Princedoms of the Atoni

Soba is one of the approximately 775 villages in Indonesian Timor that belong to the Atoni Pah Mèto. These "people of the dry land," who number about 300,000, occupy a land area of 11,799 square kilometers. Their neighbors in Timor are the Tètun, Buna', and Kémak of the Bélu district, the Hélong of Semau Island and western Timor, and the immigrant islanders of nearby Roté and Sabu. The Atoni are called Dawan by the Tètun and Rawan by the Buna', both terms of unknown etymology. The Indonesian-speaking inhabitants of Kupang town call the Atoni *orang gunung* ("mountain people"), *orang asli* ("indigenous people"), or simply *orang* Timor (Timorese). *Orang* Timor is also used generally for anyone living in the Timor region; thus many Rotenese or Sabunese living in Java call themselves *orang* Timor. The nomenclature is further complicated when Indonesians of Kupang refer to mountain people in terms of their political affiliation to a *swapradja*, or princedom (e.g., *orang* Amarasi, *orang* Amanubuan). Similarly, Kupang people refer to Tètun, Buna', and Kémak simply as *orang* Bélu. These usages are also found in Dutch literature, where the Atoni are variously referred to as Timoreesch, Atoni, or by political affiliation (e.g., Amarasiers, Amanubangers). In this chapter, I follow Ormeling (1956) in using the name Atoni ("people," "men").

[1] The field research on which this article is based was conducted between 1959 and 1961.

The Atoni occupy exclusively nine princedoms of Indonesian Timor, i.e., Amarasi, Fatu Leu, Amfoan, Mollo, Amanuban, Amanatun, Miomafo, Insana, and Beboki. They form the bulk of the population of the princedom of Kupang, exclusive of Kupang town and the island of Semau. Kupang has a highly mixed population of Atoni, Rotenese, Sabunese, Chinese, Florenese, Solorese, Alorese, Ambonese, Kisarese, Macassarese, and Javanese. Many groups have intermarried and lived there for several generations, while others are newcomers. Rotenese and Sabunese, preponderant in Kupang town, received mission education during the nineteenth century. Active Dutch administration only reached the interior of Timor in 1910–1915. Schools began shortly thereafter in the princedom centers, but their influence has only begun to reach the Atoni intensively during the past decade. Consequently, fewer Atoni have entered the civil service, teaching, the ministry, the police, or the army. Overpopulation in several princedoms has led some Atoni to migrate to Kupang town, and it is estimated that there are now about 5,000 of them, mainly doing manual labor.

When the Dutch government entered the interior in the first decade of this century, the Atoni lived in princedoms, most of which had signed contracts with the Dutch government in 1756 or earlier. Atoni princes are mentioned in Chinese travel reports as early as the fifteenth century (Groeneveldt 1960, 116–117). Subjects delivered tribute to their rulers, for which they received adjudication and supernatural benefit in return. There is a tradition of warfare between princedoms, and between their constituent villages and subdistricts, resulting at times in great alliances such as the Sonba'i empire, at other times in a fractionalized state of autonomous, warring villages.

In the twentieth century, the Dutch recognized ten indigenous princedoms, each of which they called a *landschap* and the Indonesians now call a *swapradja*. In some cases *swapradja* conform to traditional unified princedoms, while in others the Dutch government amalgamated smaller princedoms into larger units. The present *swapradja* of Amarasi, Amfoan, Amanuban, Amanatun, Insana, Beboki, and, to a lesser extent, Mollo represent unified princedoms of several centuries' antiquity, while Kupang, Fatu Leu, and Miomafo represent amalgamations of smaller princedoms under a Dutch-appointed ruler (*radja*).

Following Dutch military action in the interior and a century of warfare between the princedoms after the dissolution of the Sonba'i empire (which, at one time, comprehended Kupang, Fatu Leu, Mollo, and

Miomafo), the establishment of these ten princedoms led to many political difficulties, some of which have yet to be overcome. The settlement of borders and the elevation of ruling lines were often made in terms of inadequate information. Politics on the part of both the Dutch government and the various parties among the Atoni led to mistakes, injustices, and deceptions. The Dutch government inevitably rewarded those who cooperated and opposed those who did not. The warring period of the nineteenth century encouraged various parties among the Atoni, the Chinese, and the Rotenese and others who served as troops for the Dutch to use this situation to their advantage, promoting themselves or their allies and doing in their enemies. An arbitrary balance was maintained by the preponderance of Dutch power from 1920 to 1940. During World War II old disputes flared up, but the Japanese generally refused to become involved, for the most part, maintaining the *status quo*. In 1950, the government of the Republic of Indonesia inherited the system of administration and many of the problems consequent upon the formation of the princedoms. It has so far retained the princedoms, while weakening the power of the rulers, but is devoted to the elimination of the principalities altogether from the island.

2. The Environment and Location of Soba

Hilly loose-soiled terrain, very heavy rains from December to March, shifting cultivation by an increasingly greater population, and the expansion of cattle, which now number about 700,000 head in Indonesian Timor (about one and one-half times the human population), contribute on Timor to what the geographer Ormeling has characterized as "a deteriorating environment" (1956, 207). Particularly loose soil and hilly terrain in Amarasi, and a relatively high population density, make conditions there even worse. The former *radja* of Amarasi helped to remedy the situation by enforcing the planting of *lamtoro* (*Leucaena glauca Benth*) and by dividing the princedom into cultivation and grazing areas separated by a great fence. The results have been encouraging, particularly in the *kefettoran* (subdistrict) of Baun, but Amarasi is unique in such progressive measures.

Hamlets and fields are found along ridges and slopes, normally near sources of water. Soba is one of the twenty *ketemukungan* (villages) of the *kefettoran* Baun of the *swapradja* Amarasi.[2] This is one of four princedoms which, with the islands of Roté and Sabu, form the Regency of Kupang, headed by a *bupati* (regent).[3] In 1950, Baun had a population of 7,024 and Amarasi, 17,572 (Lobach 1951, 14).

In the village of Baun, the center of the *kefettoran*, one finds a government office, rest house, a house of the *radja* of Amarasi, the house of the *fettor* (subdistrict head), a market, a clinic, a general curriculum junior high school, an elementary school, a Protestant church, and a

Table 3. Population of Soba, West Timor

Hamlet cluster	Hamlet	Male	Female	Total
Oemoro	Boni	22	21	43
	Oemoro	27	29	56
Nunré'u	Nunré'u	30	23	53
	Kuankiu	31	44	75
	Kuanfénu	19	25	44
	Ruaputu	17	10	27
	Puru	3	2	5
	Nunko'u	6	5	11
Sonaf-Nustoi	Sonaf	24	20	44
	Nustoi	27	21	48
	Bunsibu	5	10	15
Kaidjo'o	Kuafé'u	22	18	40
	Kuanaknèté	12	21	33
	Kaidjo'o	68	53	121
	Néofmé'é	24	16	40
	Oras	19	12	31
	Kuakètun	10	8	18
Total		366	338	704

Roman Catholic chapel. A Protestant minister (a Rotenese) lives in Baun, but the Roman Catholic chapel is served by a priest from Kupang.

Soba consists of 189 households, with a total population of 704. Table 3 gives the population as of May 1961 by sex, hamlet, and hamlet cluster (my own census figures).

The village is located 2 kilometers from the village of Baun and approximately 25 kilometers southeast of Kupang town (the capital of the

[2] Early information on Amarasi is included in an anonymous article in the journal *Tijdschrift voor het Binnenlandsch Bestuur* (1892, 210–227).

[3] The district is Daerah Swatantra Tingkat II (Autonomous Region Level II), usually abbreviated Daswati II. The "province" is called Daswati I.

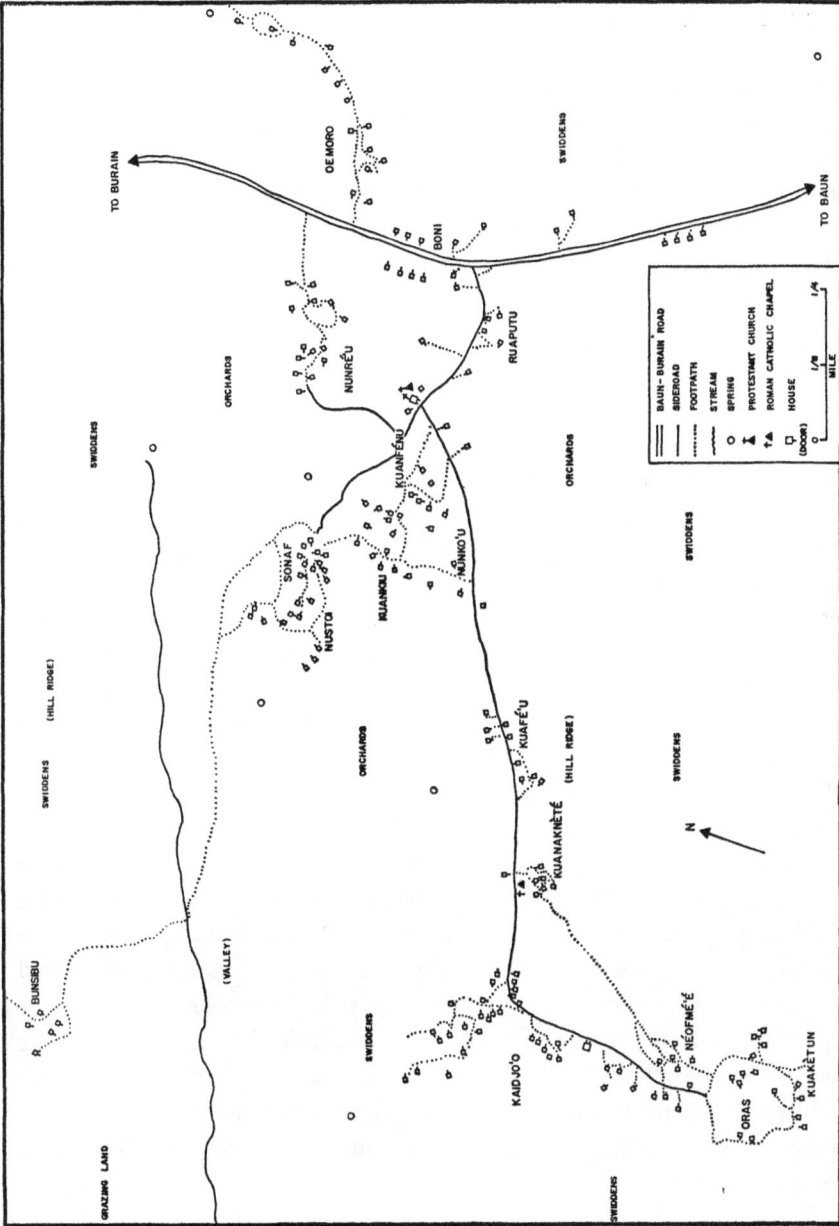

Map III. Settlement Pattern of Soba

province of the Eastern Lesser Sundas). The eastern end of Soba inter-
sects the all-weather road from Baun to Burain, the capital of Amarasi.
A side road built by villagers carries trucks a mile into the village. Such
easy access to a road and market is atypical of Timor villages. In Amarasi
itself, few villages are so favored, and the proportion is much less in
other princedoms.[4] The unique position of Soba has brought it to the
threshold of a market economy during the past two decades, but only
to the threshold. In most aspects of village organization and economy,
it varies little from areas isolated from roads.

3. Subsistence Economics

The Atoni are shifting cultivators who reside in permanent hamlets
(*kuan*). A field is cleared, fenced, and worked for several years, then
left alone. In Soba the working period is longer because soil-enriching
lamtoro is planted during the dry season, and farmers may work the
same plot for five or more years consecutively. The length of time a
field can be used varies, both over Timor and within a single village,
because of striking variation in soil, terrain, and weather. Farmers differ
in their criteria for telling when to shift a plot. Because of the variation
in initial rains, it is difficult to say when a plot has ceased to produce
well, a lower yield resulting as much from late or early planting as
from diminished soil fertility. The complexity of soil and weather provides the main Atoni argument for individual, rather than collective,
work. They prefer to stand and fall by their own decisions and efforts.

The household is the basic economic unit. There is little cooperative
effort among households at any stage of farming, except where the fields
of old people, particularly widows, are concerned. Even old people dislike
dependence and work as long as they are able. Men must first feed
their wives and children, so they may pay less attention to work for
old people. An elderly couple in Soba are admired because they make
their own field, though the man is blind. His wife leads him to their
field near the hamlet and helps him to plant, weed, and harvest, though
younger relatives clear the plot. Self-reliance is prized, and "one man,
one field" is the general rule.

[4] Of the fifty-three subdistricts of the ten princedoms occupied by Atoni,
28 per cent are served by all-season roads; 27 per cent by dry-season roads;
45 per cent by no roads at all. From late December to early March, the
main road running the length of Indonesian Timor may also be cut at the
Noelmina River, isolating six princedoms and Bélu district entirely.

Generally in Timor—Amarasi representing some exception—fields are fenced against incursions of cattle and pigs, and farmers must raid forests for timber. This requires much wood, time, and labor, thus limiting the size of the field a man can work.

Usually at the end of the dry season, around October, farmers clear plots for the planting which follows in December with the first rains. Planting is done with iron dibbles purchased in the market. During January and February, fields are weeded. Machetes are used for clearing and harvesting, and weeding is done with a short knife with a sharpened surface at the end of the blade, used with a jabbing motion. By early March, young corn can be harvested. Fields are planted with corn varying in maturation time from two and a half to four months. The corn maturing first is "for the children," breaking the period of hunger. Rice and the corn of longest maturation are normally ready in April. With rice harvest, the agricultural season ends, and stalks are left to decay in the fields.

Double cropping of corn or rice is impossible, and the success of wet-season crops is precarious, depending on careful judgment of the burning and planting times before the first rains fall. A difference of a week or two in planting may spell success or failure of crops in any village, and the first rains fall most irregularly over the whole princedom. Agriculture is mainly restricted to the wet season, though some dry-season crops such as onions and beans are grown in the Baun area for sale in Kupang. The wet season is marked by dwindling food supplies, commonly referred to on Timor as *lapar biasa*, the usual hunger.

Men normally build fences and clear and burn the fields. Women come to plant, often aided by men. Both sexes weed, but it is primarily the job of men. Women, girls, and boys predominate at harvest, but again men help. When the first fruit appears, women and children spend much time in the fields guarding against pigs, monkeys, and birds. Both sexes and all ages join in bringing the harvest home, carrying it in baskets suspended on shoulder poles or by horse.

The present *radja* has encouraged irrigated rice-growing in the small river valleys, but the steep terrain, torrential rains, and inexperience of the farmers have led to indifferent success in these first years. During 1960–1961, Soba farmers opened a forty-hectare plain of irrigated rice, encouraged by the young *radja*. Each participating household received a plot. The *radja* obtained seed from the agricultural service in Kupang and distributed it free to the villagers. Work was supervised by an older man from a nearby village who had experience near Kupang, where Rotenese have made irrigated fields for decades. Beyond canal digging, there was little cooperative effort. Disputes arose as soon as cattle were brought to turn the soil. The *radja* and the supervisor urged pooling cattle to do the whole area quickly, but many villagers preferred instead to manage their separate plots. Those with enough cattle disliked using them for the plots of relatives or friends with few or no cattle, lest it impair the health of their animals. In the end, their views prevailed. The new irrigated plots were worked like dry fields, despite the fact that uncoordinated turning of the soil upset the flow of water in secondary channels, leading to further disputes.

Most households have an orchard (*po'an*) for piper betel, areca nut, bananas, and coconut. Boundaries are recognized in terms of specific trees planted by a man. The produce is consumed by the household or used for sale. A few villagers plant gardens of tomatoes, garlic, cassava, or spring onions for the Baun market. Both sexes care for orchards and gardens, though the men climb the trees. Villagers visit the trees any time to gather fruit or clear weeds, but Sunday is the busiest day, in preparation for the Monday market. Produce is carried to the market by men, women, and children or on horseback. Village groupings cluster to display produce, which is purchased by Indonesian traders called *papalélé* who come for the day from Kupang. The produce is sold by noon, and the trucks return to Kupang in early afternoon. The traders buy most of the village produce, the rest being taken by civil servants and teachers, Indonesian and Chinese traders living permanently in Baun, or by other villagers. Men may take animals for sale on the hoof or butchered. Some villages produce specialties, such as salt, lime (for betel chewing), basketry, and carpentry, and women sell handicrafts such as baskets, cloth, and ropes. They also sell snacks for market shoppers, and women of Baun serve full meals. Some *papalélé* sell consumer goods; others buy produce for resale in Kupang.

The *papalélé*, usually Rotenese or Sabunese, wear pants, shirts, shoes, and hats. They are in their twenties and early thirties and are mainly male and bachelors, but if married may be helped by their wives. They are out to make money, are brash and contemptuous of the villagers, are normally ignorant of the Atoni language, and give neither credit nor sympathy. They have little interest in Baun but live for Kupang. Inevitably there is animosity between the villagers and the *papalélé*, particularly on the part of the older generation, who, however shrewd, are still unaccustomed to money, do not value it highly, and resent the city-slicker attitude of the young traders. Though distrusted by the older generation, the *papalélé* are increasingly emulated by the young, who have few other models of the outside where their elementary school education encourages them to look.

There are few sources of income within the village other than agriculture. Some half-dozen Soba men make and sell palm wine, either buying *lontar* (*Borassus flabellifer* L.) sugar in Baun or tapping their own coconut palms, and one man, a Rotenese, owns a small coconut-oil press. Occasionally villagers butcher and sell meat from house to house. Women proficient in elaborate basketry or tying cloth by the ikat technique for weaving[5] may sell their work to village mates or exchange it for other needs.

The Atoni have been slow to accept cattle for sale on the market. Introduced in the twenties by the Dutch, cattle have been exported mainly since World War II. The government encourages export from which the exchequer benefits. Atoni need some money to buy goods, pay taxes, and contribute to the education of their children. They are now beginning to sell cattle, which they otherwise value for slaughter at great feasts or for traditional needs such as bride wealth. Increasing numbers of cattle harm fields and forests. The three government services—animal husbandry, agriculture, and forestry—often work at cross-purposes in promoting their separate interests. Their lack of coordination, and the absence of regional planning for economic development and balancing these resources, began in Kupang in Dutch times (Ormeling 1956, 120) and still continues.

Such coordination needs greater administrative authority than the Indonesian government has commanded so far. Since independence, the government has been barely able to provide sufficient facilities for the steady export of cattle, much less tackle the greater problem of conserving resources, though the desire for economic progress is great. The government services lack money, supplies, and staff, plus the breadth of vision to initiate and conduct such a policy. As in Dutch times, technical services in Kupang are poorly coordinated by the civil government and often headed by men from other areas. Department heads often shift services or are transferred to other islands. It is significant that the only effective steps made on Timor to alter ecological imbalance and to introduce different elements into the economy have been made by

[5] For details on the ikat technique, see Bühler (1942).

Atoni rulers, often on their own initiative and utilizing traditional authority.[6]

4. Property Rights to Land and Cattle

A Soba farmer decides where to make a field, often returning to an area formerly worked, but he must inform the *temukung* (village headman). The latter should see that his villagers do not occupy land of others in his own or another village, each village having its acknowledged but unregistered borders; but the degree to which he serves as arbiter or champion of his own villagers in such issues depends upon his character. The *radja* and the *fettor* (subdistrict head) are not informed concerning allotments unless disputes arise.

The two former *radja* of Amarasi persuaded landowning lineages to cede rights over ricelands and cornfields to them and the village headmen. This weakened the authority of local lineages in respect to political figures. Atoni rulers throughout Timor have often sought to control land, and it has been done by force as well as persuasion. Authority over land, tribute, and the definition of boundaries have welded these political units and helped to overcome the socioeconomic autonomy of households, hamlets, and lineages. Rights to formerly irrigated fields and orchards were not ceded, these remaining the property of lineages which first developed them. The expansion of irrigated fields by the present *radja* has led, as we have seen, to disputes over these lands. Some headmen claim the right to dispose of these lands and organize labor on them, the former owners opposing. The *radja* has generally favored the rights of past owners who are willing to develop irrigated fields. When they are not, a headman may be favored so that the work can progress.

Orchards fall into two categories, *po pusak* (orchards of inheritance) and *po sos* (orchards of purchase).

Po pusak consist of trees inherited by a third or later generation from an ancestor who planted or otherwise acquired them. Management is normally established by primogeniture, though a group of patrilineal descendants may divide the trees for purposes of management. In the latter case, the one who manages the trees may "eat the fruit," but he

[6] I refer to the division of Amarasi into cattle and agricultural areas under the late *radja* H. A. Koroh; encouragement for the introduction of onions and other crops into Mollo by then *swapradja* head W. C. H. Oematan; the resettlement projects in Insana initiated by *radja* L. Taolin; and the new villages, irrigated rice, and sea fishing projects in Amarasi of *radja* V. Koroh.

may not bequeath the trees to his descendants, though his offspring may continue to manage them. Descendants are obligated to maintain or expand the *po pusak*. Certain heirlooms also link living members of a lineage to the ancestors. These objects (also called *pusak*) must likewise be maintained or augmented, but not diminished. It is believed that diminution provokes the spirits of ancestors (*nitu*) to retaliate by reducing the offspring of the group. If the *pusak* is lost, the group might be obliterated and the name cease to exist.

Po sos consist of trees acquired by a man or a married couple by purchase or exchange. Like other acquired possessions, they are the joint property of the household. These properties may be divided on separation or divorce and also bequeathed to the children. Neither strict patrilineal inheritance nor primogeniture need regulate the management and distribution of acquired possessions. They are associated with the elementary family (or household), in opposition to ties of descent and affinity which are expressed in *pusak* property.

Cattle are the property of individual householders and may be freely bought, sold, or exchanged for such items as coral beads (*muti-salak*), and silver coins, though rarely for economic trees or food supplies. Sons inherit the cattle of their fathers. In the absence of sons, the father's brother or the sister's son may inherit. Cattle which is inherited in this way is held by an individual who maintains the cattle; but brothers, father's brothers, and father's brother's sons have a claim on the animals if they are needed for bride-wealth payments. Animals acquired through purchase by a household are considered the joint property of husband and wife. If the husband dies, the wife cares for the animals and has the right to their disposal, usually favoring her sons. Unmarried girls very rarely inherit or obtain cattle, though unmarried youths may do so. It is the sign of a youth's maturity that he be given cattle to care for by himself, though the youth does not have the right to dispose of the animals. Men who do not have the resources to buy cattle may shepherd another man's cattle, receiving offspring for themselves and thereby building a herd.

5. Mutual Aid and Service Work

Small groupings of two to six farmers, working contiguous plots, may cooperate in fence building. Similarly small, though not necessarily concordant, groupings may use the same corral. Field or corral work groupings are composed of immediate relatives or hamlet mates but are not permanent groups. They dissolve easily when a person shifts to a more distant plot or pastures cattle elsewhere. Corral groupings endure longer, and membership is more closely determined by kinship, but tasks are normally not shared. Relatives assist an individual householder to gather wood for housebuilding, and the building is done by agnatic and affinal relatives and hamlet mates.

There is no land tenancy. Prosperous farmers may "invite" others to work for them, paying either in kind or by simply feeding them while they work. Elders "invite" such work, and villagers expect only to be fed in exchange. Relatives or friends may help each other in the same way. Such labor is normally "invited" for specific tasks, such as fence building, planting, or weeding; and different individuals may come for different tasks, depending upon their available time and inclination. Ties of affinity also create obligations for field work.

Traditionally, villagers made fields for a *radja* or *fettor*. Such fields, called *étu*, were a part of tribute which was regulated after Atoni rulers signed "short contracts" with the Dutch government. In 1949, the rulers agreed to abolish the *étu*, under urging from the Council of People's Representatives (D.P.R.) in Kupang. But it is not surprising that villagers still make fields "voluntarily" for rulers whom they hold in high regard and, in some cases, for Indonesian government leaders and Christian ministers, the provision of food being viewed as an exchange for services rendered in leadership. Corvée labor, called *herendiensten* (literally, "services for lords") by the Dutch, was abolished before World War II, but it has returned under the Indonesian government with a new name, *kerdja bakti* (literally, service work). The Atoni realistically refer to both as simply *mépu lalan*, road work. Fields may be made for the unsalaried village headman, but this was never obligatory and reflects more the influence of the man.

Contractual clientship exists in respect to cattle, a man becoming a shepherd (*atukus*) to obtain cattle for himself, receiving some offspring or even fully grown animals. The relationship is initiated voluntarily and may be broken easily. Shepherds are normally immigrants in a hamlet or those who reside uxorilocally, both subordinate status groups.

6. *Arts and Crafts*

The main Atoni crafts are weaving and basketry, both done by women, in which skillful and artistic elaboration in design and color are made. Atoni practice neither stone nor metal work, and there is no sculpture in wood or clay. Carving, done by men, is only used to decorate house posts and wooden or bone lime-holders. Both sexes value silver bracelets, and women also wear silver and gold hair ornaments and jewelry, but the work is done by silversmiths from the island of Ndau (west of Roté) who specialize and trade throughout the region. Designs on silver work emanating from other regions thus lack symbolic meaning for the Atoni.

Though men are skilled in making dishes, spoons, and water carriers from bamboo and other wood, or containers from buffalo skin, they do not decorate them with care. Women, on the other hand, decorate cloths and baskets with elaborate colored patterns. The cherished betelnut basket (*oko*) is made and carried by women. Baskets used to store household items are normally undecorated, though often intricately woven. Baskets used at feasts are woven with vividly colored fibers. Women know how to dye fiber, as for their cloth, but now they prefer to buy ready-dyed fiber from Chinese stores. Atoni men and women are skillful at beadwork for the decoration of bags, belts, lime-holders, and other ornaments, but they cannot make the beads. This art has suffered over the past decade because of limited import of these simple items.

Men and women wear cloths (*tais*) woven on a backstrap loom. Patterns distinguish political units, mainly the subdistrict and princedom, though subtleties are also peculiar to certain villages. The normal cloth is about two meters long and a meter wide. The woman's cloth is left sewn in tubular form like the Malay sarong, while the man's cloth is cut like the Malay *kain*. Formerly, Atoni women wore solid black cloth. Women still wear the black cloth in the princedoms of Amfoan and Insana, but in Soba they wear a red, black, and white cloth, wholly patterned by the ikat (tie) technique. Men wear a cloth with two red side bands (in the ikat technique) and a white center band. Men now wear shirts on daily and feast occasions. Some women wear blouses daily, but generally they wear the long cloth tied up over the breasts. At feasts, or in the presence of rulers, men and women wear a second cloth as a sign of respect. The women wear it like a skirt over another cloth; the men tie it around the waist like a sash.

The ikat technique, though not common among the Atoni, is found in Amarasi, perhaps introduced from Roté where it is used on all cloths. Pigafetta, who visited Timor in the sixteenth century, says that the Timorese were "naked" (Le Roux 1928, 31), judged from his overdressed,

Portuguese point of view. Atoni say that they formerly wore bark cloth, and that cotton cloth was introduced by their rulers. Rulers have been the vehicle of innovations in dress and other customs during the past two centuries, in that the ikat technique, uses of color, and articles of Western dress have all been derived from outside contacts.

7. Kin Groups and Kinship Relations

An Atoni household consists ideally of a man, his wife, and their unmarried children; the household is responsible for feeding and clothing its members and securing money necessary to buy goods and pay taxes. A man normally lives in his bride's household from a week to several years after marriage, before the couple returns to the man's hamlet. Bride service and return, though an ideal, is not always practiced. A couple may settle immediately in the groom's hamlet, or, after bride service, the husband may reside uxorilocally, depending upon family demands, personal inclination, or economic advantage. A couple living with in-laws changes the ideal household composition, as does the presence of old people or adopted children. No house should lack children, and childless couples or old people normally take children to live with them. Widows or widowers may live with younger relatives, but this is disliked on both sides. Elderly couples, or widows and widowers, prefer to live alone, accompanied perhaps by an unmarried child or grandchild.

Every Atoni belongs to a named patrilineage. In Soba there are representatives of forty-five such groups, but six lineages account for 78 per cent of the households. Each lineage has ritual practices and sacred objects (collectively termed *nono*), and the villagers often refer to lineages simply as "*nono* X" or "*nono* Y." Lineages may also be termed *ume* (house) or *kanan* (name). A person is said to "*su' nono* X" (carry *nono* X on the head), meaning that he or she has rights and obligations metaphorically placed on the head, as both a shelter and a weight to be borne. A child's membership is normally established in the father's lineage when a specific part of bride wealth for the mother has been paid. A wife is accepted ritually into the *nono* of her husband's lineage and henceforth observes its prescriptions (which include behavior at feasts, forbidden food—plants, birds, meats—and woods, and respect for certain objects), but she retains certain rights and obligations in her natal lineage.

Bride wealth, paid in stages, transfers rights over a woman and her children to the lineage of her husband. The degree of transfer varies in different princedoms. In one princedom, Amfoan, it is assumed that all stages of bride wealth will be paid and the transfer of rights over the bride will be complete. She is severed jurally from her natal lineage and will not secure sanctuary there in case of trouble. She is obligated to leviratic marriage on the death of her husband. In other areas, Amarasi among them, though the right to legitimize most children passes to the husband's lineage with certain bride-wealth payments, the final payment is not allowed and the woman retains rights and obligations in her natal group.

Atoni social life is normally restricted to small clusters of hamlets. (Such named clusters are indicated on Map III.) When members of a lineage move away, the tie with remaining members weakens. This has led to the formation of maximal lineage groups with the same name but with fictive or untraceable ties between their constituent lineages. Members of such groups believe they use the same *nono* ritual, but in fact separation leads to variations in practice. The members have few affective ties, though they normally respect maximal lineage exogamy. There are no leaders or common activities for maximal lineages, which are dispersed over several villages, subdistricts, and even princedoms, though a local part of a maximal lineage does have a recognized elder called *amnasi* (old father). Patrilineal local lineages of three or four generations in depth are the essential units for bride-wealth payment and collection, mutual aid in daily life and ritual, and the maintenance of certain properties.

Membership in lineages may also be acquired from the mother or through adoption. The lineage of the father is termed *nono mnuki* (young *nono*); that of the mother, *nono mnasi* (old *nono*). Although normally a child joins his father's lineage (*su' nono mnuki*, "carry the young *nono* on the head"), he may join the mother's natal lineage (*su' nono mnasi*, "carry the old *nono* on the head"). The mother's patrilineal lineage may claim an offspring of her marriage as part of bride wealth, particularly when they lack sons. A person gaining lineage membership in this way takes the name, rights, and obligations of the mother's patrilineage but nevertheless holds a subordinate position in it. He is termed *fèto* (female), while "brothers" in that lineage who obtained membership from their fathers are termed *moné* (male), the terms "female" and "male" being common Atoni expressions for subordination and superordination. In areas where such a practice is found, among them Amarasi, lineages consist of "male" and "female" branches, but though membership may be acquired from the mother, patrilineal descent is the norm in the formation of the lineage. Though a named lineage is normally exogamous, "male" and "female" branches may intermarry.

Any local lineage maintains affinal ties with other local lineages from the marriages of its ancestors and its living members. There are two affinal categories: wife-giver (*an atoni*, male child) and wife-taker (*an bifèl*, female child). At any ritual of the life cycle (birth, marriage, housebuilding, and death) for a local lineage, these two categories of affines must be invited. The feast giver is referred to as *uèm tuan* (house owner) and the groups in the two affinal categories are called *lalan* (way), meaning that they are the "way" to marriage. Groups which are invited but which cannot trace lineal descent or affinal alliance with the "house owners" are termed collectively *kotin* (outside). At rituals and in daily life, wife-givers are superordinate to wife-takers; they are honored and have particular rights and obligations in respect to the latter. Wife-takers are obligated to pay bride wealth, which consists of cattle, coral beads, silver, and money, in exchange for which they receive the wife and gifts of cloth and rice, being fed at the feast. Wife-takers serve their wife-givers at feasts and are on call for daily work. At a feast, the wife-givers are termed collectively *atoni-amaf* (literally, people-father; metaphorically, people to be treated with the respect due to fathers). Their presence is essential for the conduct of any feast. Their representatives, for example, carry out the placenta following birth, escort the bride, trim and ritually "cool" the roof of a new house, and carry the corpse for burial. In any household this affinal tie is particularized in the relationship between any boy and his mother's brother. A boy is expected to marry the daughter of his mother's brother (or any girl of equal generation in that lineage, all of whom he calls *fé lalan*, "wife way") and he owes him respect throughout his life. The mother's brother, on the other hand, is particularly responsible for the boy in ritual and daily life. Marriage to a *fé lalan* is prescribed, and marriage to a specific mother's brother is preferred, but this is not always possible for demographic reasons.

Atoni value marriage with lineages where affinal alliance already exists. They most highly value direct exchange between two lineages, the epitome being the marriage of the children of brothers and sisters, though demographic considerations make this form rare. Where groups exchange directly, the marriage at hand may determine which is to be considered wife-giver or wife-taker, or they may refer to the marriage which initiated the alliance in the past. Marriage within an established alliance requires less bride wealth, as does marriage between "male" and "female" branches of the same lineage (their relationship being based on former affinal alliance). The more distant in time the alliance to be reaffirmed, the greater the payment. Marriages to initiate an alliance require even higher payments, and payments for marriages outside the village, or between classes, are higher still, the amount varying directly with the distance. A local lineage thus has many other lineages with which affinal alliance is maintained, either in terms of living persons or former marriages. The degree to which a group can acknowledge extensive affinal ties by invitation at feasts reflects their wealth and influence and gives them prestige in return. It is for this reason that the Atoni still value cattle more for gifts or slaughter at feasts than for sale in the market. Though sale might be necessary to acquire money, it is regarded as a loss rather than a gain in traditional economic reckoning.

8. Social Stratification

Lineages are grouped in three social classes within a princedom: *usif* (noble), *tog* (commoner), and *até* (slave). The abolition of slavery in the mid-nineteenth century by the Dutch eliminated the *até*, which has now been all but absorbed in the *tog*. Noble lineages are those presently or formerly acknowledged as *radja* or *fettor* in some princedom, and their numbers are small in comparison to commoners. Class membership is determined by lineage membership at any time, but Atoni history is marked by the movement of lineages from commoner to noble status and vice versa. Atoni do not openly acknowledge this fact, and great deference is paid by commoners to ruling lines today, but rulers are always concerned with justifying the antiquity of their nobility. The classes are ideally endogamous, but rulers do give wives to commoner lines, particularly those of headmen or influential elders, and also to Chinese traders, forming affinal *cum* political alliances in which they, as wife-givers, remain superordinate. (Such marriage is quite satisfactory to Chinese, who have an opposite evaluation of status, considering wife-takers superior to wife-givers,[7] and who rarely give daughters in marriage

[7] See Leach (1951, 37) and Freedman (1958, 99).

to Indonesians.) Rulers may only take wives from other nobles or from specific lineages in the princedom termed *amfini* (fathers). An official wife must be taken from an *amfini* line, legitimate succession to rule depending upon birth from such a prescribed marriage.

Most villages consist of commoner lineages. Within villages such as Soba, there is a further three-fold categorization of lineages for political purposes: *kuatuaf* (village owner), *atoin asaut* (marrying people),[8] and *atoin anaot* (wandering people). The first consists of lineages considered to be founders of the village, with authority over land. The elders of these lineages have primary authority in decisions affecting the village. The second category consists of members of lineages that have come later to the village, taken wives, and left offspring. Men who reside uxorilocally and their descendants fall in this category. For daily work and feasts, members of these lineages are subject to the "village owner" elders. If they misbehave, they are easily expelled. The relationship of the "marrying people" to the "village owners" is analogous to that between any lineage and its wife-giving affines. Within a hamlet, one of the "marrying people" must respect the wishes of any "village owner," whether or not they are a specific wife-giver in marriage. Though subordinate, members of the "marrying people" lineages are invited to feasts in the village, and their elders are consulted in issues affecting community welfare. An elder of such a lineage may acquire great personal influence, but he may not hold a position of authority (such as headman), and he must yield to the will of the "village owners." At feasts, such an elder sits with the "old men" (*atoin mnasi*), who are respected and older men of both the "village owner" and "marrying people" lineages. Character and influence are significant factors in the recognition of men as *amnasi* of a lineage and *atoin mnasi* of a village, rather than real age, despite the Atoni symbolic characterization of men of power and authority as "old" (*mnasi*).

The third category, the "wandering people," have neither authority nor influence and are often not invited to feasts. This category consists of individual men or families who have moved into a village to farm, but who have not yet taken a wife locally. The normal assumption is that any "wandering person" must have had trouble in his home area, and they are often suspected of theft or sorcery. (The position of newly established "marrying people" is only slightly less vulnerable.) Both Atoni and other ethnic groups may fall in this category. "Wander-

[8] For the reversal of letters in Atoni, see Middelkoop (1950, 400).

ing people" normally seek to convert their status to "marrying people" by taking a wife or by marrying off a son locally. Atoni who migrate must face the fact that they will remain subordinate in this way, and so they normally leave their natal villages only when forced.

9. Ceremonial Activities and Religious Beliefs

Feasts of the life cycle occasion night-long circle dances and songs in which historical events are related; rulers, warriors, or guests praised; and comments are made on the behavior of villagers or village incidents. These feasts, with meals, prayers, rites, and the exchange of gifts, are held during the dry season, when villagers can travel to visit relatives in other hamlets and villages, and the young people court. There are few other community social occasions, though young people meet informally to sing and talk at one another's houses. In more actively Christian villages, young people gather almost nightly during the week to practice hymns, each hamlet cluster having a chapel youth choir.

There are no societies, communal houses, or youth houses with their own ceremonial. Males are normally circumcised, but it occasions no ritual and little attention, and there are no other initiation ceremonies. Before Dutch hegemony, boys were prepared for warriorhood with training, contests, and initiation ceremonies. These have disappeared with a half century of peace in the interior, but the warrior dance is still the main dance for men. Boys are still proud to claim descent from a warrior line and may become *djago* (champion) of the schoolyard for it.

Christianity has been preached among the Atoni for forty years. Less than half are church members, fewer still are regular churchgoers, and many traditional religious beliefs and rituals are still alive.

It is difficult to treat Atoni traditional beliefs in a few words, but certain general aspects can be mentioned. Traditional religion entails belief in the power of a Lord of the Upper World (Uis Néno), lesser spirits termed *pah* (literally, land) occupying particular places, tutelary spirits obtained by individuals and incarnated in animals such as crocodiles or snakes which are tended, and the ancestors (*nitu*). Prayers to Uis Néno and to ancestors are made by individuals from their houses at feasts or on occasion of private need. Prayer and sacrifice are also conducted by officials on behalf of the subdistrict or princedom at certain sacred places, often hills forbidden to agriculture or habitation. The

Lord of the Upper World is believed to be concerned primarily with creation and maintenance of life, hence prayers and sacrifice are directed to him for rain or sunshine or for procreation and health.

Lesser manifestations of Divinity occupying particular places are more active in human life, for both good and evil. Places known to be inhabited by them are respected, and offerings may be made there. Such a place—certain hills, small woods, streams, or springs—usually gives its name to the divinity who is said to be "its owner" (*in tuan*). The traditional land official (*tobé*) was primarily concerned with prayer and offering to these divinities where land was to be broken by a farmer. This earthly aspect of divinity is supplemented in Amarasi by a belief in the Lord of the Earth or Soil (Uis Afu), who is considered a female complement to the male Uis Néno and who is propitiated when land is broken. Prayers to both are made for fertility, the former providing soil fertility, the latter providing rain and sunshine. This belief in Uis Afu as a single divinity of the earth is not held by all Atoni. In other areas, the lesser divinities fulfill the same function.

Both lesser divinities and ancestors are believed to exert continuing influence on the living. Specific misfortunes (such as illness, accident, difficulties in social relations) may be attributed to their action when other agencies are not discernible. Their action is normally believed to be retribution for some human failing or ritual inattention. A diviner (*mnané* or *méo*) is called to discover the source of the difficulty and prescribe a remedy in which he often plays a part. These diviners use devices, "medicines" (*hau*, literally "wood"), and incantations and are believed to have a special relationship with a lesser spirit that assists them in combating the lesser spirit that is harming a person. Atoni, even the Christians, often believe in sorcery, and the diviner may use his spirit helper to combat the sorcerer who in turn is using a spirit helper. The diviner is proficient in the use of medicines for illness, but his medicine is more often applied ritually (by rubbing or blowing, with incantations). Other men or women may know medicines for specific illness, which they provide for a fee, but they are not considered diviners. Ancestors are propitiated at all events of the life cycle by the householders concerned, with the particular usages and prayers (*nono*) of their lineage. They must be informed of what the household is doing and given a portion of the feast, lest they be offended and seek revenge.

The inspiration to propitiate certain animals believed to be protective spirits comes in dreams or visions to which anyone is susceptible. The use or prohibition of certain foods may be similarly inspired. A person securing spiritual aid in this way normally attends to its demands by himself, but other members of the immediate family may assist or join in following necessary prescriptions or proscriptions called *nuni* (the Indonesian *pemali*, or taboo). Descendants may also follow them. These *nuni* are distinct from the *nono* ritual of the lineage, though the two are blended in daily life or at feasts. These prescriptions and proscriptions (*nuni*) derive in their most elaborate form from dreams or visions, more simply from just eating something that does not agree. They may be maintained by an individual for short periods or by descendants over generations. Thus there are many foods or practices considered dangerous for all Atoni (such as bitter vegetable leaves for a pregnant woman); others for lineages, for households, or for individuals.

In attacking the traditional religion, Protestant and Roman Catholic churchmen concentrate on the *nono* ritual of lineages, the belief in lesser spirits, and the belief in sorcery. *Nono* objects must be destroyed by families entering communion, and life-cycle ritual must incorporate Christian ceremonial, though traditional social elements may remain. The term Uis Néno is used to translate God in the Bible, with a Christian conception of the loving God being taught in contrast to the more remote figure of the traditional religion, and the vital issue of revelation in Christ is greatly stressed. (The Reverend P. Middelkoop, the chief missionary to the Atoni, first translated the New Testament to stress the revelation.) Churchmen also seek to make ritual church-centered, rather than home- or shrine-centered, but the home is still the focus of most Atoni ritual, and the minister, lay teachers, and priests often come there to officiate. The Protestant church recognizes marriage made by traditional ceremony, rather than in the church or with government registration, and most Atoni marry this way. Only those with government jobs feel compelled to have an "official marriage" before a government official and a minister, licensed with a certificate.

Though the Christian message is nominally accepted, many people still believe in lesser spirits and sorcery, with the indigenous ministers and lay teachers often assuming a role like diviners in the traditional belief. Less scrupulous or less enlightened teachers may use this to their own profit and utterly distort their Christian message, while the more enlightened often accept this confusion and utilize it skillfully in their ministry. Sorcery raises problems, however, that are difficult for them to meet, and many villagers consult a diviner when they find the minister or lay teacher of no help. Even though nominally good Christians, they believe that their faith is simply not strong enough to combat sorcery, in whose objective existence they still believe, so they must resort to diviners for help. A lay teacher I knew did this for his wife and son who were believed to be under attack from a sorcerer. He felt his own faith was adequate to protect himself, but his wife had little faith (and his young son could not understand), and he could not see them suffer continual illness. It is quite common to find a *fettor* or *radja* accept Christianity but also conduct all the rituals of the traditional religion, often with a brother in charge. It is not just their personal uncertainty involved but their need to protect both Christian and non-Christian subjects.[9]

10. Village Administration and Leadership

The government leader of Soba is the *temukung* (headman),[10] one of sixty in Amarasi. In the traditional princedom, duties were apportioned by lineages that supplied the *radja, fettor, amfini* (fathers), *tobé* (land official), warrior leaders, headmen, tribute gatherers, and priests; though duties were assigned by lineage, personal qualities helped determine the individual selected. The headman now collects taxes, allots fields, maintains order, and executes government orders and policies of the *radja* and *fettor*. He is the village magistrate in traditional law, and he reports violations of Indonesian civil and criminal law to authorities in Baun, who in turn report to the police and court in Kupang.

As magistrate, the headman handles disputes and contracts. He is simply called *nakaf* (head). He should be an arbiter within his village or *ketemukungan* but generally a champion of his own village in opposition to others. His presence at a marriage, or at any contract involving the transfer of property or rights, legalizes it and becomes the basis of appeal to the *fettor* in case it is broken. The headman receives a fee for this service. He also hears cases concerning customary law in consultation with other elders and the disputing parties. Litigants who

[9] For supplementary information on ceremonial activities, religious beliefs, and Christianity in Timor, see Middelkoop (1949, 1958).

[10] This word is related to the Javanese *tumenggung*. I do not know whether it was introduced by Europeans or predates their establishment. Paravicini, who visited Timor on a government mission in 1756, reported the word *tommagon* used on Timor and Roté for village headman (Chys 1872, 222).

do not accept his decision may appeal to the *fettor*. If they do not accept but do not appeal, they risk ostracism or perhaps violence from the injured party and other villagers. The *radja* is a further step in appeal, but this step is rarely taken; it is mainly the *fettor* who hears cases. The Dutch government made the *radja* the pinnacle of the judicial system in the princedom, but traditionally he rarely served as judge. His duty was to provide a court and food for the litigants, while the *fettor* and other elders managed adjudication.

In 1954, the judicial authority of the *radja* was seriously curtailed when the National Court (Pengadilan Negeri) assumed full authority in civil and criminal cases covered by national law.[11] The princedom may no longer levy fines or prescribe imprisonment, but only negotiate settlement of civil disputes resting in customary law (e.g., bride wealth, divorce, property). Even in these issues, villagers may appeal to the National Court in Kupang. But insufficient staff on the court delays judgment, and few villagers, even headmen, are sophisticated enough to face the complexities of court action.

The eleven hamlets of Soba are organized in four clusters, each headed by two officials: the *amnais ko'u* (great *amnasit*) and *amnais ana'* (little *amnasit*).[12] They assist the headman in government duties (e.g., tax collecting, census, order, road work) and are also unsalaried. They are magistrates for disputes within the hamlet cluster, and their presence is essential for any legal contract or feast. The men selected as *amnasit* may be members of the "village owner" lineages, with traditional authority behind them. On the other hand, they may merely be literate functionaries capable of reading instructions. This situation is not restricted to Soba but is common on Timor. Their results in respect to government duties are often closely related to their traditional authority.

[11] See *Tambahan Lembaran Negara R.I. Nr. 603: Penetapan Menteri Kehakiman tentang penghapusan Pengadilan-pengadilan swapradja diseluruh Daerah-daerah Sumbawa, Sumba, Timor, dan Flores* (Decision of the Minister of Justice concerning the abolition of *swapradja* courts throughout the areas of Sumbawa, Sumba, Timor, and Flores), Djakarta, 19 May 1954. This act was valid for Timor on September 1, 1954. I owe this reference to Mr. Rusli, head of the National Court in Kupang.

[12] The term *amnais* (or *amnasi*) means literally "old father," the title *amnasit* being derivative. *Ko'u* means "great" in Amarasi; *ana'* means "small, little," as an adjective. These *amnasit* officials should not be confused with the lineage elders called *amnasi*, though the official may also be a lineage elder.

The headman and the *amnasit* are appointed from above, the former by the *fettor* and the latter by the headman but with the agreement of the villagers, expressed normally by the elders of the leading lineages. In the government hierarchy, the headman, *amnais ko'u*, and *amnais ana'* represent three descending grades of authority, a chain of command. Government orders for such jobs as tax collection or road work are issued down this hierarchy. Above these levels, the order has come from the Kupang government to the *swapradja* office and then to the *fettor*, who passes it to the headmen. Theoretically, the consideration of local problems rises in the reverse direction.

In fact, the pattern of authority in the village is more complicated. The government system disregards status categories of lineages and combines hamlets in villages with little more than territorial unity. Hamlet clusters are essentially autonomous socioeconomic areas, and their residents are bound closely by descent and affinity. Though ties of descent and affinity also cut across hamlet-cluster and even village boundaries, members of lineages living in different hamlet clusters cooperate far less in economic, ritual, or legal affairs than those in the same hamlet cluster. Guests who are invited to a feast on the basis of common residence are usually those of the same hamlet cluster, not the village as a whole, despite the relatively small size of Atoni villages. Guests from other hamlet clusters are invited only when ties of descent and affinity exist.

The village headman must come from one local lineage. He is usually identified with his natal hamlet, where he is a member of a "village owner" lineage. (This is the case in Soba.) His acceptance in other hamlets must rest on his personality or upon hereditary rights as head. The former subdistrict of Soba (abolished in the early 1920's), in which the present village was one of six villages, had four "heads." The lineage of the present headman was one of these, and so he commands respect in all of the Soba hamlets. Two hamlet clusters, however, are headed by *amnasit* of the noble ruling line of the former subdistrict. Their authority over people and land is still recognized and surpasses that of the headman. Members of these lineages and their hamlet mates consider themselves superior to the lineage (and hamlets) of the headman, and they number 47 per cent of the village population. Consequently, the *amnasit* of these two clusters often ignore the headman and go directly to the *fettor* in disputes or government matters. After a dispute in one of these hamlets, a person will say *"Au nao on sonaf"* ("I go to the palace!"), meaning that he or she will carry the issue directly to the *fettor*, the headman not having been approached.

In such a situation, the headman's position is awkward. If he tolerates it, his authority is weak. If he exerts his will too strongly, either he is ignored or fights develop between him and the *amnasit* of the two hamlets concerned and their respective hamlet mates. The headman has even tried to establish descent in the noble lineage, but his claim was not acknowledged by most villagers. He rarely enters the hamlets where he is not accepted, and the disputes have helped split the Protestant congregation in the village.

When such a situation exists, rooted in structural rather than merely personal issues, higher political authorities must act judiciously, remembering both traditional and administrative aspects of rule. An elderly headman with a fine record of service may be bypassed by a *radja* or *fettor* in such work as the irrigation project, which demands effective daily leadership. When such disputes arise, and a ruler deals directly with leaders of hamlet clusters, the *ketemukungan* becomes a political unit in name only. Work and leadership in particular tasks matter more than the paper hierarchy of authority.

This conflict between traditional and administrative authority in the village is further exemplified in the relationship between the "great *amnasit*" and the "little *amnasit*" in a hamlet. Dual leadership is deeply rooted in Atoni ideology, whether the leadership is conceived as "ritual" and "secular" or in terms of internal and external duties. In dual leadership, Atoni do not mean that one figure is merely an assistant to the other. Instead, the two figures perform complementary functions. This is true of the indigenous conception of kingship (and the authorities now called *radja* and *fettor*), and it is true for the two *amnasit*. In a case I know of, the "great *amnasit*" is literate, a former soldier. He represents the hamlet cluster in relations with the headman and the government in Baun. He collects taxes, takes the census, and is a leader in the irrigation projects. The "little *amnasit*" is illiterate, rarely travels outside the subdistrict, helps little with taxes or census, and only occasionally meets members of the *swapradja* council. Both men are members of the noble lineage. The "little *amnasit*" is a direct descendant of the former *fettor* and acquired membership in the lineage patrilineally. The "great *amnasit*" acquired membership via his mother. In respect to corporate rights in the lineage and property rights in the hamlet cluster, the "little *amnasit*" takes precedence and is fully capable of managing them. Where disputes and customary law are concerned, both men must be informed and consulted, the "little *amnasit*" often first. The "great *amnasit*" is thus "great" only in terms of the government hierarchy, but in traditional aspects of society he is subordinate. One is a mediator with the outside, the other an arbiter on the inside. Such dual apportionment of authority reflects an evaluation of the internal and external worlds as different but necessarily joined.

Influence of the government of Kupang in Soba during the first decade of Indonesian independence has been minimal. Only four children were enrolled in the junior high school in Baun, and only one boy is enrolled in secondary school in Kupang. Few villagers visit the poorly managed and inadequately stocked clinic in Baun. Neither the information service nor the police visit the village. There are no reserve forests which might bring villagers into contact with the forestry service, though the Baun forest officer lives in the village, and there are no missions from the agriculture or animal husbandry services. The villagers pay minimal taxes annually, collected by their own men and delivered to Baun. The headman and four *amnasit* attended several lectures on "land reform" in 1960 in Baun, but nothing was done, mainly because of the vagueness of the program and its explanation and their fears of unknown implications. For one or two months during the dry season, villagers work on the road or build houses for government employees and teachers, collecting materials in the village and taking them to Baun. During our visit in Soba, about a dozen women heard a talk in Baun by a Sabunese girl from the Kupang agricultural service on "village cleanliness and hygiene," delivered in fine Indonesian which few women understand.

The influence of the *swapradja* government has been somewhat greater. The *radja* urged the building of the side road into the village, and a truck comes once a week to collect produce for the Kupang market. Villagers have profited from the planting of gardens and economic trees, directed by the former *radja* and the headman, and the increased tending of cattle. A stronger economy and the advice of the *radja* stimulated some villagers to build stone or half-stone houses, a rare phenomenon on Timor. There is pride in these achievements among the villagers, and the Kupang government has utilized this development to show rulers and headmen from other princedoms what can be done. The economic advances in Soba do not particularly favor education, many older villagers preferring to have young people tend animals or trees. There is no contact between school teachers and parents, most of the latter being illiterate and disinterested in school. Children are sent to school because the *radja* orders it, not because the parents value learning or seek to place their children in white-collar jobs.

The isolation of teachers and civil servants from villagers involves a mutual rejection of the values and ways of the other. When a person dons pants and shoes, he becomes a *kasé* (foreigner, outsider, stranger) to the villager. An advance by the villagers toward a money economy and economic betterment is not related directly to the influence of the Kupang government or their acceptance of its leadership, except to the degree that the *radja* and *fettor* accept the program and values of the government and transmit them to the villagers. Where traditional authorities oppose the outside, villagers remain isolated. The traditional Atoni authorities, particularly the *fettor*, who is nearest the villagers in daily affairs and who identifies himself with their traditions and dress rather than the *kasé* sphere of Kupang, are thus vital "cultural brokers."[13]

[13] For further information on the Atoni, see Cunningham (1964, 1965, 1965a, 1967).

Chapter IV

Telang: A Ma'anjan Village of Central Kalimantan[1]

ALFRED B. HUDSON
JUDITH M. HUDSON
CORNELL UNIVERSITY

1. The Ma'anjan of Central Kalimantan

Central Kalimantan (Borneo) is a great sprawling province of about
153,000 square kilometers, larger than the combined areas of Java and
Madura. Yet its population numbers only about 496,000, so that it has
a mean population density of only 3.26 per square kilometer. The majority
of its people are Dajaks, who are divided into many ethnic groups. They
live in villages located along the many rivers and streams that stretch
far into the interior. These villages vary in size from one to two hundred
people, in the headwaters, to five hundred to several thousand in the
wider, lower reaches of the river valleys. Most of the population still
practice a swidden-type dry-rice subsistence agriculture, although in the
last few years wet-rice cultivation has been introduced on a small scale
in a few areas.

The major elements in the life history of each village are dictated
by the demands of this swidden system, although the details may vary
from region to region. The village is born, perhaps, when a few people
hunting forest products in an area of primary jungle find a likely area
for swidden. The tall virgin timber of centuries is felled and burned,

[1] This chapter was written during the preliminary stages of a field research
project in 1963, supported by a Foreign Area Training Fellowship of the
Ford Foundation, to whom grateful acknowledgment is made.

a small hut erected, and rice planted in a small clearing. Several people remain to protect the crop from the ravages of the jungle's creatures, while the rest of the party return to the mother village. In time, more people come to the new area, and additional clearings are hewn, at great effort, from the forest host. Substantial houses are built, and a permanent population comes into being. The land is fertile, and the original swiddens may be used for as long as four or five years. But finally the repeated cropping and the torrential monsoon downpours leach the nutriments from the soil, and new clearings must be made. As the years pass, the village population grows, and generations come and go. Most of the primary jungle has been cut, and now some people are beginning to carve swiddens from the secondary forest that has grown up on the site of earlier fields. The trees are smaller, the work is easier, but the soil not so fertile as it was in its pristine state. The swiddens must now be abandoned after only two or three years of use and allowed to regenerate for ten to twenty years before they can once more be cleared and planted. Fields are located at some distance from the village, each with its own hut. At certain times of the year the village is deserted, and its people live almost continually in their fields. With the disappearance of the last remnants of primary jungle, the population is stabilized. Few new people enter the village except by marriage, and an apparently high birth rate is offset by an equally high mortality rate and the movement of pioneers from the village in search of new areas of untapped primary forest. There follow years of constant reuse of old land that accelerates the decline in soil fertility. Soon patches of white sandy wasteland appear where nothing will grow. The forest regenerates itself only with difficulty. The land is tired. And the village, too, is old and tired. The population declines rapidly as the exodus to new lands gains momentum. Swiddens and fruit trees are abandoned. Houses are deserted, left to decay, or taken down and carried to a new location. Such a village is Telang.[2]

[2] Since returning from the field, we have gained access to records indicating that Telang may not fit the ideal pattern outlined here. There is a possibility that the Telang region may have always been agriculturally marginal, and that its people are the descendants of refugees from the area of Bandjar expansion to the east. Over one hundred years ago, C. Bangert described the Telang area: "The sandy ground would appear to be unsuitable for any sort of agriculture. . . . The neighborhood of the kampong is an utter wilderness. Where the white sand has gotten the upper hand, bracken and ferns are found to a height of 10 to 12 feet. . . . As much as I have seen, the hills are covered to a depth of some feet with sand; between the crests

Ethnically, the population of Telang belongs to the Ma'anjan. As a group the Ma'anjan number probably between thirty and thirty-five thousand and are spread through much of the *kabupaten* (regency) Barito Selatan. The Ma'anjan home area lies in the *kewedanaan* (district) Barito Timur, in the drainages of the Patai and Pupuken rivers. On the east it abuts the territory of the Islamic Bandjars of the Hulu Sungai region in the province of South Kalimantan. To the west lie the Bakumpai and Bandjar peoples of the Barito River. Marshes and swamplands bound Ma'anjan territory to the south of the Patai River. To the north the Ma'anjan have spread into parts of the Karau River drainage and beyond to the Ajuh River above Buntok, the *kabupaten* capital. In the Karau and Ajuh regions they are considerably mixed with another ethnic group, the Lawangan, whose territory that region was before the Ma'anjan incursion, though there are some villages of exclusively Ma'anjan extraction. They are distinguished from adjacent ethnic groups by language, *adat* (customary law), and, to a certain extent, religion.[3] Their language is mutually unintelligible with contiguous Bakumpai, Lawangan, and Bandjarese (that of the Malay population of southeast Kalimantan), although like many other inhabitants of Central Kalimantan they are wonderful polyglots, a factor tending to minimize linguistic barriers. In religion they are generally Kaharingan (original animistic religious system)[4] or Christian, setting them off from the Islamic groups to the east and west.

---

one finds more or less extensive marshes . . . it would seem that the territory is too small in extent for the active population, considering the manner in which they work the land" (Bangert 1860, 142–151). This situation does not seem to have changed appreciably in the course of a century.

[3] References to the Ma'anjan culture and language are included in Kennedy's bibliography under the Ngadju Group. An evaluation of these sources is given with particular reference to death ceremonies, by Waldemar Stöhr (1959, 60–62). Most interesting from the historical standpoint is the civil servant C. Bangert's account (1860) of an inspection tour through the Ma'anjan territories in 1857. A later civil servant, P. te Wechel (1915), has described customs in the area, with special attention to animism and the spirit world. Te Wechel draws on data from a number of different groups in the Buntok area, making it difficult at times to distinguish between Ma'anjan practices and those of other groups. The same is true for Mallinckrodt (1927), an article that contains much inaccurate information.

[4] Kaharingan is the term applied to the animist religions of the Dajak. In the Kaharingan world, each living thing is animated by a life force peculiar to itself. The Kaharingan Dajak has developed a system of rituals to help him maintain a harmonious relationship with the spirits of his ancestors and of the trees, plants, and animals around him upon which he is dependent.

According to their traditional history, the Ma'anjan emerged as a distinct ethnic group centuries ago in Sarunai, which was located to the east between the present towns of Kelua and Amuntai in Hulu Sungai. The fact that there is still an isolated Ma'anjan group in that region gives some credence to the story. This could indicate a gradual movement of Ma'anjan people from Sarunai toward the north and west—perhaps receiving an impetus from the expanding Bandjarese to the south, perhaps owing to the search for ever-fresh swidden areas—a movement which continues to the present day.

The Ma'anjan ethnic group itself is divided into four segments. The division is made primarily along territorial lines, at least in the home region, although each segment is also set off by differences in *adat* and by slight dialectical variations in language. More important, the members of each segment feel a conscious distinction between the different groups. To the north the Ma'anjan segment of Paku Karau occupies much of the drainage of the Karau River. This area now has its own *kewedanaan* (district) with administrative headquarters in the town of Ampah. The Benua Lima (Five Villages) segment lies to the south in the extreme eastern portion of Ma'anjan territory. It occupies the parts of the Taba-long River drainage that still lie within Central Kalimantan. Benua Lima forms a separate *ketjamatan* (subdistrict) with an administrative center at Pasar Panas within the district Barito Timur. To the west of Benua Lima lies the segment Padju Sapuluh (Ten Villages), which occupies the upper reaches of the Patai River. The two main towns of Padju Sapuluh are Tamiang Lajang and Dja'ar. Still farther to the west, in the drainage of the Napu and Pupuken rivers, lies the Padju Epat (Four Villages) segment, of which Telang is the principal village, no longer in size but as an administrative and market center. The Padju Sapuluh and Padju Epat segments both lie in the subdistrict of Dusun Timur, which is administered from Tamiang Lajang. Of the *adat* differences that set off Padju Epat from the rest of the Ma'anjan groups, the most distinctive is a nine-day death ceremony, *idjambe*, which culminates in the cremation of the bones of the dead.[5]

[5] Many Dajak groups have death-ritual cycles of similar function (e.g., *tiwah* among the Ngadju, *totoh* among the Siang). Stöhr (1959) describes the various death ceremonies of the Dajak in considerable detail. Exhumed after temporary burial, in *idjambe* the bones are placed in boat-shaped coffins which are consigned to flames at the conclusion of the nine-day ceremony. After cremation, the ashes are distributed among a number of ironwood caskets called *tambak*, which are arranged in a hierarchy according to a formalized class system that existed in former days.

2. The Village Telang and Its Environment

Geographically Telang is located about 142 kilometers north of Bandjarmasin and about 15 kilometers east of the Barito River, at latitude 2° 06′ south, longitude 115° 00.5′ east. Its present population numbers 137 (Table 4).[6] The Telang River divides the village into an older and a newer section, each laid out along its own street. The older street extends 300 meters to the south of the river, the newer one an equal

Table 4. Population of Telang by age and sex

Age in years	Male	Female	Total
0–5	18	11	29
6–10	12	7	19
11–15	8	4	12
16–20	4	5	9
21–25	3	7	10
26–30	5	1	6
31–35	3	4	7
36–40	1	5	6
41–45	5	6	11
46–50	4	6	10
51–55	0	1	1
56–60	2	1	3
61–65	0	0	0
over 65	8	6	14
Total	73	64	137

distance to the northwest, where it centers on the market area and abuts the outlying houses of Siong. The majority of the buildings in the village are single-household dwellings sturdily constructed of local hardwoods and raised on piles to protect them from flooding. Such houses are to be found over much of the Dajak region of Central Kalimantan, and it is only to the north, in the more remote parts of the territory occupied

[6] All census figures for Telang that appear in the text were compiled by the authors and apply for the date August 15, 1963. The figures from the Indonesian census of 1961 give Telang a population of 278. However, this figure includes the 125 residents of Telang Baru, located some fifteen kilometers to the southwest, and the 16 residents of Luau Gador some six kilometers to the northeast.

by the Siang, Murung, and Tabojan, that the traditional Dajak longhouse may still be found. There was formerly a longhouse in Telang, but evidently it was abandoned well over a century ago, and no traces remain today. There are five buildings in the village with specialized uses: a six-year government primary school; a large *balai adat* (assembly hall) used primarily during *idjambe,* that has not been utilized in years;[7] a rice storehouse; a market shed; and a rubber smokehouse that is used occasionally.[8] In addition to these structures, there are forty-two dwellings, although at the present time sixteen of them, or almost 40 per cent, are empty and in various stages of disrepair and decay. This is one of the visible signs attesting to the gradual desertion of the village. Others tell the same story. Thirty-five years ago the village was much larger than it now is. Then the street to the south of the river continued an additional 350 meters beyond its present terminus. The houses that crowded along this extension have now disappeared entirely, but stands of neglected fruit trees still mark the outlines of this now-dead limb of the village.[9]

The village is surrounded by forest areas that have been cleared and recleared for generations. The only primary forest remaining in the vicinity is in low marshy areas unsuitable for cultivation. Much of the land consists of 25 to 30 centimeters of topsoil over a white sand or red clay base. In many places the topsoil no longer exists, and only a few hardy grasses can survive. However, most of the area around the village is still covered with forest in various stages of regrowth. There are no real hills in the region, and the land presents a gently rolling

[7] Whereas the overgrown and decaying Telang *balai* has not been used since 1951, those in Siong, Murutuwu, and Balawa were repaired for *idjambe* ceremonies held in July 1963.

[8] Two additional structures, an office for the *tjamat penghubung* and a public health clinic, were being built with *gotong-rojong* labor from the villages of Padju Epat. A Christian church was also under construction with labor contributed by the local congregation.

[9] It is estimated by knowledgeable older inhabitants that the population of Telang in 1925 was between 700 and 800. However, this number probably included a large number of people who lived almost permanently in the Paku Karau region to the north but who were kept on the Telang rolls by the Dutch administration for ease in tax collection. Because of the wholesale destruction of Dutch records during the Japanese occupation of Kalimantan, it is rather difficult to obtain documents from colonial times relating to the area.

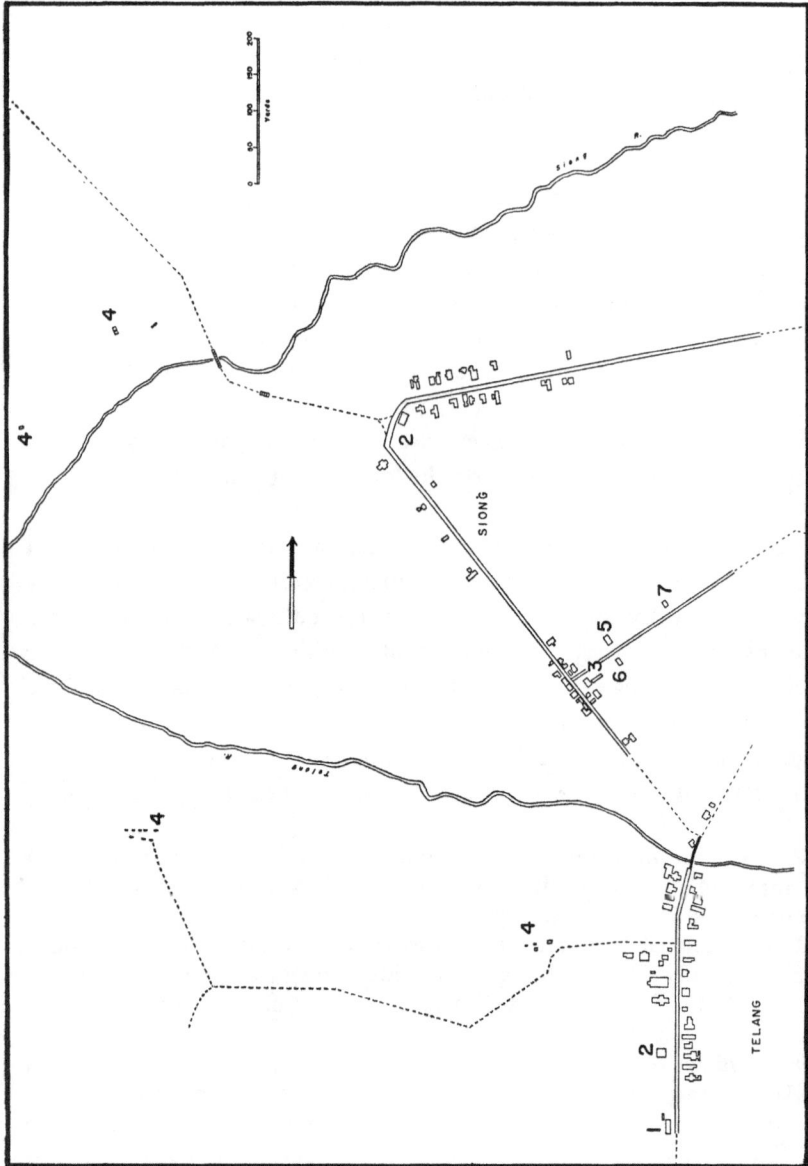

Map IV. Detail of Settlement Pattern of Telang

1. Elementary school. 2. *Balai Adat.* 3. Market sheds. 4. Burial and cremation sites. 5. *Tjamat's* office.
6. Clinic (unfinished). 7. Christian church.

contour which stretches in all directions, although it flattens out as it approaches the Barito. The Telang River flows westward through the village, becomes the Pupuken, and passes into the Barito near the town of Damparan. In the dry months, May through October, the Telang River is a narrow, tortuously meandering stream several meters in width. During that period it will allow passage of only the smallest *djukung* (canoes). In the rainy season, November through March, it overflows its banks and inundates part of the village, at the same time permitting entry of fairly large motor boats from the Barito. The river serves as a bathing place for the residents of the village and also provides drinking water, fresh-water shrimp, and an abundance of fish. The richly varied animal and bird population of the forest proves a mixed blessing, for while it serves as a potential source of meat to augment a sometimes drab diet, it also can bring ruin to an unguarded rice field in a surprisingly short time. Telang's climate is not unpleasant. The temperature usually rises to about 90 degrees F. during the day but drops into the high 60's at night, which is almost too cool for the largely blanketless population. The dry season is quite dry, and weeks may pass when no rain falls, a condition allowing new swiddens, which are cleared during this period, to receive a good burning. During the rainy season some rain falls almost every day, providing plenty of water for the rice crop but also interfering greatly with land communications.

Telang's ties with the outside world shift semiannually in response to the extreme seasonal variation in rainfall. There are two outside towns of immediate importance to Telang: Tamiang Lajang to the east, with a periodic market on Monday through which Telang can tap the resources of the Hulu Sungai and Ampah regions; and Bengkuang to the west on the Barito, with its Wednesday market, serving as a link with all the towns along the river and ultimately with Bandjarmasin. Telang lies between the two, geographically and temporally, with a Tuesday market. Tamiang Lajang can be reached effectively only by land, Bengkuang only by river. During the rainy season the trail to Tamiang Lajang is inundated, and land travel is extremely difficult. At this time the Telang River may rise six or seven meters, permitting fairly large motor boats to enter with ease from Bengkuang. The situation is reversed during the dry months. The land link to the east becomes firm, and Tamiang Lajang may be reached in an hour and a half by bicycle, while the Bengkuang water route almost ceases to exist. This seasonal juxtaposition of Tamiang Lajang and Bengkuang serves Telang very well in the economic realm. If anything, the latter connection is preferred for the simple reason that the Bengkuang people come to Telang by boat to transact business. Everything bought or sold in Tamiang Lajang has to be carried eighteen kilometers on foot or on bicycles by the Telangers themselves. But however well Bengkuang may serve Telang during the rainy season, it cannot take the place of Tamiang Lajang in the civil administrative hierarchy. Tamiang Lajang is the seat of both the *tjamat* (subdistrict head) and the *wedana* (district head) within whose jurisdiction Telang lies, while Bengkuang belongs not only to a different *ketjamatan* (subdistrict) but to a different *kewedanaan* (district) as well. Therefore the seasonal hiatus in the Tamiang Lajang land link poses problems for the effective administration of the whole Padju Epat area. It was to alleviate this situation that a *ketjamatan penghubung* (link *ketjamatan*) for Padju Epat was formed in late 1959 with headquarters in Telang.[10]

A distinction must be made between Padju Epat as an *adat* area and as an administrative unit. The former includes the Ma'anjan villages of Telang, Siong, Murutuwu, Balawa (the original "four"), and Maipe. The *ketjamatan penghubung* includes all the former plus the non-Ma'anjan villages of Tampulangit and Telang Baru, which are Bandjar in population.

In terms of political administration, then, Telang is located in the province of Central Kalimantan, *kabupaten* (regency) Barito Selatan, *kewedanaan* Barito Timur, *ketjamatan* Dusun Timur, and itself is the seat of the *ketjamatan penghubung* Padju Epat.

3. *The Household, Kinship, and Economic System*

Telang's 137 people are distributed among 26 households. Twenty-three of the households, which can be called "simple," contain a single family of one to four generations' depth. Where more than one generation exists in these simple households, the members of the second and succeeding generations, with the exception of their in-marrying spouses, are all descended ambilaterally from the members of the senior generation, the senior generation containing only siblings and their spouses. At the present

---

[10] The Indonesian governmental hierarchy usually terminates at the level of the *ketjamatan*. However, in many areas of Central Kalimantan where communication difficulties inhibit efficient administration, expediency has led to the creation of a lower unit, perhaps peculiar to this province, the *ketjamatan penghubung*.

time there are no households in Telang where two siblings coexist in the first generation, and only one, a special case on other grounds, where two married siblings coexist in the second generation. Telang's three remaining households may be termed "complex." In these households not all members belong to a single family in the sense that all are ambilaterally descended from the senior generation present. These households

Table 5. Size of households in Telang and Siong

Size of household	Number of households	
	Telang	Siong
1	2	
2	4	
3	2	1
4	3	
5	6	3
6	2	2
7	1	1
8	3	1
9	1	
10		2
11	1	1
12		2
16	1	
17		1
20		1
21		1
Total households	26	16
Mean household size	5.27	9.87
Total population	137	158

contain two or more families connected usually through a cousin relationship. There is one household containing two apparently unrelated families, although one spends most of the year in its rice field.[11] Telang's households vary in size from one to sixteen members, with a mean of 5.27 (Table 5).

[11] This description of households applies only to present-day Telang. Historically we believe that Telang households were structurally much closer to those still found in nearby Siong and Murutuwu, where households are larger and joint, or sibling-linked, families more common. Table 5 gives comparative figures for Telang and Siong.

The household is the largest corporate group. It controls most of the significant economic assets, such as hunting, fishing, and agricultural equipment. The inheritance of land-use rights (see next section) is mediated through the household. Old long-established households possess heirlooms (gongs, jars, and plates) termed *sagar abad*, which remain undispersed household property from generation to generation. The household frequently acts as a unit in the agricultural labor exchange system. The household is subdivided into constituent *perinduk* (conjugal family) units. Each *perinduk* unit usually maintains its own fields. However, some newly married couples may work in their parents' plots for a few years before branching out on their own, especially if the parents are aged and have no grandchildren old enough to help them maintain their fields. In some households all the members share their produce and eat jointly as a unit; in others each *perinduk* family eats separately. Each household has a head (*asbah*) who represents it when the occasion demands, for example in marriages, property disputes, and the completion of census forms or other government directives.

In the traditional Kaharingan world, the household acts as a ceremonial unit. Each has its own protective ancestral spirits, and several maintain spirit houses where a specific prominent household ancestor dwells. Each Kaharingan household has particular food taboos that must be observed by its members. At the time of important ceremonies, the various participating family heads in the household often combine to act as units for the contribution of food, money, and labor.

Household membership is not static, since it depends entirely on residence. When an individual changes residence, all his household relationships change too. Household affiliations are normally rearranged at the time of marriage. Both village and household are agamous. Marriage with cousins of all grades is permitted, though marriage involving patrilateral parallel cousins is not preferred. Of 59 marriages represented in Telang, 5.1 per cent are with first cousins, 18.6 per cent with second cousins, and 6.8 per cent with third cousins. Marriage between classificatory members of different generations is not preferred but is allowed with the payment of a ritual fine.[12] Although traditionally marriages were con-

---

[12] In fact almost any type of marriage is legally possible in terms of local *adat* law. The *pangulu* of Murutuwu, the most renowned *adat* law expert in Padju Epat, brought to our attention a ritual fine levied in a case of *sumbang pana' ambah*, literally a father-daughter marriage. The only case he personally knew of involved a father and a legally adopted daughter.

tracted by family representatives with or without the consent of the young people, most marriages today are arranged by the boy and girl themselves. The young couple elope (*idjari*) by going to the house of a friend or the village head and expressing their desire to marry. This individual then summons representatives (*asbah*) from the households of both bride and groom to discuss the situation. Before the marriage can take place, a contract must be negotiated between the *asbah* of the prospective spouses. This contract fixes at least the initial residence of the new couple, usually one of the households party to the contract. Residence is ambilocal or neolocal. Of the 59 marriages already referred to, 28 are uxorilocal, 26 are virilocal, 1 is equilocal (both spouses originate from the same household), 2 are neolocal, and 2 unknown.

However, individuals may join or leave the household at various times and for varying reasons. Adolescents or unmarried children often leave their natal households to help their grandparents; conflicts between household members are sometimes resolved by the departure of one of the disputing parties.

Ma'anjan kinship descends bilaterally.[13] A person's relationships outside the household seem to depend more on personal preference than on proximity of kinship. The kinship system does provide the individual with a great number of relatives with whom more personal ties may be developed as the need arises. Relatives who may live in the large towns and cities take on great importance in the matter of education. A youth wishing to progress beyond the elementary level of education provided in the village must move to an urban center, which is usually only possible when there is a relative with whom he can take up residence.

Economically, almost all households in the village engage in and derive their primary subsistence from swidden rice cultivation. The swidden

---

The *pangulu* said that he knew of no legal principle involving *sumbang pana' ineh* (mother-son marriage) but was not utterly repulsed by the idea and would be willing to hear such a case and make a decision on the basis of its particular circumstances. Naturally such marriages would be considered far from ideal. We only wish to point out the degree of latitude which people are willing to accept on principle.

[13] Ma'anjan kinship terminology may be described briefly as "lineal-Eskimo" for terms of reference and "generational-Hawaiian" for terms of address. Special kinship terminology distinguishes cousins to the third degree of collaterality, but there seems to be no concept of a kindred.

area cultivated by a *perinduk* family in a given year ranges from .22 to 4.34 hectares. The average per *perinduk* family is 1.53 hectares, and the average per capita is .38 hectare. New fields are cleared and burned between July and September. For this heavy work cooperative labor groups are formed, usually along lines of friendship and proximity of fields. These field-clearing groups, unlike the later planting and harvesting groups, are relatively smaller and more constant in membership and may consist of twelve or fifteen people who work alternately on the plots of each participating household until clearing and burning is completed. A household must furnish a full midday meal and a midafternoon snack to all those working in its field. Theoretically a household must repay a day of labor for each day it has received.

Planting begins in mid-October with the coming of the first light rains. There are two phases to the planting. In the first, fast-maturing (four-month) varieties of regular and glutinous rice are planted privately by individual *perinduk* families. Only a relatively small area of any field is sown with this fast-maturing rice. The greatest amount of field space is devoted to six-month rice, which is planted in the second phase by large cooperative work groups in a festive atmosphere. This type of cooperative work is basically a labor exchange of "a day for a day." The head of each family keeps an account of where its members have worked and of which families have sent representatives to work on its plots. In this system of credits and debts each individual is counted, rather than families as units. All "non-children" are considered equal in the system; work rendered by a man may be paid back by a woman or vice versa. Children are an ambiguous factor. Some families count them in the exchange system, others do not, which occasionally leads to hard feelings. However, many children work just as hard as adults, and especially where such children represent underpopulated households they are quite acceptable. A worker may also donate a day's labor which does not require any return. In such a case the "donation" will be explicitly stated at the time the work is performed. A day or so in advance, a prospective host will make it known that he is planning to plant a certain plot. In most instances several plots will be slated for the same day so that there is a certain amount of competition for labor. Labor groups are frequently drawn from the neighboring villages of Siong, Murutuwu, Tampulangit, and Maipe. The group working in a particular field may range in size from ten or twenty to over one hundred and fifty people, depending on the location of the plot, the number of people owing work to the host's family, the popularity of the host, and the quality and type of food anticipated. A person wishing to assure a good turnout at his own plot will announce his intention to kill a pig for the midday meal. In the actual planting work, the men form a row and go back and forth across the field, punching holes in the ground with dibble sticks. Following close behind comes a second row composed of gossiping women, jostling children, and a few unmarried men who cluster around the prettiest young girls. The people in this second row cast rice seed into the dibble holes. There are frequent rest breaks, and at least one, and perhaps two or three, meals will be served. Where only a small group appears, the work is hard and continues throughout the day with little feeling of gaiety. Where large crowds turn up, the actual work may be completed in an hour or two and the rest of the day spent in eating, gambling, and occasionally dancing.

Harvesting begins in late February with the four-month varieties and continues through March and April, when the six-month rice is cut. A cooperative labor arrangement similar to that used in planting, although usually smaller, helps in the harvest. Between the rather festive periods of planting and harvesting, each household must maintain a continual, often lonely, vigil in its swidden plots, keeping them clear of ever-encroaching weeds and protecting them from destruction by animals and birds. Night and day someone must be present in the rain-drenched huts to activate the various mechanisms used to frighten predators from distant corners of the field. This is the time when the old people pass the endless hours telling traditional stories in the smoky, crowded darkness. The neglect of a single night might spell destruction for much of the crop and a year of tight rations for the household.

It is perhaps in these days of vigilance that the value of a large household emerges. A full household has enough members to guard its fields adequately. A household consisting of a single member or a small nuclear family often finds it difficult to maintain the constant guard. When one of the unmarried men of the village decided to farm alone after an altercation with his mother, he was able to get his field cleared and planted with the aid of cooperative labor, but as a single individual he couldn't protect it, and his crop was ruined. The next year he returned to farm with his mother.

In addition to rice, other crops are raised in the swidden: pineapples, bananas, sugar cane, *ubi kaju* (cassava), eggplant, red peppers, a variety of gourds and squashes, and a few leafy vegetables, though individual families differ in the importance they assign to the last. During a good fruit season (December to March), abundant crops of durian, rambutan, *tjempedak,* and other fruits are harvested and frequently sold to Moslem groups on the Barito.

Village subsistence is rounded out by fish from the river. There are chickens and domestic pigs, but these are usually killed only on cere-monial or festive occasions. Although the forests are fairly well supplied with wild pig and various types of deer, there is only one rifle in the village, and ammunition is hard to come by. For that reason meat is a rare if much-appreciated item in the local diet.

Several sources of cash income are open to the villager. There is an old and now rapidly expanding rubber industry. A few families are tapping trees which were planted in the early part of this century; others have been planting new trees extensively for the past ten or twelve years, some of which are now coming into production. In the wet season, rubber is sold directly to buyers who come in from Bengkuang on market day. During the dry season two local entrepreneurs, one from Siong and one from Murutuwu, buy up local rubber and take it out to Bengkuang by canoe whenever the water is high enough. A local rubber smokehouse operates occasionally, but usually the latex is sold in uncured form. Four Telang households maintain small shops; another owns and rents houses locally and in Tamiang Lajang. During the rainy season young men may gain income by cutting trees in the marshy areas of primary forest and floating the logs out to the Barito, when the water is high, for ultimate sale in Bandjarmasin. The area of Padju Epat has been known for over a hundred years for its production of dugout canoes, which are sold along the Barito for supplemental income.

There are four households in Telang that do not engage in agriculture and must buy their foodstuffs. One maintains itself precariously from the proceeds of a small shop. In another, the head is an employee in the office of the government officer (*tjamat penghubung*), who also taps rubber on a profit-sharing basis for the owner of some trees. It is of interest to note that two of Telang's three Moslem families are represented in the above cases. The heads of the two remaining nonagricultural house-holds may best be described as retired from business.

4. Land Use Rights

Each village in Padju Epat has its traditional territory. According to local *adat,* an individual obtained exclusive use of village land that he himself cleared from primary forest. After the initial clearance, the use rights to the land were passed on to his descendants. There are two types of land use rights: effective or primary use rights that are inherited ambilineally through households, and latent or secondary use rights inherited bilaterally through individuals. As their names imply, primary use rights carry a stronger claim than secondary.

An individual does not begin to maintain a rice field separate from that of his parents until after his marriage. When a marriage is being arranged, the household where the new couple will take up residence and through which it will inherit its primary land use rights is stipulated in the marriage contract. When it comes time for a family to clear an additional plot, there are usually a number of suitable tracts to which it has use rights, both primary and secondary. It may choose any of the plots to which it has a primary use right. It may, with the permission of the household having primary use rights, clear a tract to which it has only secondary or, in some cases, no inherited rights at all. If a tract has not been recleared for many years, perhaps even several generations, the locus of its use rights may become obscured. If conflicting claims arise, the case is taken to the *pangulu* (see section 6) for arbitration. As a result of the recent decline in the density of Telang's population, disputes over land use rights now occur infrequently, and some people are even using land to which they hold no inherited rights whatsoever.

Fruit, coconut, and rubber trees are the property of the individuals who plant them. They generally remain attached to the household of the original owner but may be bought and sold, which is not true of swidden plots in the village *adat* system. Many people are now planting rubber trees in their swiddens. The individual first lays claim to the land according to his use rights. He usually plants rice for a year or two and then puts in several hundred to a thousand rubber trees, often interspersed with pineapples or a similar crop. The individual who plants the trees owns them outright, and since he is exercising semipermanent use of the land, in effect he owns the land for the life of the trees. Some owners of rubber trees are registering the land with the government, gaining legal title, and thereby retiring the land from the *adat* system. Like trees, such registered land may be bought and sold.

The *adat* world of the village is divided into two parts: the legal and the ceremonial. All the Ma'anjan members of the community are bound by the *adat* legal code, but only the Kaharingan segment still maintains the ceremonies related to the *adat* religious system.

5. *The Religious System, Entertainment, and Recreation*

The people of Telang are divided among three religious groups. There are 62 Kaharingan, 58 Christians, and 17 Moslems. Generally the members of a household belong to a single religion, but there are exceptions. Where a mixed marriage has occurred, the Kaharingan member has invariably converted to the religion of his Christian or Islamic spouse. There are no cases in Telang involving a Christian-Moslem marriage. The Kaharingan and Christians are all members of old Telang or Padju Epat Ma'anjan families, whereas the Islamic members of the community, except those by marriage, have their origins outside the Ma'anjan area.[14] In Telang the Moslems are by far the weakest group in terms of their participation in religious activities. The nearest mosque is located an hour's journey by canoe to the west, is attended irregularly, and only by the male heads of the Islamic families. There is no apparent adherence to a system of daily prayer or to the other requirements of the pillars of Islamic faith, although major holy days are observed with readings from the Koran and small celebrations within the household.

Christianity has fairly deep roots in the Ma'anjan region. After an early (1851) but unsuccessful start in Murutuwu, a village which to this day remains 100 per cent Kaharingan, a strong Christian mission was permanently established in Tamiang Lajang (1876). Tamiang Lajang remains the strongest Christian center among the Ma'anjan and is the local seat of Kalimantan's Protestant church (Geredja Kalimantan Evangelis).[15] No converts were obtained in Telang until the early part of the present century, but since that time the Christian community has grown steadily. The Christians of Telang and neighboring Siong hold combined religious services twice weekly in the houses of members. These services are usually led by members of the congregation, but the minister from the church in Tamiang Lajang visits Telang five or six times a year, at which times marriages and baptisms may be performed.

It is the Kaharingan segment of the population that enjoys the most active ceremonial life. There are numerous rituals to be performed, many of which normally occur during May, June, and July, the slack months in the agricultural cycle. Most require the services of a religious specialist,

[14] In general, Islam has made few inroads in the Ma'anjan region.

[15] For an excellent historical summary of the Christian movement in Central and South Kalimantan, see F. Ukur (1960). A brief history of mission activity among the Ma'anjan is given by H. Sundermann (1899, 472–478, 531–535).

the *wadian* (shaman or *balian*), for their proper accomplishment. There are five female and one male *wadian* types, each having its own characteristic spirits, rituals, and functions. There are spirit-propitiation ceremonies, village-welfare ceremonies, curing ceremonies, and life-cycle ceremonies, the most important being an elaborate cycle of death rituals which culminates in *idjambe*. The *wadian* must be able to go into trance, for trance is the door to the spirit world where, especially in healing ceremonies, the causes and cures for sickness must be sought. She must be an expert dancer, must possess the stamina to see her through a ritual that may last from one hour to nine days, and above all she must be able to master verbatim the countless chants which accompany the ceremonies she will be called upon to perform. In addition to her function as a religious practitioner and healer, the *wadian* also fills the role of local historian. Among her chants is a complete recounting of the origins and wanderings of the Ma'anjan people, the whys and wherefores of their customs and traditions, the names of their heroes, and the genealogies of their great families. Finally, the *wadian* provides the village with its primary source of entertainment. All performances are "open to the public," and it is a quiet week when there is no *wadian* ceremony in one of the villages of Padju Epat. The people of Telang, regardless of religion, will indeed travel miles to watch a famous *wadian* in action.

Christian, Moslem, and Kaharingan alike attend and appreciate the artistic features of *wadian* ritual. But for the old-time, hard-core member of the Kaharingan community, the *wadian* and her ceremonies are one of life's necessities, often a very expensive one. Not only must the *wadian's* fees be met, but the cost of sacrificial chickens, goats, pigs, and even, on great occasions, *kerbau* (water-buffalo) must be borne. The several *wadian* and frequently all the attendant spectators must be fed. This places a tremendous strain on the economy of the Kaharingan household. When the economic burden of the required ceremonials becomes too great, many Kaharingan convert to Christianity, while others only await the death of their household's older members before making a similar conversion.[16]

[16] It should be noted that the only way to rid oneself of the Kaharingan burden is to convert to another "recognized" religion. Most Dajaks consider Kaharinganism to be a real religion, and many feel that the only reason that it is not accepted officially as such by the Indonesian government is because it has no "book."

At the present time there are twelve people in the village, eight women and four men, who have mastered the art of the *wadian*, although two have subsequently retired upon conversion to Christianity. The youngest of the practicing shamans is thirty-eight years old. For the performance of certain ceremonies, only a single *wadian* in the whole of Padju Epat, a wonderfully hardy Balawa woman in her nineties, has the requisite knowledge. Young people no longer aspire to become *wadian*, and with the passing of Telang's present generation of shamans, Kaharinganism may very well die.

As a small, relatively remote village, Telang has been completely dependent on her own resources for entertainment. The arrival of the first transistor radio in July 1963 has not appreciably altered this situation. As just discussed, the *wadian* ceremonies serve as a major source of entertainment in Telang. This is especially true for the women of the village. At most times they are tied to household and agricultural tasks, but on ceremonial occasions the women gather in great numbers to gossip and to exercise their artistic abilities in the fashioning of elaborate decorations from coconut leaves and other materials.

For the older Ma'anjan members of the community, Kaharingan and Christian, male and female, there is an almost unmatched enjoyment to be garnered from the hours of extended debate that take place at all *adat* gatherings and revolve around the minute recounting of the details, history, interpretation, and application of *adat* law, together with a discussion of the ritual fine required to offset any irregularities which may have occurred on the given occasion.

For the younger people there is the institution of *kesenian*, a full night of music and dancing. *Kesenian*, held to honor a visiting dignitary or purely for its own sake, with one of the Padju Epat villages acting as host, offers traditional Ma'anjan dancing accompanied by a drum and a set of five gongs. Almost all the men in Telang are proficient musicians, although not all are equally adept at the favorite dance, *giring-giring*, an old-time dance of victory. Telang girls do not usually participate in traditional *kesenian*, although a few from Murutuwu do. During the rainy season a guitar orchestra from Bengkuang comes in once or twice a month on market night. On these occasions *kesenian* has a modern flavor, consisting of current Indonesian ballads and the dancing of *djoged*, a synthetic Indonesian national dance.

Gambling is a favorite and widely practiced masculine pastime. It is ordinarily illegal, which perhaps makes it even more attractive to the participants, but there are certain ceremonial occasions when public *"adat"* gambling is permitted. Large sums of money may be involved in the various semisecret games, especially on market nights, when itinerant gamblers come to town.[17] Another activity associated with market day is a weekly soccer game on Monday afternoon. The players are drawn from Siong and Tampulangit as well as Telang, and there are no fixed sides. Once or twice a year a composite team will go forth to do battle with Tamiang Lajang or some other distant town.

6. Village Administration and Leadership

Official leadership of the village theoretically rests in the hands of the *pembakal* (village head) and the *pangulu* (*adat* head).[18] The duty of the *pembakal* is to oversee the well-being of the village, make recommendations for improvements, organize village *gotong-rojong* (cooperative public works), collect an annual poll tax of 25 *rupiah* from adult males, and act generally as a leader. To qualify as *pembakal* an individual should be literate, own his house, and have influence in the village; he should be elected by the adult males of the village. The individual now ostensibly occupying this position performs few of the duties and fulfills none of the qualifications of office, since he has had little education, does not own a house, has practically no influence in the village, and has never been officially elected as *pembakal*. He was assistant village head at the time of his predecessor's death in 1956 and has been frozen in the job of acting *pembakal* by the civil government until a replacement comes or is pushed forward. No one else can be found in the village who is willing to become *pembakal*. In 1962 one man was elected to the post, but he immediately returned to another village far to the north.

[17] Gambling may be considered a serious problem in Telang. Many imprudent young men lose more than they can afford, and the necessity of settling such debts immediately has occasionally led them to robbery. One villager supported himself by gambling expeditions but was forced by public opinion to leave Telang after he became involved in an altercation with his first cousin following his winning 10,000 *rupiah* from the latter.

[18] The officially recognized term is *kepala kampung*, but *pembakal*, a title dating from Dutch times, is the one commonly used. Traditionally, the functions of *pembakal* and *pangulu* (*adat* head) were combined in a single individual. The separation seems to have resulted from the increased administrative responsibilities the Dutch assigned to the *pembakal*, whereas his traditional role must have been more like that of the *pangulu* today.

It is obvious that the *pembakal's* job is not a coveted one, a situation by no means confined to Telang or Kalimantan.

The *pangulu* functions as the ceremonial and legal *adat* expert in the village. As such he must officiate at all Kaharingan marriages, act as arbitrator in any local disputes that involve the interpretation or application of *adat* law, and serve as Telang's official representative at Kaharingan ceremonies held in other villages. He is entitled to receive fees for these various services. The position is still one of great respect. Like the *pembakal*, the *pangulu* is elected by Telang's adult males of all religions. The present *pangulu* is a very old man who is now practically blind. In former days he fulfilled his responsibilities admirably, but now his physical incapacities place serious limitations on the performance of his duties. He has appointed a younger man as his assistant, but this man lives some seven kilometers distant in Telang's daughter settlement, Luau Gador. Although he does represent the *pangulu* on many occasions, this man's residency outside Telang makes it difficult for him to be consulted on day-to-day matters, and he does not participate in village *gotong-rojong* activities. There have been no *adat* legal cases in Telang for some time, and the *pangulu* now only performs at the time of occasional Kaharingan marriages.[19] Since the old man seldom attends village meetings, any influence of the *pangulu* as a village leader has declined almost to the vanishing point in Telang, although the *pangulu* of Murutuwu is without doubt the most influential leader in the entire area.

Although traditionally a council of elders existed, and one still continues to operate in Murutuwu, none functions in matters of village government in Telang today. On the occasions when problems are brought to public discussion, anyone may attend and give his opinion. Younger men, especially those with outside experience, are just as likely to be heard as their elders. Women do not attend these sessions, although they participate freely in discussion on the occasion of *adat* ceremonies.

Primary leadership in Telang now lies in the hands of the two officials of the *ketjamatan penghubung* who reside in Telang. The first of these is the *tjamat penghubung* himself (who will hereafter be referred to simply as "the *tjamat*," as he is called in the village), the scion of what was formerly the first family of Telang. In the middle of the nineteenth

[19] The *pangulu* of Murutuwu, the foremost *adat* expert in Padju Epat, handles a number of *adat* legal cases each year. Many involve disputes over the ownership of fruit trees and are usually settled by the *pangulu* without the need for referral to the *demang*.

century, a Telanger named Sota'ono became the Dutch-supported leader of the whole area of Dusun Timur. The Sota'ono family maintained its close Dutch connections and its local position of leadership well into the twentieth century, sending many members to work in the colonial administration and in foreign businesses. The "Big House," an enormous dwelling which was erected by Sota'ono's sons several years after his death in 1894, is still the largest house in the whole area. Because of its Dutch ties, many of the family's members were executed during World War II by the Japanese, and it has since fallen into decline. The present *tjamat* is a great-grandson of Sota'ono; he left Telang in his youth and later entered the Indonesian civil administration. In January 1963 he was sent back to Telang, after an absence of more than twenty-five years. It was the government's hope that the appointment of a son of the Sota'ono family as *tjamat* in Telang would help stimulate the recovery of the slumping Padju Epat region.

Since his return to Telang, the *tjamat* has acted vigorously to bring "progress" to the region. His plans have included the construction of a *tjamat's* office, a new public health clinic, and vehicular roads to Tamiang Lajang and Bengkuang. All work on the various projects is carried on with *gotong-rojong* labor drawn, supposedly, from all the villages of Padju Epat. However, the farther a village is located from Telang, the less willing are its citizens to participate in such work. All of the projects have been initiated with high hopes, but up to the present time not one has been completed, all having encountered difficulties along the way. The new office has been almost, but not quite, finished for several months. Work was started on the clinic one day in March 1963 and had not yet been resumed a year later. In the meantime the Padju Epat public health nurse has removed himself from Telang and is now living in Tamiang Lajang, where he finds the living conditions better. The civil government made the completion of the Tamiang Lajang road a precondition to the granting of permits to hold *idjambe* in several of Padju Epat's villages in July 1963. Thus there was an extremely good initial turnout for *gotong-rojong* road work, especially by Murutuwu, the first village scheduled to hold *idjambe*. In early July there was much anxiety because the road was not finished on the prescribed date. The ceremony was postponed for a day or two, and then when the Murutu-wans made known their intention to go ahead with *idjambe*, with or without a permit, it was grudgingly released by the *tjamat's* office. This took the pressure off the road work, and in September 1963 the Tamiang

Lajang road remained unfinished, while work on the Bengkuang road had not yet begun. With the rains, much of the completed road was washed out. Although the present *tjamat* acts as a leader at both the village and *ketjamatan penghubung* levels, the individualistic villagers are not experienced followers, and his job is a difficult and uneviable one.

The *demang*, the second official associated with the *ketjamatan penghubung*, serves as the *adat* head for the whole of Padju Epat and receives a monthly honorarium from the provincial government. The *demang* is theoretically elected by the assembled *pangulu* and *pembakal* of the villages within the *adat* area. His office is older than the *ketjamatan penghubung* itself, for it was a creation of the former Dutch colonial administration.[20] In former days the *demang* judged *adat* legal cases referred to him by the *pangulu* of the various villages, for which he received a fee. The *demang* for Padju Epat has usually been a Telanger, and until 1949 the post was always held by a lineal descendant of Sota'ono.

The present *demang* was appointed in January 1963 by the departing former *tjamat penghubung* and was confirmed in his post by the provincial government. The various *pembakal* and *pangulu* of Padju Epat have never been convoked to "elect" him. He is not the leading *adat* expert in the area, although in the light of changing conditions this is no longer too important. Because many disputes formerly considered to be within the *demang's* jurisdiction are now being handled by the *tjamat* or referred directly to the police or civil courts, the *demang's* appellate functions in the *adat* legal system are losing their importance. These are being replaced by a new political function, that of government spokesman. Regular government officials such as the *tjamat* are committed by policy to using Indonesian in the transaction of public business. Although most villagers speak some Indonesian, there is a wide range of variability in proficiency, with the old people and most of the women at the lower end of the scale, the younger and better educated at the upper. In public discussion, even those who know Indonesian fairly well naturally feel more relaxed in Ma'anjan. This puts the *tjamat* in a difficult position, from which he is extricated by the *demang*. The *demang*, while expected to be fluent in Indonesian, does not have the official obligation to use it. Periodically all the *demang* are summoned to the *kabupaten* (regency) or provincial capitals to participate in political indoctrination

[20] There is a *demang* for each Dajak "*adat* area" in Central Kalimantan, with a total of fifty for the whole province.

courses. Upon their return they are expected to help interpret government policies for the people in their areas and to gain support for the implementation of government projects, especially at the local level.

This change in function is well illustrated in the case of the *demang* of Padju Epat. During the first eight months in which he held office he did not have a single *adat* legal case referred to him. During the same time he was extremely active in gaining support and workers for the modernization projects planned by the *tjamat*, always taking an active part in the work itself. In the role of *adat* head for the region, he visited *adat* ceremonies in the various villages and formally or informally discussed local problems, trying to make the government viewpoint known. When the *bupati* (regent) gave a speech at the recent Murutuwu *idjambe* ceremony, describing the benefits to be derived from the new Tamiang Lajang road and the need for greater sacrifices to bring the road to completion, it was the *demang*, not the *tjamat*, who interpreted and enlarged on the speech for the benefit of the Ma'anjan audience. Often after the *tjamat* has addressed a public meeting in Indonesian, the *demang* will rephrase it in Ma'anjan and lead discussion on the subject. It may well be that the *demang* now serves as the most important nonadministrative link between government and villager.

The individualistic outlook of the villagers makes the successful exercise of leadership a difficult feat. The unofficial leader in Telang is probably the teacher in the primary school, a man in his sixties and a lifelong resident of the village. He exerts leadership both in public debate and public works but is not always heeded or followed. He functions as the resident church elder in the Christian community, he was treasurer of the now defunct village consumers' cooperative, and at the time of the national elections he acted as the chairman of the local elections committee. In the political sphere he has served as the local organizer for Partai Indonesia Raja and Pakat Dajak, a Dajak nationalist group of former times. The teacher is an unusual person in this respect. Political interest is extremely low in the village at large, and there are no political parties currently active in Telang.

7. Conclusion

The picture drawn of Telang in the preceding pages is of necessity a sketchy one. The village is a willful model whose ever-changing positions and attitudes make it difficult to portray. Yet even in profile,

Telang's figure proves elusive because its outlines are obscured by the shifting environmental background. Telang is in the dying stages of the traditional swidden cycle. So too are the other Ma'anjan villages of Padju Epat, yet each has an individualistic reaction. Telang and Balawa have large Christian populations, while Murutuwu remains completely Kaharingan and Siong preponderantly so. In Telang, household size and complexity has followed the population into decline, suggesting the fragmentation of former large households. In the equally depopulated village of Siong, however, households continue to be complex, and it appears that households in that village remain or depart as units and not as individuals. How is the widespread planting of rubber going to affect the underlying swidden system? The density of population in the area has been reduced to the point where it can maintain its present level over the foundation of a mixed swidden-rubber economy if the people wish to remain. How will Telang's role as a market town affect her future, especially in an area with an expanding economy? To gain a true likeness it will be necessary in the future to view Telang not as the subject for a personal profile but as one of the constituent models for a family portrait that includes all of Padju Epat's villages.

Chapter V

Kutagamber: A Village of the Karo[1]

MASRI SINGARIMBUN
AUSTRALIAN NATIONAL UNIVERSITY

1. The Karo People

The Karo are one of the six ethnic groups that comprise the Batak, the others being the Simelungan, the Pakpak, the Toba, the Angkola, and the Mandailing. In anthropological literature the Batak are known as the Indonesian ethnic group with the strongest patrilineal system.[2] In their kinship system the Batak are also noted for the specific relation that exists between groups "providing brides" and groups "receiving brides"; the latter group, called *anakberu* among the Karo and *boru* among the Toba, pays respect in different forms to the first group, called *kalimbubu* among the Karo and *hula-hula* among the Toba.

The Karo, who inhabit the northern part of the Batak region in East Sumatra, have four ethnic groups as their neighbors: the East Sumatrans to the north, the Alas of Central Atjeh to the west, the Simelungan to the east, and the Pakpak to the south. The Karo ethnic group numbers about 300,000 people who occupy a region of about 5,000 square kilometers, an area mainly consisting of mountains and highlands. Administratively the Karo lands form the regency of Karo at Karo Highlands,

---

[1] I am grateful to the Department of Anthropology and Sociology of Australian National University in Canberra, who under the graduate assistantship program sponsored my field work in the Karo Batak country from August 1961 to July 1962.

This chapter has been translated from the Indonesian text by T. W. Kamil.

[2] For books and articles on the Batak, see Kennedy (1955, I, 145–171).

Langkat Hulu in the Langkat regency, and Deli Hulu and Serdang Hulu in the regencies of Deli and Serdang. On grounds of cultural similarity, the inhabitants of one subdistrict in Dairi (Pakpak region), the subdistrict of Tanah Pinem, can also be included in the Karo lands.

2. *Location and Settlement Pattern of Kutagamber*

The village of Kutagamber to be discussed in this chapter is located in the subdistrict of Tanah Pinem, which is found in the most northern part of Dairi, bounded on the north and east by the regency of Karo. Kutagamber is located in the eastern part of the subdistrict and is one of the villages nearest the border. Separating the regency of Karo from the Dairi region is the ridge of the Bukit Barisan (about 900 meters above sea level), approximately one hour's distance from Kutagamber. A mountain called Deleng Kempawa (1,090 meters) lies to the east of the Bukit Barisan; Kutagamber is situated on its slope, about 100 meters above the base of the mountain and 645 meters above sea level. The base of Deleng Kempawa meets with the ridge of the Bukit Barisan, forming a narrow valley through which the river Lau Rimbon flows. The subsistence activities of the people are mainly concentrated on these two mountain slopes: most of the swiddens are located on the slopes of Deleng Kempawa, while Bukit Barisan is used for cattle raising.

Like most Karo villages, Kutagamber is a village with a compact settlement pattern; almost all buildings are erected in a single area. The distance separating one house from another is between three and five meters. The ceremony houses are situated on an east-west axis, with their two doors facing in both directions. Fencing generally indicates the village limits and also functions to prevent pigs from running away, although nowadays the custom of fencing is disappearing, as pigs must be put in sties in accordance with the government's sanitation program. It is not known how long ago Kutagamber was founded, although the most significant evidence is the people's belief that their village has been occupied for seven generations, a fact which is supported by their genealogies.

The area of the village itself includes about 8,000 square meters on the slopes of the Kempawa Mountain, surrounded by coconut and citrus gardens (see Map V). The swiddens are located beyond the fruit gardens, mainly in the western, northwestern, and southwestern parts of the village. The main paths connect Kutagamber with the villages of Liren, Lau

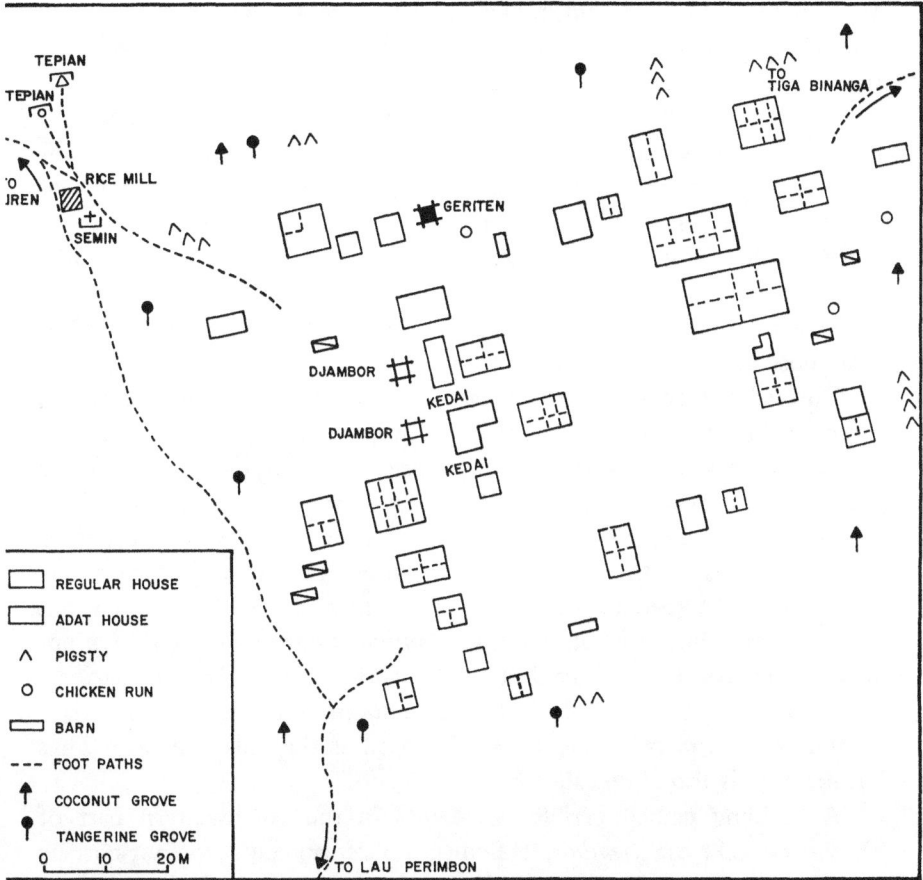

Map V. Settlement Pattern of Kutagamber

Perimbon, and Tiga Binanga. Liren is the nearest, about a fifteen-minute walk from Kutagamber, and beyond this village one finds Kuta Buluh, the capital of the subdistrict, nearly seven kilometers from Liren. A six-year elementary school is located at Lau Perimbon, about four kilometers from Kutagamber. Tiga Binanga, a small town in the regency of Karo, is the most important market for Kutagamber and the surrounding villages, lying about three and a half hours from Kutagamber by horseback, the principal means of transportation.

Architecturally the village houses can be divided into two types: *adat* and more modern houses. The *adat* house is closely related to traditional Karo *adat;* its construction is based upon certain beliefs and involves complex ceremonies. Its inhabitants usually consist of between four and eight families. The newer houses are symbolic of a new style of life, in which there is more room for the individual; there are more and larger windows, and the rooms occupied by each family are more spacious than those in the *adat* houses.

Toward the center of the village are two coffee shops which also serve as domiciles for their respective proprietors. About three meters in front of these shops are two structures named *djambor*. The lower part of the *djambor* forms a platform, on the four corners of which are poles supporting a rice storehouse. The ceiling of the rice storehouse in turn creates another floor which is often used as a sleeping place, since Karo *adat* specifies that adult young men and widowers may not sleep at home but must stay at the *djambor*. Sometimes even boys not much older than ten already sleep at the *djambor*. The *djambor* platform is also used as a place for discussions and meetings, and in the days of the colonial government it was also used as the village court.[3] Thus the *djambor* is also often called *balé*.

A building named *geriten* is situated in the northwestern part of the village. Like the *djambor*, its floor is a platform and at its four corners poles are mounted. Underneath the roof is a platform where the skulls of a famous curer and his wife are kept in a wooden box. The building was erected by the children of the curer; it displays not only the economic wealth of the founders but also reflects the high prestige of the persons to whom it was dedicated. A grave called *semin*, made of cement, is located to the northwest, somewhat outside the village limits; like the *geriten*, the *semin* is also built to honor dead of high social status.

[3] After World War II the Indonesian government abolished local courts subordinate to the regency courts.

Near the *semin* is a building housing the diesel-engine-driven rice mill owned by the village cooperative. A rice mill operated by a water wheel is found on the bank of the Lau Rimbon River; used before the engine was introduced in 1957, this mill is now closed. In addition to the specialized structures already mentioned and the regular residence houses, pig sties are scattered throughout the village. The *tepian,* or bathing place, is divided into two separate parts, one for men and one for women. The water flows from its source through a bamboo pipe to the bathing place. In addition to being the place for bathing, washing, and taking water, the *tepian* also serves in the performance of certain rituals, like taking a newborn baby to the water (*maba anak kulau*), and various purification ceremonies (*erpangir*).

At about a ten-minute walk to the northeast of Kutagamber, we find a cemetery (not included on Map V). From a distance, only forest and shrubs are visible because, according to old beliefs, clearing the cemetery is prohibited as it is thought to clear the way to the world of death. A clean cemetery would thus cause an increase in the number of deaths.

3. Some Demographic Data

Karo society consists of a segmentary social system with different levels of unilineal groups. The smallest but also the most significant economic unit in Karo society is the *djabu,* or nuclear family, which forms a unit for the consumption and production of food. Each *djabu* has its own dwelling place, either an entire house or part of a house; each has its own properties; and in certain circumstances each forms a unit in the performance of religious ceremonies. Although the *djabu* is established through the marriage bond, a newly married couple does not immediately become a *djabu* in the real sense of the word.

A newly wed couple usually continues to live with parents for about a year; ideally they should initially reside with the *djabu* of the husband's parents. During this time they depend entirely upon their parents, but as soon as they can afford to, usually after the first harvest, they establish their own *djabu.* The process of founding a separate *djabu* is called *djajo.* The husband and wife with their children create the *djabu* in its next development, and subsequently their children break away through marriage to form their own *djabu.* It is worth noting that, among the Karo, parents are inclined to be independent in their old age and do not rely upon their married children. For example, in Kutagamber four out of the six existing widows over sixty years old still maintained *djabu* of their own; the other two, although preferring to be independent, were unable to do so because of ill health. The only widower in the village also had his own *djabu*, in spite of the fact that two of his married daughters lived in the same village. Thus a number of *djabu* have only one member. Out of the 88 *djabu* in Kutagamber, the number of members in each is illustrated by Table 6.

Table 6. Size of *djabu* in Kutagamber

Number of members in one *djabu*	1	2	3	4	5	6	7	8
Frequency	8	5	19	14	23	12	3	4

The most frequent *djabu* is clearly the one with five members, composed of husband, wife, and three children. In one of the 88 *djabu* a man has two wives, each having her own rice field, house, and kitchen. According to Karo *adat*, polygyny is permitted, although it is not widely practiced. The single case in Kutagamber was a consequence of levirate (*lakoman*).

The 88 *djabu* of Kutagamber live in 32 houses, of which 22 are regular residences and 10 are *adat* houses. The residence house is occupied by one to three *djabu*, while the *adat* house contains four to eight *djabu*. On Map V the divisions into *djabu* are indicated with dotted lines. The regular residence is built by one or two families, the additional occupants being sons who have not yet been able to build a house for their own *djabu*. Table 7 shows that among the 88 *djabu*, 53, or 60 per cent, live

Table 7. Number of *djabu* per house in Kutagamber

Total of *djabu* in one house	1	2	3	4	5	6	7	8
Frequency	13	5	4	5	1	1	2	1

in *adat* houses and 35 (40 per cent) in regular houses. Of this number, only 13 *djabu* (15 per cent) occupy a separate house. In 85 per cent of the *djabu*, each house contains more than one *djabu*. The vertical line in the table indicates the division between regular and *adat* houses.

The total population numbers 371 people, excluding 27 paid workers who boarded with their employers when this census was made. The distribution of ages shows that the younger age groups are larger in number, owing mainly to the decrease in death rates with the development of modern medicines. The age and sex distribution of the population of Kutagamber is indicated in Table 8.

Table 8. Population of Kutagamber by age and sex

Age	Men	Women
0–4	34	28
5–9	21	22
10–14	23	17
15–19	15	23
20–24	17	11
25–29	15	26
30–34	13	11
35–39	15	7
40–44	7	8
45–49	8	8
50–54	5	6
55–59	7	6
60 and older	5	13
Total	185	186

4. Dry Rice Farming

Despite the fact that dry rice farming has been abandoned in most of the Karo Batak area, it is still the most important means of subsistence for the population of Kutagamber and the surrounding villages.[4] The ideal pattern is *bias nakan*, to produce enough supplies in one year to last until the next harvest. A *djabu* of five people (husband and wife with three children) needs between thirteen and fourteen quintals of rice a year, and this amount can usually be obtained from the average yield of one hectare of land.

The arrival of the Dutch in the beginning of the twentieth century changed Kutagamber and most of the Karo villages into a cash economy. Following independence this process of change has increased in intensity,

[4] In most of Karo Batak country, swidden agriculture has disappeared. Intensive rice agriculture has developed instead, while at many places intensive vegetable gardening has developed, to supply the city of Medan and even Singapore.

stimulated by new ideals of progress. The amount and variety of articles sold at Kutagamber's coffee shops reflect this fact. Cigarettes, liquor, medicine, clothes such as singlets, sarongs, and batik, and other consumer goods can be bought at both village coffee shops. Each shop subscribes to a newspaper and owns a transistor radio, while at night they are illuminated by pressure lamps. The establishment of the cooperative engine-driven rice mill already mentioned, the present construction of roads through mutual help, and the sending of children to schools in the city are all efforts to implement the new ideals of progress.

Furthermore, the villagers are beginning to attach more importance to such cash crops as tobacco than to rice, and they are expanding their fields sometimes to more than three times the former area. The disadvantage from this expansion is the disappearance of the forest and the increasing shortage of land. Consequently, fallow periods to refertilize the swiddens become more and more infrequent, and a shift to more intensive cultivation is noticeable. Expansion together with intensification of agriculture requires additional labor, a problem solved by attracting wage laborers from the adjacent areas of Toba, Pakpak, Gajo, and Singkel. These additional laborers in the village may number as many as fifty people, a situation which causes serious problems for the economy of the population in general. The need for cash to be used as capital or for other purposes is strongly felt and is clearly reflected in the increasing demand for credit, even if the interest rates are as high as 2½ to 4 per cent per month. The lowest interest rate in Kutagamber is charged by the rice cooperative: 2½ per cent a month for members and 3 per cent a month for nonmembers. On October 1, 1961, for instance, the amount of money lent from these funds at interest amounted to 85,000 *rupiah*.

In the present transitional period, many conflicts concerning land are common. In Karo *adat* law, a person may use virgin land which belongs to the village, providing he does not pawn or sell it. In this sense the village forms a corporate group of landowners. This system is most clearly seen in Kutagamber and other villages where swidden agriculture still prevails. The best pieces of land can be obtained by clearing primary forest, and this land is called *tinembak*. One who has cleared *tinembak* by felling the forest for the first time reserves full rights to cultivate this land for a second time (*balik tinembak*), despite the fact that he has abandoned it a long time since the first clearing. After the second planting, however, this individual no longer has any special claims to the field. Thus, as soon as he has abandoned it, other people from his village may use it. Productive trees planted by the previous occupant, like coconut, durian, and the like, are considered still to be his property.

As the primary forests have disappeared, the people of Kutagamber have worked the land by clearing bushes or grassland. Abandoning land for too long a period causes its eventual loss, as other people urgently need it. However, many people still tend to think in terms of the Karo *adat*, feeling that land cleared and abandoned is still theirs by right, and this has become the source of many conflicts and social tensions.

5. *Kinship System*

In the Karo community, kinship relations still form an important part of all aspects of life. This section will discuss briefly the patrilineal group and the system of marriage relations which form the basis of the Karo kinship system.

The Karo ethnic group consists of five *merga* or maximal clans: (1) Ginting, (2) Karo-karo, (3) Perangin-angin, (4) Sembiring, and (5) Tarigan. Consequently the Karo often identify their group with the name *merga si lima*, meaning the five *merga*. Exogamy is the most significant trait, as the *merga* form neither corporate groups nor units for joint activity. The members are dispersed, and a *merga* head or administration does not exist. Each clan is subdivided into subclans, also called *merga* in the Karo language. According to Tamboen (1952, 65–68), the total number of subclans among the Karo Batak is 833, with each of the five maximal clans having from 13 to 19 subclans. Each subclan has its own origin myth, and its members observe the same prohibitions. At the subclan level the ties of the membership cannot be proved genealogically. The five maximal clans each have members in Kutagamber; each maximal clan consists of several particular subclans as shown in Table 9.

According to Karo *adat*, a woman belongs to the *merga* of her husband. His death does not alter her status, as her rights and duties according to *adat* remain the same. She is fully responsible for raising her children, and the inheritance may only be divided after the death of both parents. The woman's acceptance into her husband's group also means that her own natal patrilineal group becomes her *kalimbubu* (bride-supplying group). A widow may return to her own *merga*, however, by requesting a "divorce" from her deceased husband. In Kutagamber one such return has occurred, but the other eleven widows who maintain separate *djabu* are still classified in the *merga* of their deceased husbands.

Next in importance to the patrilineal clan of the father is the patrilineal clan of the mother (*bere-bere*). Affiliations with both groups—that is, with the paternal patrilineal clan and with the maternal patrilineal

Table 9. Djabu in Kutagamber by clan and subclan

Clan and subclan	Total *djabu* in each subclan	Total *djabu* in maximal clan
Perangin-angin		28
Pinem	23	
Sebajang	4	
Bangun	1	
Ginting		23
Munte	18	
Sugihen	4	
Adjartambun	1	
Tarigan		19
Sibero	11	
Gersang	8	
Sembiring		16
Busuk	10	
Milala	6	
Karo-karo		2
Katjiribu	2	
Total	88	88

clan—can only be obtained through birth, as the institution of adoption is unknown in Karo society. The relationship between members of the same maximal clan who belong to different subclans is called *senina*, while the kinship relation between members of the same subclan is named *sembujak*. The father's and the mother's father's kin groups are called *kalimbubu*, "bride suppliers." More specifically, the former is called *kalimbubu si mupus*, meaning the *kalimbubu* who gives birth, and the latter is named *kalimbubu iperdemui*, the *kalimbubu* by marriage. On the other hand, the relation with the patrilineal group of the sister's husband and the daughter's husband is termed *anakberu*, "bride receivers." (Note that the above description has been made with reference to a male Ego). As explained above, a married woman joins her husband's group, so that her natal patrilineal group becomes her *kalimbubu*. The terms *senina, anakberu,* and *kalimbubu* denote the relations between certain groups or people, but sometimes these terms seem to have become designations for the kin groups themselves.

6. Beliefs and Ceremonies

The *adat* religon, which is called Perbegu,[5] centers about the worship of the spirits of deceased ancestors, the guardian spirits being those of patrilineal kin and their wives. Similar to the situation in the real world, in the world of spirits the wife's spirit belongs to the patrilineal group of her husband. The most prominent guardian spirit is called *si Mate Sada Wari* ("he who died in one day"), namely, the spirit of an ancestor who died suddenly—was killed in an accident, was murdered, or died while giving birth, for example. In this category are also included Batara Guru and Bitjara Guru, who are respectively the spirit of a foetus and the spirit of a baby who died before teething. All these spirits are called Dibata Djabu, the gods of the *djabu*. I might add that the spirit of an *anakberu* or *kalimbubu* may not become a Dibata Djabu.

The spirits of the Dibata Djabu may give assistance but can also cause disaster. Therefore good relations with these spirits must be maintained by the performance of various religious ceremonies and offerings. The spirits of more remote ancestors are the concern of a larger group of descendants, parallel with the branches in a genealogy. Consequently, larger patrilineal groups are formed for the worship of ancestral spirits.

The ceremony for the Dibata Djabu is led by a *guru si baso*, usually called merely *guru*. This religious specialist, always a woman, is considered to be the mediator between man and the spiritual world. The *guru si baso* knows ways to contact supernatural beings. She may become possessed (*selok*), and then people in the audience can communicate directly with or ask advice of the spirits; people may consult the guardian spirit of the *guru*, who talks by whistling through the mouth of the *guru* when she is not in a state of trance. Kutagamber has three *guru si baso* who are perpetually occupied with consultations and other religious activities.

[5] About 70 per cent of the total population of Karo Batak country are Perbegu, while about 30 per cent are either Protestants or Moslems. Kutagamber is entirely Perbegu, except for one Moslem *djabu*.

According to Perbegu belief, the spirit of a recently deceased person wanders about the world of human beings before entering the world of the spirits. In a ceremony named *perumah begu*, the spirit (*begu*) is called by the *guru;* it enters the *guru*, where it becomes aware of its death and gives advice to the mourning relatives who are left behind. Another ceremony at the time of death performed by the *guru* is to unite the new spirit with the spirits of previously deceased ancestors.

The affinal group plays an important role in ceremonies along the life cycle of the individual. At the seventh month of the first pregnancy, the *kalimbubu* performs a ceremony called *ngambahken naroh mbentar* (to present a white egg), to safeguard the birth of the child and also to protect the mother. Although the ritual is performed at the house of the mother, the *kalimbubu* are obliged to provide the food. The next ritual, held after the birth of the child, is *maba anak kulau* (taking the infant to the bathing place), with the purpose of introducing the baby to the holy spirits and the patron spirits to ask for their protection. If the child is a boy, he is carried to the *tepian* by the wife of his mother's brother (*kalimbubu*), while a girl is held by her father's sister (*anakberu*). This act symbolizes the hope for a future cross-cousin marriage with the child of the mother's brother (*impal*). This is regarded as the ideal marriage in the Karo society, as the relation between *anakberu* and *kalimbubu* is extended in the next generation.

The *kalimbubu* also plays an important part in ceremonies at later stages along the life cycle. In a ceremony called *ngembahken nakan*, conducted for a person who has reached old age, for example, the *kalimbubu* gives food to the person in question. The ceremony is therefore also called *mesur-mesuri*, meaning "to fill the stomach." In the case of a woman, the *kalimbubu* is the mother's patrilineal group. Especially for elderly, sick, and ailing people this is considered a necessity, as this ceremony will relieve their misery, by hastening either their recovery or their death.

7. *The System of Village Administration*

Descent and marriage relations also form the basic foundation for Karo political organization and village administration. Before the arrival of the Dutch in the beginning of the twentieth century, the *kampung* or village was the largest political unit in the area (Joustra 1926, 210). The patrilineal group that is considered to be directly descended from the original founders of the village forms that village's *bangsa taneh*. Almost every subclan has been responsible for the founding of certain villages, and the area where the majority of these villages is located is thought to be the homeland of the particular subclan.

The traditional *kampung* head (*pengulu*) is a member of the *bangsa taneh*, a position that is inherited by the eldest son. Together with one of his *anakberu* and one of his *senina* (see section 5), the *pengulu* runs the village administration. According to Karo beliefs, a village cannot be founded by only one person or patrilineal group but must be built with the cooperation of the *anakberu* and *senina* of that person or group. Such an *anakberu* is called *anakberu tua*, the traditional "bride-taker." The three positions of *pengulu*, *anakberu*, and *senina* are hereditary.

The *bangsa taneh* at Kutagamber is a unilineal group of the Pinem subclan, which belongs to the maximal clan Perangin-angin. Table 9 shows that this subclan claims twenty-three *djabu* in Kutagamber, the largest number of *djabu* belonging to any one subclan. Radjanangkih is the name of the ancestor who is supposed to have founded the village, and present members of Pinem represent the seventh generation of his descendants. The *anakberu tua* of this *bangsa taneh* is Munte, a subclan of Ginting, while the *senina* is Bangun.

From the political and territorial point of view, the *kampung* of Kutagamber is still intact and not broken up into parts. Another type of village in the Karo lands is a village with several *bangsa taneh* and consequently several divisions. Each division, called *kesain*, has its own administrative apparatus, a *pengulu kesain* with his *anakberu tua* and *senina*. Generally the members of a *kesain* as a corporate group own a part of the *kampung* (farming lands) and sometimes also a cemetery of its own. The head of such a village is the *pengulu* of the *kesain* which is traditionally considered the oldest. Also the *balé kuta*, where village assemblies are held, will usually be located in the territory of the senior *kesain*. Moreover, the *kampung* also will have a single ritual object for collective worship, so that ceremonies and rituals are held jointly.

This system of village administration was still in operation when the Japanese left. After the Indonesian revolution and subsequent changes in the political structure of the country, this traditional administrative system disappeared. Today the *kampung* is the smallest unit in the Karo village administration, and the *kesain* has been abolished. Moreover, to simplify the administration, the minimum unit for one *kampung* head must consist of at least one hundred families. In order to reach the re-

quired number, many small villages have been grouped together; Kutagamber (88 *djabu*) and Liren (36 *djabu*) recently were formed into
a single administrative unit under an elected *kampung* head, who resides
at Kutagamber with an assistant at Liren. Even though the political and
administrative structure has changed, the traditional system still continues
informally. Since the revolution Kutagamber has changed *pengulu* three
times, but so far the candidates elected to this position have always been
members of the *bangsa taneh*, showing the still-powerful position of this
traditional group.

Chapter VI

Allang: A Village on Ambon Island

SATYA WATJANA CHRISTIAN UNIVERSITY

INDONESIA

1. Propinsi *Maluku*

The province of Maluku (the Moluccas) is formed by the large archipelago east of Sulawesi (the Celebes), north of the Timor archipelago, and west of Irian. *Orang* Maluku, or the Moluccan people in the restricted sense, are the inhabitants of the small island of Ambon, where the capital of the province, Kota Ambon (Ambon town), is located.

The ethnic composition of the Moluccan people has as yet not been conclusively analyzed. Both in racial stock and in culture the area manifests pronounced complexity, being a transitional region between the Malayan and Melanesian areas.[1] The people throughout central and southern Maluku, together with many groups in the northern district of the province, seem to belong primarily to the Proto-Malay stock which migrated from the Asian mainland displacing the aboriginal Australoid, Pygmoid, and perhaps Veddoid inhabitants on the Indonesian archipelago. There has been considerable intermarriage with Deutero-Malay elements, particularly in northern Maluku. There seems also to be clear evidence of biological and cultural diffusion from Irian and even perhaps Melanesia, for on the whole the Moluccan peoples appear darker in skin pigment

[1] My own research leads me to conclusions substantially the same as those of A. R. Wallace, which were based on extensive observation in the Moluccan and Irian regions as well as throughout the Indonesian archipelago. See Wallace (1869).

and larger of frame than the average Indonesian. The ancestors of the inhabitants of most central Moluccan villages migrated from various areas to the north and west of Ambon no later than the fifteenth century, perhaps considerably earlier. Most of them came directly from Ceram, though many originated elsewhere. Several kin groups in those villages trace their origin to the island of Makian near Ternate. In language, folkways, and mores (*adat*), and in general cultural base, they are closely related to the peoples of West Ceram, as their legends and myths clearly demonstrate.

The total population of the province of Maluku, according to the 1961 census, was 789,534, while that of the central Moluccan district was 296,033. The 1959 census figures for Ambon Island (excluding the municipality of Ambon) show twenty-six Christian villages with a total population of 37,631, sixteen Moslem villages with a total population of 31,165, and five mixed Moslem-Christian villages with 11,568 inhabitants.

One of the twenty-six Christian villages is Allang, perched somewhat precariously on the terraced rocky slopes that rise sharply from the emerald sea on the southwest tip of the northern peninsula of Ambon Island.[2]

2. Natural Environment

Allang's site is not as precarious, however, as first impression indicates, even if one approaches it during the "east season" when the full force of the monsoon winds, which bring heavy seas and rain, is felt, for Allang has maintained its present location, guarding the entrance to Ambon Bay, for at least four centuries.

Mountains, sea, land, fresh water, and winds are the dominant features of the natural environment of Allang. The crowding of the mountains upon the shore results in the relative absence of level land, either for residential or farming areas. One who wishes to build must first create a level space by constructing a terrace. Cultivated fields are generally

[2] The description presented in this chapter refers to the situation in 1960, during the first part of which the field data were collected. Allang can be considered fairly typical of the Christian villages found in the central Moluccan region except for its larger population and slightly better economic standard. In important respects it would not be typical of Moslem villages, despite many evident similarities. Protestant villages comprise slightly more than half the total number of villages in Central Maluku.

found on the steep hillsides, where the soil is neither very fertile nor well anchored to the slope.

The only access to Allang is by shore-line path or by outrigger canoe, the latter being more popular though not necessarily more widely used. Since Allang Point lies outside the mouth of Ambon Bay, it feels the full force of winds and waves which, from June to November (throughout the wet "east season"), make the approach by sea very hazardous. During these months, the heavy swells driven by the monsoon winds break on the rocky reinforced shore line of Allang Harbor with a roar that is so prevalent and prominent a factor in daily life as to have conditioned, it is said, the quality and style of speaking of the Allangites.

Fresh water is the final factor to be mentioned. In Allang, as in many Moluccan villages, the location of the residential area is determined by streams and springs that can supply sufficient water for washing, cooking, and bathing, for fresh water is a scarce item throughout the region, especially during the dry "west season." Allang's water supply comes mainly from a couple of mountain springs, which deliver water to fixed bathing and washing places by means of a series of long bamboo pipes. There is also one stream that provides a supply of fresh water, except in the height of the dry and rainy seasons. All water for use in the home is carried by the women from these sources.

The combination of mountains, sea, soil quality, and winds have made the area well suited for the growth of both nutmegs and cloves, though the former is the more important cash crop in Allang. Topography and character of the soil mean that most cultivated plots are relatively far (in time, if not in actual distance) from the houses. During the height of the agricultural season, temporary residences are constructed near the groves and gardens; the family lives and works here during the week and returns to the village residence only for the weekend. At least half of the land owned by the village is so far back in the steep, heavily wooded hills that it is not cultivated at all. There is only a thin layer of soil covering the Moluccan Islands, and it is not very fertile. Once the luxuriant flora has been cut and burned and the soil is exposed to the leaching effects of sun and rains, plots can be cultivated only for several years before they are abandoned for a new slash. Until the present, the pattern of swidden (slash-and-burn) agriculture has been conditioned largely by the topography, the quality of the soil, the rhythm of rainy and dry seasons, and the fact that clove and nutmeg trees thrive well in Allang's environment. Tradition is of course a powerful factor, but tradition has been heavily influenced by the particular geographical conditions.

3. The Physical Appearance of the Settlement

The village proper occupies a very limited area, considering the size of its population (2,868 souls), for the steep hillsides press so closely upon the shore line that there is only a small, relatively level space suitable for settlement. Three main streets run parallel to the shore, and four streets, more or less perpendicular to the coast, lead up the hillside. Close to four hundred of the five hundred residences of Allang are found along these few streets, which run not more than five hundred meters along the shore and two hundred and fifty meters from the water's edge. (See Map VI.) The houses are extraordinarily close together, making for a population density that resembles urban more than village conditions. Only an occasional residence has any garden or yard to speak of.

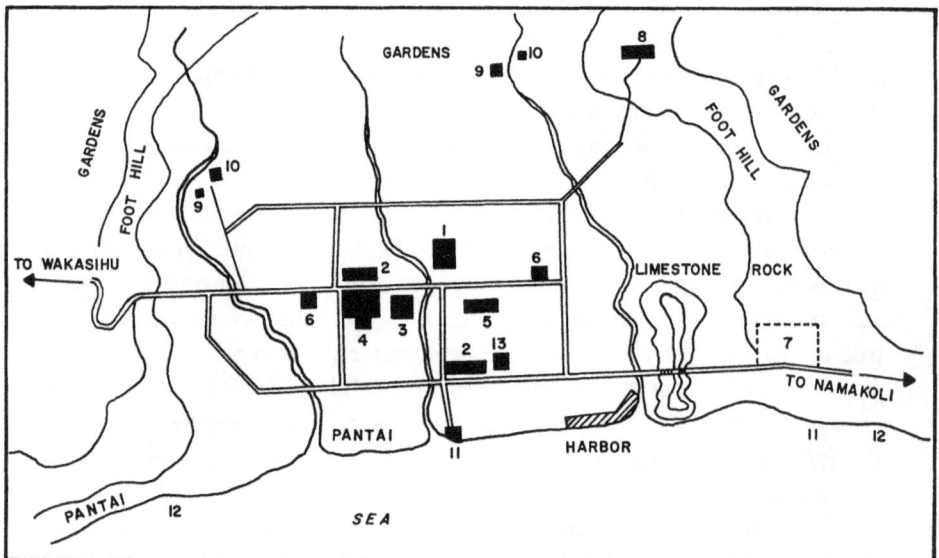

Map VI. Village Pattern of Allang
1. Ruler's residence. 2. School. 3. Baileu. 4. Church. 5. Youth hall. 6. Cooperative shop. 7. Cemetery. 8. Bungalow. 9. Men's bathroom. 10. Women's bathroom. 11. Women's restroom. 12. Men's restroom. 13. The manse.

The center of the village is defined by the presence of a group of important buildings in close proximity to each other. These are the *baileu* (a combination town hall and traditional ceremonial *adat* house), the residence of the village ruler (*radja*), the church, the village school, and, a bit farther away, the manse. Landward of the last is a youth center, recently built by the youth organization of the village congregation, which alone is not typical; the other main buildings and their arrangement are found in most villages in the region. Because of the rapidly expanding population, a new and larger school was built on the edge of the village, where pressure for land is less intense. Most of the remaining structures are residences, though half a dozen or so are stores and shops.

There are two types of building construction seen in Allang. The more common type is the traditional or indigenous style of architecture, which makes use solely of materials available in the vicinity. On a stone foundation filled with dirt, which serves as the floor, is set the frame of the house, constructed from hewn beams. The walls consist of a layer or two of plates woven from leaves of the sago palm (*Metroxylon rumphii*). This same material, called *atap*, is used for roofing. Ceiling and room partitions are made from *gaba-gaba*, stripped sago palm branches about two inches in diameter. A few windows are cut in the walls of the house, generally not more than one per room; these may be covered by bamboo shutters. There are three or four rooms with perhaps a couple of lean-tos added for special purposes such as cooking and storage or as a work area. Usually there is a covered porch on the front, where much of the living and working takes place.

The other type of construction is roughly the same in basic plan, but the materials are different. Cement is used in the foundation and probably for the floor; in rare cases a tiled floor is found. Plastered bamboo walls and ceilings replace the *gaba-gaba* and *atap* used in traditional houses. There will perhaps be glass windows, or at least wooden shutters. The roof may be of zinc plates or, more commonly, of *atap* thatch. Only occasionally is a tiled roof seen. These new-style houses, making use of modern building materials, are very popular and are replacing the traditional ones as quickly as people can save the money to build. In fact, they constitute one of the major ways in which surplus cash may be invested. It is not uncommon to see houses that combine the modern and traditional styles.

All non-indigenous buildings such as church, school, and shops are built in the new style and with an architectural pattern imported, or at least adapted, from the West. The *baileu*, however, follows the traditional architectural pattern handed down from the ancestors. Both church and *baileu* structures in Allang are unusually large and well cared for. The church building was remodeled in the 1880's when a Dutch minister was resident in the village. Its form and style are completely foreign to indigenous architectural patterns, even though the roof is of *atap*.

The *baileu*, located next to the church building, is in sharp contrast, as far as style is concerned, but similar in its size and condition. Like the church it is set in a rectangular enclosure and presents an imposing picture with its solid rough-hewn beams, raised platform, and expansive *atap* roof. All indigenous or *adat* ceremonies having to do with the village are held at the *baileu*, which may also be the meeting place of the village council on certain occasions. The location and condition of these two buildings attest dramatically to the important place both religion (Reformed Christianity) and *adat* occupy in the life of Allang people.

4. Demography

The average size of Christian, Moslem, and mixed Moslem-Christian villages on Ambon Island is 1,447, 1,948, and 2,314 inhabitants respectively. For the whole island, with its total population of 80,364, the average village size is 1,709. It is estimated that 51 per cent of the population of the island classify themselves as Christian and 49 per cent as Moslem.

Against this background, Allang emerges as one of the largest Christian villages, with a population of 2,868 in 1959, of which 1,455 were males (50.7 per cent) and 1,413 females (49.3 per cent). A breakdown of this figure according to specific age categories is given in Table 10.[3]

The population of Allang is distributed among 656 households (extended nuclear families, in many cases) with an average of 4.4 members per family. There are approximately 500 houses in the village, which means that roughly 30 per cent of the houses are occupied by more than one nuclear family. In most of these cases a recently married son and his wife constitute the second nuclear family, which generally builds and occupies its own residence within a year or so. Allang society has been strongly patrilocal in rule of residence, though in recent years a tendency toward a neolocal pattern has appeared.

[3] These figures were supplied by the village clerk. The breakdown into age groups was calculated on the basis of data from school and church records.

As to vital statistics, in 1959 there were 141 births or a birth rate of 49.1 per thousand. For the same period, 40 deaths gave a mortality rate of 13.9 per thousand. These figures yield an average increase of 3.6 per cent, which figure has prevailed annually since 1956. This startling rate of growth can be expected to continue because of the character of the population, with 58.7 per cent of the inhabitants under eighteen years of age. Thus, if there is no pronounced exodus of young people from the village and the present standard of living can be maintained, it can be expected that the population of Allang, and many other villages in central Maluku, will double in the next twenty years. Should this

Table 10. Population of Allang by age

Age	Number	Per cent
1–6	923	32.1
7–13	560	19.5
14–18	200	7.1
Over 18	1,185	41.3
Total	2,868	100.0

happen, the implications for the entire structure and functioning of Allang society as it now exists are certain to be revolutionary in the extreme. There appears to be some awareness of the increase on the part of the villagers, but as yet there has been no facing up to the problems that will undoubtedly arise.[4]

5. *Customs Along the Life Cycle*

Indigenous customs and practices surrounding birth and infancy, youth passing to adulthood, and death have been almost completely replaced, in form at least, by the Christian practices and ceremonies of baptism, confirmation, and burial. At the time of marriage the *adat* cere-

[4] The village elders estimated Allang's population at 2,000 in 1930 and 1,400 around 1900. G. E. Rumphius reports a population of 1,112 for 1691 (in an unpublished manuscript, *Ambonsche Landsbeschrijving*, in the Koninklijke Bibliotheek, The Hague) and S. A. Buddingh records 971 for 1855 (1859–1861, II, 155). This suggests that the population growth in the last thirty years has been as great as that between 1691 and 1930.

monies and traditional requirements are still widely observed, but together with civil and church ceremonies.

Indigenous customs surrounding birth were reported to have long since disappeared. Baptism ceremonies are held in the church two or three times a year for infants and small children, infant baptism being the custom in the Protestant Church of Maluku. The social or community dimension of this rite of passage is manifested by the practice of having godparents stand with the child who is to be baptized, and by the family feast following the service, for which the kindred gathers and shares in the preparations.

Indigenous initiation ceremonies have given way to Christian confirmation, which now takes place after the catechumen has completed three years of training given by the minister and successfully passed an oral examination witnessed by his parents before the Session of the congregation. During the three-year preparatory period, the candidates are subjected to close supervision by the Session, both in regard to their attendance at catechism classes and to their conduct. The confirmation ceremony takes place yearly one or two Sundays before Easter. This enables the newly received members (*sidi baru*) to take their first Communion with the congregation on Good Friday, the most important of the two annual celebrations of the Sacrament. The catechumens wear new clothes, the boys black suits and white gloves, the girls either long white gowns similar to a wedding costume or the more indigenous long black skirt and black blouse with a black shoulder-to-waist sash embroidered with black beads (*kain pikul*). The service, which takes place at the regular Sunday morning worship hour, is one of the most serious and moving in the church year, with many persons crying openly. After the service the kindred gathers for a family feast to celebrate the catechumen's successful advance in status, with the accompanying privileges accorded to full members of the congregation. The confirmation custom is Christian, yet careful observing of it will reveal many features, in both the preparatory period and the ceremonies themselves, which parallel initiation rites in many non-Christian societies, probably indicative of the initiation rites practiced in Moluccan society prior to the coming of Christianity, as described in the literature on the Kakehan of Ceram (Duyvendak 1926, Deacon 1925).

The customs and ceremonies surrounding marriage have been described and analyzed in detail in another publication (Cooley 1962, 20–54), hence only brief mention of them will be made here. Betrothal and engagement customs combine indigenous and imported elements. Elopement (*kawin lari* or *lari bini*), which occurs very frequently, seems to be largely a native custom. The actual marriage ceremony takes place three times: first, before the village chief at his residence or office, according to civil procedure specified for all Christians; second, in the church, a religious ceremony performed by the minister with immediate family and friends present, which follows the prescribed form of the Protestant Church of Maluku; last are the indigenous *adat* ceremonies, in which the groom's family and kindred carry the marriage wealth (*harta kawin*) from his home to that of the bride, where they are received by the bride's family and kindred, where they are entertained, and where the marriage wealth is transferred. After this the bride is escorted by her family and kindred to the groom's home, where a feast and entertainment take place for one or several days, depending on the status and wealth of the groom's family. All parts of the *adat* ceremonies meticulously follow forms prescribed by *adat*. The most important part of the *adat* ceremonies seems to be the paying of the marriage wealth, which functions primarily as public witness of the transference of the bride and her children from her father's to her husband's kin group.

Marriage *adat* is not considered fulfilled until the marriage wealth is given and received, even though the civil and church ceremonies have preceded it by months or even years. Probably the reason for the greater perseverance of marriage *adat* over other observances along the life cycle is the central importance of the kinship structure of Allang society, which is supported and clarified by marriage-wealth *adat*. At this point, then, there has been a compromise between the imported religion and *adat*. *Adat* related to other rites of passage served less crucial functions and hence could be replaced by appropriate Christian ceremonies.

The process of acculturation has been even more complete in regard to customs surrounding death and burial, which will be explained in Section 9 in the description of the burial societies (*muhabet*). Christian funeral services, following common Protestant practice, are held at the home and at the graveside, taken either by the minister or an elder. The family, kindred, and friends join these services and the procession escorting the deceased to his last earthly resting place. A flute orchestra from the congregation plays funeral music. The *muhabet* takes charge of all preparations and arrangements. In addition to these services, it is still quite common to observe the "third-night vigil," in which family and close friends pass the night singing, praying, reading the scripture, and eating together. The custom in its present form probably had its origin in the belief, surviving from the indigenous religion, that on the third night the spirit of the dead returned to its home, with not necessarily beneficent intentions toward the living; finding a service in progress encouraged it to continue its journey to the abode of the spirits of the dead. However, if an explanation for the observance is asked for, reference will be made, usually, to the resurrection on the third day. These vigils, together with similiar memorial feasts held on the fortieth day and on the first anniversary of the death, occur less frequently than formerly, another witness to the cultural change going on in Moluccan villages.

6. Livelihood and Occupations

Allang is predominantly and traditionally agricultural in its way of life. Products of land and sea provide a livelihood for most of the population. Almost everyone does some farming and fishing, even those who may have specialized occupations or offices. Fish caught by a variety of means provide most of the protein in the diet of the people. Fowl, and much more occasionally meat from wild game or domesticated animals, appear on the table on special occasions. Sago flour, tubers, cassava (*Manihot utilissima*), coconuts, a few leaves of vegetables or trees, nuts and fruits, in addition to fish, constitute the ordinary diet. Rice is used widely but has not yet replaced sago flour as the main carbohydrate staple.

Gardening is done by the familiar method known as shifting or swidden cultivation. A tract is cleared by slashing down the trees and brush, which are then burned. The field is encircled with a rude but strong fence made of tree branches and bamboo, to keep out the wild pigs and deer. The soil is prepared in a rough way and then planted with spinach, other greens, cucumbers, squash or other gourds, sweet potatoes, and other root crops. Cassava, the root from which tapioca is made, is planted quite widely nowadays. Sago flour is either worked up oneself or purchased already prepared. It is derived from pulverizing and straining the pulp in the stem of the sago palm, which is ready to be cut and worked after about fifteen years of growth. The flour produced from one tree, which takes two men at most two or three days to work up, will provide food for a family of six or eight for a month or more. It is either baked into hard biscuits or boiled to form a viscous jellylike mass and eaten hot (*papeda*).

Food is cooked over wood fires, which means that keeping the supply of firewood replenished is a continual part of the daily work. The men do the heavy work connected with the gardening and woodcutting, as well as working the sago. In addition to the usual household tasks, the women carry the water, tend the gardens, carry most of the produce from garden to house, and help with wood gathering. The children help in all these activities when not in school.

Besides producing food from sea and land, many families raise cash crops, mainly fruits and spices. They own tracts of land on which have been planted trees producing coconuts, bananas, mangoes, *langsat* (*Lansium domesticum*), *gandaria* (*Bouea macrophylla*), durian (*Durio ziberthinus*), mangosteens, and other types of tropical fruits and nuts. Allang is well known for its kanari nuts. It also produces a considerable amount of nutmegs and some cloves. Most families have at least a few clove (*tjengkeh*) or nutmeg (*pala*) trees on their lands. These require little care and produce spices which bring a good price. Coconuts are not in surplus supply in Central Maluku by and large, and most of Allang production is consumed as food, though a family with many coconut palms may sell a part of their crop to neighbors. In these ways the people secure cash for the payment of taxes, for school fees, and for purchasing clothing, salt, sugar, tea, kerosene, and other necessities not produced locally, such as eating and cooking utensils, furniture, and tools. The people of Allang on the whole have a level of livelihood that compares favorably with that in most other parts of rural Indonesia. And more important still, there is the possibility of improving it, given wider dissemination of knowledge and techniques and better organization of work.

In addition to the agriculture and fishing which occupy most of the population, Allang has a small percentage of people engaged in other occupations. There are two ministers (neither is an Allang man), and of the twelve schoolteachers, four, including the headmaster, originate from other places. The two cooperatives and three or four shops each have at least two more-or-less full-time employees. There are a few men who work primarily as carpenters, masons, and builders of houses. Allang is far enough from Ambon town so that there are no persons who live in the village and work in the city, though there are Allang people who have taken up residence and regular employment in Ambon, one of whom is the local ruler (*radja*). It is doubtful whether as much as 10 per cent of adult Allang males engage in primary occupations other than agriculture. Some of those with other occupations own and work land on the side so that to date there is little occupational differentiation in Allang society.

7. *The Traditional Pattern of Social Organization*

Allang society reveals two patterns of social organization, which may be characterized as traditional and emerging. The traditional pattern is so named because it is based on *adat* (folkways, mores, and customary law) and kinship, which are central elements in the tradition handed down through the generations. The emerging pattern, so called not with teleological overtones but simply because it is in the process of developing, is composed of diverse elements and structures imported from various sources and has developed distinctively within the context of Moluccan culture. It includes the following: the Protestant congregation, the village school, mutual-help associations, associations dedicated to sport and recreational interests, and cooperatives. The reason for classifying this wide variety of structures and associations into a single pattern existing alongside of, or as a counterpart to, the traditional pattern is that with certain qualifications these complexes are all constructed on a very different principle from the complexes in the traditional pattern. The complexes comprising the emerging pattern are based on the associational principle of common interest and, in most cases, common convictions. Thus the element of individual volition is prominent among the motives leading to the formation of complexes in the emerging pattern. The element of personal volition is completely absent in determining the complexes of the traditional pattern; these are created and maintained by blood ties and by obedience to the folkways and mores prescribed by the culture. The traditional pattern is being challenged by the steadily growing complexes of the emerging pattern, and it is striving to maintain itself against increasing pressures from them. We shall describe the complexes in the traditional pattern first.

Since the various types of kin groups in Ambonese society have been described in some detail in a recent publication (Cooley 1962a), only a brief summary is offered here. In addition to the bilateral *rumah tangga* or household, usually a slightly extended nuclear family, Allang society is composed of two contrasting types of kin groups, one corporate and the other noncorporate, the *mata rumah* and the *familie*.

The *mata rumah*, commonly referred to as *fam*, is a unilineal descent group organized on patrilineal and patrilocal principles. It is therefore clearly a compromise kin group and a local residence group, consisting of the males and unmarried females united by consanguineal ties and the wives of the males related by affinal ties. This kin group is thus a patrilineal residential minimal lineage.[5] In other villages, the same *mata rumah* names are found as those of one or two of the twenty-seven minimal lineages in Allang, but these *mata rumah* do not consider themselves to be related, though at one time they may have been.

The *mata rumah* is dominant in various functional areas. It regulates marriage through a rule of exogamy; it also controls the utilization of *dati* lands through the *dati* organization, which will be described in section 8; it likewise serves to fix the status or social class of its members. Traditionally *mata rumah* are differentiated by residential status into three groups: original settlers (*orang asali*), immigrants (*orang pendatang*), and foreigners (*orang asing*). The first group enjoys much higher status than the other two. Further, since the important political offices in the village are hereditary, they must be filled by men belonging to specified *mata rumah*. The *mata rumah* with which these rights and responsibilities are associated constitute a sort of ruling class in Ambonese society.

Allang is typical of central Moluccan villages in that it consists of a collection of twenty-seven minimal lineages or clans, some much larger than others. A few of the large *mata rumah* have in the distant past been subdivided into discrete *mata rumah*. The scanty data collected on this point suggest that the fission probably occurred because of differences that arose between two or more brothers, making it impossible for the lineage to continue functioning as a unified group. Where such fission has occurred, most of the functions mentioned, particularly those of an economic nature, have passed over to the sublineage, although almost invariably the original *mata rumah* remains an exogamous unit.

From this account, as well as from what will be said presently concerning the next larger subdivision of the village, the *soa*, it emerges clearly that the most basic structural and functional unit in Allang society is the unilineal descent group, the patrilineal residential minimal

---

[5] The editor of this volume prefers to designate all the unilineal kin groups by the term "lineage" and to add the various adjectives localized, residential, minimal, major, maximal, circumscriptive, matrilineal, patrilineal, etc., whenever necessary. The author of this chapter, following Murdock's system (1949, 65-69), has used in his draft the term "clan" to designate the Ambonese *mata rumah*.

lineage. But the *mata rumah* is not the only kin group, for alongside it, to some degree counterbalancing certain aspects of clan organization and serving different functions, is a cognatic or bilateral kin group known only by the Dutch term *familie*.

Familie, which clearly belongs to the kindred type (Murdock 1949, 56–62; 1960, 2–5), is neither a residential group nor an ancestor oriented group but rather a bilateral kin group, the membership of which is aggregated through affinal as well as consanguineal ties. It is organized around an individual and consists of living members of four *mata rumah*, that is, the descendants of the four great-grandfathers of that individual. Hence *familie*, like all kindreds, is Ego-oriented. As it is not a fixed, corporate group, it does not form a discrete segment in Allang society as does the *mata rumah*.

To describe its composition a bit more fully, among the components of the kindred the largest is Ego's father's *mata rumah*, all of the living members of which are included. In addition, it embraces parts of three other *mata rumah*, that of Ego's mother before she was married and those of his paternal and maternal grandmothers before they were married. Besides the women who have married into these *mata rumah*, it includes the husbands and children of the women born into these kin groups but who have married out. The total membership of the kindred may vary considerably but will normally be greater than that of the minimal lineage. It usually has a depth of at least four generations and may extend collaterally at least two and often three degrees.

The most obvious functions of *familie* are oriented to the particular individual, the Ego, who is at the center of the kindred structure. That is to say, his kindred serves to give him support and assistance, particularly at periods of crisis during the life cycle. *Familie* gathers and acts most conspicuously in connection with ceremonies and feasts surrounding birth, marriage, and death. It contributes both material and personal services which insure proper fulfillment of the needs of the individual concerned.

Aid is also forthcoming from the kindred in cases of special need such as sickness or education. The *familie* thus functions to serve the personal interests of the individual and of the members of his household. It is an expression of the bonds of unity and mutual responsibility which permeate and strengthen the fabric of social relationships.

There are, however, less obvious functions served by the kindred. For example, the sharp stress placed on the *mata rumah*, because of its economic and political functions, tends to create differences and at times serious friction between them. The *familie*, by relating members of different *mata rumah* to one another until nearly everyone in the community is related in some way to nearly everyone else, softens the competition between the *mata rumah* or at least holds it within limits, thus increasing the cohesiveness of village society and strengthening it against internal and external dangers.

Again, the *familie* can supplement or extend the *mata rumah* in regard to functions normally served by the *mata rumah*. An example relates to vacant posts in village government, such as *soa* head (head of an administrative subdivision of the village), to which succession is confined to a particular *mata rumah*. If the *mata rumah* has no male member capable of filling the vacancy, *adat* prescribes that the post may be filled by the son of a woman who was born in the proper *mata rumah* but has married out. In Allang there are two such cases, where the incumbent adds his mother's original *mata rumah* name to his own, thereby meeting the *adat* requirement.

Thus it is clear that both types of kin groups serve important though different functions. They complement each other by providing for different types of social articulation. It will be a matter of interest to see how many of the other village societies described in this book are characterized by both unilineal and cognatic types of kin groups. Firth (1936, ch. 16) has concluded that this situation is very general in Polynesia. It is here suggested that it may be more common in Indonesian societies than has yet been demonstrated. This is a subject which deserves further research.

Still another complex in the traditional pattern of social organization in Allang is the *soa*. Allang is divided into eight *soa*, or administrative subdivisions. Each *soa* consists of a group of several *mata rumah*. Some of the *soa* are much larger and more prominent in village affairs than others, a fact probably caused by historical circumstances.

Such information as is available suggests that the *soa* in more or less its present form goes back at least to the time when the village was established in its present location. In the case of Allang this would mean, at the latest, the first part of the seventeenth century. The present village was reportedly constituted by the coalescing of two or more smaller settlements that lay fairly close together. These settlements were called *aman*, indicating a group of *mata rumah* ruled over by or belonging to *ama* (father or lord in the indigenous language). At least one of these *aman*, possibly more, was located two or three kilometers from the shore, up in the hills. And the dominant one, the one from which came the *mata rumah radja* (the ruling house) and the *mata rumah tuan tanah* (the clan of the lord of the land), is called to this day *negeri lama*, the old village. The *aman*, smaller than the later village, was probably composed of two or three *soa*. We may assume that the *soa* in those days were smaller than at present, for they included only the *mata rumah asali* (native lineages) that had come in the first migration. To these, others were later added. Thus the following generalization seems justifiable: the village (*negeri*) is composed of several *aman*, each of which was made up of a group of *soa*, which are collections of lineages. *Aman* does not now appear in the structure of the village, as do *soa* and *mata rumah*, because in the uprooting during the move from the hill locations to the shore the *aman* were disrupted. It may also be that in the general confusion and instability which characterized the probable period of village formation (1480–1680) some *mata rumah* and even *soa* within an *aman* were either liquidated through war or banished to other places as a form of punishment (as was reported for Allang during the second quarter of the seventeenth century) or voluntarily moved to other places in connection with the coming of Islam and Christianity, which in some cases split the village or *aman* into two or more groups. Allang elders reported that, before the village accepted Christianity in 1622, part of the people were Moslems and the rest Alifuru (adherents to the indigenous religion). Some from each group may have emigrated rather than convert.

8. Land Tenure

There are three types of landownership found commonly in Moluccan village societies and in Allang: lands owned by the village corporately; lands owned, managed, and worked by the lineage or sublineage as an economic corporation (Befu and Plotnicov 1962); and land owned usually by the individual family head.

Lands owned by the village (*tanah negeri*) may consist of several different categories. There are fields or sections that are worked by the village as a whole for a particular purpose, for example, growing sago trees. Much of the village land is unworked because it is too steep and rugged or too far away from the village center to be reached conveniently. This is called *tanah ewang* and is usually covered by primary forest. Still another category is land which has been granted to a person or family to be cultivated while the title remains with the village government for a suitable period, during which the user demonstrates his industry and responsibility. Then the title may be transferred to the person who has used it, and it becomes *tanah pusaka*, to be described presently. In Allang it was estimated by the village official responsible for land matters (*kepala soa tanah*) that the village owned almost as much land as that owned under the other two types of arrangement combined.

Lands held by patrilineal kin groups (*tanah dati*) are also technically owned by the village, in the sense that, if all members of the kin group should die, the *dati* would return to the jurisdiction of the village government and be redistributed on the basis of priority of need or merit to landless families or those with insufficient land.

It seems clear from the *dati* register kept by the village government that the land held in the name of each patrilineal kin group consists of a number of *dusun-dati*, which refer to particular parcels of land that bear names by which their locations and boundaries can be identified. Not every patrilineal kin group holds *dati* lands, but only those that are considered native to the village. The kin groups that came after the village had been established possess or work land in other categories mentioned above. It was reported that no new *dati* lands were created after 1814.

The landholding body has its own organization consisting of *anak-anak dati*, or members of the patrilineal kin group who have rights in the *dati* land. They are headed by a *dati* chief (*kepala dati*). This corporation, so to speak, regulates the land held by the kin group. All male and unmarried female members of the patrilineal kin group have a right to *makan dati*, literally to eat from the *dati* lands. Thus the *kepala dati*, with the agreement of the group, either assigns various parcels of land to the *anak-anak dati*, so that all have a share, or divides the total produce from the *dati* lands between the *anak-anak dati*. The *kepala dati* is elected by the *anak-anak dati*, but they usually choose the eldest son of the former *dati* chief, since he will probably know most about the land held by the patrilineal kin group. In the event there should arise a dispute which cannot be settled within the *dati* group, it may be taken to the village council for adjudication.

Parcels of land from the *dati* holding may not be alienated either by sale or gift, for they do not belong to the person who works them but to the corporation, which holds them under authority from the village government. When a girl marries exogamously she loses all rights to *dati* lands held by her original patrilineal kin group, acquiring instead, through the payment of the marriage wealth by her husband's family, rights in the *dati* lands of her husband's kin group. Again, if an *anak-anak dati* leaves the village to live and work in another place, he loses the right to his share from the *dati* lands. But if he returns to the village and makes application to have his share restored, custom requires that he be accepted back into the *dati* corporation and receive his share.

Land owned by a family head (*tanah pusaka*) seems to be related in some way that is not clear to *tanah dati*, for it is sometimes referred to as *pusaka dati*. In any event, the rights to *pusaka* lands are inherited by all children of the family, whether they remain in the lineage or marry out. However, even though a married daughter is entitled to claim her share of the *pusaka* lands, it seems that she seldom does so, as this might put her husband and his *mata rumah* in an unfavorable light. It not infrequently occurs, however, that a father will present a favorite daughter who is about to be married a parcel of land to go with her into her new family. This is called *atiting*, a native term for a container for garden produce, and symbolizes the father's concern to ensure the welfare of his daughter and her family. *Pusaka* lands are also not supposed to be sold out of the family, but this does occur. Also, from his *tanah pusaka* a person may give a parcel of land to another because of some merit or indebtedness to that person. This is called *dusun pengasihan*, or gift plot. In most villages, the *dati* register has a column for the registration of *pusaka* lands.

Most land disputes are caused by the lack of clear-cut recorded boundaries around the *dati* lands. Plots were originally described by natural boundaries, such as big trees, rocks, and streams, but in the course of time these have changed, and the chances for misunderstanding and dispute are numerous. In each village government there is an officer with the title *kepala soa tanah*—a council member responsible for land matters, who is supposed to be an expert on questions of land boundaries and rights, so that he is able to clear up any problems or disputes that may arise in this sphere. Notwithstanding, land disputes frequently find their way into the district courts.

9. The Emerging Pattern of Social Organization

The Protestant congregation is the largest and most influential of the complexes in the emerging pattern. This is symbolized by the fact that the church building stands in the center of the village, its largest and most elaborate structure. Allang is homogeneous in religion. All of the inhabitants are considered members of the congregation, though of course not all are faithful or active participants in congregational life. The nature and activities of the congregation are based on cultural materials (beliefs, language, ceremonies, attitudes, symbols, dogmas, conceptual system, patterns of organization, etc.) that are non-indigenous: they have been imported from outside the region; in fact, from outside the original cultural continuum of Indonesia and Asia.

The congregation is one but has within it various subgroupings, each of which performs specialized functions within the whole. For example, there is a Sunday school to educate and train the children; three years of catechism classes are required of those in their middle and late teens to prepare them for full membership. There is a youth organizaton to meet the special needs of young people fifteen to thirty-five years of age. The women, in their own organization, have opportunity for self-expression, fellowship, and service. Finally, the ruling body, the Session, is responsible for the life and work of the entire congregation. The only activity that takes place in the homes and on a family basis is the prayer meeting held on specified evenings in several homes in different parts of the village. All other church activities, with the exception of Sunday worship (and even this to a certain degree, since it is primarily for adults), seem to be organized on age and sex criteria, a principle of organization in some contrast to that found in the traditional pattern.

However, there is one similarity to the traditional pattern, and that is the *adat*-like character of religious participation. The congregation is based on very different principles from those of the traditional institutions in the village, yet the spirit and character of the activities, as well as the motivation and attitudes of the participants, carry a strong traditional flavor. Beliefs, and practices associated with them, are accepted from the older generation and passed on to the youth not because they are felt to be rationally compelling, volitionally or emotionally satisfying, but simply because these are elements in the pattern of religious tradition that has characterized the society for generations and centuries. Allang is a Christian village, and holding these beliefs and understandings is part of what that means. The same is true of participation in religious acts, whether corporate or private. These things are done not so much because the doer is consciously aware of the meaning and result of doing them—though, of course, many are—but because this is the way such things should be done. Perhaps it does not go too far to say that the spirit and the manner of observing the *adat*, which is part of the traditional pattern, have come to characterize the way in which Christianity is conceived as well. Some observers have even referred to a "Christian *adat*," which they claim to find in Ambonese society. The term is not without its basis, even though it may not be entirely appropriate.

How and why this situation has come about is apparent if one recalls that in the seventeenth century Christianity replaced an indigenous religion that was closely united with the *adat* system. For a long time, apparently, the leaders of the new religion did not feel it necessary to be critical of the *adat* system, even though *adat* was based on the indigenous religion and relied on sanctions that to this day are still derived from that sphere. The potential incompatibility of the two was reduced by a process, probably unconscious, of indigenization of the immigrant religion. Thus Protestant Christianity in Maluku has constantly been subject to "*adat*ization," if the term may be allowed, as the acculturation process has proceeded. The form and structures of the new cultural element (Protestant Christianity) passed over into Ambonese culture more fully and easily than did its functions and meanings, which encountered more resistance from the indigenous culture. To make this observation is not to imply that the Christian faith and practice of Allang people is nominal or purely formal. There is much sincere piety and faithful devotion to be found in the local congregation, which possibly has more vigorous life and activity than the average Moluccan congregation. Both the ministers and the officers of the congregation show some awareness of the social and cultural context of the congregation's life and work, which is in turn reflected in the scope and conception of its program. This fact is sufficient to demonstrate with certainty that the Protestant congregation in Allang belongs to the emerging rather than the traditional pattern of social organization. It also has resulted in a need for achieving better understanding and cooperation between the village council, which represents most fully the traditional pattern, and the Session of the congregation, which is the main representative of the emerging pattern.

In terms of organization, the Protestant congregation is the most complex unit in Allang and at the same time carries on the most extensive program of activities. Well over half the population of the village participate at least once a week in a church activity, many more frequently. The activities of the congregation are primarily religious in function, though some serve other functions as well. Probably a higher percentage of the younger and older age groups participate regularly than those in the middle age group. The Allang congregation, which because of its size has two ministers, both young and vigorous, seems to be better organized and more active than the average Moluccan congregation. More important still, it is conscious of some of the problems and challenges facing it in a rapidly changing situation and is trying in various ways to meet them. The congregation is part of a district and regional and national Christian community, which gives it contacts and experience beyond the limits of Allang society. Thus the Protestant congregation may be seen as a force for social as well as cultural change, helping to draw the village out of its traditionalistic atmosphere and isolation into the growing stream of regional and national life.

A second complex in the emerging pattern of social organization is the mutual-help associations, voluntary societies organized for the fulfillment of particular functions. Allang boasts several *muhabet*, or burial associations, composed of heads of families who have joined together to share the expenses and work involved in funerals. When a person related to a member dies, the *muhabet* takes over all arrangements for the funeral: the provision of food and drink (for those who come to express sympathy as well as for the bereaved family), the preparation of the coffin and grave clothes, the digging of the grave, the arrangement of funeral service details, and so on. The *muhabet* has its own organization, with a charter and elected officers, most of them closely connected with and considered an adjunct of the village congregation.

Another type of mutual-help association centers around the functional concern of repairing or putting new thatch on the houses of members. The thatch is made from the leaves of the sago palm, which are plaited to form shingles that are bound with bamboo strips to the wooden rafters of the roof. It takes several hundred of these plates or shingles, which are roughly four feet long and sixteen inches wide, to thatch a small house. From the point of view of cost, labor, and time it is a task that lends itself to cooperative efforts. So a group of men form a roof-thatching association, which endeavors, for example, to put a new thatch, or make necessary repairs, on the roof of one of the members every two months. Each of the members prepares an agreed-upon number of bundles of palm-leaf shingles. On a given day, all the members gather to take off the old thatch and put on the new, with much joking and singing. This organized approach, a good example of the *gotong-rojong* principle found widely in Indonesian societies, makes possible the sharing of labor and expense of roofing all the members' houses on a regular basis, thus guaranteeing security, spreading the cost over a period of time, and considerably lightening the burden on the individual. These associations are organized along the same lines as the *muhabet,* except that their charters and regulations are approved by the village council.

These types of mutual-help associations, illustrating collective efforts, are organized on voluntary principles, not necessarily on *mata rumah* or *soa* lines. Data were not collected on their history, but the impression is very strong that they do not go back for more than a century. One may suspect that they represent forms of collective insurance that developed around functions formerly served by other means. Thus they may be viewed as creative responses to social and cultural change, particularly in the realms of family relationship and *adat,* which have been considerably influenced by acculturation. In the case of the *muhabet,* it is fairly clear that the "bear ye one another's burdens" principle of Christianity has been an important force in creating the institution, almost certainly to replace more indigenous ways, unacceptable to the Church, of fulfilling the function.

Allang also has associations dedicated to the pursuit of particular interests such as soccer, boat racing, and music. Several of these are carried on within the youth organization of the congregation, which also boasts a number of choirs and flute orchestras that take part in the church services. With the exception of musical activities, associations based on common interest are quite recent. The general pattern of life in Allang is such that in individual activities, or those involving a very small group, usually close relatives, predominate. The farming, hunting, fishing, fruit gathering, and other daily occupations are generally carried out either alone or in groups of two or three. Allang's environment has stimulated individual rather than team or group activities. It may be concluded, therefore, that the association for expressing common interest is only beginning to develop and assume importance in the emerging pattern of organization.

Consumer cooperatives represent another complex in the emerging pattern of social organization in Allang. There are two cooperatives, MEMPEKI and COOPAL, as they are abbreviated. Their original function was to meet the villagers' needs for consumer commodities. In addition to handling consumer goods, the cooperatives are now increasingly serving to collect local produce to be marketed in Ambon. For example, cloves, nutmegs, mace, and other commodities are sold to the local cooperative, or at least turned over to it for sale on a commission basis. Formerly a person either took his own product to Ambon for marketing or sold it to a Chinese, Arab, or other merchant who periodically visited

Allang. The cooperatives are rapidly taking over this entrepreneurial function, which is greatly enlarging their operation as well as their profit. They reported a profit of 7 million *rupiah* in 1959. This profit, most of which formerly went out of the village, now remains either in the form of dividends to the members or in the form of reinvestment. In either case it represents an advance in the village economy. The success of the cooperatives also provides a number of jobs for villagers, since several full-time persons are needed to tend the store, transport produce to the market, and carry commodities back to the village. Hence the development of these cooperative associations is a welcome sign of change and growth in a society which, for reasons we cannot explore here, formerly discouraged Christian villagers from engaging in trade and commerce. It suggests that the population is beginning to shake itself free of the limitation of traditional attitudes to seek a broader and more secure base in Moluccan society. Together with the other complexes already mentioned, the cooperative association constitutes an emerging pattern that increasingly challenges the traditional pattern of social structure that has dominated central Moluccan Protestant village society for centuries.

10. Education, Recreational Activities, and Artistic Expression

In 1960, Allang had a primary school of six grades with two classes for each grade. Since then, in collaboration with the neighboring village, a junior high school (grades 7–9) has been opened in a new building originally erected by the Allang village council to replace the already old and too-small primary school structures. Of the twelve teachers in the primary school, which enrolls around 560 children (roughly 20 per cent of Allang's population), eight are natives of Allang; four, including the principal, come from other villages. They are appointed, supervised, and salaried by the district education authority, which also determines the curriculum and supplies the materials. The village is responsible for erecting, equipping, and maintaining the school building.

The villagers, and the village council, were reported to take little part or interest in the school and what goes on therein—except for close attention paid to the conduct and appearance of the teachers, especially those from outside the village, who do not come within the communal control inherent in the traditional pattern. There was no parent-teacher group in Allang. In 1960, very few pupils who finished primary school went on to secondary school. This has probably changed, now that the village has its own junior high school, though the teachers observed that Allang parents did not seem to value formal education very highly, as evidenced by their willingness to take their children out of school before they completed the sixth grade and by their failure to encourage them to continue with secondary schooling.

Allang is typical of Moluccan villages in general, in that it is sufficiently distant from a city or town so as not to have recreational facilities easily available outside its own sphere. One form of recreation in which the people of Allang do participate is singing and social dancing (the latter not generally approved in Allang) in connection with a marriage feast or some village festival, or singing activities in connection with the congregation's life, such as informal classes and group activities held at the youth center under the auspices of the congregation's youth group. Mentioned previously were various associations for athletics, such as soccer and boat racing. The most common way of passing the time, however, seems to be informal visiting and conversation among friends after the day's work is done. The young women like to gather and sing. The young men prefer talking or more active sport, although singing with a guitar is also popular. Festivals connected with the church year, especially Christmas, New Year, and Easter, provide a break in the usual round of life. The same holds for feasts or parties held in connection with events in the life cycle, such as baptism, confirmation, marriage, and birthdays.

We find little organized recreation and none at all on a regular basis in Allang. This means that many other activities, such as church events, economic endeavors, and informal social gatherings, have recreation as an important latent function. It should be added that the young people of Allang are reading more than is generally reported to be the case in other villages.

There is little artistic expression manifest in Allang society, except for church music. There are several choirs and three or four flute orchestras that take turns providing special music for the services in the church. Allang residents like to sing and have considerable musical talent. The leaders of the choirs frequently compose their own songs or adapt or arrange other songs. In addition to church music, some playing and singing of folk songs is done. There is a fairly rich folk music in the central Moluccan region, but most of the truly indigenous music has disappeared. Folk dancing occurs infrequently. Social dancing is popular among the youth but generally frowned upon by the older members of the congregation. Dancing at a wedding feast, for example, may be a mixture of social and folk dancing, some of the eighteenth-century folk dancing of Europe having been adapted and made their own. Painting, wood carving, and other artistic media are not found. In both the spheres of artistic expression and recreation, with the exception of music, Allang society appears to be relatively undeveloped.

11. Village Government and Social Control

In Moluccan societies the structure and functions of village government are still largely rooted in the traditional system of social control, that is, in the *adat* system (see Cooley 1962a), so these two topics belong together.

Adat refers to obligatory behavior that is held essential to the well-being and security of individuals and, generally, of the whole community. Ambonese villages are discrete *adat* communities. While there is much similarity throughout the region regarding the specific requirements of *adat* in a particular case, there are distinctive features in each village. The *adat* of each village is obligatory for all its members, but only for them. The reason for this is the belief that the *adat* was fixed by the ancestors, the village founders, for their own welfare and that of their descendants; it represents their judgment, or will, and its observance is an expression of respect for them. Ignoring or flouting the will of the ancestors is a hazardous undertaking because of the power their spirits are believed to hold over the members of the community. Thus the sanctions of *adat* are rooted in the beliefs and attitudes that surround the ancestors. The community, acting through the village government, which is the successor to the ancestors, applies human sanctions prescribed in *adat* in cases of violation where the offenders are apprehended. Nevertheless, it is still very widely believed that the spirits of the ancestors will visit suffering and tragedy upon violators of *adat* and/or their offspring, whether or not they are apprehended. One of the main functions of the village council, therefore, is to supervise and guarantee the observance of *adat*, upon which the welfare of the community is believed to depend. Before considering further social control in Allang, we shall describe the structure and functions of village government.

Allang is governed by a village council called *Badan Saniri Negeri,* more commonly simply *Saniri.* Its members consist of the hereditary ruler (now popularly elected but still generally chosen from the lineage which, according to *adat,* is designated to rule the village, as are the *soa* heads, *tuan tanah,* and *kapitan* also), the eight heads of *soa* (see section 7), together with certain other traditional officers, such as the lord of the land (*tuan tanah*), the *adat* chief, the war leader (*kapitan,* now a purely ceremonial office), the chief of the forest police (*kepala kewang*), and the village messenger (*marinjo*). The two last-named officers are not actually members of *Saniri,* but in view of their duties usually attend meetings. The *adat* chief is also not officially a member of *Saniri,* but may be asked to sit with that body when his advice is required.

Present regulations provide for electing and seating, as *Saniri* members, certain officers who represent functional groupings in society, to balance the hereditary rule represented in the traditional membership of the *Saniri,* but Allang has not yet implemented these regulations.

Allang is atypical also in that the ruler is not resident in the village but works in Ambon, coming to the village only when his presence is absolutely required. At other times his authority and function rest with the two *soa* chiefs who serve as officers of the month (*kepala soa djaga bulan*), which office is found in village organization throughout the region. Allang has two because it is a large village, each of the eight *soa* chiefs serving in this capacity once every four months, for which he receives a small honorarium. The *kepala soa djaga bulan,* sometimes referred to as *bapak djou* (together with the ruler in most Moluccan villages), serve as the executive arm of government and deal primarily with routine internal matters, freeing the ruler for larger concerns, especially external relationships, largely with the district office.

The *Saniri* functions at three levels: the *Saniri Radjapatih,* consisting of the *radja* and the *kepala soa,* who form the administrative branch of the village council and are the main core of village government; the *Saniri Negeri Lengkap* or full *Saniri,* composed of all members of the *Saniri,* as listed previously, who form the legislative branch of village government, making policy decisions and issuing regulations; and the *Saniri Negeri Besar,* or great *Saniri,* consisting of the *Saniri Negeri Lengkap,* meeting with all males over eighteen years of age on occasions when it is necessary to consult the whole electorate. In Allang, for all practical purposes, the *Saniri Radjapatih* governs the village.

The functions of village government include supervising and guaranteeing the carrying out of all *adat;* defending the community against dangers from without and within (particularly illegal occupation or exploitation of land); providing for fulfillment of the demands and expectations of the villagers in pressing toward progress and welfare in all spheres; and finally, of equal importance, implementing instructions and regulations issued by the higher civil and military authorities. In summary, the *Saniri* is charged with preserving and furthering the security and prosperity of the village. These functions are carried out through a distinctly authoritarian pattern of leadership, perhaps partly developed under the influence of the policy of indirect rule practiced by the Dutch during the colonial period, a policy that reinforced tendencies present in the indigenous culture. We cannot here go more deeply into why the giving and receiving of commands appears to be the usual way of getting things done in Allang, as it is in Moluccan villages generally.

The village government is, of course, not the only instrument or channel of social control in Allang. Along with it, and within the same traditional pattern, are the two kin groupings mentioned earlier, the patrilineal residential minimal lineage (*mata rumah*) and the kindred (*familie*), which function significantly in matters of social control, particularly in regard to behavior surrounding marriage and land. These forms of social control operate mainly through *adat*, which, though it has undergone extensive changes, particularly in the last century, is still a powerful force in shaping and directing behavior in Allang society.

Worthy of further mention is the manifest weakening of the authority of the village government. Owing to various factors, among them the weakening of *adat* in general, the changed status of village officers accompanying the development of new patterns of village government under the Republic of Indonesia since independence, the changing pattern of economic relationships, the changes and advances in education at the village level, and, last but not least, the increased stature and more vigorous activity of the village congregation, a notable change is taking place in the scope and weight of the authority attached to the village government and its various officers. Social control is becoming more complex and diffused, with institutions other than *adat* and the village council gradually growing in influence. This process is manifested, among other ways, in the growing self-consciousness and desire for independence from direct control of the village government on the part of the congregation and, less obviously, of the village school. While these changes are already being felt both by village officers and congregation and school leaders, to date there has been little evidence of a serious wrestling with the problem.

The village congregation is itself an instrument of social control. Christian moral teaching is carried on through various aspects of the program of the congregation, and the Session endeavors more or less directly to supervise the moral behavior of its members. Those whose moral conduct is at variance with the standards approved by the Protestant Church of Maluku are given pastoral guidance by the minister and Session. If they refuse to conform, they are publicly declared ineligible to receive the Holy Communion.

It would be difficult—and hazardous—to generalize about the relative influences of traditional norms and indigenous values, Christian values and norms, and secular values and norms upon the behavior of the people of Allang. It should not be thought that these three dimensions of the system of social control exist separately or independently from one another. They are in fact interwoven so as to be indistinguishable to all but the most discriminating eye. Allangites on the whole consider themselves to be loyal both to their indigenous cultural tradition and to their Christian faith. Only among the young people is there any awareness that there may be tension between the values and norms of *adat* and those of the Church and the Gospel. To date, secular values and norms have only been felt in a peripheral fashion, although the situation is rapidly changing. Recent historical developments, including the disappearance of the colonial regime, the Japanese occupation, the Republic of South Maluku affair, and the introduction of guided democracy and Indonesian socialism, have resulted in a situation of flux so far as social control is concerned. It is difficult both to predict what direction will predominate, and to escape the conclusion that traditional patterns of social control seem to be increasingly on the defensive and that secular patterns will make themselves felt more strongly as the present national trend continues. In this sphere, as in many others, the process of acculturation continues apace, both as the newly developing Indonesian national culture influences Moluccan culture and as external cultural influences from various quarters make themselves felt as well. For Allang, the former, however, is undoubtedly more important than the latter, under present circumstances.

Chapter VII

Muremarēw: A Dual Organized Village on the Mamberamo, West Irian[1]

GOTTFRIED OOSTERWAL

SCHOOL OF GRADUATE STUDIES

PHILIPPINE UNION COLLEGE

1. Introduction

The Mamberamo, the largest river in the northern part of West Irian, forms a borderline between two culture areas. People living on its western banks, such as the Bawjee, the Borromesso, the Seewaya, and the Banowa, are culturally related to the inhabitants of the Geelvink Bay (Serui, Waropen). Those living east of the Mamberamo belong to the vast culture

[1] The data for this chapter were collected during three field trips to the Mamberamo area. From June to August 1959, preliminary general research was carried out in the eastern Mamberamo area. This field work was made possible by the Netherlands Organization for the Advancement of Pure Research (ZWO, The Hague), to which body grateful acknowledgment is made. A further investigation into the social and religious organization of the people living east and west of the Mamberamo was made in January and February 1962. A year later, from January to March 1963, a special study was made of the mythology and the ritual of the *kone* (cult house) complex, especially in the upper Mamberamo area. This research was made possible by a grant from the Netherlands Foundation for Scientific Research in New Guinea (WONG, The Hague). The author would like to express his sincere gratitude toward this body for its generous allowance, and to Drs. J. van Baal and J. H. Westermann in particular for their stimulating help.

area of the "Western Interior of Sarmi" (see section 6). Between these there are contrasts in language, social structure, religious beliefs and mythology, and material culture. Also, racial differences exist. Almost every investigator, including Le Roux (1935, 58–76) has noted the occurrence of at least two physical types in the area, a rather tall and robust type and one of slender, medium build. All people living west of the Mamberamo belong to the first type, as do also some from the eastern bank. The slender, medium type, however, is found exclusively among the people east of the Mamberamo. In a village such as Muremarēw, on the east bank of the Mamberamo, about 25 per cent of the people are tall and robust, dolichocephalic, with a broad nose and wide nostrils, a rather broad mouth, crisp, frizzy hair, and a very dark skin; while more than 40 per cent of the inhabitants are shorter and rather slender, dolichocephalic or mesocephalic. Especially characteristic of the latter type are their rather pointed faces. They have a nose with relatively narrow nostrils, and thin lips. Their hair is crisp and wooly, but their skin is brown and lighter than the first type.

The Mamberamo River rises in the Central Mountains, southeast of the Lake Plain. Its upper end, called the Idenburg, flows westward through the eastern Lake Plain. Near the place where it is joined by the large Rouffaer River, the Idenburg suddenly turns northward to become the Mamberamo and to flow through the Van Rees Mountains to the Pacific Ocean (see Map VII).

About 80 kilometers downstream from this confluence the river Marēw, a righthand tributary, converges with the Mamberamo. Such a confluence is called a *mure* (*murra, muris*). This explains the name of the village of Muremarēw and those of the many other villages in this area with names starting or ending with the word *mure*.

2. *Location and Settlement Pattern of the Village*

The swift Marēw River pours out great amounts of sand and gravel into the Mamberamo. Thus in the course of time a sand shelf has been deposited along the eastern bank of the Mamberamo. When the people of Muremarēw built their village, some of the houses were built on the bank itself whereas others were constructed on this sand shelf, which lies about three and a half meters below the bank of the Mamberamo. This natural division of the village into a higher and a lower section corresponds with a similar dualism in its social system.

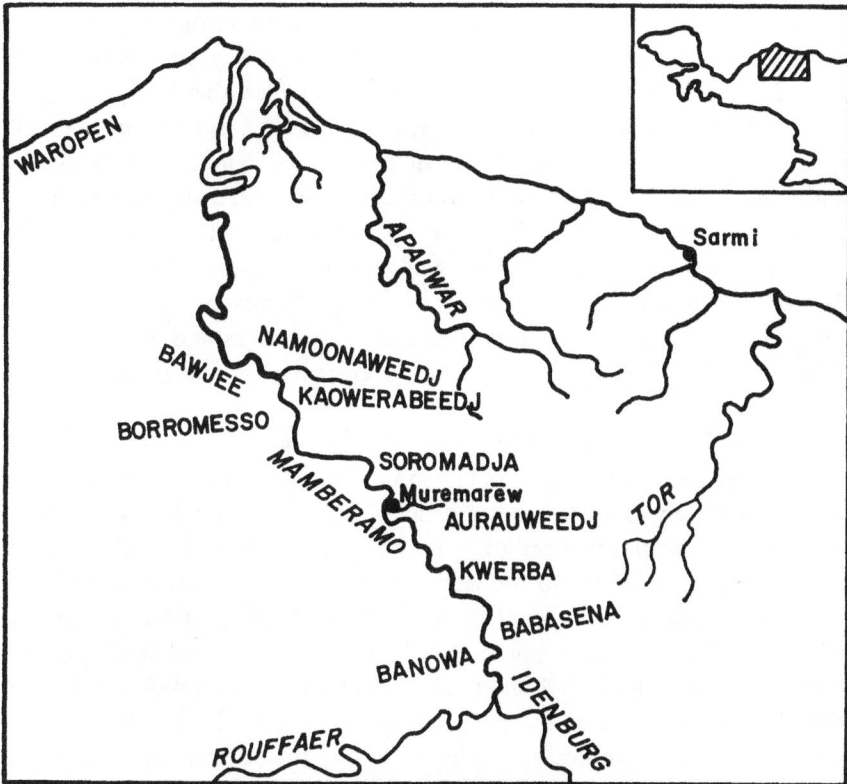

Map VII. The Mamberamo River and Its Ethnic Groups

Ideally, the villages of the upper Mamberamo area have a circular design: in the center stands the *kone*, a huge, circular-shaped cult house; around the *kone* is a large, open space, the *konnebonees;* and around the *konnebonees*, in two concentric circles, are built the houses of the people. The houses in the inner circle belong to the married people. In the outer circle are located the houses of the lower social groups: the bachelors' houses, the guest houses, and the *nawatshiu,* the houses where women retreat during their monthly periods and at childbirth. An excellent example of such a circular village is that of Minekwa, east of Muremarēw. Usually, however, the shape of the village must be adapted to the geographical environment. Thus the village of

Muremarēw forms only a large segment of a circle. The center is formed by a hill (named Serraree), about fourteen meters high, on the top of which the *kone* is built. Two rows of dwellings, one on the bank and the other on the lower sandy shelf, form the arcs (see Map VIII).

On the higher level of the village, called *peejawoom*, are nine dwellings for the married people. These houses rest on poles, are rectangular, and consist of a floor made of strips of tree bark, with a sloped, overhanging roof of palm leaves. There are no walls, nor any visible partition, although two or three families usually reside together. Some of these houses, which vary in size from 7 to 40 square meters, have a cooking place on the floor: a square area covered with ashes and three or four stones on top. Usually, however, the fireplace is on the ground, under the floor.

At the foot of the hill Serraree, on the highest and driest part of the *peejawoom*, is a large, open space described by the villagers as *booneeseebeeter*. It serves as the dancing square and as the place where the villagers regularly meet to talk about serious village affairs. On its northwestern corner stands the largest and most solid house in the village, in which drums and all other equipment for dancing, such as feathers, plumes, and shell strings, are stored. The house is owned by Sersa, the war leader and the best hunter. It is also Sersa who takes the lead in the dances and, assisted by other villagers, sweeps the *booneeseebeeter* with *sabar* leaves before festivities start. At the eastern border of the *booneeseebeeter*, at the foot of the hill Serraree, stands a long table (*gwereetsh*) with benches (*metshareetsh*) on both sides, where the people eat before and between the dances.

About 3½ meters below the *peejawoom* lies the lower section of the village, denoted as *tawanawoom*. In early 1963, seven houses stood there: two *nawatshiu*, two bachelors' houses, a large guesthouse, and two smaller houses used for various purposes. This lower section differs in many respects from the higher section. During the day the *tawanawoom* is neglected as much as possible. Men are not allowed to go near the *nawatshiu*, as they would spoil their hunting luck forever. No children play there; no shouting or laughing is heard. In short, it is in every respect the lower and inferior section of the village: a place for women, bachelors, and strangers.

The two terms *peejawoom* and *tawanawoom* refer not only to the higher and lower sections of the village but have a much wider application. The terms denote a dualism and are used to refer to everything

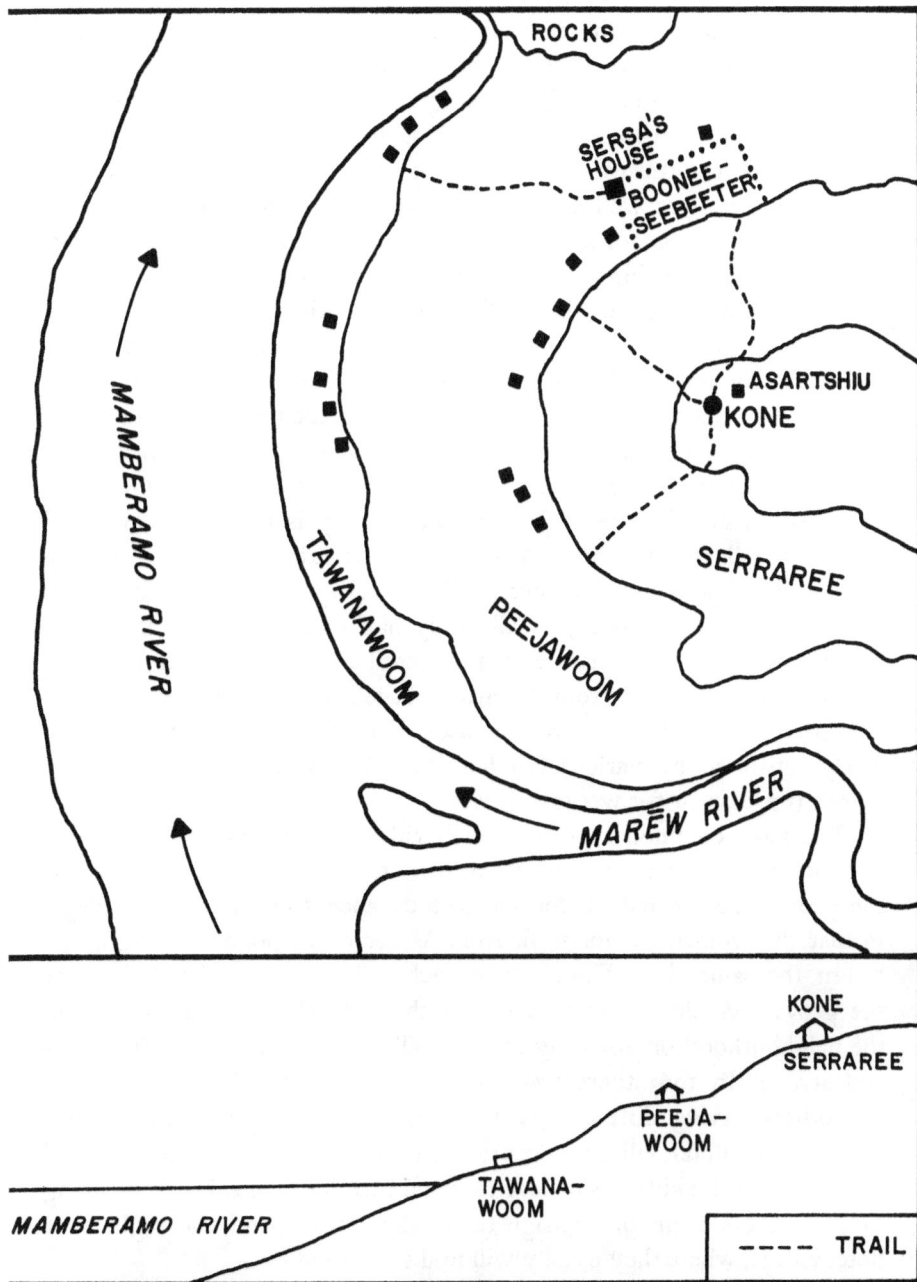

Map VIII. Pattern and Elevation of Muremarēw

and everybody considered the higher or the lower part of a unit. The sky is *peejawoom* and the earth is *tawanawoom*. The upstream section of the river Marēw is *peejawoom*, the downstream, *tawanawoom*. Therefore men always bathe in the upper part of the river and women in the lower part, as men are considered *peejawoom* and women *tawanawoom*. These two terms also are used to denote the difference between senior and junior as well as the two sexes. The whole universe is thus divided into *peejawoom* and *tawanawoom*, and the dualism in Muremarēw (see Section 7) is a reflection of this concept.

In their study called "Local Grouping in Melanesia," Hogbin and Wedgwood (1953, 58) suggested that the term "village" be used for the settlement only and that the term "parish" be used to refer to the social group. Such "a parish is a local group which is distinguished by political unity and the occupation and overlordship of a defined territory." The terms village and parish will be used here in this sense.

A remarkable feature of Muremarēw society is that it is composed of several villages. The main village is Muremarēw, the center of the social and religious life. However, only on rare occasions is it inhabited by all 94 members at once; usually only half of that number is present and at that, only from late afternoon until the following morning.

At various distances from the main village are smaller branch villages, consisting of only three or four houses. These branch villages are alternately inhabited by various families from Muremarēw, who may stay there a few days or for weeks on end.

The most common type of branch village is the sago village, which is built in or near a sago grove. Sago is the staple food, and most of the groves are located at considerable distance from the main village, so that the women cannot walk from Muremarēw, pound the sago, and return the same day. Therefore, branch villages have been built near the groves. While the women pound the pith, their husbands hunt in the neighborhood or just hang around, talking, sleeping, or cutting bows and arrows. In 1963 there were four of these sago villages, as well as five others serving different purposes, such as hunting villages, security villages, and hotel villages. Security villages are built in very isolated places, which the villagers believe to be safe from sorcery. People walking long distances from one village to another may spend the night in a hotel village, where they usually will find some food.

A noteworthy contrast between the larger main village and the branch villages is in their sanitation. Nowhere is any garbage or refuse found in the village of Muremarēw. Inhabitants defecate in the river Marēw; the men upstream, the women downstream. Even the excrement of dogs is immediately removed, a practice which stems from the parishioners' tremendous fear of sorcery. It is generally believed that people—and even animals—can bring sickness and death to others if they can acquire body wastes. Inasmuch as Muremarēw is often visited by people from other parishes, the villagers very strictly remove any refuse. But in most branch villages, where strangers never come, vermin-attracting filth is allowed to accumulate.

Under this village system these (semi) nomadic people have the advantages of a settled life, despite the very harsh natural circumstances and the low level of their technology, which make truly permanent residence impossible.

3. Demographic Notes

In February 1962, the parish of Muremarēw numbered 94 souls: 53 males and 41 females. It is evident that these numbers are far too small for any statistical analysis. However, they do show clearly that the community of Muremarēw is a small-scale society, where life is strongly influenced by personal preferences and needs, and there is great variability. A comparison with other parishes on the Mamberamo shows that Muremarēw is bigger than the average (see Tables 11 and 12).[2]

One fact seems to be evident from these figures: all parishes show a majority of males. In the lower age groups it is greater than in the higher. The physician Van der Hoeven states that in the villages east of the Mamberamo, there are 128 males to every 100 females. But for the age group up to 15 years the ratio of males to females is 143 to 100 (Hoeven 1950).

As a result, every parish has a large number of bachelors. There were 13 in Muremarēw, 10 of whom were over twenty-one. However, there were only two unmarried girls, of about seventeen years of age, and one widow. The result is that in Muremarēw—and in other Mamberamo societies—a tendency can be observed similar to that in the Tor territory (see Oosterwal 1959). Bachelors are gradually developing into

[2] The figures on the Babasena are from a mimeographed report by A. Thenu and J. M. Kröschell (1958). The figures on the Aurauweedj are from H. R. Karstel (1956), also mimeographed.

a social group with its own set of values and mores. Because of their specific economic activities—the hunting of crocodiles—the bachelors have become the wealthiest people in Muremarēw and have an abundance of food, such as rice and tinned fish. Chinese traders offer fair prices for good crocodile skins, and the bachelors' houses are well equipped. They have mosquito nets, suitcases, chopping knives and clothing, which

Table 11. Population figures of Muremarēw (1962)

Age	Males	Females
0–6	7	4
6–12	8	6
12–18	9	7
Over 18	29	24
Total	53	41

Table 12. Population figures of the Mamberamo area (1962)

Name of people	Males	Females	Total
Babasena	27	24	51
Kwerba (Taberee)	49	41	90
Kwerba (Bowaree)	47	40	87
Aurauweedj	31	23	54
Kaowerabeedj	55	50	105
Namoonaweedj	29	24	53
Marēwbeedj	53	41	94
Total	291	243	534

has aggravated the antagonism in Muremarēw society between the bachelors (*tawanawoom*) and the married people (*peejawoom*).[3]

Little can be said of other demographic aspects of Muremarēw society, as there are not enough comparative data available. There were

[3] This unbalanced sex ratio has been observed now by many investigators in the whole north of West Irian, from the Mamberamo to the Tor River and beyond. There seems to be a whole complex of causes: cultural, psychical, nutritional, and medical. It seems desirable that this phenomenon should be investigated by a team of workers, comprising at the least an anthropologist, a physician, and a nutritionist. (See the population research project among the Marind-Anim and Jeei-nan people in Netherlands South New Guinea, S-18 project of the South Pacific Commission).

19 married males and 24 married females, including one widow. Of these males, 16 had one wife, 2 had two wives, and 1 had three. Polygyny is considered exceptional and occurs mainly when a man's first wife is too weak, because of age or sickness, to supply him with enough food. Successive polygyny, however, is a very common feature, because women die earlier than men. Almost 40 per cent of all married men were married for the second time; about 10 per cent for the third time.

The 24 married women had had 51 children. However, it is possible that not all their deceased children were included in the genealogies. Also, the death rates are not reliable. My general observation was that it is about as high as the birth rate. From January 1962 until March 1963 there were 4 babies born in Muremarēw: one died immediately; another died after six months. That same year the parish also lost a boy about seventeen years old.

4. Subsistence

The people of Muremarēw subsist upon sago. Since its preparation is (almost) exclusively a feminine duty, the whole parish depends largely upon the women for its food. The production of sago is so closely related to women that the sago itself and its attributes have become symbols of femininity. For this reason, any woman who gives sago to a man other than her husband or brother is considered to have an adulterous relation with him.

Hunting is exclusively a masculine pursuit, but because animal life is rather scarce—there are some wild pigs, marsupials, rodents, and reptiles, and quite a number of bird species—hunting yields but little. The significance of hunting in Muremarēw is social rather than economic, as hunting and its attributes are equivalent to masculinity and virility. Hunting adds to the status of a man. Its significance is rooted in tradition and, even more than with sago, hunting is embedded in myth and ritual.

Of minor importance are fishing, gardening, and collecting forest products, which, however, do augment the rather meager diet. But *ab-beejewedjos* ("I go collecting") is an acceptable excuse for any man who wishes to leave the village without revealing his real reason or who is caught at places where women are working.

Sago and hunting are complementary activities that form the economic base, and on many occasions it is even prohibited to eat sago without pork. On the other hand, production of sago (female) and hunting (male), with their respective traditions and mythology, are also in conflict with each other and largely accentuate and aggravate the antagonism between the sexes in Muremarēw society.

5. The Village Community

The inhabitants of Muremarēw call themselves Marēwbeedj, people of the (river) Marēw. In this name the great significance of the parish community is reflected. The parishioners consider themselves first of all as members of a local group, which stands for unity, safety, and continuity. Muremarēw society is composed of several localized lineages and other corporate groups, between which opposing interests and strong antagonisms exist. Consequently, disputes between these kin groups become so severe that there is always imminent danger of splitting up the parish. Only the parishioners' own strong conviction that "there is no life outside the community"—this is how they express themselves—ultimately guarantees the stability of the group.

The parish is the only place where people feel safe. When in 1962 the young man Seebaya died, all parish members automatically were above suspicion, but for various reasons his own kinsmen from another village were accused of sorcery. Therefore Sersa, the leader of the Soromadja lineage, went to the village of Seewano, where he killed his own classificatory brother. The result was a war in which the Soromadja of Muremarēw fought against the Soromadja of Seewano, each assisted by members of the other kin groups in their respective communities.

The parish is a strong in-group with a highly developed *esprit de corps* and a common opinion to which young and old, male and female, contribute. Since there is no monocratic authority in Muremarēw, not even a gerontocratic leadership, life is highly regulated by general opinion and tradition. This opinion is formed both informally and formally. At regular intervals the parishioners come together on the *booneeseebeeter* to discuss important village affairs, and when very weighty problems need to be discussed, the inhabitants sit on two special logs (*attis*), which normally are kept in the cult house.

All parishioners have equal say in village affairs, although some elders are more respected because of their great knowledge of myths and traditions, while the opinion of a great hunter or mighty warrior weighs heavier than anybody else's. Nevertheless the influential members of the group are considered no more than *primus inter pares;* they cannot force the group—or even an individual—to adopt a particular opinion. The lack of chieftainship and the strong individualism of the members, who often prefer to live on their own in the jungle rather than submit to the general consensus, create serious problems in the daily life of Muremarēw. For example, endless discussions are necessary before every body agrees on a project. In January 1962, the villagers decided to organize a big feast, but the question arose of who should be invited and who should not. Three months later the question had not been answered, which is typical of almost every important event. And when agreement has finally been reached on some project, endless discussions follow on how to do it. The people of Muremarēw are well aware of these drawbacks, so that when they recently were brought under government control, and the government appointed Sersa as official headman (*korano*) of the village, they willingly accepted the arrangement.

The parish of Muremarēw has its roots in the land. It was here, people believe, that the ancestors came into being, created the pigs and fish and sago, and used to live. Therefore in principle this land is inalienable; only parish members share the collective right to cut sago trees, to hunt, to fish, and to collect forest products. Within this well-defined territory every lineage has its own section, although the division is not rigid. As long as at least some Marēwbeedj keep their actual residences on this particular piece of land, their parish is the sole owner. It is the land, therefore, that gives continuity to the parish, even though the villages are often moved.

The Muremarēw community is an almost closed group, as its members should only marry fellow parishioners. Almost 95 per cent of all marriages are contracted within the village. Exceptions are the man Derate, who married a woman from the Kaowerabeedj, and the woman Seesah, who married a Soromadja from Seewano. Derate stayed at Muremarēw but Seesah went to live with her husband, the prevailing rule of residence after marriage being patrilocal. Seesah, however, remains a member of the parish of Muremarēw, and her children are also considered potential members. In reality, however, they will belong to their father's parish because their actual residence is there, and thus their rights in their mother's parish may never become effective. It is because of this patrilocal residence pattern that parishes—and lineages, as well—are structurally patrilineal. But it is an open patrilineal system. Any man or woman who can trace his or her relationship with the ancestors of Muremarēw, either through a male or a female, has a right by birth to membership.

But it depends (mainly) upon a man's own choice (of residence) whether he will actually become a member. For example: the woman Wogeeye married Kawee, a man from the Kaowerabeedj, and went to live in his village. Their son, Kabeere, was about seventeen years of age when he made Muremarēw his permanent abode. He is now considered a Marēwbeedj. Though kinship structure in Muremarēw is based on patri-local residence and patrilineal descent, the right to become a member of the parish is not always transmitted strictly unilineally. With A. C. van der Leeden (1956, 171), I believe that this structural incoherence should be considered as a type of adjustment to the harsh circumstances in which these people live. The open group system is far more suited to conditions in this area than the rigid (lineage) system.

6. The Sociocultural Context

The community of Muremarēw, though a world in itself, is also part of a greater cultural and social unit, and an understanding of this particular community can greatly contribute to an understanding of the larger unit. However, a certain knowledge of the larger culture area also seems desirable for a better understanding of Muremarēw. This is particularly the case with regard to its social structure.

Situated on the eastern bank of the Mamberamo, Muremarēw forms part of the culture area of the "Western Interior of Sarmi." Van der Leeden defined this area as "the territory in northern New Guinea which is bounded in the west by the Mamberamo River and in the east by the river Woske" (A. C. van der Leeden 1956, 7). In the north this culture area is bounded by the Pacific Ocean. The southern boundary runs somewhere in the eastern Lake Plain.

The western interior of Sarmi is a very sparsely populated area, especially in the south. Sometimes a walk of two or more days separates one small parish from another. The isolation has been responsible for many differences between the people, although on the whole the cultural unity is far greater than the diversity.

In the northern part of this vast area a number of dialects can be distinguished, all of which are closely related, however (A. C. van der Leeden 1956, 23–28). In the southern and western parts, the linguistic unity is still greater. People living on the eastern banks of the Mamberamo, from the Bagoosa in the north to the Kwerba in the south, speak the same language. This language is also spoken by the people in the southern hinterland of Sarmi, from the village of Muremarēw to the village of Messentifereh on the eastern bank of the Tor River. This large language area—rather an exception in the north of West Irian—includes people such as the Kaowerabeedj, Aurauweedj, Meta-weedj, Murenyerwa, Airmati, Segar, and many others. There are some minor differences in dialect, but these are so slight that the people themselves are not aware of them. *Nogookwabai* is the term the people use to denote this unity. Literally, this means, "We speak the same language," although it refers to their common way of life, based on the same sago and hunting economy, the same social structure, and the same religious concepts.

This great unity is ascribed by them to their common origins and is supported by their myths and traditions. These myths invariably point to Muremarēw as the place from which the people and their culture originated. They relate how the man Mammowsoh once went out to cut ferns for a new *kanieyew* (stomach shield of twisted fern fibers, a common men's dress in this area).

When he returned to his village, built on the hill Serraree, he discovered that he had forgotten the bone of the cassowary which he had used to cut the ferns. Going back to retrieve it, he found a giant waiting for him. The stranger had no *kanieyew*, neither did he wear a *nabodjow* (common men's headdress). Mammowsoh became afraid of him. "Yes, it is me," the stranger said. "I have brought you pigs and dogs. Kill a pig and take it home. But remember that the pig's heart is mine. Bring it back to me." Mammowsoh did as he was told. He killed his first pig and made a big feast. But he kept the pig's heart in the *kone*. The giant became very angry. He disappeared into the air, taking the *kone* with him. Suddenly he released the *kone*. The wind scattered all the people in it over the earth. They became the ancestors of all the different people on earth with their great variety of cultures, languages, and skin colors. The cult house itself crashed on top of the hill Serraree. When the *kone* touched the ground, its center pole broke into two pieces. Out of it came the Soromadja, now living in the villages of Muremarēw and Seewano. Mammowsoh and Adjaw[4] then went to the east, and wherever they stopped they built huge cult houses. When a

---

[4] This myth does not explain where Adjaw suddenly comes from. He is one of the first men on earth and known in the whole interior of Sarmi as the (co-) builder of the *kone*.

building was finished Adjaw cut the lower part of the center pole, and out of it came the various people now living in the western interior of Sarmi, such as the Nawkena, Kwerba, Sarma, Seereejenne, Mararena. After they had finished their "creation," Mammowsoh and Adjaw disappeared.

This is only a small part of a complex of myths telling how the world came into being, how the first people came on earth, how they quarreled, and how they laid the basis for the present culture in the hinterland of Sarmi. "Man should never forget what happened in that first village," informants told me, over and over again, because here they found the basis for their whole culture and social life. And this first village where man and his culture came into existence is supposed to have been on the very spot where Muremarēw is now situated. This belief makes Muremarēw the basis, the guardian, and the model of tradition in the hinterland of Sarmi, and most of the inhabitants of that area look upon the Soromadja of Muremarēw as their cultural leaders and the keepers of their great secret.[5] Every feast, religious or profane, that is organized by the people of Muremarēw reaffirms this great cultural unity. And as their food situation is not as precarious as in most of the other villages, the people of Muremarēw can afford to give more feasts than any other. This fact contributes greatly to the high esteem in which they are held by all the inhabitants of the hinterland of Sarmi.

7. Dualism in Muremarēw Social Structure

People live in small independent communities, where the nuclear family and the open patrilineage are the most important groups. The number of patrilineages varies from parish to parish. There are, however, mythological and other indications that suggest an original structural pattern of two patrilineal and two matrilineal units. These patrilineal groups, though open and in some parishes rather vague, have very distinct functions in society. Each lineage has its own name by which its members identify themselves. Usually the lineage also has its own territory. For what has been said about the parish also applies—to a lesser extent—to the lineage: it is rooted in the land.

---

[5] A similar position is held by the Kwerba-Bowaree. It is on the territory of the Soromadja that Mammowsoh started his work of creation. But he went to the Kwerba, where he disappeared. The Kwerba still keep a wooden image in their village that is considered to be a representation of Mammowsoh.

Another important function of the lineages emerges in the organization of feasts, either religious or profane. Some lineages even have their own *kone*. The most important function of the lineage, however, is in the regulation of marriages. Everywhere in the Sarmi area marriages are contracted by exchange, ideally a sister exchange. But if a man has no sister, he can give another younger female relative in exchange for his bride. Generally this exchange is made on an individual basis, although in some parishes, particularly in Muremarēw, other members of the lineage may strongly influence decisions. Custom also requires a person to marry outside his own lineage; consequently the various lineages within the parish are united by the mutual ties of marriage relations. The very small size of the local lineages and the inability to exist independently contributes to the strong unity and continuity of the community, in spite of the antagonisms and conflicts between its groups.

In addition to the strong unity within the village community, the people of the western interior of Sarmi know of larger associations between various lineages and parishes. In the northern part these associations are rather vague and indefinite, but in the area between Muremarēw and the Upper Apauwar basin the existence of two distinct associations of lineages presents a clear picture of a moiety system. One moiety is female and bears the name Jowesso; its male counterpart is the Adjaw moiety.[6] To the Jowesso, for instance, belong the Kaowerabeedj, the Waseera, the Namoonaweedj and the Egonneebeedj. The Adjaw moiety includes the Soromadja, the Kwerba, and even the Mararena, living on the coast a few miles east of Sarmi.

Despite the fact that these moieties do not form well-integrated units in all aspects of life, they can be clearly distinguished during the various feasts, during the ceremonial exchange of gifts between the lineages, and sometimes during wars. They emerge most prominently in mythology and in the *kone* ceremonies. Adjaw and Jowesso are considered husband and wife. The Adjaw insist that it was Adjaw who built the *kone*, whereas the Jowesso are of the opinion that it was Jowesso who did so. The songs of the *kone* complex are a reflection of this great controversy (see Section 9).

[6] Adjaw and Jowesso are mythical ancestors, husband and wife, whose real names are Sekotshee and Beneene, respectively. But their names are sacred: women, children, and bachelors (!) are not allowed to hear them or they will "loose their teeth." Hence people always speak about Adjaw and Jowesso.

As the villagers understand it themselves, this dual division in society is a reflection of the dualism in the whole universe:

Adjaw	*—Jowesso*
sky	—earth
sun	—moon
peejawoom	*—tawanawoom*
high	—low
upstream	—downstream
elder	—younger
kinsman	—stranger
male	—female
hunting	—sago

In no other village in the (southern) hinterland of Sarmi is this dual organization so clearly seen as in the parish of Muremarēw. Hence, a study of this community can contribute greatly to an understanding of the dualism in the whole western interior of Sarmi.

The dualism in Muremarēw social structure is clearly incorporated in mythology. One of the origin myths, for instance, explains:

In the beginning the sky and the earth were not yet separated. There were two villages in the world: Werreeuw and Eebleeyaaitsh. Man should always remember them! One day, a woman named Commatter visited the village of Eebleeyaaitsh. There was nobody to greet her. As she stood looking at the *kone*, suddenly she saw the *kwettar* [the pole used as a staircase for the *kone*] become smaller and smaller. Finally it was only two feet long. Commatter took some red clay and rubbed the shrunken *kwettar* with it. Then she took the pole to her home, which was somewhere in the river Kaowera. There she wrapped the piece of wood in a bark cloth and slept with it. The following day the woman went out to pound the sago. On her return she noticed drops falling from her house. Rushing in, she saw that the *kwettar* had become a man, named Moronee. He became Commatter's husband. . . . One day a quarrel arose between husband and wife. This quarrel was much worse than all the preceeding ones. "I have made you," Commatter shouted, "but you behave as though you were the master!" Moronee felt ashamed. He went back to his own village and fell asleep. Commatter followed him and woke him up. They fought together. Moronee fled and jumped into the lake. Commatter then was sad and cried for many days. When Moronee heard his wife cry, he came out of the lake. Commatter took his arm in a firm grip. But Moronee jumped into the lake again. This broke the woman's heart. Immediately she changed into a white stone. Her people took the stone back home. "Our mother," they cried, "our mother Commatter. Moronee killed you. He is our enemy. Our mother Commatter." [These are still the words of a very important song.]

At present this white stone is kept in the house of Keyapee, one of the oldest inhabitants of the village of Muremarēw. It constantly reminds him and the other members of his lineage (the Waseera lineage) of their ancestor Commatter and how she was killed by her own husband. "Man should always remember those events in that first village," these Waseera people repeated over and over again.

The myth continues:

Moronee has never come back. However, he sent his son Mammowsoh. The latter went to Eebleeyaaitsh, his father's village, and made a new *kwettar* for the *kone*. [As was described in Section 6, Mammowsoh became the ancestor of the Soromadja, who were "born" from the center pole of the same *kone* in the first village.]

The Soromadja also live in the village of Muremarēw, which is situated on the "historical" spot where the village of Eebleeyaaitsh was once located. Thus the descendants of the mythical quarreling husband and wife are here united in a permanent marriage alliance that represents the unity between the two opposite parts of the whole universe. In their conflict and cooperation the two lineages of Muremarēw reflect the dualism of the universe, which thus has its focus in Muremarēw.

The parishioners of Muremarēw belong either to the Soromadja lineage or to the Waseera.[7] The Soromadja are considered the owners of the village and its environs. They are also the owners of the *kone* on top of the hill Serraree. The Waseera have their territory in the basin of the river Kaowera, about one day's walk from Muremarēw. Ownership of the two distinct territories is strictly respected but occasionally leads also to severe conflicts. Antagonism between the two kin groups comes most noticeably to the fore at festivities and ceremonies. Every dancing feast is a "fight" between the two lineages, which is especially true of the Djame and Warabeeree dances.

The Djame dance is known in the whole hinterland of Sarmi and

[7] A couple of years ago a (nuclear) family from the Peerassee lineage—one of the four lineages of the Kaowerabeedja—settled in Muremarēw. However, their presence in no way disturbs the dualistic pattern as described in this chapter; they even marry outside the village of Muremarēw.

beyond. Djame is a mythical female cannibal who used to live in the village of Wereeuw, "one of the first two villages in the world." A Soromadja from the village of Eebleeyaaitsh finally killed her. The whole story is included in the songs that accompany the Djame dance.

The Warabeeree is different. The "fight" is even more realistic as the songs don't tell that a Soromadja should win, as is the case with the Djame dance. The songs accompanying the Warabeeree dance tell of a tree, called *warabeeree*. Whoever owns this tree—and can therefore make use of its bark—will have great success in hunting. It is this success in hunting that adds to the prestige of the individual and the entire lineage to which he belongs. Consequently, both groups try to take possession of the tree by dancing. At least twice a week the men must perform this dance, in which two parties again are involved, each facing the other. Since none of the members likes to give up first, it becomes very exhausting, especially for the first two rows of dancers, who hold drums between their legs while dancing and singing. Generally, in about an hour the first "casualty" occurs. Totally exhausted, a man falls to the ground and is considered "dead." To prove that he is not dead, members of his lineage press a burning stick against the soles of his feet. When he does not show any reaction, they press it against his wrists. Sometimes a man is so exhausted that he remains unconscious for quite a while. But his fellow dancers continue all night, and the next as well. Sometimes the "fight" is so severe that the dance is prolonged for a week or more.

However, there is cooperation as well as conflict between the two lineages. Or, as informants expressed themselves: "Children need a father and a mother." In other words, the continuance of the community of Muremarēw, and of the whole universe, depends upon the cooperation between husband and wife, between the male and the female, between the *peejawoom* and the *tawanawoom*, between the Soromadja and the Waseera. In Muremarēw this becomes evident in the economic cooperation during feasts and ceremonies, the greatest of which is the inauguration of the *kone*, and in the marriage alliance.

Neither of the lineages alone would be able to produce and store enough food for the whole community. If a man of the Soromadja happens to find traces of a boar in the Waseera territory, he is allowed to hunt it there. If he kills the boar on Waseera land, half of the spoils belongs to the other lineage. During feasts the lineages complement each other in the same way. If the Soromadja organize a feast, the Waseera will help them to produce the amount of food necessary to make it successful. During dances and other ceremonies the two lineages, the male and the female, complement and need each other.

It is noteworthy that this dual organization of Muremarēw is not reflected by partition of the village. In one house Soromadja people live together with Waseera. This confirms the idea that the unity of the community, and the cooperation between the opposite lineages, must be greater than the antagonisms and conflicts. The community's great significance as the social and political landowning unit has caused blurring of the dualism in many parts of the hinterland of Sarmi. It is common residence that counts. Under the harsh circumstances of the environment, the neighbor is more important than the faraway kinsman. The reason that accounts for the strong lineage consciousness in the community of Muremarēw is that there are only two lineages from opposite moieties living together in a small spot. This creates a front mentality. Moreover, each of these two lineages is considered to be the keeper and the guardian of their group's secrets: the Soromadja of the Adjaw moiety and the Waseera of the Jowesso moiety. And both lineages are well aware of their important position.

8. *Kinship and Marriage*

Cooperation and conflict between the two lineages are most clearly evident in marriage arrangements. The lineages are strictly exogamous. Although it is true that a Soromadja man of Muremarēw married a Soromadja woman of Seewano, the latter are not considered as belonging to the same lineage. To repeat Sersa's own words: "Those are different." The maximal lineage is not an exogamous unit here.

Because of the strong tendency toward local endogamy—almost 95 per cent of the marriages were contracted within the parish—and because of lineage exogamy, a particular situation is created: the two lineages have become entirely committed to each other. Thus a symmetric marriage alliance has come into being between the two opposite parts of Muremarēw society, which again is a reflection of the relationship between Adjaw and Jowesso, Moronee and Commatter, heaven and earth, male and female.

Therefore, the marriage arrangement, which in the hinterland of Sarmi is largely a matter of two individuals exchanging their sisters, in Muremarēw is contracted by the whole lineage. Consequently, many of the problems that result from individual exchange do not occur in

Muremarēw (cf. A. C. van der Leeden 1956, 142–151; Oosterwal 1961, 99–112). When the Soromadja man Sapharee recently married the Waseera woman Babysaya, the latter had no brother. But the whole Waseera lineage now has a claim to Sapharee's sister Ertemet. And when last year the Soromadja man Ereit married the Waseera woman Sassareeuw, he had no younger female relative to give in exchange for his bride. During the marriage talks, however, the Soromadja gave the Waseera the assurance that in due time they would provide another woman. The ideal of an immediate, symmetric exchange between individuals still prevails, but as this is well-nigh impossible in such small-scale societies, the lineages arrange for it. Thus the levirate has become a lineage levirate as well: all the classificatory brothers of the deceased have a title to the widow.

Between two men exchanging sisters a special relationship exists, called the *mommoitsh* relationship (*mommoitsh* means literally exchange, also balance, reciprocity, equality). One would expect to find this *mommoitsh* relationship between the two lineages of Muremarēw also. Informants unanimously agreed that this relation could exist, but it does not at present. They denoted the relationship between the two lineages as a *gèmmez* relationship (*gèmmez:* "debt," also moral debt, guilt, wrong; in short, anything that has to be made up for). The *mommoitsh* relationship suggests a balance, a reciprocity, which does not exist between the two lineages. The *gèmmez* relationship suggests that there is no social balance between the two lineages. The main reason for this seems to be that the Soromadja have given more women to the Waseera than they have received. In this Irian culture, where every good relationship is based on exchange and reciprocity, the Waseera therefore have to offer food and other valuable gifts to the Soromadja on various occasions. In addition, when the latter organize a feast—and they are master feast givers—the Waseera have to render all kinds of services, such as the preparation of food, the building of the wooden structures where the boar are roasted, the collection of *damar* resin for illumination during the festivities, and so on. This disturbance in the social balance is one of the main reasons for really serious conflicts between the two lineages. Fortunately, however, this balance is "restored" in myth and ritual (see section 9).

The symmetric marriage alliance between the male and female lineages of Muremarēw has greatly influenced kinship relations and terminology. Thus most men now marry a (classificatory) MoBrDa or

FaSiDa, which coincidentally are denoted by the same kinship term. That means also that a man gets a (classificatory) FaSi or MoBrWi (same term because of coincidence) as his mother-in-law, while his brothers- and sisters-in-law are at the same time his cousins and classificatory siblings. The result is that many taboo relations between in-laws become blurred, and affinal kin are denoted by the same term as consanguinal relatives. Officially a strong avoidance relationship exists between a man and his mother-in-law, daughter-in-law and his younger brother's wife: he is not allowed to talk with them or to mention their names. Even words which sound similar to these in-laws' names are not to be uttered. It is clearly hard for a man not to talk to his mother- and sister-in-law when he lives with them in the same small house. But if these in-laws are, in addition, his classificatory mother and sister with whom he has played since boyhood, this avoidance tends to be neglected. Were it not for the strong lineage consciousness, even more kinship distinctions would have been blurred than are at present.

9. *Religion and Society*

Religious life has its center in the representations and rituals of the *kone*, which stands on top of the hill Serraree. This *kone* is a huge circular building with a conical roof.[8] The interior is very dark, there being only two openings, opposite one another, which serve as the entrance and exit. But even these openings are closed by doors. Directly crossing the circular interior are two parallel rows of poles forming a kind of passageway from the entrance to the back door. Thus the interior is composed of three parts: in the center is the corridor, about one and a half meters wide, with an open space on either side. In each quadrant of the floor a square opening is reserved for a fireplace. (During festivities in the *kone* these four fires burn constantly, and their choking smoke makes it well-nigh impossible for the unaccustomed to stay very long.) In the center of the *kone*, reaching from the top of the building down to the middle of the floor, is a long center pole, called the *tome*. At the inauguration of the *kone* it will be chopped off at about a man's height.

Of particular interest are the many symbols hanging in the *kone*, such as the *nawotsh, koiseenemetak, kwitshekorah, surah, maratooken,*

[8] For a detailed description of the *kone* see J. P. K. van Eechoud (1962, 89–105) and G. Oosterwal (1961, 212–228).

tabyeen, kamamotteen, tome, and others. The *nawotsh* is the symbol for the moon; many discs of different sizes made from plaited rattan, hang from the ceiling of the *kone*. The *nawotsh* also serve as rattan connections between the two cross beams. The villagers believe that the moon has creative power: just as it waxes from a crescent to a round disc, so small children will become adults, young pigs will grow fat, and sago trees will ripen (see Oosterwal 1961, 217–223). The *koiseeneme-tak,* a square of plaited rattan, represents the bat (flying fox), the animal that plays so prominent a role in the whole culture of the western interior of Sarmi and generally throughout Irian. In the Mamberamo area, bats are believed responsible for the planting of sago trees; they are considered as symbols of life. The *kwitshekorah, surah,* and *maratooken* are similar rattan figures that hang on the ceiling of the *kone,* symbolizing pigs and sago trees.

Of great importance are the sexual symbols of the *kone*—the *tabyeen,* the *kamamotteen,* and the *tome*—respectively standing for woman's breast, female genital, and male genital. The form of the *tabyeen,* also hanging from the ceiling of the *kone,* is similar to that of the *nawotsh* (moon). *Kamamotteen* means literally the anus of the cassowary, but from mythology and the construction of the *kone* it is clear that this symbol stands for the female genital. The *tome* occurs in two forms in the *kone:* as a carved wooden penis about ten centimeters long and as the center pole of the *kone* (Oosterwal 1961, 221–228). In the ritual of the *kone,* all these symbols are believed to stimulate fertility, creative power, and hunting luck; in short, the health, wealth, and continuance of the parish and the "good cosmos."

The *kone* cults, however, mean more than just fertility; they also reflect the social structure of the parish. This becomes evident even during the construction of the *kone.* As soon as a stage in the construction is completed, a feast is organized; the more important the newly finished part of the *kone,* the longer the feast. Thus there are festivities as soon as the ground plan has been laid out and the sixteen poles that mark its outline have been driven into the ground. Then follow feasts for the finishing of the rafters, of the roofing, and so forth. When the building is finally finished the significant inaugural feast follows.

Long before this great event takes place, the Muremarēw people start preparing food. The women spend weeks preparing sago. The men organize big drives to kill as many animals as they can. Delegates are sent to invite lineages from the Jowesso and Adjaw moieties to attend.

The details of the ceremonies have to be omitted in this chapter, except for a description of the most important ritual, the truncation of the center pole (*tome*). The young men sit in the corridor of the *kone* around this pole, eating small portions of sago and pork. The elderly men sit on either side of the corridor. Women are not allowed to be present. When the leader gives the sign, eight young men leave the *kone* to blow the sacred flutes which are kept in a small, closed house, the *asartshiu* (*asar* or *ahaar*, flute; *tshiu*, house), near the *kone*. Then six young strong men take hold of the *tome*, which has received two deep incisions at the place where it will be chopped off. The strongest man stands on the first floor of the *kone* and, at the sign from the leader, truncates the *tome* with one blow of his chopper. At the very moment he hits the *tome* the other men holding it make a skillful rotating movement and "screw off" the *tome*. This is a thrilling moment. All noise and hilarity cease. Evidently it is a very significant act upon which much depends.

Immediately after the chopping the men start a wild dance, carrying the cut-off piece of the *tome* (*tommattekar*) between their legs. Facing toward the entrance, they dance four times forward and four times backward through the middle corridor of the *kone*. Then the flutes are put away in the *asartshiu*, and the women crowd into the *kone*. Wild dancing and singing start, the women dancing in the open spaces on either side of the corridor. During the dancing and singing, eight elderly men sit along the dividing lines between the corridor and the two open spaces. Their faces are turned toward the men who dance in the corridor, although informants said that these eight men were there to watch the women. In the meantime they prepare tobacco, which they pass alternately to the men and women.

At midnight food and betel nuts are distributed. Then the dancing and the singing resume, continuing until dawn. In the morning, after a very short sleep, the women prepare food again: sago porridge and pork and, unlike the first night, any other food that is available. During these *kone* festivities almost the whole food supply of the parish is exhausted. For weeks and months thereafter there is hardly any food for the parishioners; but "a man does not live by bread only," and the parish has gained prestige by distributing so much food.

On the second and on subsequent nights of the festivities, the food is not brought into the *kone* but is prepared and left in the gallery around the *kone*. Six fires are made there, which burn all night: two on either side of both the entrance and the back door, the other two in the intervening spaces. Near the fires at the entrance and the back door lie the *attis,* two logs that are used as sitting places for important events in the village. The *attis* lying at the entrance belongs to the Soromadja, the one at the back door to the Waseera.

Any parishioner, asked about the significance of the *kone* ritual, could only explain that "it was the custom." However, from the myths it seems evident that the inauguration of the *kone* is primarily a re-enactment of the most important event from the past, namely, the creation of man. This idea fits into the whole mythology and ritual of the *kone* complex. The myth of Mammowsoh has been described in Section 6. Other myths tell about the mythical man, Omayaaitsh, a personification of the sky, who had a very long penis. It reached from the sky to the earth, where the women lived. Coitus took place in an indirect way: Omayaaitsh put his penis into the earth, it appeared at another place on earth, and there the women had intercourse if they wished. When Omayaaitsh came to earth he was badly handicapped by his long penis, which "dragged behind him like a tail." The penis was then cut off, which made coitus and the conception of man possible. On the other hand, sky and earth have been separated since then. This important event is also mentioned in those myths in which the *tome* itself is considered as the link between sky and earth. In these myths man faced a great dilemma: to remain separated from woman, with all the consequent advantages (e.g., no wars, no death), or to live with woman, have normal coitus, but with the sky separated from the earth.[9] Man chose the latter. But informants from the various parishes on the Mamberamo emphatically stated that there are still places where people have not made that decision, where men and women live completely separately. Coitus takes place only when "the men put their long penises into the ground and when these penises break through the earth at the place where the women reside." These women are said to live south of the Van Rees Mountains in the Western Lake Plain and are called: Aesabeedja (*aes,* woman; *beedja,* people). The men are said to live somewhere on the (high) mountain ranges west of the Mamberamo. They are called Tettabeedja ("men with the long penis").

[9] These myths—and the others related in this chapter—were told by different men from the various parishes where the field work was done. Sometimes the myths were told in the Indonesian language; often, however, the informants told them in their own vernacular. The myths were recorded on tape, translated, and verified on the spot during the different field trips.

Small children remain with their mothers; but when boys reach the age of about six years they are sent to their "fathers" to live. The Toribeedja, a group of people living at the confluence of the Rouffaer and Idenburg rivers, are said to have regular contact with the Aesabeedja in order to exchange tobacco for choppers and knives. This information of the informants fits into the mythology and traditions of the *kone* complex.[10] The act of chopping off the *tome* is therefore a re-enactment of the most significant event of creation. It also upholds and justifies the special status of man in Muremarēw society (see Oosterwal 1961, 228, 237, 239).

The inauguration of the *kone* also throws light on the other dualism in Muremarēw society: the male and the female lineage and the Jowesso and Adjaw moiety in the whole hinterland of Sarmi. The most important songs of the *kone* ritual are those of Adjaw and Jowesso, believed to have been sung once by Adjaw and Jowesso themselves and later taught to their own people. Van Eechoud mentions in his ethnography that the Kaowerabeedj indeed speak about Adjaw and Oewiejeho (Jowesso), but that Adjaw is unimportant and that all songs are "Jowesso-songs" (1962, 164–165). As the Kaowerabeedj belong to the Jowesso moiety, there is naturally no place for Adjaw, who was a Soromadja. The latter, on the other hand, claim that they do not know anything about Jowesso songs and call all songs Adjaw songs. This is but another example of the antagonism between the two moieties.

During the *kone* festivities at Muremarēw the villagers start with the Adjaw songs. These songs narrate how Adjaw catches a *weeuwwaroo*, a cicada, and how he then imitates the cicada in his song, as do all the people dancing in the *kone*. Adjaw sings about the rivers, how they came into being, and about the rain and the fishes. He sings about people and tobacco and coitus. Adjaw would like to have intercourse with his wife, Jowesso, but she refuses. Then the villagers begin to sing the answer of Jowesso. The Waseera (and the other lineages of the Jowesso moiety)

[10] In these "stories" seems to lie the origin of the very bold statement made by Ruth Benedict that "many tribes in Dutch New Guinea . . . have strong clans, . . . who solve their marital problems by ignoring marriage alliances. . . . In these tribes the maternal line lives together, harvests together, and shares economic undertakings. The women's husbands visit them secretly at night or in the bush. They are "visiting husbands" and in no way disturb the self-sufficiency of the matrilineal line" (1947, 125). Benedict probably heard about this from P. Wirz and M. Moszkowski. The latter visited the Mamberamo about 1910 (see M. Moszkowski 1911, 315–346).

try to outdo the Soromadja (and Kwerba, etc.) with their singing. They raise their voices suddenly when they start to sing what Jowesso once sang: "Jowesso was in her own village. She pounded the sago, she caught the fish, she shot the boar and roasted them on the mountain. The rain was coming, and many birds came flying to (the village of) Moomae. There were also cassowaries. They 'sang' in the jungle. Jowesso imitated the sound of the cassowary and killed one." From this point the people imitate the voice and the walking of the cassowary. Big cassowary tails are attached to the backs of the dancers. "Jowesso picked the fruit of a *ganemo* tree. Then she stood in the doorway of the *serraaitsh* tree." With a loud voice, the Soromadja then start to sing again: "Adjaw put his finger into the anus of the cassowary. Then he built the first *kone*." Thereupon the Waseera answer: "Jowesso came to the Mamberamo, where she built the first *kone*." Now a real contest starts about who in fact did build the first *kone*. "As the river Mamberamo meanders from left to right, thus the songs of Adjaw and Jowesso alternate," informants used to say. This contest goes on for weeks and the songs are repeated every night, during which time the villagers become more and more excited over the question, "Who built the first *kone*?" for that ultimately decides the status and position of the moiety and the lineage in Muremarēw.

After weeks of dancing and singing—the period depends upon the amount of food available—it is time to bring the sacred flutes into the *kone*. When the leader of ceremonies gives the sign everybody has to leave the *kone*, which will remain empty for a couple of days. During that time the Soromadja and Waseera (with their guests) organize a big drive to shoot the flute pig. Women are not allowed to see this pig or to eat of it. When the boar is prepared, the dancing and singing start anew, but only for four nights. The fifth night the flutes must be brought into the *kone*. During the course of those four nights, more and more women stay away from the *kone*, and at the beginning of the fifth night there are only a few elderly women left. Then, about midnight, the strongest and youngest men leave the *kone* to get the flutes (*asar*) from the *asartshiu*. The older men now warn the few elderly women to leave also. When the flutes are blown for the first time in the *asartshiu*, the men in the *kone* will get a piece of burning firewood to chase the women out. No woman is allowed to see the flutes; if they did, the rains would come, the Mamberamo would rise, and a great flood would destroy all life on earth.

The strong men carry the notched flutes in their left hands in a procession from the *asartshiu* to the *kone*. While they carry the *asar* their heads are bowed. They stop at the eastern side of the *kone* and blow the flutes, the notches pointed toward the sky. At that time, there are only four elderly women in the *kone*. When the sound of the flutes is heard these women immediately turn their faces to the opposite side. The procession with the flutes around the *kone* goes on. The men stop for a second time at the main entrance of the *kone* and blow the flutes again. The four women in the *kone* now turn their faces toward the back door. A third and fourth time the flutes are blown at the western side of the *kone* and at the back door. Then they are carried into the *kone*. When they enter, the men suddenly pretend to see the women and get very excited. They start shouting and screaming furiously, and the four old women, their faces covered with their hands, flee from the place, pursued by a number of enraged men waving sticks and burning pieces of wood. The *kone* has now definitely become the possession of the men.

This ceremony is also a re-enactment of an event that happened in the mythical past. Myths tell that formerly two (or four) women were the owners of the *kone* and the sacred flutes. Then the men fought a real battle to conquer them. One myth relates, however, that two women managed to escape, taking the sacred flutes with them. These women are said to be the ancestors of the previously mentioned Aesabeedja.

When the flutes are blown inside the *kone* the men stand in two rows opposite each other. Each row consists of Soromadja and Waseera, alternately. The Waseera men have female flutes, the Soromadja carry the male counterparts. The Waseera men first lift the female flutes and start blowing them, and then they lower them; then the Soromadja lift their flutes and start blowing them; consequently the female and male flutes play alternately, on and on. At the end of the first part of the ceremony, all male and female flutes are blown at the same time, all pointed toward the floor of the *kone*. Then the flutes are put down beside the four *kone* fires, and the Soromadja exchange betel nut and tobacco with the Waseera.

The whole flute ceremony, from now on held in the *kone*, involves the following elements: the killing of the flute pig and its preparation; the feeding of the flutes; the many different ways of blowing on the eight different types of flutes, which vary in size from about ½ to

2½ meters; the ceremonial exchange; and communal eating. An important question remains, however: "Why are the flutes blown?" The answer given was almost always the same: "But we must live," or, "We have to eat and be happy."[11] And indeed, in its more exoteric aspects, the cult is certainly a fertility rite, a means to procure and maintain life and, as they believe, to prevent the cosmic order from becoming chaotic. The men said: "When we blow the flutes, the sago will grow; the rain will fall; the pigs will multiply; the trees will bear fruit." They know very well that they depend on the women for their food and for the continuity of the whole parish, but by their ownership of the sacred flutes the balance is restored, as the flutes are considered to be the first cause of all things. The men used to say: "Women can only work on things that we have created."

Flutes are not the personal property of individual men but symbolize the whole lineage. A man gets his first flute from his own father and has to pass it down to his sons; but as the whole lineage is the owner, no one can give away a flute to somebody who is not a member of the lineage without the consent of the whole lineage. The passing down of a flute is a very solemn act and occurs at the end of the initiation ceremony. Boys are initiated into the secrets of the economic, social, and religious life of the community when they are between twelve and fourteen years of age. Throughout a two-month period of hardship and seclusion, they must stay in the *kone;* they are not allowed to meet women, and they have to suffer and to endure hunger and cold. However, their mother's brother supervises them and takes care that no real harm is done to his sister's children. At the end of the period the boys are "killed." They have to lie down and are not allowed to move, even though they are beaten and frightened. Then the father blows on a newly made flute and "revives" the spirit of his son, who will thus learn to believe that the flutes are the givers of life.

Finally, another religious ceremony, which is also of extreme importance in Muremarēw social life, has to be mentioned: the *ennemaree,* the burial of the bones. When a person dies, his corpse is wrapped in banana leaves and placed without much ceremony on a *nensar* tree or on a high scaffolding made of *nensar* trees. People believe that death ends only the life in the parish but not the eternal life in *oonoosoobert,* where an individual continues to live as *gwaria* or *warria.* The Marēwbeedj believe that their "village of the dead" is located somewhere

[11] See the information from the Tor area reported in G. Oosterwal (1961, 228–239).

above the clouds and that Djeeuwme is its ruler. The road to the village goes through Djeeuwme's house, a tall tree called *seraaitsh*, but nobody can enter there empty-handed. "When many pigs are killed, a man is permitted to ascend to *oonoosoobert* through the *seraaitsh*" (Oosterwal 1963).

After several months, when the corpse on the *nensar* tree has almost decomposed, the bones are removed, wrapped in new banana leaves, and buried. This burial of the bones is an opportunity for a big feast, to which many guests from nearby as well as faraway places are invited. On top of the spot where the bones are buried, a small house is built to store food for the ceremony. On the night when the *ennemaree* starts, the Soromadja offer food to the Waseera and vice versa. Then betel nuts and other gifts, such as arrows, pig's teeth, and shells, are exchanged. This is a token of the great solidarity between the two opposite groups of Muremarēw society and a sign that none of them is suspected of having practiced sorcery, which, according to the general belief, is the main cause of death.

An *ennemaree* is never characterized by an atmosphere of grief and sadness, but by gaiety and merriness. After the ceremonial food exchange and the communal meal, people start to dance and sing, expressing their belief that the dead will be raised and that Djeeuwme will soon come to Muremarēw with all the *gwaria* and *warria* to establish a new order. Then there will be no more misery, illness, or death; there will only be abundance of food and wealth or *poona* (Oosterwal 1963). In 1961–62, under the impact of certain social and political events, these old beliefs gave rise to a large-scale cargo cult in Muremarēw and the whole area of the southern hinterland of Sarmi.[12]

10. Conflicts and Conciliation

The attention of many investigators in the hinterland of Sarmi has been attracted to the tendencies of parishes to split up, as well as the frequency with which this process occurs. The greatest dangers to life and to the continuity of the Muremarēw parish are the many tensions and frictions between the antagonistic groupings. Fortunately, the general

---

[12] These "cargo" beliefs are of genuine native character. In 1961–62, the people of Muremarēw for the first time came in contact with Christian missions. Since 1962 a teacher-evangelist (*guru*) of the Seventh-Day Adventist mission has been stationed in Muremarēw.

feeling that life is impossible without the parish suppresses many conflicts. Yet these tensions make themselves felt in almost every aspect of daily life. And even joking, witticisms, and teasing, also institutionalized, are too small outlets to disperse them. The situation in the parish of Muremarēw is worse than in most of the other villages. But the Marēw-beedja have also found their own strong ways to counteract the menaces of splitting and extinction, thereby guaranteeing the continuity of their parish.

February 5, 1963, is marked in my diary as a day in which all the pent-up emotions and ill feelings burst forth. The outburst started in a rather innocent way. At about four o'clock in the afternoon the Waseera man Bennai gave his wife Orae a sound thrashing because of her laziness, as he said. For days she had not gone out to collect food. "I don't feel well," was Orae's excuse. Bennai was forced to beg some sago from his mother; that's why he told his wife frankly that he had not married her simply because of her nice face and breasts. She commented that she did not need *him*, and that he had better take another wife. No insult is more serious in Muremarēw than when a woman lets her husband feel that she can do without him. The man's whole position is then at stake, and he can only answer by brute force. Totowa, another Soromadja, almost killed his wife in 1962 when she said similar things to him. The men know how weak and vulnerable they are, economically.

When Bennai started to beat his wife, everybody felt that he was right. Orae had neglected and insulted him. Customarily in Muremarēw nobody interferes in conflicts between two people, which is one way to prevent it from spreading all over the parish, where everyone is related to everyone else in more than one way. However, Bennai's sister told Orae that she indeed was a very bad wife and did not deserve such an excellent husband as her elder brother. Orae ran up to her and started to beat her with a piece of wood. Then Bennai's mother became enraged, and mother and daughter fought with Orae. Although the men tried to stop the women by persuasion, the old woman Sabeesae, normally too weak to walk, stood in the middle of the village and roused the women to fight. The men were in a desperate position. None of them wanted to approach old Sabeesae, who, unhindered, could stir up all the other women. Finally, the old man Moppa took a piece of wood and threatened to beat her if she did not "shut up." Unintimidated, Sabeesae continued to call the women to fight. Then Moppa lost his temper and hit her arm. A tremendous tumult was the result. Sabeesae was the "leader" of the women, and she therefore ran upon Moppa and scratched and bit him. Now the honor of the women was at stake! But the men had to rescue old Moppa. So the battle started; all men against all women, as in mythical times. Suddenly Sersa shouted, "Sapharee, get the flutes!" Two or three strong young men ran up to the *kone* and returned with the sacred flutes uncovered in their hands. Screaming and shrieking, the women ran out of the village into the jungle, some of them leaving their children behind. Sabeesae, "knowing" the secret of the flutes, merely turned her back and continued to call to the women, "Beat them; scratch them; defeat them!" But no woman dared to stay behind, for six sacred flutes were placed next to each other in the center of the village.

Late at night, Eraya took up the flutes to return them to the *kone;* his children were crying for their mother. Kureddee tried to stop him. "Let the women cool off," he said. "Otherwise they will start again tomorrow." Eraya, however, wanted his wife back, so he took the flutes. Kureddee, however, snatched the flutes out of his hand, shouting, "Don't touch them. They are mine!" Indeed, the flutes did belong to the Soromadja, and Eraya is a Waseera. A very serious fight arose. Some men got their bows and arrows, others took their axes or choppers or clubs, and they flew at each other, Soromadja fighting against Waseera. The old woman Sabeesae tried to intervene, but nobody could stop the fight, as there was no central authority. The whole parish split into two groups.

Totowa and Moppa were seriously wounded. Nokwew and Sapharee were eliminated. Then Sabeesae, daringly, threw herself between the fighting men. Other women, returning from the jungle, persuaded their husbands, many of whom were wounded, to stop. "Cut the *sabar*!" they shouted. "Cut the *sabar*!" Slowly, the men went one by one into the jungle. They stopped at a big tree, the *sabar* tree, and started to cut it. One after the other took his chopper, stone ax, or even wooden stick and hit the tree, thus "blowing off steam." Bennai cut so heavily that his strength gave way and he fell unconscious to the ground.

When the tree finally fell, a big "boo" was raised. Then, as if a fight had never taken place between them, they lifted the tree to their shoulders and carried it to the river. With much laughter and shouting, the *sabar* tree was thrown into the Mamberamo; the current took it away. There was a moment of deep silence, during which they all watched after the trunk. Then the talking, laughing, and shouting started again. "It is gone," they said. "It is gone." By this they meant the *sabar* tree and the whole conflict and all the hatred. Nobody will talk about this conflict again.

With fiery torches—it was then about midnight—the men went to the *kone* to get the *attis*. They laid these logs opposite each other on the *booneeseebeeter*. In between they spread a new cloth of tree bark. The men sat on the *attis* or around them; the women sat on their heels alongside. A few pieces of burning *damar* resin lighted the place. Eraya rose to his feet and said, "I have offended Kureddee. Now I give my shells." He laid a beautiful string of shells on the bark cloth. Next Kureddee said, "I lost my temper. I give my arrows." In the same way all the men laid the best they had on the cloth. The whole ceremony took place in great silence and reverence. Then betel nuts and tobacco were exchanged. Those who had most gave most; those who had nothing only received. But nobody counted the number of gifts. This exchange between the Soromadja and Waseera symbolized the equality of both groups and restored balance. "We must give the best we have," Sersa commented. "That makes living together possible again."

Very early the next morning all the men and women made hasty preparations for a big drive. "We must kill a pig," they shouted. "We must kill many pigs!" For there is no reconciliation without a feast. When everyone was about ready to go, five men suddenly appeared, clothed in women's attire. They even imitated the women in their way of walking. Some of the transvestites had made artificial breasts, which caused much laughing and joking. Only the five "women" remained solemn. They took their bows and arrows and went off. The others followed, still laughing.

When asked the reason for this transvestitism, the answer was: "Just fun. We always do that when we go out hunting after a big conflict." They seem to do it to deceive Djeeuwme, the goddess of the afterworld and the owner of the pigs. Somebody had to be killed during the conflict as an appeasement. But they only "killed" a tree. "Djeeuwme would not allow us to kill a pig now," Berya told me. But, of course, Djeeuwme would not do any harm to "women," for women never kill pigs.

That very night a big feast was held. All the men and women sat at the long table on the *booneeseebeeter* to eat sago and pork. The festive spirit was heightened when, during the eating, the seats could no longer support the noisy feasters and tumbled down. When the Djame and Warabeeree dances started, the whole conflict was forgotten, but subsequent conflict and cooperation will continue in Muremarēw.

Chapter VIII

Bontoramba: A Village of Goa, South Sulawesi

HENDRIK T. CHABOT
INSTITUTE OF SOCIAL STUDIES
THE NETHERLANDS

1. The Macassarese and Buginese

The peculiar shape of Sulawesi (Celebes), with its four peninsulas, is caused by mountainous formations branching off in four directions from the center of the island. The mountain massif in the center makes communication between the different parts of the island difficult, whereas the population has been too sparse and the technical obstacles too great to make road building economically advisable, at least in the recent past. Relative isolation has contributed to the considerable variation in language and culture among the population of the four peninsulas.

The southern peninsula, which concerns us most in this chapter, is characterized geographically by an impressive chain of old extinct volcanoes, surrounded by lowlands along the coast. From the slopes of the highest volcanoes (approximately 3,000 meters), one has a beautiful view of the hills and coastal lowlands that stretch down to the coast on the west, south, and east sides. The distance between the western and eastern coastlines is about 150 kilometers. The rivers are short and unnavigable, while the water distribution is uneven. The soil is generally fertile, but deficient crops resulted from the shortage of water. Small irrigation works, however, have improved the situation considerably, making South Sulawesi self-supporting, as far as the staple food, rice, is concerned, and the Sadang River dam in the southern hills of the central massif is intended to change this part of the country into one of the rice-export-ing regions of Indonesia. The long coastline and Tempe Lake give the population extensive opportunities for various fishing activities. Hunger indeed does not have to be the main concern of the population of South Sulawesi.

The area, consisting of approximately 5,000 square kilometers, is inhabited by about five million people: Macassarese (about two million) in the south, and Buginese (more than three million) in the north. The main difference between the two ethnic groups is in their languages; although the differences may seem impressive at first sight, the common underlying structure is easily found. Both languages have had their own script since time immemorial; the written literature, incised on *lontar* palm leaves, includes various versions of the old *I La Galigo* epic and the diaries of kings, recorded by court secretaries, which contain the most important events of the respective kingdoms.

South Sulawesi was converted to Islam during the first decade of the seventeenth century. The king of Goa, a powerful Macassarese maritime kingdom of that period, was the first to embrace the new faith; he afterwards subdued the other Macassarese and Buginese kings and forced them to become Moslems. The old ancestor cult, however, has never disappeared completely and still continues to play an important role in the life of many Macassarese.

During the seventeenth century, Goa had many contacts with Portuguese and English, as well as Dutch, traders, but in the second half of the century the Dutch managed to get a foothold in South Sulawesi. They built a strong fortress that formed the beginning of what is now Macassar town, and from there they directed their commerce and played their role in the struggle for power in South Sulawesi. This struggle between the Macassarese king of Goa and the Buginese king of Bone had already been going on for centuries, and it lasted another two centuries, until in the beginning of the twentieth century the Dutch were able to penetrate more deeply into the interior to subdue the two kingdoms, which in those days had become weakened from various causes. From 1910 on, the lower levels of the Dutch colonial government gradually extended into even the small towns and villages of the region. This chapter will focus on one of the villages of the kingdom of Goa, or, more precisely, on one of the original nine banner communities which federated into the Goa kingdom. Only recently, under the Indonesian government, have the kingdoms, which have become small principalities, been transformed into administrative units.

Macassarese and Buginese society is characterized by its highly formalized class structure. Small and large principalities took part in the game that interests every individual in South Sulawesi, the struggle for hegemony. In each principality I noted a social pyramid with the prince, his council, and the members of his kin group at its top, the nobility; at its bottom, the large mass of peasants; and in between the heads of the banner communities (later officially called "*adat* communities") and their extensive kin groups. The higher classes in a stratified society always tend to keep the borderlines between the social levels as rigid as possible. To the average Macassarese peasant, members of the prince's kin group seem to be people of a different and definitely higher order, but even so, stories of commoners who have become war leaders, religious leaders, or wealthy men do exist, thus indicating that there are possibilities for people from lower classes to move up to become members of the higher classes. The prestige of a person from the lower levels is also increased if he can show an even remote kinship affiliation with some person from the higher levels. From the standpoint of the lower people, social levels seem to be less rigid.

Members of the various noble families in the various kingdoms are related by marriage. To a limited extent, this also holds for members of the kin groups of the *adat* community heads. The common people in the villages also tend to marry within their own kin groups, although some marriages between different kin groups do occur. We shall return to this issue later, but for the moment it is sufficient to say that the first impression one obtains by observing Macassarese society or by studying the available literature[1] is a picture of a highly stratified society.

2. Location, Settlement, and Demography of the Village

One of the thousands of villages of the Macassarese area is Bontoramba. This village, where I did my field work in recurrent periods totaling more than one year, before and after World War II, is one of the fourteen villages of the *adat* community or traditional administrative area of Borongloë (with approximately 14,000 inhabitants), which

[1] Kennedy's bibliography of the Macassarese (1955, II, 332–345) and the one included in my dissertation (Chabot 1950, 260–274) may very well supplement each other.

together with ten other *adat* communities comprise the principality of Goa (with more than 200,000 inhabitants).

Bontoramba is situated in the lowlands. The southern mountain massif is vaguely visible on the distant horizon, while the hills are nearby. The main road, which connects Macassar town with the villages in the mountains, goes for about 15 kilometers through a varying landscape of rice fields, pastures, bush, and forests. The only big, but still unnavigable, river in this part of Sulawesi, the Djeneberang, just bypasses the southwestern outskirts of the village.

According to a census taken in July 1948, the village consists of 129 houses with 787 inhabitants, of whom 384 are males and 403 females. They belong to fifteen different larger and smaller kin groups. Within the context of the village territory, one family living in one house is considered as a very small kin group. Members of all these groups, however, have their co-members in other villages, other *adat* communities, and other principalities.

Bontoramba has one large kin group occupying 81 houses and fourteen smaller kin groups occupying the other 48 houses. Four of these occupied respectively 18, 9, 5, and 3 houses; three kin groups occupied 2 houses each; while seven consisted of just 1 house each. Map IX shows that the settlement pattern of the village is quite compact. The houses of the group of 81, especially, and also those of the other smaller groups, are rather close together. People seem to feel more secure and comfortable when living right next to relatives, which facilitates mutual help in everyday life. The very small kin groups usually consist of people who have run away from other villages, because they eloped, or of people who were looking for a better living in Bontoramba. As the economic conditions in most Macassarese villages are about the same, and in some even better than in Bontoramba, we may conclude that problems of individual adjustment may have been the main reason that these people left their large kin groups to settle in Bontoramba in small groups.

Despite the general preference among Macassarese villagers to stick to their own kin groups, demographic data from Bontoramba from the year 1948 indicate a certain frequency of migration and a tendency toward constant intra-village moving. Of the inhabitants of Bontoramba, 73 per cent were born in the village; 14 per cent were born outside the village but within the *adat* community Borongloë; 10 per cent were born outside the *adat* community but still within the kingdom of Goa; 3 per cent were born outside Goa.

The kin group of 81 houses has the highest percentage of members who were born in Bontoramba (89 per cent), compared with the others (53 per cent). The large kin group is thus a rather stable group, as far as staying within the village territory is concerned. For a number of reasons there exists, however, a tendency for people to move frequently from house to house. An old widower wanted to live alternately with his married children; a young boy who had been constantly ill went

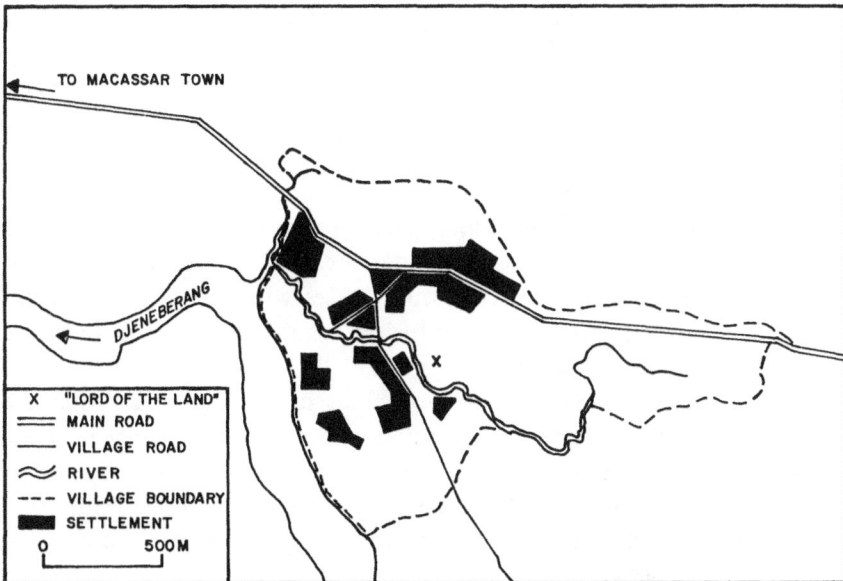

Map IX. Settlement Pattern of Bontoramba

to live with his grandfather to "improve health"; a difficult child was sent to an uncle, as a new environment is believed to be more conducive to better social adjustment; a young girl joined her newly married sister for companionship; a woman who had quarreled with her husband asked one of her female neighbors to join her for the night, thus indicating her rejection of her husband. These, and many more, are sufficient reasons for moving, so that the composition of households changes frequently. A change of environment seems to provide an easy solution for individual problems of social adjustment. Frequent moving from one house to another does not involve important consequences in cases of young children and old people, but it does create certain problems for the average adult. Custom requires that an adult should live in his own house, and despite the fact that moving away from the main group is made easy, it does mean a lowering in status for the individual concerned. These are the consequences that members of the small kin groups have to face.

3. *Kinship and Marriage*

Kinship relations are an important aspect of Macassarese society in general. Regardless of administratively maintained village boundaries, *adat* communities, or principalities, the members of one bilateral kin group can be found scattered all over the country. This tendency for spreading, for group fission, has already been indicated. There also is a tendency, however, for fusion, for living closely together in large numbers on a few territories. Thus the core of the bilateral kin group usually occupies certain specific territories, including parts of two or three villages. Here a constant struggle for status and power exists. The great frequency of endogamous marriages between the families within these bilateral kin groups and the recurrent ceremonies for the worship of common ancestors tend to maintain the solidarity of the groups.

An insight into the nature of two kinds of relationships within the nuclear family will give us a deeper understanding of the social relations between relatives, in the broader sense, and also between members of the community in general. One is the relationship between father and son and consequently between older and younger brother; the other is the relationship between brother and sister.

The relationship between father and son is characterized by the traditional dominance and patriarchal authority of the father within the nuclear family. In a conversation, it is improper for a son to contradict his father; he should listen quietly and respond in a respectful and formal way. Very often a son feels uneasy when facing his father, as if afraid of making mistakes in his speech and behavior. An observer will very soon notice a tendency for the son to avoid his father; the son always tries to seek an excuse for leaving when his father enters the room. An adult son who wants to communicate with his father concerning important decisions, as, for instance, on arrangements for working in the rice fields or for the circumcision of a child, seldom addresses the old man directly but usually through his wife or other persons.

A similarly constrained, although less formal, relationship exists between older and younger brothers. The possibilities for conflict between brothers are great in this society where competition, endeavor to improve status, and struggle for power are important elements, particularly for the young men. This pattern of relationship between young men in general, which includes possibilities for conflicts, extends far beyond the range of the nuclear family and the bilateral kin group.

The relationship between women seems to be different. Daughters behave in a far less formal manner toward their mothers, in comparison with that of sons toward their fathers. However, although mutual help and cooperation between daughter and mother is highly valued, girls tend to develop more frequent relationships of friendship and intimacy with their aunts or grandmothers than with their mothers.

Another basic principle, important to the understanding of Macassarese social relations in general, is the brother-sister relationship. According to Macassarese custom, a brother is the protector and guardian of his sister. This relationship is also the leading motive of the great Macassarese epic, *I La Galigo*, which narrates the separation of Sawerigading and his twin sister Tenriabeng, their efforts to find and to join each other, and all their experiences and adventures when trying to overcome the many obstacles that prevent their coming together.

The relationship between the sexes is also highly conditioned by this brother-sister ideal, the main idea being that the sexes should remain separate, as a meeting would necessarily produce bad results. According to Macassarese public opinion, a man and a married or unmarried young woman cannot meet each other alone without further consequences. Although the meeting may have been purely accidental, the situation could be considered as a heavy insult by the brother, husband, or other male relatives of the woman and will involve serious consequences. The situation counts, not the intention of (one of) the parties. Custom requires the insulted party to seek vengeance by killing the offender with a dagger. It is especially the brother of the woman who has the obligation to protect her from offenses and insults. Until recently, quite a number of cases of killing by brothers of insulted women have been reported, some from Bontoramba.

Macassarese etiquette has thus incorporated several rules of avoidance, which have to be taken into consideration by men and women in contact situations. A man who visits a house, for example, has to stop in front of the door and cough, in order to give the women who might be present in the house the opportunity to leave the place.

The usual consequence of an accidental or deliberately arranged individual contact between male and female, if noticed by somebody else, is elopement. The marriage contract in case of elopement is made according to Islamic rules, with the lowest possible bride-price rate of 20 *real*. The couple married in this way, however, still has to face the anger of the wife's relatives, and the husband has to be careful not to encounter his wife's male relatives, as they should kill him according to custom. Even if the anger has diminished after a period of time, the couple will only be accepted by the wife's kin group after a reconciliation ceremony. It may take months or even years before the wife's relatives are persuaded by mediators, usually influential persons who belong to kin groups of higher status than the wife's relatives, to accept a reconciliation. The reason for marriage by elopement is hardly, if ever, an economic one, and only occasionally do love motives prevail. It is always possible in Macassarese society for either a man or a woman to force the other party into a situation that will necessarily result in an elopement, with its extensive consequences. In Bontoramba, marriage by elopement was quite a frequent occurrence. Of the 89 married couples of the kin group of 81 houses, 15 were married by elopement. All the couples except one had performed the reconciliation ceremony, and the wife's relatives of this certainly exceptional couple tried to overlook the fact by not mentioning their names.

The coherence of large kin groups is maintained, as previously mentioned, by a tendency to keep marriages endogamous. Of the eighty-nine married couples of the large kin group of 81 houses, seventy-nine were endogamous (89 per cent). Of these, sixty-nine had been arranged by parents or other influential people, and ten were the result of elopement. The arranged marriages were greatly influenced by the traditional concepts of approved marriages: sixty were between young people of the same generation; the nine marriages between people of different generations were, with one exception, between people of approximately the same age group. Eight marriages were between kin of the "fourth grade" (first cousins), thirty between "sixth grade" (second cousins), and twenty-five between "eighth grade" (third cousins). More distant kinship relations are not indicated by a specific term but only by the attribute *bella* (distant). It is possible that, among the eighth-grade cousins who were selected to marry each other, several were actually more "distant" cousins. Even the old people, experts in kinship matters, may not have a clear conception of very distant kinship relations, and it does not take much effort to create fictive connections in order to achieve the required relationship between the prospective marriage partners.

Within the large kin groups, people favor strong ties with the leading members. Despite the general conception that all members of a kin group are equals, people are clearly aware of the fact that several relatives are economically, socially, or politically more successful than others. It is with these relatives that people try to strengthen relationships through marriage. In practice this means that influential members of one and the same kin group tend to arrange marriages between their children. It means, in other words, that we found a tendency for clustering around the influential members of the kin group. When an influential member has died somewhere in the kin group, young influential people elsewhere may assume power; some individual families decline while others rise in status. This rise and decline and constant mobility are characteristics of the kin group.

Beside the general tendency to marry within one's own kin group, many people also seek to establish marriage relations with other kin groups in order to enhance status. In addition, exogamous marriages also occur when influential members of the nobility or heads of *adat* communities arrange marriages between children of their followers. In such cases the will of the influential personality of the lord is a more decisive factor than kinship relations between the prospective marriage partners.

In addition to kinship affiliation and status, the personality of the boy or young man is also taken into consideration in the selection of a marriage partner. An ambitious individual with a competitive and aggressive personality, with status consciousness and pride, is a much-favored marriage partner. The inert, restrained, and diffident young man is not very much appreciated; he is considered unable to defend the name and to increase the prestige of his kin group. A person with such a personality is also expected to be unsuccessful in his marriage, because he fears failure in sexual relations and is thus considered unable to win his wife.

A girl is expected to have the complementary personality. The obedient and timid girl is the ideal. But more aggressive types, deviants though they may be, will also have a chance to marry, either by elopement or because parents are much more willing to concede to the girl's wishes in order to avoid the troubles of an eventual elopement.

In Bontoramba, 5 per cent of the people who had long passed marriageable age were still unmarried. Among them were 15 men who were beyond the age of thirty-five and 24 women who had passed the age of thirty. Some had bodily defects, were deaf-mute, blind, or albino; most of them, however, seemed to have had difficulties in having their marriage arranged by older people because of their extremely hesitant and overly modest characters.

A wedding is one of the most important social events in a Macassarese community. To celebrate the marriage of a daughter, an elaborate wedding party that lasts three days, a week, or even a fortnight, with many buffaloes killed, with a great number of guests, and with a great variety of elaborate ceremonies, indicates the high social status of the host.

The amount of the bride price (*sunrang*), however, is the most important status indicator. The amount of the bride price is fixed by custom and varies in accordance with the social status of those who pay or receive it. The rates are expressed in terms of *real*, a coin of former days no longer in use for regular financial transactions. According to the custom of the kingdom of Goa, the bride-price rate for members of the royal kin group or nobility is 28 *real*, for heads of *adat* communities 26 *real*, and for the commoners 20 *real*. In actual monetary value, these differences are insignificant; much more important, however, are the status differences symbolized by the rates. In addition, the payment is usually only partly made in coins; the greater part consists of pieces of land. Very often, the bride price actually paid is much higher than the amount customary for the payer's status. Many other criteria, such as affiliations with important kin groups, high social position, high occupation or rank, political power, and strong economic position, will favorably influence the raising of the bride price beyond the fixed amount. The rate of the bride price mainly relates to the social class of the bride's kin group. "A woman's status should never decrease," i.e., a woman's bride price should never be less than the one paid for her mother.

Most marriages that take place in the average Macassarese village community are of the 20-*real* category, while bride prices of 24 *real* are often exceptional. The registers of the *imang* of Borongloë (the Moslem official in charge of the registration of marriages), recorded 107 marriages that had taken place in the *adat* community during the period between July 1948 and July 1949. Two of these marriages were of the 26-*real* category, twenty-four of the 24-*real* category, two of the 22-*real* category, and seventy-seven of the 20-*real* category. In two other exceptional cases, concerning Javanese immigrants, 22 *real* and 5 *rupiah* were paid. Of those 107 marriages, nine took place in the village of Bontoramba, and of these nine, seven were based on a 24-*real* bride price, one on a 22-*real* bride price, and actually only one on the 20-*real* bride price. If we consider that most marriages in the average Macassarese village community outside Borongloë are of the 20-*real* category, while bride prices of 24 *real* already indicate exceptional cases, the Bontoramba situation is very striking indeed. The reason for this situation seems to be the fact that several years ago the head of the *adat* community married one of his cousins to the daughter of the village head of Bontoramba, who is one of the influential people in the large kin group of 81 houses. Thus the other members of this group now consider themselves to be related to the head of the *adat* community.

The customary rules concerning the bride-price rates in relation to the various social classes differ from principality to principality. For a person belonging to a certain principality who marries within its boundaries, this fact does not create any difficulties, but for those who marry persons from other principalities it requires real effort from both sides to arrive at a compromise. A Buginese immigrant in Bontoramba who initially insisted on a bride price of 44 *real*, based on the customary rules in his own principality, finally had to be satisfied by raising the 20 *real* to 22 *real*.

As a consequence of the custom of arranged marriages, many prospective brides and grooms have never seen each other or are not very well acquainted with each other. A few days before the wedding ceremonies start, the marriage is announced to the prospective bride and groom in their respective homes. The announcer is the person who has taken the responsibility for the ultimate success of the marriage arrangement. This is never the father or the mother but usually some older female relative. Through various means she has to persuade the girl and the young man to accept the arrangement. Generally she will succeed, but there were several cases where it took weeks, months, or even longer before the couple consented. Refusal is indeed extremely difficult for everyone concerned, as those who make the announcement and who attempt the persuasion are very often people of high status, sometimes even of slightly higher status than the parents. Young people are always taught to obey people of higher status. Whenever they refuse, the resulting question, "Do you intend to bring shame upon me?" will raise intense psychological conflict in their minds, which they often solve by consenting.

The *nikka*, the contract concluded between the groom and the father of the bride in the presence of the *imang*, the Islamic official of the *adat* community, is simply one of many ceremonies, although it is the most essential one. Sprinkling with water on various occasions, fumigating the bride and groom at the beginning of the event in their respective homes, are meant to make them and all the things they use ritually clean. The traditional speech to welcome the groom when he arrives at the house of the bride, escorted by his relatives, the ritual of the first "touching" of the bride, the first common meal, and the first "common bath" merely symbolize the intimate relations between husband and wife, which in reality do not yet exist. They all attempt to persuade the young couple to accept each other as husband and wife.

Custom requires that the bride should initially reject the advances of her new husband, because the groom is supposed to win his wife. Not all young husbands, however, seem to be able to live up to these expectations. If he is not successful, he may react in the opposite way by further avoiding his wife. If a man is not able to win his wife, his marriage is considered unsuccessful, and consequently a divorce according to Islamic law may be one of the solutions.

The person who has been responsible for the success of the marriage arrangements, however, will always attempt to avoid a divorce by various means, which may explain the fact that the divorce rate is extremely low in Macassarese society. The registers of the *imang* of the *adat* community (approximately 14,000 inhabitants) reported 107 marriages in the period between July 1948 and July 1949, against 7 divorces. In Bontoramba (787 inhabitants), I registered 3 cases of divorce according to Islamic law and 6 cases of separation. More than half of these cases resulted from the failure to produce children.

The incidence of polygyny also seems to be rather low in Macassarese society. In 1949 the *adat* community of Borongloë had among its population of 14,000 only 34 people who practiced polygyny, 27 of whom had married their second wife by elopement. These individuals had probably been forced to do so, because only in exceptional cases are people able to plan deliberately to take a second wife. In Borongloë only very powerful people or aliens, namely the head of Borongloë himself, an Arab Sayid, and two Chinese shopkeepers, were able to practice polygyny. A second wife in a polygynous marriage always lives in a separate house, preferably in another village, since a friendly relationship between the co-wives never seems to exist. In Bontoramba there was only one case of polygyny, the result of an elopement. The second wife lived in an adjacent village with one of her relatives and was only visited occasionally, after long intervals, by her husband. This case of polygyny did not seem to increase the man's prestige, because polygyny in Macassarese society is only considered as a status symbol if a person already possesses the means and the power to organize matters with his own efforts.

4. Religious Activities

I have mentioned the existence of various forces that have induced factionalism of large kin groups, and how a policy tending to keep marriages endogamous seems to maintain coherence within these groups. Similarly, recurrent ceremonies for the worship of common ancestors seem to have the same function. These religious activities center on sacred objects. The heirlooms of the kin group of the prince of Goa, the heirlooms of the *adat* communities, and the heirlooms of several village heads are worshiped not only by the members of the kin groups involved but also by the dependents and followers of these people. The holy objects of the princes of Goa are thus officially worshiped not only by the members of their kin groups but by all of the approximately 200,000 inhabitants of Goa. Religious activities take place at large annual celebrations for planting and harvesting, but they also occur to celebrate such critical events along the individual's life cycle as childbirth, circumcision, and marriage, and occasionally when a person has to fulfill a vow or leave on a long journey. Large ceremonies involving the whole principality or the total *adat* community are performed on important occasions: the inauguration of a prince or *adat* head, for example, or the beginning of a war.

At religious celebrations the sacred object (a flag, a sword, or other object) is ritually taken from its usual place, the attic, and displayed to the guests. It is then smeared with the blood of a sacrificial animal, and the important persons of the princedom of the *adat* community may deliver an oath of loyalty in traditional phrases but in an emotional way. Occasionally a sacred object will be displayed together with another sacred object of a subordinate community or kin group. The rituals will thus also demonstrate and confirm, in a symbolic way, the superiority of one group over the other.

At the village level, however, few kin groups possess holy heirlooms. When sacred objects are present, people are free to choose on their own which kin group they want to join for ceremonial activities. The possibility for choice is derived from the fact that some persons belong to more than one kin group, as a result of an exogamous marriage of grandparents or great-grandparents. People are free to attend rituals at two or even more places, while they can even join rituals performed by families in other villages; their choice, however, is often determined to a considerable extent by the leading personalities guiding these rituals.

In Bontoramba, within the large kin group of 81 houses, no single family possesses sacred heirlooms.[2] Ceremonial activities have usually centered about several popular and influential individuals within the kin group, who compete with one another for the leading position in one way by trying to get the greatest number of participants at their rituals. A large concentration of people will make a group feel powerful; in turn, a large, cohesive, and well-organized group will attract still more followers.

A kin group that possesses a sacred object will usually be better integrated than a kin group without one, as no doubts concerning leadership and no competition for power will exist within such a group. The family that possesses the heirlooms will automatically be considered its leader by virtue of the sacred customs established by the ancestors, and most will join that family for ceremonial activities. Consequently such kin groups or families are considered with suspicion by the heads of *adat* communities, as they are potential rivals who could achieve a status that might challenge their position.

In addition to these religious rituals centered on sacred objects and oriented according to kin group, another public ceremony, the harvest ritual, seems also to function to improve cohesiveness among groups. In Bontoramba the harvest ritual is always performed at a sacred spot called "The Lord of the Land," under a big mango tree where a small shelter (*saukang*) has been erected, and where several large flat stones lie scattered about.[3] The shelter, which is erected on four piles with

[2] The village chief of Bontoramba, who belongs to the large kin group, once showed me a small wooden statue which he considered, in rather vague terms as a holy object. In fact it is a sacred object *in statu nescendi*.

[3] Several elaborate myths try to explain that the sacred place is the spot where the ancestors departed for heaven. Long ago—so runs the story—there was a man who told the people, "When I am not here any longer, when I shall have gone to heaven, and if you would like to offer me something, then you must perform the rituals on that stone in the middle of the country."

a fifth one truncated in the center, is just large enough for one man to sit in. It is the place where the *pinati*, the religious specialist, sits when he performs the rituals. All the households in the village are expected to contribute a plate containing rice, eggs, and meat, decorated according to detailed prescriptions (which also leave room for the display of considerable imagination) with a number of specific kinds of leaves, folded in a special way. The plates are prepared by women who are supposed to have extensive knowledge of the prescriptions dealing with the preparation of ceremonial food for the ancestral cults.[4] After the ritual the food will be consumed in a communal meal by the participants.

In Bontoramba the ceremony has become less popular than it must once have been. Only a small number of families still contribute the ceremonial food. At one of the harvest rituals I attended, I observed only forty-five plates, although 129 families were supposed to live in the village. Most of the plates came from families belonging to the large kin group of 81,[5] which, as the dominant kin group, had the greatest interest in the preservation of this public ritual. The other kin groups seemed to be less interested, and only some of them participated in order to remain on good terms with the leading people of the village.

5. Status and Class

The drive to improve status seems to be an important stimulus for action in the average Macassarese male. Within the family we have noticed competitive tendencies in the relationship between brothers, while within the large kin groups we have also seen the ambition of particular families to achieve positions of leadership. A society that favors competition, however, also seems to place tremendous pressure on its individuals, many of whom develop a fear of failure when they feel unable to live up to expectations. Failure will bring shame (*siri'*) upon them, and this is considered a very serious matter.

The competitive attitude, however, can only be exhibited in the relationship between equals, because in dealing with a person who has estab-

---

[4] The Macassarese used to say, "The ancestor cult is the religion of women, Islam the religion of men."

[5] Of the forty-five plates offered, thirty-seven were presented by families belonging to the group of 81, one from the kin group of 18 (who were Buginese immigrants), five from still another group, and two from people living in other villages but owning land in Bontoramba's territory.

lished a superior status, a man is supposed to be submissive and obedient. This attitude is the basis for an important institution in Macassarese society, the relationship that exists between retainer and lord. According to this system, a man who is striving for influence and power may collect about him a group of retainers who have accepted his superiority and who will thus help him increase his power; the clients will, in turn, also improve their own status. The bigger the group of retainers, the greater the power of the lord and consequently, also, the higher the status and prestige of the retainers. The awareness that high and low need each other in their struggle for power underlies the retainer-lord relationship. In addition, the retainer-lord system can also be used as a means to recruit manpower for the completion of projects that, for various reasons, cannot be carried out on a kinship basis. Very often a group of retainers remains demobilized and inactive, but the lord may summon them any time collective action is needed.

The required characteristics for a potential leader in Macassarese society is generosity in dealing with others, courage to take risks, eloquence in speech and debate, the capacity to organize and stimulate action among other people, and also, as we have seen, the ability to organize celebrations and rituals. On the other hand, retainers should be loyal to their lords, should show courage, and should react immediately and effectively in case of insult.

An ambitious man will have the greatest opportunity to develop a large group of followers in periods of crisis or disaster, in times of war, and in many other cases of emergency. In normal circumstances, however, the persons who have the most favorable opportunities to develop a group of retainers, provided that they possess the required qualities for leadership, are persons who possess sacred heirlooms, wealthy landowners, and persons of high rank.

The really large and wealthy landowners are usually found among the nobility and the heads of *adat* communities and their relatives. Such people own large tracts of land in different villages, *adat* communities, and even princedoms, where relatives and local representatives organize matters for them. In Bontoramba there are no pieces of land belonging to members of the nobility or other important persons; the biggest pieces of land belong to members of the large kin group of 81.

According to the 1949 land rent registers of the *adat* community of Borongloë, the average land holdings per house amounted to .54 hectare of wet rice fields and .69 hectare of dry fields. The average number of inhabitants per house was 6.1, so that the average land holding per person came to .09 hectare of rice fields and .11 hectare of dry fields; all in all .2 hectare of land per person, which gives the picture of a small peasant society.

In looking at the figures for each house in more detail, we find that the members of the large kin group possessed .77 hectare of rice fields and .88 hectare of dry fields per house, whereas the average for all other kin groups amounts to .17 hectare of rice fields and .38 hectare of dry fields per house. It should be taken into consideration, however, that the latter group also included a few individuals in the village who were not engaged in agriculture but in other occupations: for instance, there were three small shopkeepers, the owner of a repair shop, and several carriers (people who hire themselves out to carry other people's goods to and from the markets in adjacent villages).[6] From these figures it also may be clear that the possession of land contributes to status in the village.

In approaching the same subject matter from a slightly different angle, we may say that 25 of the total number of 129 village houses (21 of these belonged to the large, 81-house kin group) possessed more than one hectare. And furthermore, that 8 of the 129 houses possessed more than two hectares apiece, 7 of these 8 again belonging to the large kin group. Only one individual possessed more than three hectares. He belonged to the large kin group, and in describing his character in general terms we approach the ideal of the strong leader: industrious, eloquent, modest, and difficult to find because always on his way. Consequently he was a very prominent man whose advice in important matters frequently was seriously considered by the villagers.

Landownership is not limited to the borders of the village as an administrative unit. Most people own additional pieces of land in other villages, and a few even have property outside the territory of Borongloë. Usually, however, people try to keep their landholdings nearby, and they sometimes manage to exchange their distant holdings for pieces of land situated conveniently close to Bontoramba.

[6] The market of the *adat* community of Borongloë is located along the main road in a village four and a half kilometers east of Bontoramba. Fish and salt from the coast is sold here, to be transported to the mountain villages, which in turn supply tobacco, vegetables, fruits, and pottery. During market days, which occur once a week, approximately 800 to 1,000 people, of whom most are men and only a few older women, gather there, because additionally it is the right place to hear the latest rumors and gossip.

Other indicators of wealth and status are houses, number of buffaloes, and specific kinds of equipment, such as long heavy rice blocks for pounding rice and looms. In these possessions, the village census figures also showed the dominance of the large kin group. During my field work I counted 238 buffaloes and 11 horses belonging to members of the large kin group, as opposed to 45 buffaloes and 1 horse for the rest of the population. There were also 53 rice blocks and 73 looms owned by persons belonging to the large kin group, but only 22 rice blocks and 28 looms owned by members of the other fourteen kin groups. A big kin group at the village level thus means a rich group and, consequently, one of relatively high status.

6. *Important Village Functionaries*

Most of the leading figures in the village belong to the dominant kin group. The most important is the village headman (*kapala*), a functionary who is elected by male members of the village who possess a "labor card," a card indicating age of eighteen years or older, thus a potential worker whose services can be used for the labor force of the village. When a new headman is to be elected, the various kin groups nominate one of their leading members as a candidate, usually a man who is expected to be able to get along well with the head of the *adat* community. Usually the candidate of the dominant group will be elected without much opposition. The recent village head of Bontoramba, naturally a member of the kin group of 81 houses, did not even have any rivals during his election. A small kin group would not have the slightest chance to win an election, as people automatically vote for the candidate of their own kin group. A group without power therefore will consider it wiser to refrain from any attempts to propose their own candidate, since such an act will be considered as an offense by the prospective village head, who will punish the little group later by suppression and opposition.

In villages where two or more kin groups of approximately equal power exist, the smaller ones take sides, and the candidates must campaign in order to win their support. In addition, a candidate must also achieve the favor of the head of the *adat* community; his powerful position can strongly influence the election, since the villagers require the consent of the *adat* head for the new village head. On the other hand, heads of *adat* communities often try to increase their power by nominating their relatives as candidates for village headmen within their territories. The head of Borongloë for instance, once tried to have one of his cousins elected as *kapala* of Bontoramba, but his campaign failed, even after a re-election. The establishment of marriage relations between his kin group with powerful kin groups in the village might have produced better results.

The village head is charged with administrative responsibilities by the central government: he has to collect the land tax, and he has to organize and recruit the labor force required by the *adat* head and the prince for work on public projects. In addition he has the final authority over internal village matters; for instance, he is the man who gives permission to aliens who want to settle in the village, he decides on the opening of new swiddens, and he gives important suggestions in cases of land disputes. Within his own kin group he will be considered as a member of the group of elders, regardless of his actual age, and his authority will even extend to internal kinship affairs; he is not supposed to interfere in the internal affairs of kin groups outside his own, however. As the final link in the hierarchic chain between the central government and the rural population, he is a representative of that government, and as such he has numerous responsibilities; on the other hand, he is also a member of the village community and, as such, their representative in dealing with levels above the village. Nonetheless he will be involved also in the local struggle for power which concerns basically all Macassarese males.

Another important leading figure in the community is the *guru*, the Moslem religious official of the village. He occupies the lowest rank in a hierarchic chain of officials, of whom the *imang* represents the level of the *adat* community; the *kali* of the principality ranks highest. The *guru* is responsible to the *imang* for the registration of births, marriages, divorces, and deaths. The minimum requirement for such a position is the ability to recite several of the most important Koran verses, and the *guru* is thus often called upon by individual families to attend celebrations or rituals where the reciting of Koran verses is required, as, for instance, circumcisions, weddings, funerals, or visits to graves. Thus a *guru* will often develop close personal relations with particular families. A *guru* who is unpopular will be avoided, and many families will prefer to have their own Koran specialist. It has often happened that villages have one or more persons as *guru* in addition to the official village *guru*. Bontoramba also has one additional *guru* who is a member of the small kin group consisting of 18 houses. This man has managed to establish direct contact with the *imang* of Borongloë and for several reasons seemed to be tolerated by the *kapala* and official *guru* of Bontoramba. In other cases, however, much more friction and tension exist within the village community as a consequence of the presence of two or more *guru*, each belonging to powerful kin groups.

A third functionary to be mentioned is the *pinati*, the specialist of the original religion, the ancestor cult. This man is supposed to have extensive knowledge concerning the care of sacred objects, the details of rituals to be performed at various occasions, and also the formulas to be pronounced at these rituals. He thus has a leading role not only in the preparation of important celebrations of events along the individual's life cycle but also on more public occasions such as the harvest ritual described in Section 4. As an expert in rituals, the *pinati* is also supposed to possess knowledge of indigenous herbs and drugs, which enables him to practice curing and healing. Not all families have a *pinati* among their members, although some villages have more than one recognized *pinati*. Generally, women are also supposed to know about the details of the rituals, and several of them even know about curing. When the leading *pinati* of the village (who usually belongs to the dominant kin group) is an unpopular man, the families who dislike him may go to another *pinati*, either in the village or elsewhere, or call upon one of the female curers. The *pinati* of Bontoramba, who does belong to the often-mentioned large kin group of 81 families, is the only one in the whole village.

7. Conclusion

Within the near future, we may expect changes in several areas of village life. The frequency of elopements will probably decrease, while the number of divorces has shown a tendency to increase. The Macassarese traditional bride price is tending to develop into the Moslem *mahr*, while ancestor worship is definitely declining. All this means that the cohesion between members of the kin group is decreasing, without necessarily implying that the kin group will disappear.

Increasing intensification of school education will very likely affect the customary seclusion of women. Curiously enough, one of the two public schools of Borongloë, which was situated in the village of Bontoramba, counted 100 girls among its 226 pupils in 1949. Most of these girls, however, were not allowed to continue their education in the high school in Macassar town, and, after graduating from elementary school at the age of eleven to twelve, they were forced to continue the traditional secluded life of the average Macassarese rural woman. When I revisited Bontoramba in 1953, not much seemed to have changed. The tremendous increase of school education in subsequent years, however, may have brought about changes on the surface of Macassarese village life; but the fundamental values mentioned in this chapter will continue to operate for quite some time.

In summarizing our main argument, we may conclude by saying that a closer observation of Macassarese rural life in one of its many villages does not confirm the first impression that one obtains when studying the literature on two counts. The literature time and again gives the impression of a strict social hierarchy, whereas in reality we find much uncertainty about the lines dividing the various layers of society from each other. It becomes clear that the picture one obtains depends on the point of view from which one observes the situation. If seen from above, one notices strict lines, barriers to hinder the commoner wanting to climb the social ladder, whereas, if seen from below, we find several ties between low and high people that give the low ones increased status. This contributes to the uncertainty which is always present when matters of status are discussed. One's place in the hierarchy depends on various imponderables.

The literature also treats villagers as an undifferentiated mass, whereas again during field work we found a great many subtle differences in social status as well as a constant moving up and down the village hierarchy, with the possibility for the gifted person to rise through the use of social institutions. It is not by accident that we referred here to what people do or could do, as, generally speaking, we may say that men are supposed to be the agents of enhancing status and women the agents of maintaining status in Macassarese society.

Chapter IX

Tihingan: A Balinese Village

CLIFFORD GEERTZ
UNIVERSITY OF CHICAGO

1. Bali

Bali is Indonesia's most famous island. As possessor of the only explicitly Hindu culture remaining in the archipelago, its temples have been photographed, its rituals described, its art analyzed, its psychological depths probed, and the beauty of its women praised by a long series of gifted ethnographers until today the anthropological literature on it is more developed than on any other part of the country.[1] But, for all this, aside from Korn's monograph on Tnganan (1933), a community as atypical as it is interesting, and a few scattered papers on so-called Bali Aga mountain settlements, detailed and systematic descriptions of particular villages from a sociological point of view are still lacking. It is toward the filling of this gap that the following brief description of a South Bali gong-making village is intended to contribute. Though something will be said about religious and artistic life, as breath-taking here as elsewhere on the island, the main emphasis will be on political, social, and economic structure.

2. Environment, House Land, and Field Land

In 1957-58, the year in which my wife and I studied Bali, the island's population was about 1.7 million, of which some 80 per cent or so was concentrated in the southern heartland of Tabanan, Badung, Gianjar,

---

[1] For references, see Kennedy's bibliography (1955, II, 544-567).

Bangli, Klungkung, and Karengasem.[2] Geographically, this heartland consists of a sloping, volcanic hill mass running down from a complex of
huge fifteen-hundred- to three-thousand-meter cones in the north center
of the island and leveling out to a flat piedmont only within eight to sixteen kilometers of the southern coast. The whole area (some 3,450 square
kilometers) is striated lengthwise by dozens of narrow, very deep-cut
river gorges a few hundred meters apart, spreading out from one another
like the ribs of an opened fan as they run downward to the sea. Settlements are strung one below the other down the slope, along the spurs
between these gorges, separated by wet rice fields and coconut gardens.
North–south—or up–down—relationships between settlements have consequently always been much closer than east–west ones, and each spur,
drawing water from a common source, has tended to form a natural
ecologic unit. The main traditional (i.e., pre-1906) court centers tended,
in turn, to be located toward the lower ends of the more important of
such spurs, but still well back from the coast at about the place where
the hills begin to level out into plains, from which vantage points they
vied ceaselessly with one another for control of peasant communities both
above and below them. Some seven kilometers mountainward from
Klungkung, one of the most illustrious of these ancient courts but today
a sleepy small town and regional (*swapradja*) seat, lies Tihingan: population 720.

You cannot see Tihingan until, coming upward along the road from
another settlement a few hundred meters across the rice terraces below
it, you are already in its midst, for it is wrapped in a blanket of coconut
trees. Even then you will not at first see very much—the people live
concealed behind high brick and mud walls, which, lining the narrow,
crisscrossed streets and pathways, give the forbidding effect of a repeating
labyrinth. Halfway up the north–south road the monotony is relieved
momentarily by an open-sided, vaguely Polynesian-looking meeting house
(*balé bandjar*), a few temples (*pura*) also largely concealed by walls,
a towering waringin tree, a small cleared space for petty trading, and
a ramshackle bamboo-shed coffee stand. And then the unbroken walls—
unbroken save for narrowed, screened-off doorways—begin again. A fur-

[2] These estimates are based on 1954 election statistics data as given in
I Gusti Gde Raka's monograph (1955, 10). Our study was supported by
a grant from the social sciences section of the Rockefeller Foundation, administered by the Center for International Studies, Massachusetts Institute of
Technology.

ther climb of a few hundred meters and you are out of Tihingan as suddenly as you came into it; another few hundred and you are in another settlement, physically (but not socially) its twin. Except for a few people moving self-absorbed along the roadway, grooming fighting cocks in the shade of the meeting house, or chatting indolently at the coffee stand (and if it is midday, even these may not be present), you would hardly know, despite the frenzied yapping of the emaciated dogs, that you had been in a village.

Actually, whether or not Tihingan *is* a village depends upon how you choose to define the term, for, as I have tried to show in more general terms elsewhere, the notion of a single, uniform social referent for this word (*desa*) cannot be defended when actual social relationships and not merely ideal cultural conceptions are considered (C. Geertz 1959, 991–1012; 1961, 498–502). Tihingan has an origin temple and a death temple of its own (Pura Puseh, Pura Dalem), but it shares its third main temple (Pura Balé Agung) with the settlement below it; it is the headquarters of a man the government (and, on occasion, the population) refers to as a "village head," but his bailiwick includes three other settlements besides Tihingan; the rice fields of its inhabitants are scattered around among several nearby irrigation societies (*subak*), mixed in with those of people from dozens of other communities; and so on. But the people of Tihingan call it a village, as do their immediate neighbors, and for practical purposes this will perhaps suffice. It must not be assumed, however, that the social entity referred to as a village in other Balinese communities will necessarily be the same sort of entity Tihingan represents. For all the visual monotony of its settlements, Bali's social structure is a complex of contrasts, a tissue of irregularities.

The definition of the "village" of Tihingan (or of any Balinese "village") is further complicated by an odd, peculiarly decisive structural fact: unlike peasant communities in most parts of the world, there is not in Bali any simple enfoldment of both house land and field land into a single corporate or semicorporate unit. On the contrary, a sharp distinction is drawn between the settlement unit, the *bandjar*, or hamlet, and the agricultural unit, the *subak*, or irrigation society. The organization and regulation of daily social life is severed from the organization and regulation of cultivation; though the hamlet and irrigation society are built on similar principles, they are built separately and function autonomously. We have two sorts of customs, the Balinese say: dry ones for the *bandjar* and wet ones for the *subak*.

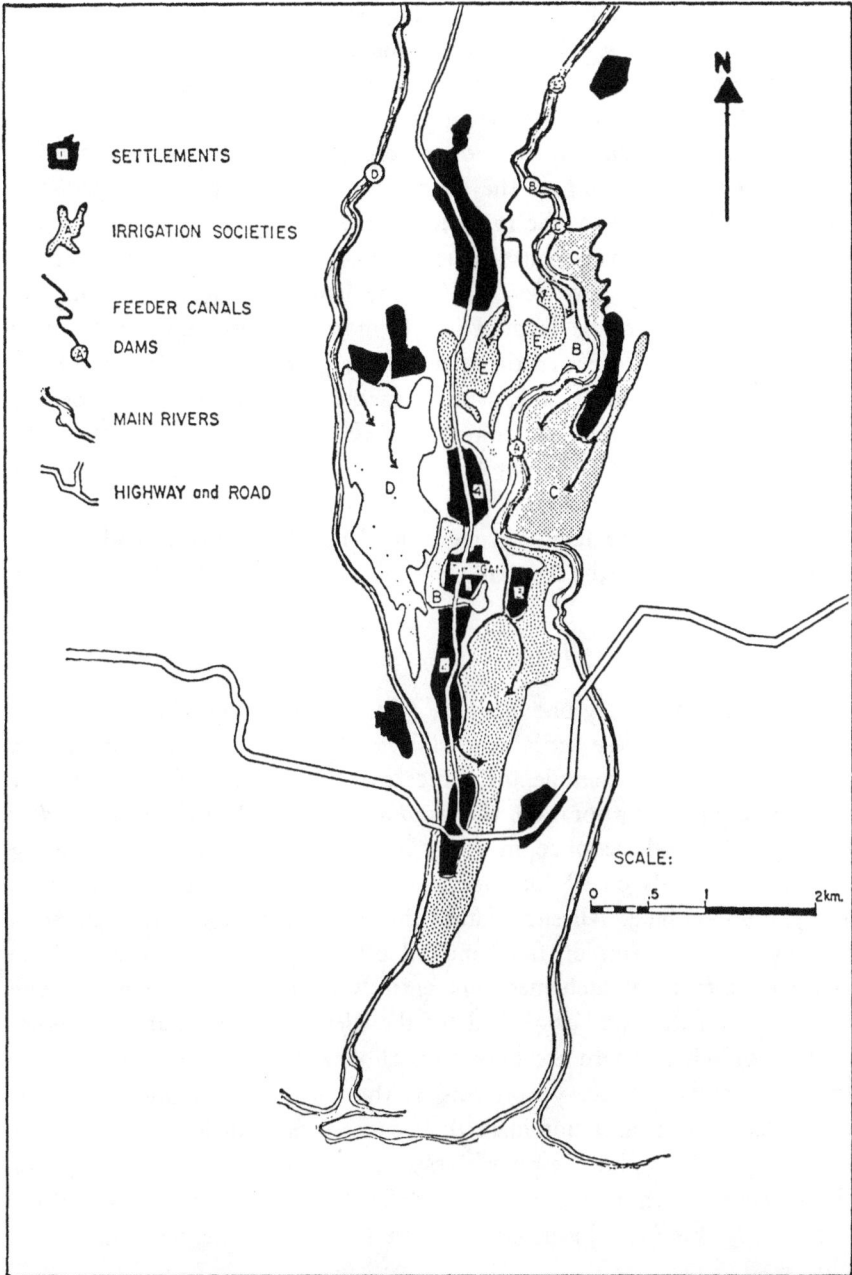

Map X. *Bandjar* and *Subak* in the Tihingan Area (simplified); from Peta Pengairan, Swapradja Klungkung, Djawatan Pengairan, Den Pasar, Bali

This division can be seen in ecological terms if one looks to Map X, which depicts a segment of the Tihingan spur running from about 75 meters above sea level to around 300. The various *subak* line either of the bounding river gorges, growing generally larger in size as one moves down the slope—a simple function of topography. The various *bandjar* are strung up the center of the spur along a dirt, but usually passable, road branching off from the main east–west Dutch-built highway which now connects the main court-center towns. Though there is a natural tendency (but only a tendency) for the land of people living in any particular *bandjar* to be located in the more near-at-hand *subak*, there is no unique or well-defined tie between any given hamlet and any given *subak*. From the hamlet side, land is spread out through a number of different irrigation societies; from the *subak* side, land is owned by members of a number of different hamlets. To get a perspective image of Balinese "village" life one must take, therefore, a stereoscopic view, looking at it on the one hand through the lens of the *subak* and on the other through that of the *bandjar*.

3. The Settlement Unit

In consisting of only one *bandjar*, Tihingan (see Map XI) is somewhat atypical for a Balinese settlement cluster. The cluster to the immediate south consists, for example, of three; that to the immediate north, of four. As a public corporation, the *bandjar* is centered in the *balé bandjar* meeting house where once in every 35-day Balinese month a meeting of the male heads of all the independent families of the hamlet—some 138 people—is held. All such family heads must attend (or, if ill, send a substitute) on pain of fine, and all official policy decisions for the *bandjar* are taken at such meetings, entirely by unanimous decision. The meeting—and the *bandjar*—is led by the *klian bandjar* (literally, hamlet elders), of whom there are here five, chosen also on a consensual basis by the meeting for five-year terms, at the end of which they may not be re-elected but must nominate their successors in order to avoid electioneering. The rights, responsibilities, and limitations of the scope of the meeting's authority are strictly defined in a written "constitution" (*awig-awig bandjar*) inscribed at some forgotten time on palm leaves (*lontar*).

As a social institution, the *bandjar*, or the *bandjar* government, is but one corporate unit among many others in the village, and its powers,

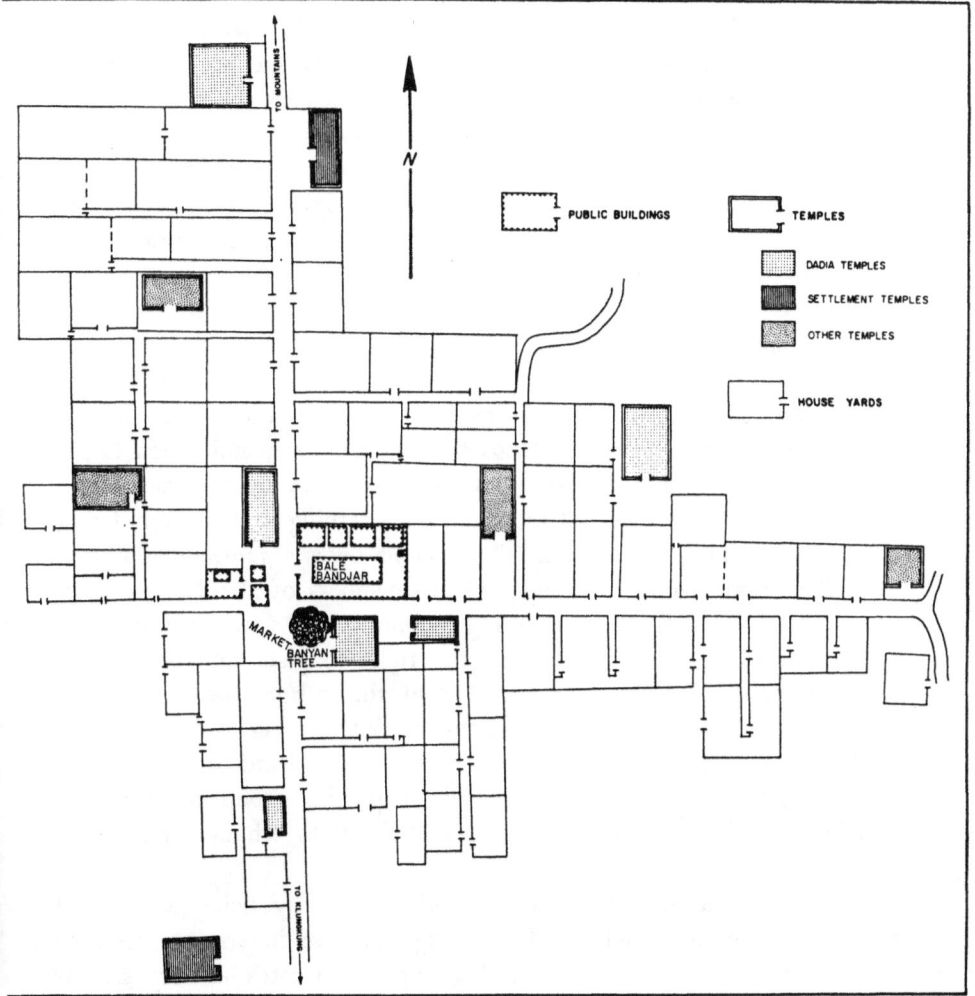

Map XI. Settlement Pattern of Tihingan

though great, are neither unbounded nor all-pervasive. Its major powers focus around collective worship, public works, and civil order. The *bandjar* as a whole is responsible for maintaining and repairing the origin and death temples and for carrying out the elaborate ceremonies which are performed in them every 210 days. The *balé bandjar* must also be kept up by the hamlet, as must various other public facilities: the house in which the statues of the gods are kept, the sheds in the small market place, the graveyard, the roads and paths, and so on. In 1957–58 a school building—located in the next settlement southward—was built by hamlet labor and money in cooperation with several neighboring *bandjar*. The hamlet membership is responsible for night guard and must respond to alarms for fire and theft. If any hamlet member is holding a cremation (an increasingly rare, but still occurring, event), each family unit must give ten days' work toward its preparation to the family involved, and at death itself the hamlet as a body is responsible for making the death litter, digging the grave, and sitting all night with the bereaved.

All land in the *bandjar* belongs to it as a whole, and when house sites or coconut groves fall vacant they are allotted by the meeting to certain families, the rules and regulations concerning such matters being very precise and very complex. The *bandjar* owns a *gamelan* orchestra, as well as some dance costumes, which members of the *bandjar* may use, contributing a fixed share of any income gained from performances to the hamlet treasury. It also has the right to plant and/or harvest, as a group, the fields of any member of the village, the one-twelfth or whatever crop-share payment for this work becoming part of the public fund also. It even owns a one-third interest in a hand cart (the other two-thirds are owned by a private coconut-picking group in the village and by a single rich man), which is rented out to whoever may need it for transporting goods.

All important legal matters are made official by being announced to the assembled household heads: marriage, divorce, inheritance, transfer of property (except rice land), and so forth; and oaths—a very serious matter—are sworn before the same body. It has important sanctions with respect to crimes, ranging from fines all the way up to total exclusion from the hamlet. (A few years ago, in a hamlet a few kilometers from Tihingan, a man was even stoned to death at a *bandjar* meeting for certain improprieties.) And finally, the *bandjar* sponsors dance and drama productions, hiring outside groups from the public treasury, holds cock-fights, and conducts special purification rituals in the case of epidemics, social upheavals, crop failures, or other disasters. All in all, the Tihingan *bandjar*, like most of those of Bali, seems hyperactive. It is always planning something, building something, debating something, performing something.

Actually, this heavy burden of public duty is somewhat lightened so far as the individual family is concerned by dividing the *bandjar* on the one hand into two halves and on the other into three thirds on a simply territorial basis (see Map XII). For very large jobs—for example, repairing the road or building a new wall around a temple—the whole hamlet will be used as a unit in a mass attack on the task. For others—such as preparing offerings for the origin temple—only one "half" will be used, the other "half" being used the next time around. And for smaller, more routine tasks—grave digging, for example—only one of the thirds will be activated, in a similar rotation system. The result is a very complex and shifting pattern of almost continual public activities regulated by the several *klian* under the general policy direction of the meeting. And as these territorial divisions coincide, as we shall see, with no other social grouping in the hamlet, but have been in fact deliberately designed to crosscut them, they act, as does the *bandjar* government in general, as an important integrative mechanism in this otherwise faction-prone village.

Citizenship in the hamlet (or, as the Balinese put it, in the *adat*— roughly, the legal community) always involves an adult man and woman, bound together as an indivisible unit, because there are two kinds of work to be performed: men's and women's. Usually when a young man has been married for about a year he and his wife "go down into the *adat*" (*tedun ke adat*) per decision of the hamlet meeting. At divorce or at the death of one of the pair, those involved will usually leave the *adat* because, now only a half person, so to speak, they are no longer competent to carry out the duties involved. However, several other arrangements are possible for adults who, for one reason or another, lack spouses. Unmarried adult brothers and sisters, a widower and her son (if he is at least adolescent), even two unrelated people living, for some reason, in the same compound, may pair up to enter the *adat*. When a couple's youngest son is married and enters the *adat*, they may, if they wish, leave it—a process called *ngarepan panak*, "pushing one's child forward." But even though this means an escape from a good deal of labor and other obligations, most people are reluctant to take advantage of it; "to leave the *adat* means to lie down and die," and there is therefore

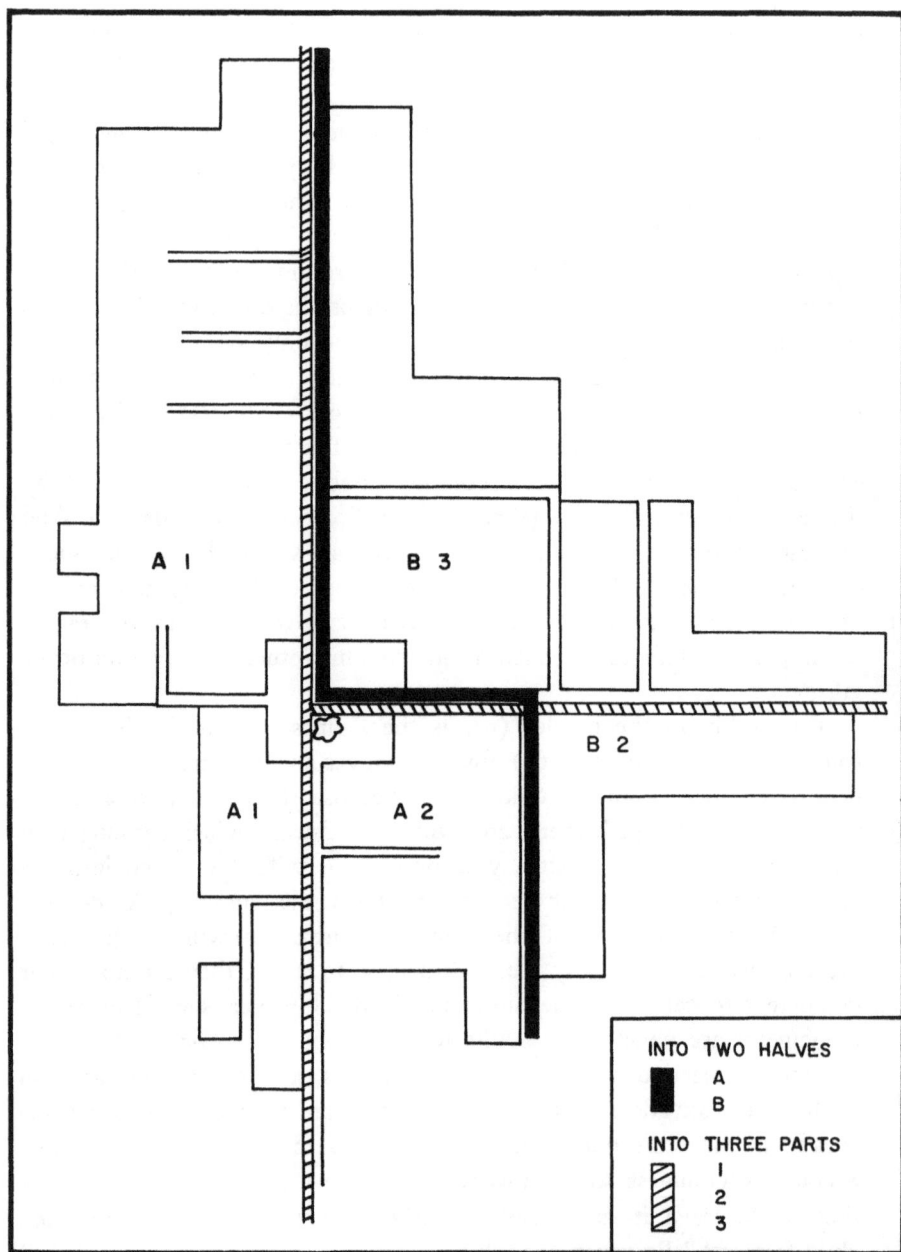

Map XII. Divisions of the *Adat Bandjar*, Tihingan

a tendency to stay in as long as physically possible, even though the work is explicitly not lightened in deference to age or infirmity—a social policy toward senescence upon which a good many of the aged seem, indeed, to thrive. In any case, the parents' remaining in the *adat* does not prevent their married youngest son from entering himself.

Beside the five *klian*, there are a number of other officials chosen by the hamlet (secretaries, messengers, etc.), but the administrative apparatus is in general quite rudimentary and the *klian* follow the public will rather more than, at least as *klian*, they lead it. The actual political process, here a very lively one, revolves more around kin groupings, "caste," class, and, latterly, education and national parties than it does around the formal govermental structure. The hamlet is a legally very carefully defined arena (the "constitution," a sacred as well as a secular object, runs to more than 6,000 precise words), within which the political factions of the hamlet compete rather fiercely for influence, wealth, and, especially, prestige.

Finally, superimposed over the top of this whole, very localized, political system (Tihingan is 70 per cent endogamous, the three neighboring settlements 77, 80, and 95 per cent) is a central government-appointed "village" bureaucracy headed by a salaried official called *perbekel*.[3] His domain (called a *perbekelan*) includes not only Tihingan but the immediately surrounding settlements as well (numbers 2, 3, and 4 on Map X). In each settlement there is a *pengliman* appointed to assist the *perbekel*. (In Tihingan this is at the moment one of the present *klian*, but such a coincidence is not inevitably, not even usually, the case.) The main function of this miniature bureaucracy is to relay information, regulations, exhortations, and commands from the central bureaucracy to the populace—that is, to talk rather more than to listen—and its role in village life remains, as a consequence, rather limited.

4. The Title System and Social Stratification

Aside from their common citizenship in the *adat*, with respect to which they are all, by explicit constitutional provision as well as by

[3] In making comparisons I will, for the sake of simplicity, compare Tihingan, in which the *bandjar* and the settlement happen to be identical, with settlements (i.e., nucleated residential units) rather than neighboring *bandjar*, though the latter sort of comparison would be more proper technically.

deeply rooted moral convention, absolutely equal in legal status, the members of the *bandjar* are discriminated with respect to general social status in terms of two different, completely independent, and unrelated title systems. Where the sense of community generated by the *bandjar* as an overarching political unit suppresses, or at least minimizes, differences in social condition among the members of the hamlet, the title systems provide symbolic mechanisms in terms of which such differences are expressed and underlined.

The first of these is a rigorous system of teknonymy applied both comprehensively and with undeviating regularity to the entire population. A child and a childless man or woman are referred to and (unless close kin) addressed simply by their given name, preceded by a sex and/or a birth-order title. A man with children is universally called "father of" (*pan*) his eldest child; a woman "mother of" (*men*) the same child. When the man or woman has a grandchild they then shift to being addressed as "grandfather of" (*kaki*) or "grandmother of" (*tjutjun*) the new baby; similarly, on the great-grandparental level (*kumpi*, both sexes).

Details of this somewhat complicated practice aside, such a uniformly applied teknonymous system has at least two important implications so far as the symbolic classification of individuals in the hamlet is concerned.[4] First, it isolates a husband-wife pair terminologically (for they are referred to as "father of" and "mother of" the same child), thus emphasizing once again the fact that the couple is an indivisible unit for most social purposes, not only with respect to hamlet citizenship but also temple allegiance, kin-group affiliation, voluntary society membership, and so on. Second, and perhaps even more crucially, it introduces an implicit (but noncorporate) age-class system into village society. It is the group of "fathers of" that is looked upon as the leading group in the society; the "grandfathers of" are respected elders and advisers counseling wisely behind the scenes; the "great-grandfathers of" are senile dependents; those without teknonyms are juvenile dependents. (A man, or woman, who never has a child remains terminologically all his life himself a child, and the shame of this is often deeply felt, so that the teknonymy system also stresses the Balinese high valuation of fertility.) A very great part of the everyday life of the community, is patterned in terms of this age-set type of distinction, and "father of," "grandfather of," etc.,

[4] A full description and analysis of this system will be presented in a forthcoming monograph, *The Balinese Kinship System*, by my wife and myself.

are quite definite, if only implicitly defined, social roles. Tihingan is a rigorously age-graded society.

The second type of title system in terms of which individuals are status ranked in Tihingan is what has usually been called "caste" in the literature on Bali. As the system was borrowed, at least indirectly, from India, as many of the terms and practices connected with it are generally reminiscent of those of India, and as the Balinese themselves consider that they have, being "Hindus," a caste (*wangsa*, literally, people, nation, kind) system, such usage is reasonable enough as a first approximation. But in sociological terms, the difference between the ways in which the Indian and Balinese systems are organized and function are so great that one might question the appropriateness of the term altogether. The several *wangsa* are not occupational groups, do not form corporate wholes crosscutting village lines, are not linked with one another through traditional patron-dependent service relationships, and do not provide the basic structural setting for all aspects of ordinary interpersonal behavior. Balinese "caste," if that is what it is, is not the master institution of Tihingan society but just one more among the bewildering variety of overlapping social forms that compete for the allegiance of the average citizen.

In Tihingan, every person has a title indicating his *wangsa* that he inherits from his father. There are two main sorts of such titles: *triwangsa* and *djaba*. *Triwangsa* ("three peoples") titles are those whose bearers are considered to belong to one of the three twice-born varna of traditional Hindu theory: Brahmana, Satria, Vesia. The *djaba* ones are those whose bearers are considered to belong to the fourth varna, the Sudra. (*Djaba* literally means "outside," but this has nothing to do with the notion of "outcastes," of which there are none in Bali.) For the island as a whole, it has been estimated that about a tenth of the population is *triwangsa*, the rest *djaba;* but a true census either of titles or the numbers of people bearing each of them has never been made. In Tihingan three different *triwangsa* titles are represented, accounting for 13 per cent of the households, and nine different *djaba* titles, accounting for 87 per cent. (See Table 13, in which are shown, for comparison, the title compositions of settlements 2, 3, and 4—in which, it so happens, there are no *triwangsa*—on Map X as well.)

This *wangsa* title system is to a rather surprising extent a pure prestige system—that is, it functions mainly to establish a hereditarily ascribed public status to individuals independent of political, economic, or moral considerations. It is, of course, not unrelated to such matters. A *triwangsa* title was (and to a large extent still is) a prerequisite to political office at the supra-village level. Only men with Brahmana titles can become high priests (*pedanda*). And there is a general notion that the present differences in rank among the three *wangsa* are owing to a lowering

Table 13. Title-group composition of Tihingan and three neighboring settlements.

Tihingan		Settlement 2		Settlement 3		Settlement 4	
Name	Per cent of families	Name	Per cent of families	Name	Per cent of families	Name	Per cent of families
SUDRA		SUDRA		SUDRA		SUDRA	
Pandé Tosan	32	Pasek Gèlgèl	24	Maspadan	51	Pasek Gèlgèl	39
Kebun Tubuh	19	Dukuh	9	Pulasari	16	Pemedilan	17
Pasek Kaju-		Tangkaban	9	Pandé Tosan	14	Badeg	13
selem	17	Kebun Tubuh	8	Daoh	9	Kebun	
Pulasari	10	Pandé Bedaga	8	Kedisan	8	Tubuh	10
Pasek Gadoh	4	Manikan	7	Sawan	2	Selain	7
Pasek Gèlgèl	2	Kedisan	7			Pring	6
Bagus*	1.5	nameless**	7			Madang	2.5
Pertéka	1.5	Pasek Bendesa	3			Bendul	2.5
Tianjar	1	Bali Mula	3			Bendesa	1.5
		Daoh	3			Dankang	.75
TRIWANGSA		Pandé Tosan	3			Bonden	.75
Sang	5	nameless**	2.5				
Brahmana	4	Sangging	2				
Gusti	4	Tegeh	2				
		Pulasari	2				
		nameless**	2				
		Pring	.5				
		Tangkas	.5				

  * Strictly, Bagus is a *triwangsa* title, but this group of them was lowered to Sudra status during the Japanese occupation because of a sexual scandal; those unwilling to accept the *bandjar*'s decision migrated elsewhere.
  ** These groups have forgotten their name, but not that they have one.

of the *djaba* groups from a previously high position as a result of some misdeeds by their mythological ancestors, which diminished the moral stature of their whole line. But the corollaries do not hold. The overwhelming bulk of the *triwangsa*, both now and in the past, do not have any supra-village political importance at all and are indistinguishable from, sometimes even subservient to, their *djaba* neighbors. The impoverished head of one of the village's higher *triwangsa* families served as a man of all work for my fairly well-off *djaba* landlord. Similarly, only a small proportion of the Brahmana become priests, and most live a relatively ordinary life as peasants or artisans, some being considered quite unspiritual types indeed. And as for moral character, the area's most notorious gambler and general ne'er-do-well (a member of a nearby *bandjar*) was the possessor of a very high Satria title. Though the prestige system which the institution of *wangsa* titles supports interacts with the political, economic, religious, and, as we shall see, especially the kinship systems of Tihingan, it is in no way a simple reflex of them but rather, in this most status conscious of societies, a powerful autonomous force.

The main content of this prestige system is, naturally, symbolic deference. People with lower titles speak in a more polite form of language (*alus*) to ones of higher and are spoken to in a less polite form (*kasar*). People with lower titles always sit lower than people with higher ones, follow them through passageways, speak after them at public gatherings, smother them in decorous gestures, and so on. Indic notions of pollution, much attenuated and redefined, are also involved: the period of ritual uncleanness following death, both for the survivor's family in particular and the hamlet in general, shortens with rank; lower people can accept food from higher but not vice versa; lower people must be very circumspect about touching higher ones. And there is a tremendous elaboration of sumptuary rules: certain people may have certain sorts of pavilions in their compounds, altars in their temples, or fences around their graves, others not; higher people may have higher cremation towers than lower people; a great many ritual details differ with rank. And all these matters are, again, totally independent of any considerations other than inherited title. The ne'er-do-well gambler was addressed in the appropriately elevated language of respect, though opinions of him were a good deal less than elevated. My *djaba* landlord treated his menial with the deference proper to the latter's rank and was treated with due familiarity in return, so that to watch them you might well confuse employer with employee. The title system establishes an authoritative allocation of cultural prestige that is acknowledged and maintained in terms of the symbols of propriety and politesse, no matter how well or poorly it happens to fit with the realities of power, wealth, or character.

But perhaps the major expression of the Balinese title system appears in marriage. *Djaba* title groups are preferentially endogamous, *triwangsa* ones prescriptively so, with the exception that under a rule of hypergamy a man may marry a woman of lower rank than himself. In Tihingan, with one scandalous exception in which a Brahmana woman married a *djaba* man and was instantly expelled from her group, all *triwangsa* marriages for the past four generations have been either title-group endogamous (70 per cent) or hypergamous. *Djaba* marriages have been only 49 per cent title-group endogamous (the question of hypergamy is, as we shall see in a moment, rather more complicated among *djaba*); but this figure is somewhat misleading because it is lowered by the fact that very small *djaba* groups have difficulty maintaining exact endogamy, given the concurrent strong, even overriding, preference for hamlet endogamy. Eliminating such small groups, *djaba* title endogamy climbs to nearly 70 per cent. The same effect does not occur for *triwangsa* title groups, because, unlike the *djaba*, they do not emphasize hamlet endogamy over title group but rather title group over hamlet, and so they tend to marry outside the hamlet but within their own group. Tihingan *djaba* were 75 per cent hamlet endogamous, *triwangsa* 32 per cent.

All this is not merely a matter of ethnographic detail, for it reveals one of the major structural tensions in the village. The *triwangsa* regard themselves—or would like to—as, in a quite literal sense, above the hamlet. They wish to form alliances across its boundaries and so lift themselves up as a regional elite, operating in a social, cultural, and political sphere outside the hamlet's purview entirely. *Djaba* regard themselves—or claim to—as first and foremost hamlet citizens, and they resist all efforts of the *triwangsa* to extricate themselves from the local context. In Tihingan, where the *djaba* are so strong and the *triwangsa* so generally unimpressive, being genealogically rather distant from the main ruling lines, the victory tends usually to go to the hamlet, in that the constantly pressed claims of *triwangsa* people for escape from certain public responsibilities, particularly in the ritual field, are effectively rejected. But in other hamlets with other title-group compositions, the reverse could be found; and even in Tihingan, the populace has not yet been able to force the Brahmana family to participate in the rituals at the death temple, and some minor political concessions to *triwangsa* status have been made. The differing view of the privileges of title is thus one of the animating forces of village politics, though rather less prominently here than in many other *bandjar* where the power of the antagonists in this "caste war" is more evenly balanced.

In Tihingan, status rivalry takes on its sharpest form among the different *djaba* groups rather than between them and the *triwangsa*. Though the Pandé and Pasek groups have a certain cultural claim to higher status than the others, in general no group will openly grant superiority to any other and in fact will privately regard itself as "really higher." Thus, whenever a title-group exogamous marriage takes place, the group from which the woman comes must at least profess to regard it as a mis-caste alliance, for to do otherwise would be to admit officially to a lower status under the hypergamy rule.[5] As a result, almost all title-group exogamous marriages are, in form at any rate, marriage by capture, in which the group from which the woman is ostensibly "stolen" (more frequently she has, in fact, eloped) puts up a great show of outrage, the hamlet is alarmed, and a search organized. With smaller groups the outrage tends to be *pro forma* only, and even with the larger ones the excitement usually soon dies down and the marriage is accepted as a simple fact of life by the woman's group, at least so long as a general balance of exogamous marriages between the groups involved is maintained so that there is no net loss of women from one to the other over time. When hamlet exogamous marriages occur in which a local woman is "stolen," the whole hamlet may rise in anger, and such cases sometimes come very close to mass violence. Usually such marriages, too, are accepted after a time, however.

5. Kinship System

All this status rivalry is further reinforced by the way in which the Balinese kinship system plays into the title-group system. The Balinese are patrilineal and virilocal (kin terminology is, however, purely generational), and the basic residence unit is either some form of patrilineal extended (or joint) family or nuclear family with various dependent adult relatives attached.[6] In addition to these domestic units, however, there are

---

[5] Actually, marriage in Tihingan is not only preferentially within title group but, even more preferentially, with a patri-parallel cousin (FaBroDa, FaFaBroSoDa, etc.). Only about 15 per cent of the marriages were of this sort, however.

[6] In Tihingan, about 60 per cent of the residence compounds, or house yards, contain more than one nuclear family (and 15 per cent more than two), the male heads of such component families being agnates—Fa and So, Bro and Bro, FaBro–BroSo, FaBroSo–FaBroSo, etc. In Tihingan, no compound contains four families, but in other hamlets compounds with up to six families are frequently encountered, and a few very large compounds of more than ten families exist.

also large patrilineal descent groups, called *dadia*. In Tihingan there are four such *dadia*, though in other hamlets there may be anywhere from zero up to eight or ten of them. The formation, composition, and precise structure of these groups cannot be described in any detail here, but the sociologically most relevant features of them may be mentioned. First, they are highly corporate and multifunctional, engaging in important religious, political, and economic activities. Second, they are completely localized, not extending, as do title groups, across hamlet boundaries. Third, not everyone in Tihingan belongs to such a group, but only about three-quarters of the population, the other quarter belonging to no kinship group larger than an extended family. Fourth, though formed on a kinship basis, they tend to absorb into themselves any other local family with the same title, even if it is unrelated to the agnatic core. And fifth, they are, of course, also endogamous and in fact to a greater degree than title groups that are not *dadia*.[7] It is around the *dadia*, then, that the main struggle for status in *Tihingan* revolves.[8]

Each of these *dadia* is the proud possessor of a large temple somewhere in the hamlet (see Map XI). At this temple the members of the group hold the usual ceremonies every 210 days, at which they propitiate their ancestors, and each group vies jealously with the others with respect to the elaborateness of its ceremonies and the fineness of its temple. In fact, the existence of such a temple is the critical index of the existence of such a *dadia*. It is the transfer of a house-yard shrine of an agnatic line from what is considered to be the original compound of that line to a compound of its own, comparable to that of the hamlet temples, that signifies that the group is no longer merely a domestic entity but a civic one, an institutionalized faction within the framework of the *bandjar*, the superordinate political unit. Moving the temple out of a house yard onto a separate compound (which must, of course, be granted it by the hamlet as a whole) heralds the movement of an agnatic line out of the private world of family life into the public world of community life, a distinction that in Tihingan is, in fact, a very sharply drawn one.

[7] The methodological questions involved in the assessment of "degree of endogamy" are both statistically and conceptually complex and will be discussed in full in the aforementioned monograph on Balinese kinship.

[8] The strength and importance of these corporate descent groups varies greatly from *bandjar* to *bandjar* and is rather greater than average in Tihingan. In settlement 2, for example, there are only three such groups, to which only 41 per cent of the population belongs, the other 59 per cent being "unattached."

The political significance of the four *dadia* is clear from the fact that the five *klian* as well as the *perbekel* and *pengliman* are all members of them. The *perbekel* is from the most powerful group (the Pandé), the *pengliman*—who is also one of the *klian*—from the second most powerful (the Pasek Kajuselem). The other four *klian* are drawn one from each group (Pandé, Pasek Kajuselem, Kebun Tubuh, and Pulasari), so that the composition of formal hamlet leadership reflects exactly the relative political strengths of the four *dadia*. Also, there are—or were in 1958—two national political parties in the hamlet: the Socialists (Partai Sosialis Indonesia) and the Nationalists (Partai Nasional Indonesia). All members of the Pandé and Pasek Kajuselem *dadia* belonged to the Socialist party; all the members of the Kebun Tubuh and Pulasari plus all the unaffiliated people (including the *triwangsa*) belonged to the Nationalist. The actual local political process is most complex and variable, and only an extended analysis of cases could reveal its basic dynamics. But that hamlet politics in Tihingan are to a significant (but *not* exclusive) extent descent-group politics is apparent.

Finally, the four *dadia* form the framework within which work is organized in the hamlet's artisan specialization: the manufacture of *gamelan* orchestral instruments. Tihingan is the only hamlet in Bali that still produces such instruments (though far from the only hamlet that is highly craft specialized), and as the instruments are brass metallophones, gongs, cymbals, and the like the craft involved is a smithing one. The title Pandé literally means "smith," and it is possible that in the past the making of *gamelan* was a "caste" monopoly of this group. But today, and for as long as anyone can remember, people from every *djaba* title group in Tihingan participate in their manufacture. Individuals who do not belong to the four *dadia* are fairly well restricted to small-scale repair work, or occasional hire work for larger groups, but the *dadia* are organized for the production of new orchestras. Within one *dadia* there are several forges, located within one or another of the compounds occupied by members of the group and worked by subgroups whose composition is determined genealogically and residentially. For the really major effort, the forging of the larger gongs, however, the men of the entire *dadia* cooperate in order to provide a labor force large enough for this very arduous job. Each *dadia* has traditional relationships with the hamlets for whom it provides *gamelan* sets, has its own techniques and modes of tuning, and competes with the others with respect to the fineness of its work. The pounding of a rival's hammers is one of the most galling sounds to a

Tihingan smith, driving him to work the harder to maintain his descent group's reputation. And as such pounding can be heard almost every day, this is a very industrious and, in the aggregate, wealthy hamlet.

6. *Associational Groups*

Not all sociologically significant alliances in Tihingan hamlet are formed in terms of ascriptive ties of residence, age, title, or descent; some are optional. The main structural settings for such "free" alliances are the associational groups called *seka*, literally "to be as one." Though the term may be applied to any group (for example, the group making up a *dadia* is sometimes called a *seka dadia*), strictly speaking a *seka* is a voluntary group, a sodality, organized for some particular purpose. It may be temporary or it may last for years, even generations; it may be *ad hoc*, or it may move from one task to the next; it may be very large, or it may contain only a half-dozen people. But it is never fully coordinate with any other principle of affiliation in the society—it deliberately crosscuts them so as to bring individuals of different groups together on the basis of a sentiment of personal friendship and common need alone.

There are a number of such *seka* in Tihingan. For example, there is a *seka gong*—that is, a group which, using the hamlet *gamelan* (*gong*), hires out to play and dance at fetes of various sorts. It includes 25 *gamelan* players from virtually all the various title groups, *dadia*, and sections of the hamlet, three female *legong* dancers, one male *kebiar* dancer, and ten or so "extras" who carry the instruments and fill in when someone is absent. The money received for playing should go half to the *bandjar* and half to the *seka* on a "share-cropping" arrangement, but, as the members of the *seka* are also mostly smiths, they have been able to repair and improve the *gamelan* so that the hamlet has agreed to take only one-fifth the proceeds. Within the hamlet the *seka* performs for 12.50 *rupiah* (i.e., for individuals; for the *bandjar* as a corporation it plays free), a nominal sum, though the hirer has to pay 15 *rupiah* to the hamlet for the rent of the dancers' costumes if he wants them too. Outside the hamlet it plays for as much as it can bargain for and at one glorious point received 250 *rupiah* for an hour's work at the Klungkung court. The money received has been used to buy uniform clothes for the players, spent for a large pig feast at Galunggan, the major calendrical holiday, and on occasion has been divided equally among the members.

As a matter of fact, this *seka* has now dissolved, in part as a result of the adolescent dancers growing up and new ones not being trained and of personal quarrels among the members. But people feel that it, or one like it, will relatively soon re-form.

Another important *seka* in the hamlet is the *seka buruh*, "the workers' *seka*." This *seka* organized originally during the Japanese period, consists of twenty men, again fairly randomly distributed so far as other social identifications are concerned (except that none of them is *triwangsa*). Its main job is to harvest the coconut trees belonging to the hamlet for one-half the proceeds. It also owns, as mentioned earlier, a third share in a hand cart, which it either rents out or uses to transport items on contract. It will, in fact, for a fee, take on virtually any labor task from housebuilding to field harvesting. Proceeds are again used for a Galunggan feast or divided evenly among the members.

There are a number of other *seka:* for making thatch roofing, for various sorts of agricultural work, for brick manufacture, and other purposes. There is a *seka* formed of the young men of the village that is more designed to inculcate a sense of public responsibility in them by putting them to work repairing the roadway than anything else. There are, or have been, various *seka* to teach children dancing and *gamelan* playing, to sponsor cockfights, to buy and manage rice land collectively, and to maintain special temples of one sort or another. The voluntary association is not just a peripheral or residual element in Tihingan village life but, like all the other angulate pieces of this intricate social jigsaw, an essential one.

7. The Agricultural Unit

Each major drainage of Bali—running again lengthwise from the mountains toward the sea—is considered by the population to be a single self-contained ecological unit. This unit, a long, narrow strip centered around a larger river, is called a *sedahan*, after a traditional tax collection official now transformed into a government functionary, and over all such units in the general region where once a local court held sway and today a regency (*swapradja*) government does, there is a *sedahan agung* (great *sedahan*), a chief tax collector. Each *sedahan* is broken down into a large number of *subak*, and these are the fundamental elements of the whole system. The term *subak* is commonly translated as "irrigation society," because of the central role this institution plays in the regulation of water supply. But the *subak* is in fact very much more: an agricultural planning unit, an autonomous legal corporation, and a religious community. Aside from house gardening, virtually everything having to do with cultivation lies within its purview. Effective power with respect to agricultural matters lies and seems always to have lain in the *subak;* it is thus not a mere appendage of the larger order units, which as political entities are hardly more than tax districts. Theories of "hydraulic despotism" to the contrary notwithstanding, water control in Bali is an overwhelmingly local and intensely democratic matter.

A *subak* is defined as all the rice terraces irrigated from a single dam (*empelan*) and major canal (*telabah gde*). All individuals owning such land (with some minor exceptions, it is all in freehold tenure) are citizens of the *subak*, or *krama subak*, just as all those living on the land of a *bandjar* are its citizens, or *krama bandjar*. As there are *klian bandjar*, so there are *klian subak;* as there are *bandjar* meetings, so there are *subak* meetings; and as there is a *bandjar* legal code, or constitution, so also there is a *subak* one. Public obligations enforceable by fines, regulations concerning land use, legal transactions having to do with land transfer, collective ritual for group ends (such as fertility)—all these fall within the domain of the *subak* government as their counterparts fall within the domain of the *bandjar* government.

The ecological and engineering details of the *subak* irrigation system are far too complex to be described in any fullness here. The main feature is the one-dam–one-*subak* relationship. As can be seen from Map X, the dams are arranged one below the other down the river canyons, a single canal, usually of some length, carrying the diverted water to the *subak*, often with the aid of overhead aquaducts or long tunnels. After the water arrives at the *subak* it is successively partitioned by an extended series of carefully graduated bamboo water dividers distributed over the whole area in such a way that what was a single broad incoming artery veins out into dozens—in larger *subak*, even hundreds—of small rivulets directly feeding one terrace or a small group of them. This final unit of water, *and* the amount of land it irrigates, *and* the amount of rice seedlings needed to plant that land, *and* the amount of (unthreshed) paddy harvested from it are known as one *tenah*. Thus, the sum total of *tenah* in a *subak* adds up to its total water supply, to its total area, to its total rice-seed demands, and to its total rice production—depending upon whether you interpret the *tenah* in its water, areal, seedling, or rice-harvest meaning. For any one *subak* the number of *tenah* is fixed by the concrete pattern of successive water division whose form is determined by the *subak* as a corporate group (for the most part relatively few changes in the established pattern are introduced, however), but between various *subak* it will of course, differ. *Subak* B in Map X contains 160 *tenah*, making a single one about .45 hectare in areal terms; *subak* A has 530, making a single one about .30 hectare areally. Also, as the total water supply varies from *subak* to *subak* according to ecological factors (in general, higher ones tend to be better off), the size of a *tenah* in water also varies. The number of cubic feet per year in a *tenah* may—and commonly will—differ between two *subak* even if their number of *tenah* is the same.[9] The *tenah* is fundamentally a water unit, sliced out of the entire water supply available from the *subak*'s main dam and canal by a fixed pattern of successive divisions of flow, and thus varies as that supply and that pattern varies. It is a maddeningly irregular system for one who wants to make any sort of analysis, but a remarkably ingenious, just, and effective one so far as the peasants are concerned.

The *tenah* becomes, then, the basic unit for *subak* taxation (labor or monetary), agricultural planning, and land transfer. Though quite aware that metric units are more comparable between *subak* than *tenah* ones, the peasant nonetheless thinks of his land holdings entirely in *tenah* terms. Inheritance divisions and tenancy grants are expressed in *tenah*, agricultural wealth is calculated in terms of *tenah* (though, naturally, with rule of thumb adjustments with respect to their location, etc.), one's rights and obligations within the *subak* are expressed in *tenah*. The one exception is in voting. In determination of *subak* policy and election of *subak* leaders, each owner is legally entitled to a single vote no matter how many *tenah* he holds. In fact, of course, large holders tend to carry rather more weight for the usual economic and social class reasons. In the majority of cases, however, what is remarkable is not how much wealth differences account for but how little. If anything, the *subak* organization as such tends to act against the interests of the well-off rather than in their favor; to counter the political forces, real enough

[9] Owing to intra*subak* ecological differences, custom based on assumed precedence in clearing, and other factors, the areal extent of a *tenah* may vary slightly within a single *subak* also. And as field fertility naturally varies somewhat, a *tenah* as a volume of rice also, of course, varies—but generally not too widely.

in themselves, stemming from economic inequality. Like the *bandjar,* the *subak* is deliberately blind to any other basis of social status but membership in itself, and like the *bandjar* it is ultimately sovereign.

As mentioned, the *subak* head, elected by all the members of the *subak,* is called, at least in Tihingan, the *klian subak.* Under him are a series of (also elected) *klian tempek.* A *tempek* is a territorial (that is, water) subdivision of the *subak* but is in no way independent of the whole; its role is merely administrative. In *subak* A there are four such *tempek;* in *subak* B, seven. Below the *klian tempek,* and under their direction, are a large number of men called *pekaseh,* a term that in some parts of Bali is synonymous with *klian subak* but in Klungkung denotes a member of the "water group," the *seka jeh.* In *subak* A, 160 of the 455 members are *pekaseh;* in *subak* B, 60 of 222. It is this group that, as its name implies, performs the actual tasks of water regulation and irrigation system upkeep.

These tasks range from the constant clearing of the small field canals and minor repairs on the water dividers, and the daily, even hourly, shifting of channels of flow that is necessary to make the whole system work, to the guarding of the fields at harvest to prevent theft. The members of the *subak* as a whole are taxed, according to number of *tenah* owned, for these services, the rate differing from *subak* to *subak* but being, in any case, far from nominal. (In *subak* A, for example, it is 30 *rupiah* a season, in *subak* B, 20 *rupiah.*) The proceeds from this "water tax" (*pengot*) are first applied to general *subak* needs, and then any remainder is divided among the *pekaseh,* who are, in any case, excused from one *tenah*'s worth of tax. For performance of the unending everyday tasks, the *pekaseh* usually serve a daily "watch" in pairs. Thus, in a *tempek* in *subak* A, for example, where there are twenty-four *pekaseh,* each *pekaseh* is "on duty" with a fixed partner one day in every twelve. Once every two weeks or so the entire twenty-four are mobilized for some piece of heavier work, and for even larger tasks—such as the clearing of the main canal or repairs on the main dam—all the *pekaseh* of the whole *subak* may be mobilized. Finally, if the task involved is very heavy, the whole *subak* membership may be called upon, but this is quite rare. The role of the *pekaseh* is so great that people often refer to them as the "*subak* members" without qualification, although everyone is aware that legally this is not the case and in important policy decisions (e.g., adding new terraces to the *subak*) all owners, *pekaseh* or not, have a right to participate and usually do so.

There are a number of other important aspects of *subak* organization, but they can only be mentioned here in passing. On the one hand, there is the obvious problem of inter*subak* coordination. By and large this is accomplished through a process of collective bargaining among the various *subak* themselves, under the governance of an explicit code of customary law (*adat*) to which all in one drainage adhere, and not by any administrative dictation from above. Rules for the amount of water that must be allowed at all times to bypass any dam, patterns for the borrowing and lending of water rights, and ritual systems regulating the order of planting (higher *subak* plant earlier than lower ones so as to stagger peak water requirements over time) are all firmly established and strictly observed. On the other hand, there is a complex intra*subak* ritual pattern centering around two sorts of temples, one (*pura mastjeti*) set in the midst of the field and dedicated to the goddess of fertility and one (*pura ulun suwi*) set near the main dam and dedicated to the god of water. In addition there are the usual Malaysian rice-mother rites carried out by individual farmers, seasonal-round ceremonies for each stage of (rice) cultivation usually carried out by all the *pekaseh* as a group for the whole *subak*, and occasional mass processionals down to the sea by the entire membership to cure a crop epidemic or relieve a mice plague, for example. This developed ritual pattern, matching with fine precision the actual flow of agricultural activity, is one of the major regulating mechanisms in the whole, marvelously intricate ecological system the *subak* represents.

The extent of the intricacy is perhaps most clearly dramatized by the so-called *masa* (roughly, month, time) system of planting in effect in the various *subak* around Tihingan. There are four such *masa*—the "eighth," "sixth," "fourth," and "second," named after the Balinese months (how *those* are determined we had perhaps best ignore here)—in which rice is planted in each system. Table 14 compares the four systems (in a very oversimplified form). Now, within any one *subak* some *tempek* will, per *subak* decision, follow the "eighth" system, some the "sixth," some the "fourth," and the others the "second," though all of these may not be in force at once. The point of this arrangement is, again, to stagger the peak water demands, this time within one *subak* rather than among a set of them. In *subak* A, for example, there are seven *tempek*, one of them on the "second" system, two on the "eighth," and three on the "sixth"; the seventh *tempek* alternates from year to year, as a sort of wild card, among the "sixth," "second," and "eighth" systems, depend-

Table 14. The *masa* system

Masa system	Month											
	1	2	3	4	5	6	7	8	9	10	11	12
"Second"	plant rice						harvest rice	plant dry crops				harvest dry crops
"Fourth"		harvest dry crops		plant rice					harvest rice	plant dry crops		
"Sixth"				harvest dry crops		plant rice					harvest rice	plant dry crops
"Eighth"	harvest rice	plant dry crops				harvest dry crops		plant rice				

ing on what the water situation happens that year to be. *Subak* B, on
the other hand, is divided right in half, two of its four *tempek* being
on the "fourth" system and the other two on the "eighth." The details
of all this—how it is determined who will follow which system, the means
of enforcement, comparative advantages of the various systems from the
ecological point of view, and the ways in which compensations are made—
need not be pursued here. But it should be clear that the control of
cultivation around Tihingan is fairly exact. In fact, as—somewhat in
contrast to most parts of Bali—the *subak* as a whole often decides even
which dry crops are to be planted at which times, the control is exact
indeed. To call the *subak* merely an irrigation society is thus to underesti-
mate its scope rather seriously.

Turning to the social composition of the various *subak* around
Tihingan, the first point that has to be re-emphasized is the lack of
any straightforward correlation between the place of a person's residence
and the location of his rice fields. Of course, most of his fields will
be somewhere reasonably nearby, but they will not as a rule be confined
to one, or often even two, *subak*. Thus residents of the *bandjar* of
Tihingan own land in significant amounts in five different *subak* lying
both to the north and the south of them, as well as having scattered
holdings in several others more distant. "Large" landowners (i.e., those
with between 1.5 and 3.5 hectares) all have land in more than one *subak*,
and most have some in three or four. *Subak* A (see Map X), in which
more Tihingan land is located than any other, only contains 47 per cent
of the total land owned by residents of the *bandjar*. And, to put the
matter the other way around, this land accounts for only 5 per cent
of the total land in that *subak*. Altogether, no less than thirty-eight
bandjar are represented in the membership of this *subak*, and the *bandjar*
with the largest amount of land in it owns only about a quarter of its
total. This dispersive pattern is summed up in Tables 15 and 16, in which
the scatter of holdings is depicted from both the *bandjar* and *subak*
perspectives.[10]

As Tihingan is basically an artisan *bandjar*, its relations with the
realm of the *subak* are actually somewhat anomalous. In the first place,
the proportion of its members holding wet rice land is comparatively
low: of the total 138 family heads, only 46 or 30 per cent own rice land,
as compared to 47 per cent, 67 per cent, and 72 per cent in settlements

[10] Were the percentages to be adjusted to *bandjar* population on the one
hand and *subak* areas on the other, the picture would be even more striking.

2, 3, and 4 respectively. In per capita terms, this works out to .19 hectare in Tihingan, against .24, .32, and .53 hectare for the neighboring settlements; so that, in gross terms, Tihingan is not in any sense a land-rich village. So far as rice land *per owner* is concerned, however, Tihingan is around, or even slightly above, the local average: .61 hectare against .50, .59, and .73—a fact that indicates, of course, that in Tihingan one tends either to have a significant amount of land (though the term "significant" is a most relative one: even the largest holder has only 3.3 hectares) or to have none whatsoever, in contrast to the more graded

Table 15. Location of land owned by members of Tihingan *bandjar*

Subak	Per cent of land
A	47
B	21
C	7
D	13
E	10
other	2

Table 16. Distribution of land ownership in *subak* A

Bandjar	Per cent of *subak* A land
Most-represented	24
Tihingan	5
36 other	71

distributional patterns characteristic of the other settlements. And finally, those Tihingan people who do own land—mostly the more accomplished smiths—tend not to work it themselves but to give it out in various sorts of tenancy arrangements, mostly to members of surrounding *bandjar*. In Table 17, which compares the per cent of *bandjar* owned land worked by members of the *bandjar* as against the per cent worked by nonmembers, Tihingan's role as a "landlord village" is quite apparent.

The tenancy patterns through which the relations between landholder and tenant (*sakap*) are actualized (wage labor in agriculture is very rare around Tihingan) are, again, complex in the extreme. There are four main sharecrop systems found in Bali: *nandu*, under which the tenant receives half the crop; *nelon*, under which he receives two-fifths; *ngapit*, under which he receives one-third; and *merapat*, under which he receives one-quarter. In the Klungkung region the *ngapit*, or one-third, system is standard; but, as Balinese only maintain standards so as to be able to vary them, the actual arrangements differ almost from case to case. Social relations between the contracting parties, location and quality of the land, type of crop involved, current economic conditions, source of such capital as seeds and cattle, and sheer love of complication combine to produce a range of tenancy institutions whose adaptability to particular circumstances is endless.

Aside from the basic two-to-one crop-sharing pattern, three other institutions regulating access to land ought to be briefly mentioned. The first is the pawning or *gadé* system. Under this practice the owner of

Table 17. Owner-tenant percentages

	Per cent of owner-worked land	Per cent of tenant-worked land inside *bandjar*	outside *bandjar*
Tihingan	11	36	53
Settlement 2	73	26	1
Settlement 3	57	36	7
Settlement 4	63	27	10

a piece of land surrenders it to another man for a cash sum, but the title is not transferred. Instead, the pawn taker works the land until the owner is able to repay the loan, at which time the land returns to the control of its proper owner. The amount of the repayment is the same as that of the original loan; the lender's interest is considered to consist of the returns from the land while he has it in his possession. In many cases (about 80 per cent of those in Tihingan and the three surrounding settlements), the owner will only consent to pawn his land with the express understanding that he will be employed as a *sakap* sharecrop tenant on that land for the duration of the pawn, in which case the amount of cash involved is much smaller. Again, as a relatively well-to-do *bandjar*—or, rather as a *bandjar* with a number of well-to-do individuals in it—Tihingan is primarily a giver of money and a receiver of land in *gadé* transactions. Over all, it shows a net gain of seventeen *tenah* of land (or about 12 per cent of the total amount of land owned by its residents as such) by means of the *gadé* process, as against net losses of fifteen, seventeen, and nineteen *tenah* for settlements 2, 3, and 4.

Second, there is *plais,* a kind of key-money system with respect to tenancy. The man who wishes to become a tenant must "lend" a fixed sum of money to the owner at the outset of the relationship. Usually this sum is returned in full to the tenant when and if the tenancy is ended; less often the principle slowly depreciates over time until after a number of years the owner's debt is liquidated entirely. Owners claim that the *plais* system—particularly the nondepreciating sort—protects the tenant's rights, for the owner will not usually wish, or often even be able, to repay the loan, as he must do if he displaces the tenant. Tenants claim it is mere extortion by landlords. As land is short, the landowner may accept a higher *plais* from another bidder, expel the tenant already on the land, and pocket the difference between the old *plais* and the new one. This can be a quite vicious system once it begins to roll; but such auctioning happens less often than one might expect, in part because it is so universally disapproved of and in part because the reaction of the tenant may well be violent. In any case, not all tenancies involve *plais* (from the government's point of view, it is illegal), for one does not demand such payments from relatives or close friends; and the degree to which it is protective or oppressive so far as the tenant is concerned varies a good deal from case to case.[11]

Finally, there is a very popular system in the Tihingan area—and particularly in Tihingan itself—called *melanjain,* in which the tenant is responsible for growing dry crops but not rice. He receives one half of the dry-crop product, but after harvesting it he must prepare the field—plow it, etc.—for rice. The owner then takes over, and the tenant receives no share of the rice crop at all. The *melanjain* system is considered to be more a "worker" than a "tenant" system, for what you are really doing is hiring a man's labor and, especially, his cattle for the preparation of one's rice field, giving him half the dry-season crop as payment. Only poor men will accept *melanjain* contracts, and the system is generally regarded as a means by which people who are not themselves farmers can nevertheless avoid sharing their rice returns with a tenant. In fact, as planting, weeding, and harvesting are all commonly done by *seka* of one sort or another—*bandjar,* kin group, voluntary—one

---

[11] The very existence of *plais* might be held as evidence for the fact that share rents are, in purely economic terms, "too low." And, to maintain perspective, it must be remembered that a landlord here will be a man holding one or two hectares of land and may well be himself a tenant on someone else's land.

can, by using the *melanjain* system, "cultivate" a rice field without ever actually doing any serious work in it oneself. For Tihingan smiths, busy in their forges, such an arrangement is very attractive; though many Tihingan people do themselves farm and some of the poorer ones even serve as tenants or *melanjain* workers.

All these patterns, and a large number of others, are combined in various ways to yield a dense network of land rights and labor obligations that is, of course, at the same time a social network. Sharecrop arrangement, *plais* payment, pawn contract, *melanjain* relationship—all have different meanings in terms of what they imply with respect to economic class, mutual obligation, and social alliance. In the context of "village" life generally, the ties between economic patron and economic dependent growing out of the structure of productive organization in agriculture entwine with those growing out of residence, age, title, kinship, and personal friendship to join *subak* and *bandjar* together, not into a single, bounded, self-contained unit but as strands in a web of social interconnections that spreads out in countless crisscrossing lines and in all directions over the entire countryside.

8. The Temple System and Social Integration

The begetter of order in this otherwise rather particulate social field is the temple system. Arguments from functional potency to functional necessity are both empirically dangerous and logically suspect, but it is nonetheless difficult to see how a social system of the Balinese sort could possibly operate without something very much like the temple system to give it form and outline. A society consisting of a multiplicity of overlapping groups, each directed to a distinct and fairly specific end—a pattern I have called elsewhere "pluralistic collectivism"—would seem to need some ritual expression of the elemental components of its structure in order to maintain a level of conceptual precision sufficient to permit its participants to find their way around in it. The temple system provides both a simplified model of Balinese social structure and a schoolroom in which the kinds of attitudes and values necessary to sustain it are inculcated and celebrated. Without it, it seems certain that Balinese society would be a good deal less intricate and a good deal less interesting.

On the other hand, all Balinese temples are pretty much alike. The architecture—the split gate, the walled courtyard, the small altars to various gods and godlings—is about the same from one temple to the next; only the scale and, to some extent, the particular altar vary. The ceremonies—the invocation of the appropriate gods of the temple's "birthday," the presentation of offerings, the performance of obeisance rituals by the (usually hereditary) temple priest (*pemangku*)—differ mainly in their degree of elaborateness and in the number of people caught up in them. But yet, for all this outward similarity, the temples differ sharply with respect to the purposes to which they are dedicated and the social composition of the congregations they serve. There are houseyard temples to honor direct ancestors; descent-group temples to proclaim the importance of the patriline; *subak* temples to ensure fertility and an adequate water supply; "state" temples to legitimize traditional patterns of political loyalty; "title" (or "caste") temples to uphold the privileges of rank; and special "voluntary" temples to mark a holy place, commemorate a historical event, or fulfill a personal vow. Each of these temples marks out the boundaries and stresses the significance of one or another sort of tie, whether of kinship, ecology, status, or whatever, and taken together they sketch out a general map of the social terrain through which, in his secular life, the Balinese moves. In these terms, perhaps the most important landmarks of all are the so-called "Three Great Temples" (Kahyangan-Tiga)—the origin temple (Pura Puseh), the death temple (Pura Dalem), and what can be translated, a little awkwardly, as the great council temple (Pura Balé Agung).

In Tihingan, the origin temple is located at the extreme northern edge of the village, the death temple at the extreme southern edge (see Map XI), a pattern that is, however, in no way standard. In the every-210-day ceremonies (called *odalan* and falling at different times for the two temples), the entire *bandjar* participates, for the origin temple commemorates the first settlement in the area and is dedicated to the general welfare of the inhabitants, and the death temple is concerned with honoring the dead and appeasing the divinities of evil and destruction. It is not always, however—not even usually—the case that the congregations of an origin or a death temple coincide with the citizenry of a single *bandjar*, or even with one another. In most cases, several *bandjar* are included in one congregation, and sometimes congregation lines actually cut across *bandjar* lines, dividing the citizenry with respect to temple allegiance. The ceremonial pattern carried out in such temples has been described several times in the literature, and the Tihingan pattern shows no significant deviations from the norm—there is the same joyous reception of the visiting gods, descendent from the holy mountain, Agung, in the center of the island; the same Hindu-style ritual obeisance under the leadership of the *pemangku;* the same sad, muffled-drum departure of the gods after three days; and so on. The famous ritual combat between the witch Rangda and the dragon Barong which is associated with death-temple *odalan* in many places in Bali is absent here, because, the villagers say, the king at Klungkung took their Rangda and Barong paraphernalia away at some distant time in the past for rebellious activity; but in settlement 2 there is such a combat, known over much of Bali for its fervency, which virtually all Tihingan people attend.

As for the third of the great temples, the great council temple, it is, as noted in section 2, shared with settlement 2 and is, in fact, located midway between them. This temple has an *odalan* not every 210 days but only once in a lunar year and is, rather vaguely, dedicated both to the fertility of the fields and the vigor of the *bandjar.* (Not only members of the two *bandjar* which "carry" it participate in its *odalan* but, secondarily, representatives from the various surrounding *subak* as well.) It thus relates, in symbolic terms, the, in structural terms, disjunct entities of hamlet and irrigation society and expresses the general unity, or at least the continuity, of what I referred to as the extended field of village life.

From the social point of view, what is perhaps most important to emphasize is the extraordinary preparatory effort that goes into the making of an *odalan.* The Pueblo Indians of the southwestern United States have often been remarked as considering the really crucial part of a ritual the extended and meticulous preparations leading up to it; and, though the Balinese do draw great rewards from participation in the ceremony itself, the same sort of thing is true of them. For literally weeks ahead of time, the members of the congregation are preparing offerings, repairing and decorating the temple, discussing who will do what, and practicing *gamelan* pieces, so that by the time the ritual itself comes it is something of an anticlimax, or at least hardly more than the final phases of preparation. During the period prior to the *odalan* proper, the intense cooperation among female members of the congregation (who make most of the offerings) and male ones (who do most everything else) clearly acts to bind them together into a whole. In fact, given the great number of temples in the area (all of whose *odalan* usually fall at different times), Tihingan people seem to be always either preparing for a temple ceremony or cleaning up after one, and the integrative force of this continual collective effort, as it moves from one social context to another, is the linchpin of the entire system.

9. The Balinese Village

Tihingan shares with the other "villages" of Bali not so much a specific concrete form as a set of characteristics, general principles of social organization, which, though they work out variously in different places—even, as we have seen, in immediately adjoining settlements—are nonetheless common over the whole southern heartland area. Among the more important of these are the following:

(1) There is a marked tendency to perform particular social activities in groups specifically designed for those activities and for them alone. The view of a peasant village as a functionally diffuse, all-purpose social form does not, whatever its value may or may not be elsewhere, apply at all in Bali.

(2) There is a related and equally marked tendency to deny all other bases of social demarcation save those immediately relevant to the situation or task at hand. In a *gamelan seka* it doesn't matter what your title is; at a *bandjar* meeting it doesn't, at least legally, matter what your kin group is; in a *subak* it doesn't, or at least shouldn't, matter where you reside.

(3) As a corollary, social activities tend to be relatively "pure" in nature: status (or, better, rank) relationships are a matter of pure prestige; economic relationships of pure wealth; political relationship of pure power; religious ones of pure ritual. The various systems interact and influence one another significantly, but they never (or almost never) fuse.

(4) There is a very sharp line between the worlds of private life, conducted behind the house-yard walls (and which I have not been able to describe in any detail here), and that of public life, which goes on outside of them. Public obligations are heavy, unevadable, but nonethelesss strictly limited, and there are specific mechanisms (also not described here) for adjusting between them.

(5) Activity and elaborateness are valued for their own sake. A Balinese "village" is a very busy place, and the complexity of the ways in which people are, even in formal terms, related to one another is staggering. If one were to apply stylistic categories to social structures—probably not too good an idea—the Balinese would surely be classed as rococo.

(6) The crisscrossed maze of specific, strictly defined, highly autonomous, and largely collective social ties that all this subtlety and industry produce is held within a general form by the temple system, in which the elements that make it up are both expressed and strengthened.

There is much more to Balinese village structure than this, to say nothing of the actual processes in terms of which it functions. But in a microscopic examination of what is really only one, in no sense independent, part of a much larger whole, perhaps some starting points for a more thorough analysis can be located. And knowing where, in the whole mass of overlapping alliances, to begin is half the battle in any effort to lay bare the underlying form of Balinese social organization. In Bali, the term "village" is perhaps best reserved (as the Balinese themselves often reserve it) not for a particular social body but for the entire plexus of discrete interpersonal and intergroup relationships that honeycombs the whole island from Djembrana on the west to Karangasem on the east. Properly conceived, the Balinese village is not a circumscribed community but an extended field.

Chapter X

Tjelapar: A Village in South Central Java

KOENTJARANINGRAT

UNIVERSITY OF INDONESIA

1. The Javanese

There exists a vast published literature on Javanese culture. A large number of books and articles deal with the Javanese language and both ancient and recent court literature, art, and drama; many others describe and analyze folklore and folk art; much is written on the Javanese art of batik, on the Javanese kris, on Javanese music, and on Javanese clothing; piles of notes and information exist on various aspects of Javanese *adat* law; there are publications on Javanese Islam and on Javanese history, ancient as well as modern; many books and articles focus on village life and agriculture (Kennedy 1955, II, 387–512). As far as I know, however, no comprehensive published description exists on particular Javanese village communities.[1]

The rural Javanese, who, according to a 1958 census, form a large percentage of Java's 56.5 million inhabitants,[2] occupy the central and eastern parts of the island of Java. The extreme northwestern part is populated by Javanese-speaking peasants, with a Sundanese-speaking or

[1] Bachtiar Rifai's comparative study on forms of land ownership in the two villages Bulungan and Ngurensiti in North Central Java (1958) is still unpublished.

[2] The population of Java plus that of Madura, according to the Labor Force Sample Survey of the Ministry of Labor of the Republic of Indonesia, 1958.

a bilingual Javanese-Sundanese elite in towns and cities. Usually they are rice cultivators (*tani*) working on very small plots of irrigated land (*sawah*), but a portion of these peasants, inhabiting the mountainous and hilly regions that stretch across the center of the island from the west to the extreme east, in several places practice agriculture on dry fields (*tegalan*) using manioc, rather than rice, as their principal crop. Tjelapar, the village to be described in this chapter, is situated in the hilly region of South Central Java and is inhabited by peasants who consider manioc as their staple food.

According to the Javanese conception of social classes, the village is populated by *wong tjilik* or "little people." However, there are also *wong tjilik* in the towns and cities, where they form the lower strata of the urban population and follow a great range of occupations, most of them based on manual labor. Javanese who consider themselves as belonging to a higher social level are the *prijaji*. These include members of the administrative bureaucracy, holding positions ranging from government clerks in small towns to officials of superior rank in larger cities. In rural Java the traditional administrative personnel, or *pamong pradja*, constitute the core of the *prijaji*. Only in very exceptional cases do *prijaji* live in the village, usually retired government officials who have bought a few hectares of land for cultivation. There are also Javanese engaged in trade. These *wong sudagar*, or small traders and merchants, who also may live in the villages, have their locus primarily in the more urban centers, where they occupy separate quarters called *kauman*. A rather limited upper class or nobility, *ndara*, which has lost much of its traditional prestige since World War II and the Indonesian revolution, is mainly concentrated in the four court centers of South Central Java (Jogjakarta, Surakarta, Mangkunegaran, and Paku Alaman), into which the Javanese state Mataram split subsequent to 1755.

Apart from this horizontal stratification there exists a vertical division of Javanese society, based upon the degree of participation in Islam, distinguishing the *wong abangan* from the *santri*. The former are those who do not live according to the basic principles of Islam as understood by the Javanese, that is, who do not perform the *salat* five times a day, who do not fast in the month of Pasa (Ramadan), who have no desire to make the pilgrimage to Mecca, and for whom pork is not a taboo. The *santri* are people who follow Islamic principles seriously and hence differ sharply in all these respects. Although the criterion of differentiation is basically the degree of participation in Islam, the two groups can certainly also be regarded as two subcultures with contrasting world views, values, and orientations within the Javanese culture as a whole.

Like the *abangan*, *santri* are present among all social levels. There are *abangan* and *santri* among both rural and urban *wong tjilik;* there are *abangan* and *santri* among the rural and urban *wong sudagar;* there are *abangan* and *santri* among the *prijaji;* and members of both categories are even present among the nobility. Geographically, however, many areas of Java have a dominantly *abangan* population, while many others consist mainly of *santri.* Tjelapar, although dominantly an *abangan* village, also has a small number of *santri* among its population.

2. Location, Settlement Pattern, and Houses of Tjelapar

In the hilly region south of the Seraju River of South Central Java, in the valley of a little river, Kali Tjelapar, seventeen kilometers to the north of the district town Karanganjar (regency of Kebumen, residency of Kedu), is located a widely scattered cluster of hamlets that comprise the village of Tjelapar. The road leading to Tjelapar from Karanganjar, which before the Indonesian revolution could be used by automobiles, is badly damaged in many places and has lost most of its bridges. By *déleman*, a type of pony cart, a vehicle of considerable importance in the vicinity of Karanganjar, or by jeep, one can reach the nearby village of Kaligutji; the rest of the way one must either walk or go by bicycle. This transportation problem contributes to the relative isolation of Tjelapar and many of the other villages in the South Seraju Hills area. In contrast, the villages of the lowlands to the south of the district town, railroad, and highway running along the southern part of Central Java are easily accessible for all types of vehicles.

The total area of Tjelapar consists of some 560 hectares of land. About 40 hectares are occupied by houses and courtyards; the rest includes 390 hectares of *sawah* (irrigated rice fields), 71 hectares of *tegalan* (dry fields), and 15 hectares of teak forest, part of a large government-owned forest area in the hilly region of South Seraju.

The teak-forest vegetation to the north of the village is relatively more dense than the forest to the south. As a consequence, land on the north side of the Tjelapar River is relatively more fertile and more suitable for irrigation than the land south of it. Most of the dry *tegalan*

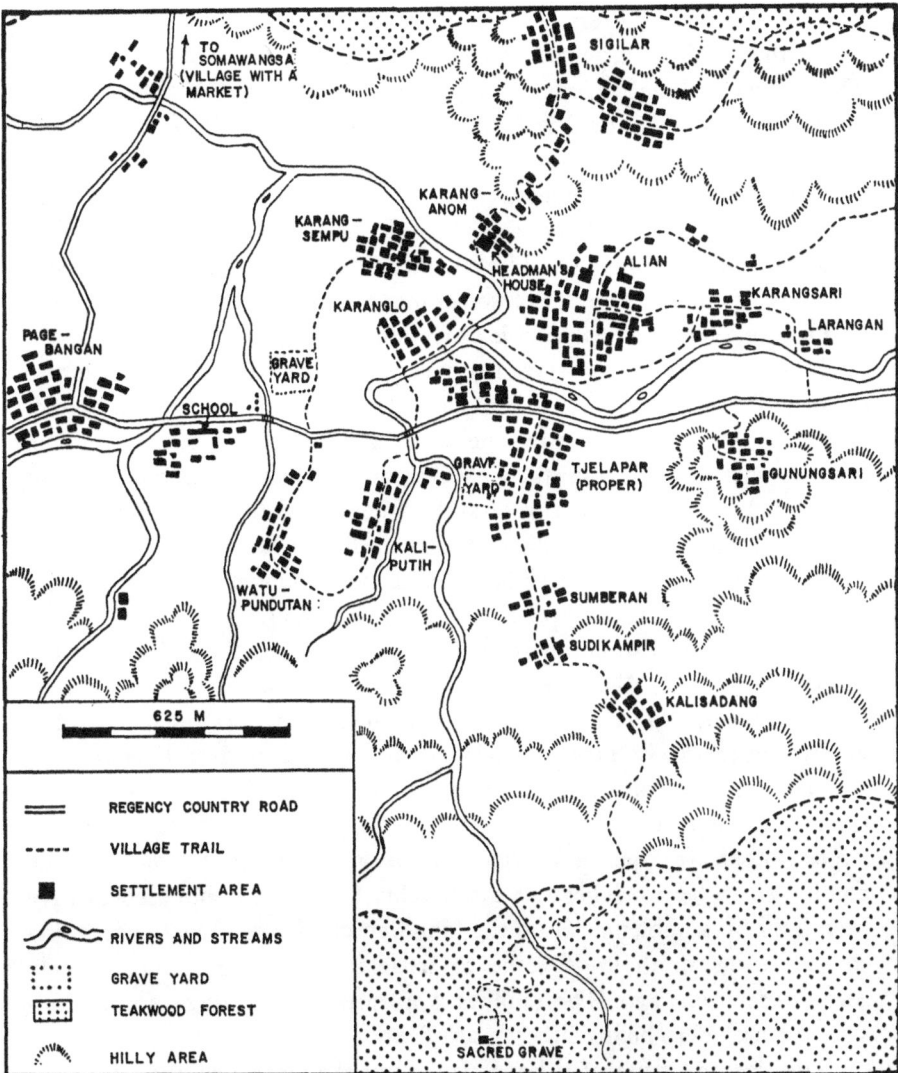

Map XIII. Location of the Various Hamlets of Tjelapar

land is situated in the southern portions of the village, and the plots of irrigated land are usually poor *sawah*.

The settlement pattern of Tjelapar shows a scattered design of thirteen rather widely dispersed hamlets, with cultivated fields in between. This differs strikingly from the settlement patterns of the villages south of the railroad, which tend to form compact nucleated villages comprising three or four rows of houses strung along a road or a river. Tjelapar hamlets (*dukuh*) have names of their own, and the core of the village consists of the rather densely populated ones: Tjelapar proper, Alian, Karanglo, and Karangsempu. These hamlets are crowded compounds, with houses built closely together or sometimes even contiguous to each other, thus forming long houses occupied by ambilocal extended families.

The average house in a Javanese village is a small rectangular structure of approximately four by five meters. The frame is made of a system of wooden pillars and beams, the walls are panels of plaited bamboo, and the thatch roof consists of overlapping layers of plaited coconut leaves, tied with bamboo strips onto the wooden rafters of the roof frame. The inside of the house is divided into small compartments by movable bamboo panels. There are sliding doors, no windows, and light enters through large holes in the upper part of the side walls.

The Javanese distinguish several styles of house, determined by the shape of the roof. The average villager of Tjelapar has a house with a *srotong* roof. A *trodjogan* roof, although quite general in many other villages, is relatively rare in Tjelapar, and houses with a *limasan* roof are restricted to those families who consider themselves descendants of the original inhabitants and the village's "upper class." Three relatively larger houses are Tjelapar's pride, because of their *djoglo* roofs, a style considered to be a privilege of the nobility.[a] These are supposed to have been built by a nobleman from the kingdom of Mataram, who, according to the village mythology, came to settle in the village approximately seven generations ago. The families who now occupy these houses consider themselves to be his direct descendants.

The size and style of a house is a symbol of prestige and class, but the wealth of Javanese villagers cannot be judged in this way. Very well-to-do people may occupy quite simple *srotong* houses, whereas others less wealthy may occupy larger houses with *limasan* roofs. Sometimes, however, an outside observer may consider the house material as an

[a] For further information on Javanese houses, see H. Maclaine Pont (1924, 44–73) and Sastra Amidjaja (1924, 105–118).

indication of wealth. Villagers who can afford to buy construction materials more common in towns and cities, such as bricks or wooden boards for the walls, tiles or zinc plates for the roofs, wood and glass for doors, concrete or tiles for the floors, are usually relatively wealthy villagers. Several houses of Tjelapar are indeed constructed with building materials from the city.

3. Demographic Data

In July 1959 the village counted 1,891 inhabitants.[4] A breakdown according to sex and a distinction between children and non-children appears in Table 18.

Table 18. Population of Tjelapar in July 1959

	Children	Non-children	Total
Male	407	550	957
Female	339	595	934
Total	746	1,145	1,891

By the term "non-children" I designate villagers above the age of fourteen to fifteen years, who usually begin very soon to participate heavily in adult activities, whether within the household or outside in agriculture and cattle raising. Furthermore, many children marry at the age of fifteen or even younger.[5] Despite their participation in adult activi-

[4] The village registers were very inaccurate. A quick survey of these registers showed many inconsistencies and errors, while comparison with the 1959 figures provided by the subdistrict office, which is located in the village Karanggajam about twelve kilometers to the south of Tjelapar, revealed a difference of about 60 individuals.

[5] Village people rarely know their age. They are able to fix the time of their birth only if it is associated with some important or extraordinary event in the past. Such an event will still be remembered and can be used as a chronological guide. In checking the age of the children in the village, I could fortunately use such a guide in the beginning of the Indonesian armed revolution, which was approximately fourteen years previous to my field work in 1958–1959. Thus I was able to complete a list quickly by dividing all the children into those born before and those born after the outbreak of the revolution, i.e., children above and below fourteen years of age.

ties and the adult status they have achieved through marriage, these villagers very often still behave like children until they have reached actual maturity.

The 1,891 people of Tjelapar are divided into 369 nuclear families (*batih*) and live in 351 houses (*omah*). Often two or three nuclear families live in a single house, all sharing one kitchen; on the other hand, there are also houses with two to three nuclear families in which each nuclear family conducts its own household economy using a separate kitchen. Those houses occupied by one, two, or three nuclear families, or by two to three households, are often built very close to each other. Especially in the crowded core hamlets, there are practically no courtyards for planting because of the close proximity of the houses.

During the period between January 1958 and August 1959, 114 infants were born; 12 of them, and 48 other children and adults, died. (The figures on infant mortality in the village were very inadequate according to my impression.) Recently more people have tended to leave the village than move into it. During the same one-and-a-half-year period, only 10 people moved in, while 28 people, comprising 10 families, left the village either to transmigrate to South Sumatra or to start a new life in urban areas of Java. In addition, an unlisted number of individuals are seasonal or occasional migrants, moving recurrently back and forth for shorter or longer periods.

One of the reasons for the tendency to leave the village is pressure caused by the land shortage. This holds true for most of the South Seraju region as well as for a large part of South Central Java. The regency of Kebumen, for instance, was already one of the most densely populated areas in Java before the war. The district of Karanganjar now counts more than eight hundred souls per square kilometer, whereas in the adjacent district of Pedjagoan, the density of population exceeds one thousand per square kilometer (Widjojo Nitisastro 1956).

Of Tjelapar's 1,145 inhabitants in the "non-child" category, 259 persons were holders of a *petuk*, a government certificate giving the dimensions of their land property for purposes of tax assessment.[6] In reality the number of landowners is much larger, because usually each *petuk*

---

[6] Most villagers regard the *petuk* certificate as a document that proves their property rights. According to the village land register in 1959, there were 187 persons who held a *petuk*. As I did not trust the register, I checked for myself on the total of such landholders and arrived at this figure of 259.

is held by several people, often the younger siblings of the registered owner. It is customary among the people of Tjelapar, and in many other villages in the hilly regions north of the railroad, that heirs do not apply at once for individual *peṭuk* certificates to their respective shares of inherited land, but that only one of them, usually the eldest son, has the responsibility for doing so. This man registers not the separate pieces of land to which his siblings are individually entitled but rather the entire estate of his deceased father, as a single unit for which he himself holds the collective *peṭuk*. Later, when a co-owner or *ponḍok* feels capable of assuming independent status in the village community because he has increased his landholdings through purchase or other means, he usually separates his own landholdings from the collective estate and acquires a land certificate of his own. The majority of the landholders own between 1.5 and 2 hectares of dry land, or *tegalan*, in addition to about .25 to 1 hectare of wet rice fields or *sawah*. The holders of *peṭuk* covering 1.5 hectares had three or even up to five *ponḍok*, whereas some holders of *peṭuk* for 2.5 hectares had as many as ten *ponḍok*.

In fact, by Central Javanese standards two hectares of land is considered a large holding, and this is usually subdivided into small parcels that are cultivated by others, following the various sharecropping systems (*maro, mertelu,* etc.),[7] by renting, or by pawning. These systems are very similar to those that exist in Bali, which are described in Chapter IX of this book. Thus among the peasants who do not own either *tegalan* or *sawah*, and who in the village community are called *linḍung*,[8] there are still quite a number who are able to cultivate land according to the various ways mentioned. Those remaining, who are really too poor to rent any land at all, are forced to work as agricultural laborers, or *buruh tani*, and to receive as wages either money or a portion of the crop.

4. Peasant Life and Daily Habits

Deeply concerned with the well-being of the family, the Javanese peasant strives within the family to create a state of *slamet*, or emotional

[7] Extensive information on the share-cropping system, in Java in particular and in Indonesia in general, can be found in Scheltema (1931).

[8] In other areas in rural Java, the terms *ponḍok* and *linḍung* seem to have other meanings: cf. Djojodigoeno and Tirtawinata (1940).

calm, in which nothing unfortunate will happen to anyone. Emotional upsets and other disturbing experiences expose the family to supernatural dangers, which find expression in accidents, sickness, and death. One of the most important ways in preventing anxiety because of such dangers is to achieve the spiritual state of *préhatin*, the essence of which is that an individual is aware of the range of possible disturbing events and thus strives to adjust his behavior to this awareness. Though not expressed in particularly concrete ways, this spiritual state must be maintained by the observance of various taboos and by the performance of socioreligious rituals called *slametan*, which have the function of reinforcing the state of *préhatin* and promoting *slamet*. The *slametan*, which is the central ritual in Javanese peasant life, involves a communal sacred meal, either very simple or very elaborate depending on the importance of the occasion (see C. Geertz 1960, 11–15). A *slametan* performed within the household is usually attended by the closest neighbors, but sometimes no guests at all are invited and only sacred food distributed to the homes of the neighbors. These household *slametan* rituals are performed at various points in the individual's life cycle.

In anticipation of childbirth, the entire family enters the state of *préhatin* beginning with the third and fourth months of pregnancy, and this is sometimes enforced by simple *slametan* rituals. The prospective mother now begins to observe a series of food taboos, although she continues to carry on her ordinary duties until the actual confinement. During the seventh month of pregnancy a ceremony called *tingkeban* or *mitoni* is performed, including an elaborate *slametan mitoni* meal. The ceremony is supposed to assure a successful delivery and to bring *slamet* to the unborn child and to the family, but in addition it serves as an anticipatory announcement of the prospective birth. Another *slametan* during the ninth month is given in honor of the prospective child's symbolic siblings, the amniotic fluid and the placenta, which are supposed to be his intimate guides throughout life.

Childbirth (*babaran*) is the climax of a period of crisis within the household that begins in the third month of pregnancy. For assistance in delivery the peasant family calls in a *ḍukun*, a midwife, who is often also a specialist in magical, shamanistic, and curing practices. She will receive a fee consisting of food and money for her aid. Mayer has described in detail many of the protective charms, spells, and other symbolic acts formerly performed by a *ḍukun* to ward off supernatural dangers from mother and child (1897, I, 279–285). Although these have now been largely abandoned in village communities, most of the traditional medicines and practices used by the *ḍukun* in treating mother and child, such as massage, as well as most of her traditional equipment, such as the bamboo knife for cutting the umbilical cord, are still in use.

Special care is taken of the placenta, which is deposited in an earthenware jar and ceremoniously buried in the back yard of the house. A series of small *slametan* ceremonies follow: one, in connection with the ritual cutting of the child's hair; one on the day when the stump of the umbilical cord falls off; and one on the thirty-fifth day of life. The number 35 is obtained by combining the five-day and seven-day weeks. Every 35 days there recurs the same combination of days as those on which an individual was born. This is called the *weton* ("the day the child came out") and is important in scheduling magical practices and ceremonies throughout his life cycle.

According to Islamic religious law, a mother is unclean and subject to a series of taboos for a period of forty days after childbirth. Sexual intercourse is prohibited, and mother and child are supposed to remain under the care of the *ḍukun*, although in practice this responsibility is usually assumed by the woman's mother.

In normal circumstances the infant is breast-fed for fourteen to eighteen months or sometimes even longer. Supplementary solid food such as soft cooked rice, mashed bananas, or maize pudding is given soon after the second week. Feeding follows a demand schedule: the infant gets food or the breast whenever it cries. Weaning in the sense of achieving emotional independence from the mother does not usually occur until long after breast-feeding has ceased.

A Javanese infant spends most of its waking hours in someone's arms—mother, grandmother, elder sibling, or father—where it is fondled tenderly, or else it is carried in a sling (*sléndang*) securely fastened to the left side of its carrier, as the latter goes about the daily activities or visits the market about two hours' walking distance from Tjelapar.

Small *slametan* ceremonies similar to that on the thirty-fifth day are also held on the infant's third *weton* (105th day) and on its fifth *weton* (175th day). On the seventh *weton* day occurs an especially important ceremony called *teḍak sitèn* (going down on the earth), which is followed by an elaborate *slametan*. Besides establishing the first contact of the infant with the earth, the ceremony marks the end of the crisis period following childbirth and symbolizes the ability of the child to stay alive on its own.

Small village children go naked, sometimes with a pubic cover. They are toilet trained gradually with a minimum of punishment. Up to the age of two the child is petted and appeased, but thereafter he is expected to adjust gradually to his social environment. The usual method of inculcation and discipline includes snarling, corporal punishment, and invidious comparisons with the superior behavior of siblings and others in order to encourage pride. Another common method is to threaten the child with external sanctioning agents, such as ghosts, evil spirits, bogeymen, or strangers. This has serious drawbacks; one result is that most Javanese peasant children are shy, afraid of strangers, and slow to make acquaintances outside the family.

As the child grows up he gradually extends the range of his social relations, while learning to adjust himself to social realities and to shape his behavior according to prevailing social standards. The range of social contacts for boys as well as for girls expands through school and through herding or market activities.

The village school is situated in the nearby village of Pagebangan, which for many Tjelapar children is approximately one hour's walking distance from their homes. In 1959 only 169 Tjelapar children were registered as pupils of the village schools, and only a small number of these attended school regularly. The majority of the girls are given increasing responsibilities in the home in matters such as cooking, threshing paddy, and tending younger siblings, while many boys have to collect twigs and teak leaves in the forest (used for wrapping material), cut *puḍak* leaves (used for plaiting), assist in agricultural activities, or run all sorts of errands. In addition, many boys and girls hire themselves out as buffalo, cattle, goat, or duck herders (*angon*). Most parents in Tjelapar are aware of the importance of a school education for their children, and they do start sending them to school at the age of eight, nine, or ten years. However, the parents are faced with the fact that many children are reluctant to work as peasants after graduating from school.

The onset of adolescence for girls is marked by a simple *slametan* at the first menstruation, but in general the transition to adult status is a gradual one. For boys, however, circumcision, which occurs between the ages of six to twelve, is an important event, dramatizing a sharp transition from childhood to adolescence. The circumcision ceremony, called *tetak* or *sunat*, is regarded by most Javanese, even in Tjelapar where the notion of Islam is very superficial, as an initiation rite whereby the boy is "made a Moslem." The operation is performed by a professional circumciser (*bong*), who has the requisite skill and also knows how to treat wounds, especially in emergency cases when serious bleeding occurs. There are good descriptions of Javanese circumcision rituals (Inggris 1921), and regional variations in details are reported by Schrieke (1921). The important event is often celebrated with a party and a *wajang*[9] or *angguk* performance (see Section 9).

The transition at puberty does not necessarily involve the imparting of sexual knowledge. Parents avoid mentioning matters of sexual significance in the presence of their children. This adult attitude does not, of course, prevent the acquisition of sexual knowledge through indirect observation, the overhearing of adult conversations, or the imparting of information by older people such as grandparents.

Premarital sexual relations are prohibited in village society, and the methods of controlling the sexual behavior of adolescents involve a certain amount of segregation of the sexes and chaperonage of girls. Boys and girls have the opportunity for contact at school, in planting and harvesting groups, and in particular at parties and festivals. Although clandestine meetings between the sexes and sexual intercourse before marriage do occur, generally girls are expected to be chaste at marriage. An unmarried girl who becomes pregnant brings shame upon her family. Abortion, however, is not practiced in such cases, because it is considered an even greater sin. The only practical solution to the problem is to compel the boy to marry the girl before her condition becomes public knowledge.

[9] The *wajang* is a Javanese folk puppet play. Of its several types, the two-dimensional leather puppet play is the most popular today. The central actor not only recites the story and sings the songs but also manipulates the puppets and directs the *gamelan* orchestra, which provides the sound effects to accompany the movements of the puppets. A good storyteller must have a variety of artistic talents. In addition to knowing the story, the songs, and their sequence by heart, he must be able to improvise personal remarks, jokes, and satirical comments on current events in harmony with the characters of the puppets and in time with the music. Many anthropological theories have been advanced to account for the integration of the *wajang* into the social life of the people. To the Javanese these puppet plays have both an artistic and a ritual value, which helps to explain their popularity. In addition to a wide repertory of stories, there are several kinds of *wajang*. Plays with three-dimensional wooden puppets are popular among the Sundanese of western Java. South Sumatra, Bali, and Lombok have plays with two-dimensional leather puppets resembling those of the Javanese. A huge literature exists on the subject: see, in particular, Hazeu (1897).

The village youth often do their own courting and may make their own choice of a mate with parental consent. In Tjelapar, however, many marriages are arranged by the parents. Of the 51 marriages that occurred during 1958 and early 1959, 23 were between very young people,[10] all of which were arranged without consent of either the girl or the boy. Culturally defined rules concerning prohibited, disapproved, and permitted marriages play an important role in contracting marriages, and parental approval indicates that these rules have been complied with.

Prohibited marriages (*sirikan djedjoḍoan*) are those which are considered really incestuous. These include unions between siblings or other members of the same nuclear family. There is no conception of supernatural punishment for unions of this type; they are merely considered so absurd that nobody even thinks of the possibility. Javanese mythology, however, includes several accounts of incestuous unions between mother and son; the offspring are always magically potent heroes. There are two other types of prohibited marriage, both of which are negatively sanctioned by threat of supernatural punishment. These are unions between a grandparent and grandchild and those with a *misan* (second cousin). The latter prohibition is very striking in Tjelapar and apparently also in many other peasant communities of rural Java. The Javanese are not able to give an explanation for this prohibition, but a Dutch scholar, Bertling (1936), has attempted a structural interpretation.

Disapproved marriages are those which, though theoretically prohibited and also threatened by supernatural punishment, can nevertheless be arranged by performing a variety of preventive rituals designed to protect the couple against supernatural reprisal. Unions of this category include: (1) those between consanguineal relatives where the groom belongs to a younger generation than the bride (e.g., between nephew and aunt); (2) marriages between paternal parallel cousins (*pantjer wali*); (3) sororate unions and in general any marriage with a relative of a deceased spouse; (4) marriages between individuals whose *weton* days do not harmonize according to the Javanese *pétungan* or numerological system.

Marriage is permitted between adopted children in the same nuclear family and between maternal parallel cousins. In general, the Javanese peasants do not have a clear notion of preferred marriages. In several

[10] One marriage involved a girl of about eleven years and a boy of about thirteen years of age.

areas, marriages between cross cousins are regarded with positive favor, but in other regions this type is simply a frequent form of permitted marriage. In Tjelapar there exists a special type of approved marriage, namely between *mindoan* (third cousins).

Village communities usually have a number of older people who are generally considered experts in marriage customs and whose advice in decisions concerning marriage arrangements is frequently requested. In Tjelapar the village headman is considered the authority in such matters, and his advice often is decisive in character. Experts in marriage customs often act as intermediaries. When a decision is reached, the boy's parents or their representative pays a ceremonial visit to request the girl's hand (*nglamar*). The girl's parents, when they have given their formal consent, accept a betrothal gift (*paningset*), after which an engagement period of several months or longer follows.

A village wedding ceremony involves the following elements: (1) the procession of the groom's paternal and maternal relatives, on the afternoon before the wedding day, to the bride's house to offer the bridal gift (*sasrahan*) consisting of cattle, foodstuffs, textiles, and money; (2) the *reresik*, or visits to the ancestral graves by two or three of the bride's patrilineal relatives, on the afternoon before the wedding day; (3) the gathering of the bride's kindred at her house, the evening before the wedding, to receive the blessings of the good spirits, the *widadari;* (4) the procession of the couple, the bride's guardian, two witnesses, and escort, on the next morning, to conclude the marriage contract and to register (*idjab*) at the office of the *pengulu*, or Moslem religious official, at the subdistrict town; (5) an elaborate *slametan* ceremony at the bride's house in the afternoon; (6) an elaborate party beginning around eight at night and lasting until about six the next morning, at which the guests are entertained with food, drinks, and a puppet play, and at which many have the opportunity to enjoy a card game.

There is no fixed rule of residence determining where a married couple should live. The ideal is to set up an independent household, but as many villagers marry between the ages of thirteen to eighteen, for girls, and fifteen to twenty, for boys, a young couple is not considered able to manage their own living. Consequently they reside in the house of one set of parents until they are considered fully adult, usually for a period of three to five years. According to informants from Tjelapar, a young couple always chooses the home of the wife's parents to stay, since the young wife naturally prefers to stay with her own mother rather than with her mother-in-law.[11] After the initial period a new house is built for the couple, usually by the wife's but sometimes by the husband's parents, who also assign the couple the use of a garden plot and a few fruit trees. It frequently happens that the new dwelling is built immediately adjacent to that of the wife's parents, sometimes even sharing the same roof, although with a separate kitchen. Many of the 103 large houses in Tjelapar were occupied by two, three, sometimes even four nuclear families forming matrilocal or patrilocal extended families. Shifts in residence after the initial period may occur, and quite often the couple leaves the parental compound to live neolocally in another hamlet or even in another village. In any event, however, one married daughter always resides permanently with her parents, caring for them in their old age and eventually inheriting their house.

Polygyny is rare in Tjelapar and apparently in most of rural Java. According to the census of 1930, only 2 per cent of all marriages in Java were polygynous. Widjojo Nitisastro (1956, 6) reports an incidence of 6 to 7 per cent in the village of Djabres in the same general area of South Central Java, although Tjelapar had only three polygynous families in 1959.

In regard to divorce (*pegatan*), the Javanese follow the rules and procedure laid down by Moslem law of the Sjafi'itic school. Consequently divorce may be granted upon the request of the husband without the consent of his wife. There is no definite rule determining which of the divorced parents the children should follow, but infants who still require maternal care always follow the mother. No matter with whom the children reside, however, both divorced parents have the obligation to provide for their maintenance until they reach adulthood. When a divorce occurs, each spouse retains the property he or she brought into the mar-

[11] I checked this information concerning initial uxorilocal residence by considering 457 marriages in Tjelapar's village register. It appeared that quite a number of couples had not followed the custom as stated by the informants but had resided according to the initial virilocal pattern.

	Married outside Tjelapar	Married in Tjelapar
Initial uxorilocal	59	322
Initial virilocal	29	47
Total	88	369

riage, but the property they acquired together during the marriage (called *banḍa srajan*) is divided according to the principle of *sagénḍong-sepikul*, which allocates one-third to the wife and two-thirds to the husband.

The incidence of divorce appears to be quite high in Java, especially in rural areas. One reason is probably the high frequency of traditional arranged marriages and the consequent lack of deep emotional ties in the early years of married life. Another factor is the absence among the Javanese of any conception that divorce is morally wrong.

The peasant family does not have fixed daily activities, but a certain rhythm is nevertheless observable. People of Tjelapar awake at sunrise and, after having taken a bath in the river or at the well, they start on their daily round of activities until about noon. Besides work in the *sawah* or *tegalan*, there is always much work around the house. Household utensils and other implements need repairs; there is some sewing of clothes to be done; sometimes people weave material, plait mats, or work on a piece of batik. The children are at school or help in the fields and around the house.

After a lunch of *sega ojèk* (gruel of manioc eaten with various side dishes), the staple food of the people of Tjelapar, the adults usually return to work and the children, who have returned from school, go to herd the animals. If we stroll in the village toward sundown, when the people have returned from their various activities, we will find them seated in their courtyards, chatting and gossiping with animation, while waiting for the sun to set. Sometimes we may encounter groups of children with water buffaloes, cows, or goats, returning from their pasture.

After the evening meal of *sega ojèk*, men will go to the guardhouse of the night watchman (*garḍu*) or to a coffee shop, essentially to a place where they can meet other people, to sit and talk about the daily events in the village. If a person is a member of the various village art clubs, the group of *angguk* players or the group of *selawatan* singers, the group of *gamelan* players, or the group of *wajang wong* actors, he may go to practice or to rehearse his art (see Section 9). Many of the men and boys in Tjelapar like to play *tjeki* (a Chinese card game) or dominoes, and they may go to meet their friends to play cards until late into the night.[12]

[12] Playing cards or other games formed a very important daily recreation in a Javanese *prijaji* or nobility household, particularly before World War II (see Tjan Tjoe Siem 1941). In the villages it is still important today.

5. *The Household and Its Social Relations*

The *somah*, or household, which is the basic unit in Javanese society, is not always characterized by a separate dwelling but invariably by a separate kitchen, for each Javanese household cooks its own meal. Most Javanese desire a large family, because of the general belief that many children are a blessing and because of the practical consideration that children can take care of their old parents. Because of the high infant mortality rate, generally similar to other rural areas, the average Tjelapar household is small. Larger households, which occupy "long houses" or the same compound, usually consist of nuclear families (*batih*) who are closely related to one another. Old couples with married daughters or sons who reside matrilocally or patrilocally for the initial period of marriage may form temporary as well as permanent matrilocal, patrilocal, or ambilocal extended families. Larger households or those of more prosperous and prestigeful villagers may also include one or more pre-adolescent relatives in the status of *ngèngèr*, a term meaning "taking a child to serve in the house." According to this custom, which should not be confused with adoption, a pre-adolescent child (nearly always a girl) may be placed in the house of an older married sibling, uncle, or aunt who provides for her maintenance. This may be done for several reasons: the family may need additional household help, or it may be prosperous and thus in a position to render aid to relatives in less fortunate circumstances. A child in this status does not sever her ties with her own parents, and she acquires no inheritance rights in her foster home.

Although the husband is the head of the household, the wife does not have an inferior status. According to the Javanese point of view, husband and wife are expected to work together for the maintenance of the family. In the villages both cooperate in agriculture. Preparation of the soil for tillage, plowing, harrowing, and the repair of irrigation works fall primarily within the masculine sphere of activities, whereas women do most of the planting, weeding, harvesting, and threshing, as well as the further processing, preservation, and preparing of food. Both sexes transport crops from the field to the home, and products from home to the market, but in many market centers one notices a predominance of female buyers and sellers. In public and political affairs, however, the village women do not play a leading role, and, although female landholders have the same voting rights as men, they are usually not interested in such matters, preferring to send sons or brothers as their representatives to village meetings.

The Javanese peasant household is expected in the first place to maintain good relations with its immediate neighbors, then with the other households in the same neighborhood and in the same hamlet, and finally with households in other hamlets. These good relations are expressed in various systems of mutual aid, which have recently been termed *gotong-rojong*. Javanese etiquette incorporates this idea into a number of formal obligations toward neighbors that must be taken into consideration by every household head. Although a person may not be on particularly familiar terms with his neighbors, he is obligated to invite them or send them food when performing a *slametan;* he has to offer them small presents when returning from a journey (*olèh-olèh*)[13]; he must render them assistance in case of sickness, accidents, or death; finally, he may not refuse a request for assistance in work around the household of a neighbor.

In the case of a death, the neighbors are expected to do all the work in preparation for the funeral; thus the family and the relatives of the deceased can concern themselves with their grief and tend to the corpse of the deceased. In addition to their contributions of labor, the neighbors often donate money, to help meet the expenses of the funeral, or food for the *slametan* and for guests. All this aid is usually rendered wholeheartedly, without the expectation of its return. The custom of mutual aid in case of death (*tetulung lajat*) is indeed very spontaneous in nature.

Quite often neighbors need assistance for different kinds of work around the household, for instance, for repairing the roof, renovating the bamboo walls of the house, ridding the house of mice, digging a well in the yard, or pounding rice in preparation of a feast.[14] The request, when made in a specific conventional polite form by means of a visit (*njambat*), may not be refused. The villager who is asked to work by his neighbor feels that this neighbor now owes him a debt of labor too. The labor debt of his neighbor is never forgotten by the person who has been asked for help, and its extent is always carefully calculated.

[13] *Olèh-olèh* are small presents consisting of food or articles which are supposed to be characteristic of the area where someone has traveled.

[14] Rice not intended for a feast may not be pounded with the assistance of a neighbor but, if done with help from outside the household, must be pounded by hired labor.

When he later needs assistance for work around his own household, he knows precisely whom he can *njambat*. This custom of mutual aid, which is in Tjelapar generally known as *sambat-sinambat* ("mutual asking for help"), has a much less spontaneous character than the *tetulung lajat* discussed in the previous paragraph.

Outside the nuclear family, or sometimes the extended family, the significance of kinship ties at the village level is very limited. A Javanese peasant very rarely knows about kinsmen of his grandfather's generation, and even sometimes only little about those of his father's generation. The kindred consists of local relatives up to three generations removed, usually direct descendants of Ego's great-grandfather on his father's as well as his mother's side. Actually, however, the effective kindred mainly includes members of Ego's generation to the third degree of collaterality, and only occasionally is it extended to kin of the parents' generation. In addition, the kindred also includes several close local relatives of the wife. This kin group meets occasionally at specific events for celebration of important events along the life cycle of Ego's children and other household members (*pitonan* or *tingkeban*, *tedak sitèn*, *sunat*, and weddings), for funerals, and for annual celebrations like *bakda* (end of the fasting month)[15] and Suran (Moslem New Year). A specific term for kindred does not exist, except the rather vague *sedulur* ("relative").

In Tjelapar and most other villages in the hilly regions of South Seraju, one may observe special ancestor-oriented kin groups, called *alur waris*, which usually include six to seven generations. These groups are obliged to care for the graves of common ancestors and to contribute to the expenses of the *slametan* ceremonies accompanying such care. Each *alur waris* usually has a member in the village who is actually responsible for the graves. This man has to contact the other members of the bilateral kin group. He knows in the first place those bilateral descendants who reside in his own and in the neighboring villages, usually as far as the third generation. However, often he has lost track of many relatives who may have left the village long ago for faraway places, and similarly his knowledge of the descendants beyond the third generation may become quite vague. The *alur waris* is thus an ancestor-oriented, bilateral occasional kin group, which usually becomes ambilineal after the fourth generation. The cohesiveness and activeness of the group depend to a great extent upon the person who is the family representative

[15] Elsewhere in Indonesia called Lebaran.

in the village of origin. From the individual's standpoint, the members of his *alur waris* are in greater part also members of his kindred. In some cases the *alur waris* is larger, while in others the kindred is larger, especially when a marriage with a third cousin (*mindoan*) has occurred, thus including the relatives of the third cousin. When the representative of the *alur waris* has lost track of the descendants of his ancestor, the *alur waris* will be identical with his kindred.

In many villages of South Central Java with dominant *santri* populations, the *alur waris* is not responsible for the care of the ancestral graves, and the term simply means "traceable heirs." Islam generally discourages rituals related to the maintenance of ancestral graves, and this seems to explain the fact that the *santri* villages in the Kebumen regency south of the railroad lack an active *alur waris*, while their graveyards look neglected, dilapidated, and damaged.

Apart from the neighborhood, the kindred, and the *alur waris*, the villager has another type of social relations: those with other members of his hamlet. These relations are of a more or less formal character. Theoretically the residents of the hamlet are all descendants of the original settlers, have land in the vicinity of the hamlet, and thus should cooperate with each other intensively in agricultural and other activities. In reality, however, many hamlet residents have plots of land elsewhere, while many nearby pieces of land belong to or are cultivated by people from other hamlets. Furthermore, in the course of time many hamlet residents have moved out, and aliens have come in to settle. Activities directed by central government agencies, however, tend to operate within the formal hamlet bonds.

More important for the villagers are the social relations and cooperative activities with other peasants who possess irrigated or dry fields in the same locality. Peasants who own fields close to each other tend to assist each other in agricultural activities like hoeing, planting of rice seedlings, care of the young shoots, and weeding the *sawah* while the rice plants grow. This type of mutual aid, called *grodjogan* or *gentosan* in Tjelapar, may be arranged in two ways. In one arrangement, a group of peasants, A, B, C, and D, perform some work together, as for example hoeing in A's field; this man A, in turn, will help B in weeding or something else. The other way is when the group of peasants hoe successively, first on A's field, then on B's field, on C's, and so on. It is this latter arrangement which is called *gentosan* ("alternate in shifts").

The *grodjogan* groups of peasants form more or less permanent work teams, who, although informal in character, easily serve as nuclei for the formation of agricultural or other cooperatives, which promote, for instance, the rent of agricultural implements (such as a plow), the cultivation of fish in ponds, the raising of goats, and sale of copra, and so on.

Several large *grodjogan* groups in Tjelapar do have a formal character. These groups consist of peasants who own plots of land in areas of the village considered to be sacred. Such groups often collectively perform calendrical *slametan* rituals, organized by the oldest member of the group, who often acts as host, with all members contributing to the expenses. The leader of a group of peasants who work fields on the slope of a sacred hill north of the village is not the oldest man of the group, however, but a man considered to possess extensive knowledge of the Javanese traditional system of numerology and astrology in connection with the agricultural cycle.[16]

Finally, the village wards are also important to social relations within the village. Large villages like Tjelapar can be divided into wards, within which people tend to associate more frequently with one another rather than with people from other sections of the village. These wards are often determined by *gardu* (guardhouses) or *warung* (coffee shops), which, because of their location in particular sections of the village, can be considered as the central but informal meeting places of these respective sections. The three *santri* hamlets Sumberan, Sudikampir, and Kalisadang in the southern part of Tjelapar, for example, also form one ward, although with a different type of meeting place, the mosque and the adjacent *pesantrèn* (school for reciting the Koran).

Regular gatherings at guardhouses, coffee shops, or the *pesantrèn*, where people associate informally after work to talk about the daily events in the village, tend to determine the general political viewpoints of those who reside in the respective wards. In matters of local village politics such as elections or appointments of village heads or officials, or in cases of land disputes between families, the village splits into oppos-

[16] This peasant was also the village blacksmith, which in Javanese culture is considered a prestigeful occupation, very often connected with the knowledge of magical practices and curing. The man was, in addition, the technical expert of the village. He was also able to undertake a variety of repair work, from bicycles, sewing machines, and pressure lamps to small mechanisms such as wristwatches.

ing factions that conform to the pattern of the wards. National political parties have also penetrated the village through the ward meeting places; a party will have members predominantly in certain wards but not in others.

6. *Occupations*

Most of the villagers of Tjelapar engage in agriculture, either working their own land or somebody else's on a sharecropping basis or renting land. However, most of the landholdings are very small, much of the land is in dry fields (*tegalan*), and much of the *sawah* land does not produce good crops because of deficient irrigation. The people of Tjelapar, and most of the peasants inhabiting the Seraju Mountain area, cultivate *bodin* (manioc), which constitutes their staple food. The *sawah* are planted with rice, which is not a basic food but one of honor that is offered to visitors, to guests at celebrations, or to neighbors who come to assist in mutual-aid activities. In addition to the main crops, people employ a large variety of secondary crops (*palawidja*), which are cultivated in rotation with the main crops. Several villagers of Tjelapar have become quite wealthy by concentrating in their *tegalan* on the cultivation and trade of *kentjur*, a root widely used in Java for spices or as an important ingredient in various kinds of traditional Javanese medicines. *Kentjur* roots from the villages in the South Seraju Mountain area are transported by carriers and sold to middlemen at the railroad junction in the district town Karanganjar. With the capital accumulated, these peasants have started money lending or house renting or have left the village to start various enterprises in the towns, often supported by initial capital from Chinese.

Generally, however, the peasants of Tjelapar are not wealthy, because most of the landholdings are very small. Thus, many who work their own land act as sharecroppers, or who rent land, must seek additional income. One of the several ways is to hire out as an agricultural laborer. Many of the landowning as well as the landless agricultural laborers (*buruh tani*) of Tjelapar seek employment much more often in other villages outside Tjelapar, especially in those south of the railroad. This tendency to hire out as a laborer outside of Tjelapar is perhaps caused by the lack of esteem attached to working for wages (in the form of money) on somebody else's land. By going away from their village, people can avoid humiliation.

In addition to agricultural labor, there are other modes of supplementary work in which people engage. Several kinds of trades serve the needs of the village. Many women as well as men plait mats, hats, or basketry made of the fiber of the *puḍak* plant (see Section 4) for sale in the market in Somawangsa (a village at an hour's walking distance to the north of Tjelapar). Many men and women make pottery. Twelve carpenters can be employed by the villagers to build frames of houses and furniture. The one blacksmith may be asked to make or repair a hoe or other iron implements. Twelve villagers work as barbers in their spare time. Seven women who own sewing machines may be asked to make children's school clothing. Many women possess looms, but, because yarn is difficult to procure, woven textiles are seldom produced. Many women are skillful at batik work, but, because white muslin is also scarce and difficult to obtain, only a few actually make batik.

More and more people are leaving the village to seek employment elsewhere, either occasionally or permanently. Many villagers, especially young men, migrate seasonally for several months or more to work as rubber tappers or in Chinese enterprises in South Sumatra (Palembang). A number of these were married men who have already stayed in South Sumatra several years; they have ceased to keep in touch with their wife and children, who have thus developed into matrilocal families. On the other hand, I was also told of four cases in which married women have left their husbands and children. Villagers who can afford the costs have sent their sons to attend the junior high school of the junior teacher's school at Karanganjar. Once graduated from these schools, young men usually do not return to the village, and since 1958 an increasing number of young people have left Tjelapar permanently, to work in remote cities such as Bandung or Djakarta, either as servants or as clerks in government service; some have joined the Indonesian army, navy, or air force.

7. Social Classes of the Village

Within the context of Javanese culture as a whole, most villagers are considered only "little people" or *wong tjilik* (see Section 1). Within their own community, however, the villagers of Tjelapar also distinguish three social levels: the *linḍung*, or landless villagers; the *kuli*, or landowning peasants; and the *kénṭol*, or descendants of an original village upper class.

The landless immigrants and landless people in general are considered to be at the bottom of the scale. The term *lindung* to designate these people seems to be restricted to Tjelapar and the villages in the area of the South Seraju Hills; in other places of Java such terms as *pondok*, *pondok selusup*, *glongsor*, or *rangkepan*, are more frequent. Most *lindung* of Tjelapar are poor agricultural laborers who work on other people's land. Several, who do not even have their own house in which to stay, work and live as servants (*rajat*) in the larger households of the village head, the retired former village head, the religious teacher, or several other village notables.

Landless people often may acquire land by purchase or by other means and thus move up in status from *lindung* to *kuli*. The term *kuli* to designate landowning peasants may be different in other areas of Java where terms like *gogol* or others exist. According to the size of landholdings and often accompanying differences in wealth, the *kuli* are subdivided into several levels, ranging from "weak *kuli*" (*kuli kendo*) up to "leading *kuli*" (*kuli pengarep*). Apart from the size of their landholdings and the amount of their wealth, the *kuli* of Tjelapar are also divided into a lower and a higher category based upon the difference between original settlers and newcomers. In the eyes of many villagers, the criterion of seniority is considered even more important than the criterion of wealth.

In Tjelapar the term *kuli* is restricted to those people who possess a *petuk* certificate. As mentioned in Section 3, these certificates describe a collective property of the titleholder and his siblings, who form his dependents or *pondok*. No important differences in terms of social level exist between *kuli* and *pondok*. In other areas of Java, however, where the term *pondok* has the same meaning as *lindung* does in Tjelapar, *pondok* and *kuli* belong to two different social levels.

Every individual landowner, male as well as female, has a number of rights that are confirmed by an ordinance issued by the Dutch colonial government (*Staatsblad 1906 No. 83 jo. bijblad 6576*). Most important is the right to vote for a candidate in the election of village heads or officials; next is the right to petition the district head; then the right to dismiss a village head who has lost the confidence of his villagers; and finally the right to participate in important discussions of the village administration concerning matters within the community. On the other hand, the status of *kuli* also involves a number of community responsibilities: (1) *kerigan*, or supplying labor for the village community, the village officials, and the public works of the government; (2) *tuguran*, or taking care of the night watch in the village; and (3) *palagara*, or supporting the village head and officials with foodstuffs and money on fixed occasions, determined by local customs (see Section 8). Despite its heavy burdens, however, the position of *kuli* still remains a desirable social status in Javanese village communities, since it implies a certain amount of local prestige.

In former times, the concept of *kuli* was probably not identical with that of landowner. Besides the original landowners, who were usually descendants of the original settlers (*wong baku*), most Javanese villages included a group of people who comprised the productive labor force (*kuli*) of the village. These *kuli* were very important, since village heads who had the obligation to recruit and to organize manpower from their respective villages for the Javanese princes and feudal lords, or, under the Dutch colonial government, to work on the construction and upkeep of roads, bridges, and irrigation structures, and also to collect the land tax and large parts of the village crops, had to rely on the *kuli*. In the first place the village heads naturally must have assigned the landowning villagers with the heavy burdens, but in addition they may have called on many other villagers who may not have been landowners. For compensation, many Javanese village communities allotted the *kuli* plots of land for usufruct during their period of service. Such plots of communal land, which are called *siti pekulèn* or *siti gogol*, had to be returned to the village when the *kuli* retired. In many areas of Java where obligations became too heavy, many *kuli* in fact did resign and thus returned their *siti pekulèn* to the village for allotment to other people who were willing to take their place. In Tjelapar and other villages of the South Seraju Hills region, however, *kuli* became a hereditary status, descending together with the *siti pekulèn* to the eldest son of the previous occupant. Not infrequently a younger son is elected, and in default of sons a daughter may succeed to the position, so that not all *kuli* are males. Since the *siti pekulèn* also became inherited land, most people of Tjelapar, although still aware of the existence of the term, could not explain the difference between *siti pekulèn* and the actual inherited land, or *siti jasan*.

The highest social level in Javanese village communities is usually those who consider themselves the direct descendants of the original first settlers. These original settlers are often known as the *tjakal bakal*, or the common ancestors of the community, and their graves are frequently the centers of local public worship. The direct descendants consider themselves as the core of the village (*wong baku*), and they pretend to be the village upper class. In Tjelapar, however, the original settlers are not considered to be the *tjakal bakal*. They are replaced by a semihistorical figure called Untung Surapati. Despite five variants of the myth recorded from five informants in Tjelapar and neighboring villages, all versions describe Utung Surapati as a son of one of the Javanese rulers of the ancient Central Javanese kingdom of Mataram, who was hunted by the Dutch and who, after an adventurous life as an outlaw, wandering about the rural areas of Central Java, finally settled near Tjelapar as a hermit.[17] Based upon this myth, the worship of Untung Surapati (locally called Panembahan), developed in the Tjelapar region, replacing the

[17] All variants of the myth agree in the following particulars: (1) Untung Surapati was the son of the king of Mataram, Sunan Mangkurat Tegalrum; (2) he was born with a helmet and therefore taken to the home of the *patih* (prime minister) to be released, but was switched with the infant of the *patih*, who was also born at approximately the same time; (3) he was raised by a brother of the king named Pangeran Kadjoran; (4) he traveled much as a young man and led an adventurous life; (5) he spent a long time in Bali and went to Djakarta; (6) he worked as a servant with a Dutch family and had a secret affair with the daughter of his master; (7) he was imprisoned and became leader of forty other convicts; (8) he and his forty followers managed to break out of prison; (9) they led an adventurous life as outlaws in the surroundings of Djakarta; (10) later they were driven to the east by Dutch troops but received aid from Javanese kings, such as the Sultan of Tjirebon, and later the Sunan of Mataram; (11) the king of Mataram concealed Untung Surapati, gave orders to kill a convict who very much looked like him, and showed the Dutch troops who arrived at Mataram in search of Untung Surapati the corpse of the convict; (12) the king of Mataram sent a force under command of Pangeran Puger to East Java to suppress a revolt in Pasuruhan, and Untung Surapati joined the force; (13) he was able to defeat the head of the rebels, Bupati Tjakranegara, in a duel; (14) as a reward, Untung Surapati was granted the status of *bupati* (regent) of Pasuruhan; (15) later the Dutch identified the regent of Pasuruhan as Untung Surapati, who was supposed to have been killed by the king of Mataram; (16) they attacked Pasuruhan and defeated Untung Surapati's armed forces; (17) Untung Surapati fled and continued a hunted and adventurous life as an outlaw, wandering about the rural areas of Java; (18) he became a servant and student of a famous hermit and thus became a hermit himself; (19) he settled in the South Seraju Hills at a place, Depok, near the recent village Tjelapar; (20) in Depok the hermit Untung Surapati became also widely known by the name of Ki Pemandangan; (21) he married five women—four local women from nearby villages, of whom two were spirits (one a *peri*, and one a *siluman simau*), and a princess from Mataram; (22) a son named Ki Somadiwangsa, who was born from the princess, married the daughter of Ki Wanahita, the original settler of the village Tjelapar.

worship of the original *tjakal bakal* of the village. A sacred grave, hidden in the forest south of Tjelapar is considered to be Panembahan's grave, and a large ambilineal kin group, which orients itself toward the sacred ancestor Panembahan Untung Surapati, forms the *kéntol*, a powerful village nobility. The village head of Tjelapar, most of his village officials, the retired head, many Tjelapar families, the village heads of six other adjacent villages, the village officials, and a great number of families in many other neighboring villages all consider themselves as belonging to the Tjelapar *kéntol*. Genealogies in poetic form written in Javanese script, showing kinship relations with Panembahan, are kept as sacred heirlooms by the headman of Tjelapar and by several other of the important *kéntol* families. Several members of their younger generation, who have had the opportunity to enjoy a relatively advanced school education, have left the village to go into government service or into the Indonesian army or air force. They thus have obtained a *prijaji* status.

Apart from political power, the *kéntol* also enjoy great prestige within the village community, manifested by the formal style of speech and the respectful attitude adopted by the villagers in dealing with them. The superior status is also evident from the distinctive seats occupied by the *kéntol* at feasts, *slametan* ceremonies, and other public occasions.[18]

Tjelapar also counts among its residents a number of lower-ranking government officials: the government teak forest supervisor, the irrigation supervisor, a village health officer, three village schoolteachers, and three retired government officials, who have bought land in Tjelapar and who plan to stay in the village for the rest of their lives. The *prijaji* status of all these people puts them on a level with the *kéntol* in the community, but the villagers will always consider them as outsiders. They do not have the same rights and duties as the other villagers: for instance, they may not participate in the elections of a village headman, and they do not have to work at *kerigan*.

8. The Village Administration

Tjelapar forms the center of an administrative unit consisting of five villages called *glondongan*. From the standpoint of village administration, the recent significance of such units does not seem to be very great. Each of the four other village heads makes decisions autonomously and

[18] Earlier information about these *kéntol* are included in A. van der Poel (1846, 173–180) and Pranahadikoesoema (1939, 153–160).

does not depend whatsoever on the village head of Tjelapar; at meetings of village heads in the subdistrict or district office, each of the five headmen appears individually. A brief investigation of the contacts between Tjelapar and its neighbors has shown much more intensive relations with a market village to the north than with two of Tjelapar's subordinate villages. The association between the five villages of the *glonḍongan* seems only to have a traditional and symbolic meaning. In many other areas of Java, indeed, similar confederative associations of villages do exist, of which two types are the most frequent. One type, called *mantjapat*, is similar to the *glonḍongan* Tjelapar, an association of five villages; the second type, called *mantjalima*, is an association of nine villages, with one in the center and eight surrounding it.[19] There seems to have been a period in which the administrative units had some significance for cooperation in times of natural disaster and insecurity or when joint efforts and cooperation between the villages concerned were needed for purposes of irrigation. In many areas of Java, the Dutch colonial government long neglected the system of Javanese village confederations but never abolished it. Although it has now lost its function in most areas of Java, its outward form, like the *glonḍongan* Tjelapar, still exists.

Although, in matters of village administration, Tjelapar's headman has no authority over the other four headmen of the dependent villages, socially he is their superior. He may demand their respect according to Javanese etiquette, and at public gatherings he ranks higher.

Besides being nominal head with the title *glonḍong* of the four villages, Tjelapar's headman is the actual headman or *lurah* of his own village. In different areas of Java he would be called by other terms, such as *bekel, perbekel, ḍemang, penatus, kuwu,* or *petinggi.* From time immemorial, village heads have been elected by the adult inhabitants of their village, very often without formal consent of the king. Only in areas of direct concern to the king, as in those villages situated near

[19] The term *mantjapat* means "four outgroups," while *mantjalima* means "five out-groups." The *mantjalima* confederative system seems thus to be an extension of the *mantjapat* system. The first circle of four villages is considered as one unit while, together with the four other villages of the second concentric circle, the whole system will thus consist of five out-groups. Dutch specialists on Indonesia have speculated a great deal on the real meaning of these systems of village confederations. Probably influenced by the frequent occurrence of the number five and of concentric circles in Javanese mysticism and magical practices, these scholars try to relate the *mantjapat* system of village confederacies with the Javanese primitive mentality.

the court town, was royal approval of the candidate required. In areas allotted by the king to his relatives and to members of the nobility for appanage (*lungguh*), however, village heads were often appointed by the lord or his officials. When Java came under direct control of the Dutch colonial government, the elected headman had to be approved by the district head (*wedana*), and with the abolishment of the appanage system (from 1918 on) the election and appointment of village headmen became uniform throughout most of Java.

Once elected, the headman continues in office without re-election as long as he retains the confidence and respect of his villagers, often until his death. It has been mentioned, however, that if he loses this confidence, the *kuli* of the village can petition the district head, who has the power to dismiss the incumbent and to call a meeting of the *kuli* to elect a new *lurah*. A headman who retires voluntarily usually nominates one or two candidates from among the more respected men of the village—often one of the local officials or a relative who has served without pay as the headman's assistant (*magang*)—and the villagers choose the successor by vote. Candidates for *lurah* campaign through many informal means of persuasion and conciliation, such as feast giving or house-to-house visits. Membership in the *kéntol* class is still an important requirement for candidacy as village head in the South Seraju Hills, while in Tjelapar and villages in the same general area several *lurah* belong to the kin group who consider themselves the direct descendants of Panembahan.

Aside from membership in the *kéntol* class and in the prestigeful Panembahan *alur waris* kin group, the *glondong* of Tjelapar also derives his power from his position as guardian of Panembahan's sacred grave. Through this function he is believed to be in close contact with the ancestral spirits and thus to possess magical power, which enables him to practice curing and sorcery. He enjoys a wide reputation as *kijahi* or *dukun*, the *abangan* type of religious specialist, and people come to visit him not only from the surrounding villages but also from areas and cities throughout Central and East Java, and even from Djakarta, in order to be cured from diseases, to obtain advice on love matters, family problems, and failures in business enterprises, to consult him concerning magical practices to injure competitors and rivals, or to get magical formulas and amulets for many other purposes. His Java-wide reputation has placed the *kijahi* of Tjelapar in contact with many *prijaji* and urban people and has brought him a certain amount of material wealth.

As village administrator, Tjelapar's headman is assisted by a staff of fifteen village officials (*prabot desa*), most of whom are appointed, although several are elected. There are two deputy village headman (*tjongkok*), one village clerk (*tjarik*), two village treasurers (*kamituwa*), two religious officials (*kaum*), whose main function is to register divorces, four village marshals (*pulisi* or *djagabaja*), and four village announcers or messengers (*kebajan*). Another important functionary usually present in most Javanese villages, the man in charge of the distribution of water for irrigation (*ulu-ulu, andjir,* or *reksabumi*) is traditionally absent in Tjelapar.

The headman and his officials receive no salaries from the government but are supported in part by the usufruct from plots of land (*siti bengkok*) that are allotted to them during their period of office and in part by a variety of traditional duties and services owed to them by the villagers. These duties and services are called *palagara* and consist of the following obligations: (1) to pay the village officials a fixed amount of rice per year (*djanggolan*); (2) to offer the village officials food at celebrations (*pundjungan*); (3) to offer a village official a small percentage of the total payment when he is called upon to witness transactions like purchases, sales, leases, loans, or pawning (*panjeksèn*); (4) to pay the village head when a local exogamous marriage occurs and when a bride is moved away from the village community (*pengandjal*); and finally (5) to work in the household of a village official for a certain amount of time (*kuduran*).

In addition to the *lurah* and his *prabot desa*, there exists a council of elders or *kasepuhan*, a highly respected but informal group. Tjelapar has a council of twenty-one elders, of whom eighteen are residents and three, peculiarly enough, nonresidents. The *kasepuhan* of Tjelapar are *abangan*, except one man who is a *santri*. This man lives in one of the southern hamlets of Tjelapar called Sumberan and is a religious teacher and an expert in reciting the Koran. Most of Tjelapar's *santri* are indeed concentrated in Sumberan and two adjacent hamlets, although several other *santri* families live scattered in the other parts of the village. Unlike in other Javanese village communities, where the council of elders is usually an advisory body to the village head, the Tjelapar council includes the village head himself. The council meets very irregularly, according to informants, only when disasters occur or only to discuss *adat* matters in the abstract. Personal controversies between several of the members of the council have created factionalism, and the group apparently does not exercise much influence on the village administration or on its social and political life. Every one of the twenty-one old men, however, is considered to be an expert on Javanese *adat*, and the villagers may consult any one of them individually on such matters.

The headman and his staff hold regular meetings with the villagers every thirty-five days. The traditional meeting, usually called *rapat selapanan*, is according to Javanese *adat* supposed to be attended by the responsible landowning inhabitants, which would include only the *kuli*. In Tjelapar, where one can be a landowner without being a *kuli*, the villagers who attend the meetings and who have the right to vote are the *kepala somah* (heads of households). The meetings, held in the spacious front veranda of the headman's house (*pendapa*), are usually discussions of domestic matters within the village community, joint village projects, land disputes, and other problems of general interest. Several meetings that I attended during my field work considered the plan to improve irrigation by building a dam in one of the little rivers south of the village, formed a committee to organize a feast for the village school, reported on public safety to a subdistrict police officer who happened to be present, discussed a land dispute, and planned to raise funds for the Organisasi Pertahanan Rakjat, or village defense organization. In addition, at every meeting various government announcements and instructions, from both district and subdistrict, were made.

In village meetings in Central Java, the headman often appears to determine everything in an authoritative manner, while the heads of the households serve only to approve his decisions. Those who attend seem passive, and no opposition is apparent. Careful observation, however, exposes the considerable opposition that does exist in Javanese village communities, although it is rarely discernible from the outside. Efforts are made behind the scenes to reduce the differences between conflicting viewpoints, during the discussions and gossip in the guardhouses or coffee shops. The village head, who actively participates in these operations, knows every development; at the official meeting his announcements are nothing but the final resolution of preliminary discussions, and as such are naturally acceptable to a majority of the assembled people. This system of conducting meetings is probably derived from a corresponding element in Javanese social behavior, in which public controversy must be avoided at all costs. This attitude is further strengthened by the patriarchal figure of the village head; like a father, he should never be directly contradicted. Apparently this old system is being abandoned in places where village assemblies are presided over by younger men.

The young village head does not inspire fatherly respect, and he may in addition, having been educated in the town and usually having taken part in meetings of political parties or other organizations, himself change the mode for conducting a village assembly.

Other meetings are held occasionally in between the thirty-five-day intervals, in cases of emergency, for example, or more frequently when announcements must be made on behalf of the central government, the district or subdistrict administration.

9. Associational Groups

The associations that serve specific village interests can mainly be divided into four types: economic, aesthetic-recreational, religious, and educational.

The economic associations take the form of village cooperatives. Such organizations existed long before World War II, both in Tjelapar and in Javanese village communities in general. After the war, the Indonesian central government made efforts to intensify the development of cooperatives down to the village level. A cooperative service was established as part of the Ministry of Economic Affairs to sponsor, support, and supervise this development. As a result of continuous propaganda and directives from both the cooperative service and the administration, many cooperative organizations have arisen in Tjelapar. Each hamlet counts at least one cooperative, established under government instructions to promote the conservation of *pari* (paddy). These, however, are nothing but modern versions of the traditional *lumbung pari* system, in which members stored unthreshed rice to provide seed for the next planting season and inexpensive rice for celebrations and feasts or as preparation against times of scarcity. The rice borrowed by members from the storehouse must be returned with a small amount of interest. Other cooperatives have not been established along hamlet lines but have long been developed among the cooperative *grodjogan* work groups of peasants (see Section 5). Most of these cooperatives in Tjelapar are established to promote the raising of goats, as the meat is in great demand for feasts, while others aim at the cultivation of fish in ponds to provide additional food. These associations in Tjelapar function both as credit and as consumption cooperatives. Recurrent credit, however, is very rarely used by the peasants for improvement or expansion of existing enterprises. The establishment of cooperatives for renting agricultural or other implements, such as plows, large hand saws to cut timber, or plates, drinking glasses, spoons, and gas lamps for feasts, is a very recent development. Usually *grodjogan* groups jointly own plows or other equipment, which is lent to others on a mutual-aid basis, while necessities for feasts are owned and rented by enterprising individuals.

Aesthetic and recreational associations have also existed since much earlier than World War II. Most important are the several art groups: nine *selawatan* groups, two *angguk* groups, and one *wajang wong* group. *Selawatan* groups consist of ten to fifteen members, with an instructor who is often also the leader. At *selawatan* performances the participants in turn sing chants of Arabic origin, accompanied by five drums and tambourines. The chants retell narratives taken from the Javanese Islamic folk literature. *Angguk* is a Javanese folk play based on Javanese Islamic folk history, the Anbija and Menak stories, performed by boys or young men who act, dance, and sing to the accompaniment of drums and tambourines. The group may consist of ten to fifteen persons, also under the leadership of one person who is considered the most expert on the plays.[20] The *wajang wong* group is much bigger than all the other art groups, having more than thirty members with a leader and several instructors. The *wajang wong* is a Javanese folk play that is much influenced by the Hindu epics Mahabharata and Ramayana. The play is performed by males as well as females, who act, dance, and sing to the accompaniment of a complete Javanese orchestra. A village *gamelan* orchestra employs about ten musicians who play xylophones, gongs, and other percussion instruments. The village art groups are usually hired to provide entertainment at feasts. The actors rehearse regularly at the leader's house.

Many inhabitants, especially the younger people of the three *santri* hamlets in the southern part of Tjelapar, are affiliated with the *pesantrèn* school. A group of twenty to thirty boys gathers regularly each evening for two to three hours at the *medjid* (mosque) after *magrib*, or sunset prayer, to practice reciting verses from the Koran. They are also taught writing in Arabic script. The teacher is an old *santri* peasant of the *kéntol* class, who has made the pilgrimage to Mecca and who is also considered as leader of the Tjelapar *santri*. Being a minority, this group exhibits great solidarity and often opposes the village headman.

Youth organizations of traditional character are the *sinoman* for boys and *bijada* for girls. The original purpose was probably educational. Among others, these groups were often initiated to perform preparatory

[20] For further information on *selawatan* and *angguk* see T. Pigeaud (1938, 103–104, 272–273, 282–283, 290–295).

work for feasts and celebrations. The headman of Tjelapar has made unsuccessful attempts to organize a *bijada* group for girls exclusively from the *kénṭol* group, and instructions to form *sinoman* groups have not been received with great enthusiasm by the Tjelapar youth. Most girls from the *kénṭol* class have attended the village school and form cliques that concentrate on activities like sewing and child care. Most boys of Tjelapar are organized into the village defense organization, which was established at government instruction to give village youth some military training and to teach them some military discipline. In addition, the Tjelapar defense or youth organization is very active in sports and recreation as well as in social activities, such as in rendering aid at feast preparations and in cases of sickness, accident, or death.

10. Relations with the Supravillage World

From time immemorial, Javanese village communities have been subordinate to a supreme government, controlled by a hierarchic administrative system of which they knew only the lowest reaches. Although several studies have been made by sociologists or historians on the structure of this ancient administrative system (Schrieke 1957, I, 167–227; II, 1–267; Boechari 1963, 122–133), we possess concrete knowledge of the administration only from the Dutch colonial period. In certain areas of Java, and very likely in the South Seraju Hills region, the system developed as late as the second half of the eighteenth century. The bureaucracy, called *pamong pradja*, consists of a highly developed chain of command, a pyramid whose lowest layer is comprised of subdistrict heads (*onder*, *setèn*, *tjamat*, or *penèwu*) who receive orders from district heads (*wedana*), who in turn are subordinate to regency heads (*bupati*). These indigenous civil administrators were supervised by Dutch officials and were subservient to Dutch residency heads (*residenten*), and these in turn to Dutch provincial heads (governors), who formed the top of the pyramid and were in direct contact with the Department of Inland Administration (Legge 1961, 1–20). The subdistrict usually includes twenty to thirty villages, while the district controls five to ten subdistricts. Tjelapar, together with twenty-six other villages, belongs to the subdistrict of Karanggajam, one of the five subdistricts of the district Karanganjar.

The villagers have most frequent contact with the subdistrict heads and the members of his staff, the intensiveness of the relationship depending on the industriousness of the local officials. Less important will be contact with the district officer, who only infrequently pays visits to villages; however, occasional meetings of village heads do occur at the district office. The least frequent contact will be with the regency officers. Except for villages near the regency capital, most villagers have never even seen the regent to whose territory their village belongs, and not many people are aware of the existence of still higher levels.

Members of the *pamong pradja* belong to the highly respected *prijaji* class and are considered greatly superior in status to village people of even the highest levels. *Pamong pradja* possess extensive power and authority within their own territories and enjoy great prestige among the rural population. *Pamong pradja* administrators express their superiority in the patriarchal attitude that they assume in dealing with village heads and officials. The village administrators, in fact, are accustomed to receiving orders only from the *pamong pradja*, and consequently other departments or ministries of the central government have to make use of the *pamong pradja* to communicate their instructions to village levels. Thus a *pamong pradja* administrator, particularly the subdistrict head, is relied on for communications with the villagers not only by the more recently established local bureaus of many new Indonesian ministries or local branches of national political parties but even by local government departments which had already been in existence under the colonial administration.

The Indonesian government has attempted to introduce a new democratic administrative system based on regional and local autonomy. In Indonesia in general, and in Java in particular, these efforts were felt by the *pamong pradja* to represent a serious threat to their position, and they were not understood very well by many members of the bureaucracy. Investigations concerning the development of regional and local autonomy had begun under the Dutch colonial government; preparations for the system's introduction lasted almost a decade, while the actual efforts to develop it had in 1954 not yet reached the village or the so-called third level,[21] except as an experiment in the special region of Jogjakarta (principality of South Central Java).[22] Tjelapar belongs

[21] Much has been written on the plans and preparations for the development of regional authority in Indonesia, although concentrating mainly on the legal aspects of the matter. For references see the bibliography in Legge (1961, 281–289). In addition, see The Liang Gie (1958). For the more sociological aspects of regional authority in the case of Jogjakarta, see Selosoemardjan (1962).

[22] For the development of regional authority in Jogjakarta, see Soenarjo Dipodiningrat (1954).

to an area that still continues under the old system of village administration. Consequently the subdistrict head of Karanggajam is still one of the most important men, through whom national ideologies and concepts deriving from the central government are filtered down to the village.

In matters of party politics in Tjelapar, the *pamong pradja* also plays a formulative role, since the villagers consider relations with a superior much more important than commitment to a party ideology. Despite the fact that the village had been an important base for guerrilla units during the Indonesian armed revolution, and despite the fact that during this period the village population had been exposed to the influences of national and political ideologies, the population of Tjelapar, like most traditional villages of the South Seraju Hills region, still is largely very unsophisticated in matters of national politics. Consequently many people simply follow the *pamong pradja*, who in South Central Java belong predominantly to the Nationalist Party (PNI). During the 1955 elections for Parliament and the Constitutional Assembly, the village head of Tjelapar, his staff, and the majority of the population voted for the PNI. The immediate and most vigorous rival of the PNI in the South Seraju Hill region at that time was the Communist Party (PKI). In Tjelapar this party naturally incorporated the opponents, personal rivals, and enemies of the village head, people who live mainly in the southern hamlets of the village. This group included the Moslem religious teacher and most of Tjelapar's *santri*, thus bringing about a situation in which pious Moslems voted for the Communists.[23]

Since 1955 the *pamong pradja* have also been entrusted with the very important but difficult task of implementing the government's community development program in cooperation with the Djawatan Pendidikan Masjarakat (Bureau of Community Education) of the Ministry of Education and, recently, with the local Biro Pembangunan Masjarakat Desa (Bureau for Community Development) of the Ministry of Cooperatives. Particularly in the South Seraju Hills region, the *pamong pradja* often have had to do the major part of the work themselves. In Tjelapar, for instance, the subdistrict administration had to organize the literacy courses, as well as courses on community leadership, which for particular reasons were not very successful at that time. The government has based its program of community development on the principle that a great

[23] Three years after the election, when I did my field work in Tjelapar, the excitement of political antagonisms and the activities of the political parties had altogether disappeared.

deal must be left to the initiative of the villagers themselves,[24] but the traditional patriarchal attitude of the *pamong pradja* toward the rural population has not left much room for the development of individual initiative. In addition, the civil servants are often too soon satisfied with superficial results; for example, the results of the literacy campaign in the villages of the South Seraju Hills region has been very striking indeed, but little attention has been paid to following it up. In Tjelapar, for instance, I noticed in 1959 that many of the illiterate peasants of the village, who had attended the courses one or two years before, had already lost the ability to read, because the lack of relatively simple reading material did not give them any opportunity to use their new education. In general, very little reading material enters the village regularly. Only the village teachers and one of the retired government officials subscribe to newspapers and magazines, which are delivered at the subdistrict post office. A village messenger goes there three times a week to obtain the papers and also the mail, which must be delivered to various individuals in the village.

Although the community's channels of contact with the outside world are very limited, on an individual basis the villagers have extensive relations with their acquaintances in South Sumatra or with their friends and relatives in Djakarta, Bandung, Jogjakarta, or other cities. However, those villagers who through school education or extensive contact with the outside world have become receptive to change, as well as the more enterprising and progressive individuals, tend to leave the village to seek their futures elsewhere. For the time being Tjelapar will probably not have much opportunity to develop into a strong autonomous community within the framework of the modern Indonesian state, because it constantly loses its best people.

As a result of centuries of domination by a patriarchal administrative system, directed from the top by Javanese supreme rulers or by the colonial government, Javanese village communities have developed into clear-cut and discrete territorially based administrative units, a fact which will make it harder to amalgamate them into larger communities able to support a more effective, modern democratic administrative system. This will be the biggest problem in the development of regional autonomy on the third level in Java.

[24] This aspect of community development in Indonesia is also described by Selosoemardjan (1963).

Chapter XI

Villages of Unplanned Resettlers in the Subdistrict Kaliredjo, Central Lampung[1]

KAMPTO UTOMO

UNIVERSITY OF INDONESIA

1. Javanese Resettlement in the Lampung Area

The Netherlands East Indies government began the resettlement of Javanese peasants in Lampung, South Sumatra, in 1905. Owing to these efforts, an enclave of what are known as Javanese "colonization villages" was created in the surroundings of Gedongtataan, twenty kilometers west of Tandjungkarang, the capital of Lampung with its port Teluk-betung. Later, in 1926, the resettlement villages were expanded, and the community of Pringsewu came into being about thirty kilometers to the west. Thus in the heart of Lampung with its swiddens, coffee gardens, and pepper groves, Javanese communities have emerged with their distinct social, cultural, and ecologic patterns.

South of Pringsewu at the fertile edges of Rawa Kementara (Kementara marshes), more resettlement villages sprang up even during World War II, under the influence of the Lampung *marga* system. These new villages to the south accommodated in part the Javanese resettlers who had abandoned the large-scale settlements of Sukadana and Metro, which the colonial government from 1935 had established on the plains of Cen-

[1] This chapter has been translated from the original Indonesian text by T. W. Kamil.

281

tral Lampung[2] (see Map XIV). In addition, quite a few of the earlier resettlers from the Gedongtataan-Pringsewu region moved to these southern border areas because of the "population pressure" in the older

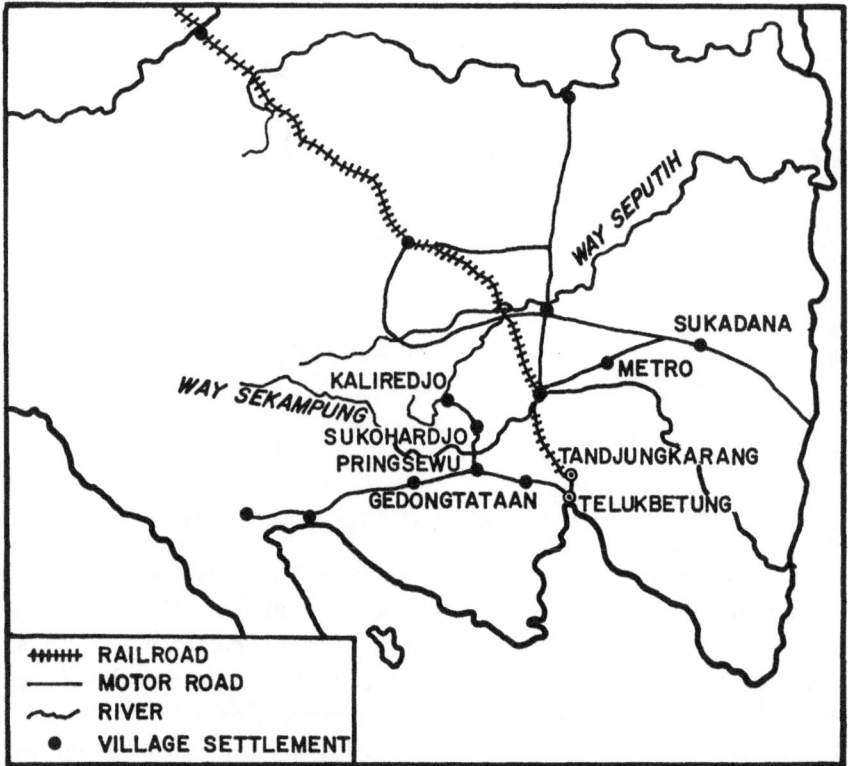

Map XIV. Javanese Resettlement Area of Lampung

colonization villages, similar to the situation in rural Java. In 1938 it was noted that in the "old" colonization villages, approximately 73 per cent of the landholders owned less than .7 hectare, whereas 32 per cent of the heads of families owned no land at all. It may even be asserted that it was the old settlements themselves that generated the leadership for new pioneer villages.

[2] For further information about the implications of resettlement programs, see Heyting (1938), Leeden (1952), Pelzer (1945), Soekasno (1941), and Verstappen (1956).

In the first years of the Indonesian revolution, before the Dutch military action between 1948 and 1949, and following the restoration of interregional communications after the transfer of sovereignty in 1950, the Javanese of the old colonization villages Gedongtataan and Pringsewu began to search for new land to settle and cultivate. Permission to clear land to the north of the Way Sekampung River, which for the most part consisted of vast forests, was obtained both from the *marga* heads in the southern section of Lampung (the *marga* Way Semah and the *marga* Pogung) and from those who resided in the villages of the Way Seputih Valley about fifty kilometers to the north (the *marga* Pubian and the *marga* Anak Tuha).

Simultaneously the Indonesian government began a resettlement program for people from Java. In part, this measure was merely a continuation of the old program, that is, the transplanting of wet rice cultivation to the Central Lampung plains. A second, more important endeavor, was the beginning of new clearings in the western part of Lampung by the Biro Rekonstruksi Nasional, or B.R.N. (National Reconstruction Bureau), as part of the rehabilitation program for Javanese revolutionary veterans. The B.R.N. project included, among others, the upstream land between the valleys of the Way Sekampung in the south and the Way Seputih in the north, with Sukohardjo, an early (1939) colonization village on the north bank of the Way Sekampung River, as the starting point.

Encouraged both by the willingness of the various *marga* to accommodate pioneers and by the activities of the government, the population of the old villages Gedongtataan and Pringsewu became involved in the northward movement, crossing the Way Sekampung River. The new settlements became known as the "Way Sekampung area." Remarkably, it was the old and middle-aged people who spurred this activity. Originally this spontaneous pioneering was local in character, including people who moved from older villages to new Lampung areas, but the restoration of communications with Java, by mail and by visiting, soon produced results. The flow of spontaneous self-supporting settlers coming directly from Java grew rapidly, until it became even stronger than the movement of local pioneers.[3]

[3] For further information about these unplanned resettlements in Lampung see Djoko Santoso and Ali Wardhana (1957) and Kampto Utomo (1957, 1958).

2. *The Subdistrict of Kaliredjo,*
Way Sekampung Area

Six and a half years later, as of July 1957, it was estimated that the settlers who had moved into the villages north of the Way Sekampung numbered between thirty-five and forty thousand people (about 8,500 family heads), distributed among eighteen new villages. At that time the number who had come directly from Java as spontaneous settlers was thought to be at least twice that of the local pioneers. Among the local pioneers, it was also found that the older age groups dominated. Table 19 is based on records giving the ages of family heads in the four original pioneer villages around Kaliredjo.

Table 19. Settlers in the Kaliredjo area by age and origin

	Under 35 years	35 to 45 years	Over 45 years
Local pioneers	44%	34%	22%
Spontaneous settlers	57%	28%	15%

During field work consisting of several months in three subsequent periods in the years 1956 and 1957, I attempted to study the development of these various Javanese pioneer villages (which I will subsequently call *desa* Djawa to differentiate them from the native Sumatran *kampung* Lampung). I was particularly concerned with patterns of leadership, seen first between the *kepala tebang* (chief clearers) and their followers and subsequently, as the population grew steadily during the period of expansion and consolidation that led to the formation or organization of villages, in the relationship of the *lurah* or village heads with their people (in the initial stages the village heads were former chief clearers).

Within the traditional Lampung *marga* system, which since 1954 has seen the addition of the *negeri*, a third autonomous region generally consisting of several *marga*, the community of Javanese pioneers from the beginning was equated with the small Lampung village or *kampung*. During my field work, it was apparent that the Javanese villages had reached a point of self-sufficiency where they were no longer dependent upon the *negeri*. Other than the initial permission for land use from the *marga,* no significant relation between the *marga* and the pioneers has ever developed; the pioneers have never been influenced by *marga* leadership. With common aspirations for development under the leadership of their own *pamong desa* (village administrators) and *lurah,* the pioneers created separate communities. Subsequently they demanded government acknowledgment of their achievements in their insistence upon the formation of their own separate subdistrict. In this way the pioneers hoped to communicate directly with government authorities, thus gaining access to any government aid available on the subdistrict level, help which they thought would not be forthcoming if they were under *marga* or *negeri* leadership. Thus at the end of 1957 the district administration of Central Lampung agreed to form the subdistrict of Kaliredjo, which included about half of the new residents in the Way Sekampung area, eleven villages with a population of about eighteen thousand (with approximately 4,500 family heads). The name had been derived from that of the first pioneer village in the area. Considering this united action by the pioneer villages, clearly evident during the period of my research, I have decided to choose as the object of my study the group of pioneer villages as a whole rather than one particular village.

Another factor to be discussed in this chapter is the pattern of ecologic adaptation, in particular the various ways and forms the peasants employed in starting their work on newly cleared land, from the moment they arrived as pioneers and obtained a piece of land to be cleared and cultivated up to their efforts to sell produce on the market. I will also survey the extent to which differentiation occurred in the economy of the new villages. In drawing comparisons with the farming methods of the original Lampung population, with their swidden farming and dry rice cultivation, I hope to gain an insight into the prospects, as well as the limitations and obstacles, encountered by the Javanese pioneers in their introduction of wet rice farming in the new area. In my field work I made qualitative comparisons of conditions in various villages; the figures presented in this chapter were taken from records available in one particular village, as I did not have the opportunity at the time to do a special survey to collect complete census material.

The villages in the new subdistrict of Kaliredjo originally belonged to the Lampung district Padangratu. After division, the old subdistrict was left with 12,500 residents (about 3,000 family heads), distributed among twenty-two *kampung* in the upper valley of the Way Seputih: 84 per cent consisted of Lampungese, while 16 per cent were Javanese.

The average village in the old Lampung subdistrict contained 136 family heads and 564 residents (15 per cent nonindigenous), while the average *desa* Djawa in the new subdistrict of Kaliredjo counted 459 family heads and 1,794 residents, more than three times the number found in the average Lampung *kampung*. The average old colonization village in the Pringsewu area contained 460 family heads and 2,308 residents. The average family in the Lampung Padangratu subdistrict numbered 3.9 members, whereas the figure for the new Javanese villages was 4.1.

3. The Pattern of Leadership in the
Pioneer Communities

The first clearing permit for the initial Kaliredjo pioneers was granted in 1950 by the head of *marga* Anak Tuha, who at the time lived at Hadujangratu, a *kampung* in the valley of Way Seputih. The leader of the pioneers who obtained the permit, called *kepala tebang* (chief clearer), was an elderly man who twenty-five years previously had already experienced the first pioneering in the Pringsewu area. He had traveled more than forty kilometers in order to obtain the permit from the *marga* head. Subsequently other people came forward to request land-clearing permits, each thus becoming *kepala tebang* of a group that would then select a particular area in the forest, collect supplies from their old village, clear the land, and start dry rice farming, each individual with his own section. If the harvest was good, the *kepala tebang* would increase the number of his followers and expand the field area in the coming years. These followers became the populations of the new villages, with each pioneer settled on his own share of land. Village territories with their boundaries clearly drawn were created, but since the clearing permits never specified a particular plot within the forest area, conflicts very often arose among the chief clearers and later among the new villages as well.

After their wives and children had joined them, the pioneers built houses, and a new village came into being. The *kepala tebang*, who was always considered the leader of the group, often automatically became the *lurah* (village head). He would appoint a *tjarik* (village secretary), usually a young man with some school education, to help him in keeping records of the ever-increasing population. He also would appoint a *kamitua* (treasurer) and other assistants, called *kebajan*, to take charge of the respective *peḍukuhan* (hamlets). The village administration was responsible for the further development of the village: it had to distribute land for dwelling places as well as for farming, and it had to organize and direct the construction of roads between the various *peḍukuhan* and even from village to village.

There indeed is an urgent need for communications between the new Javanese pioneer villages as well as with the old villages and the nearby towns. Roads, village market squares, school buildings, and other public utilities are usually built on a *gotong-rojong* (mutual-help) basis, in terms directed by the respective *kebajan*. In the case of road construction, for example, every pioneer whose land borders on the road must clear it and help remove the big tree trunks remaining from the forest. In this way people also collect wood for building material, either for their own use or for sale. The sale of wood produces money, which then can be contributed to the funds needed for paying workers who build bridges over small streams.

The new villages opened elementary schools, with the expenses for buildings and for teachers' salaries shouldered collectively. The teachers, recruited from the newcomers, were often not properly qualified. When funds were short, social-minded village heads frequently took care of part of the teachers' wages, by giving them free room and board, or turned sections of their houses into classrooms: "noblesse oblige."

Some pioneer villages derived profits from building markets, first clearing part of the village land for the purpose and then collecting money from the retailers who were given licenses to build shops or booths. Not every village succeeded, for the already large number of existing markets, often at only short distances from one another, and the system of quite frequent market days, recurring twice a week with different schedules for each market, make it unprofitable for newer villages to establish a market. In 1957 only one village had managed to build a mosque, apparently because it had a relatively large number of *santri* among its population. There was also a village that built a clinic at the initiative of a *mantri kesehatan* (head nurse and administrator for health affairs) from the village of Sukohardjo.

What do the village people conceive as the ideal *pamong desa* (village adminstration) and village head? The term *pamong desa*, derived from the Javanese verb *momong* (literally, take care of, foster), implies the concept of directing and guiding the people. A leader who understands people's needs thus will know how to direct the people in his community, but there should be a mutual relationship. Not only should the leader make sure that the people act in accordance with his directions for the common good, but conversely the people should have some control over his guidance and his services for the community. Indeed, in the later development of a pioneer village the village head has often been replaced by another man who has greater ability to guide the further progress and stabilization of the community.

The members of the village administration receive compensation in the form of rice, which the people present once a year (*djanggolan*). In the old prewar colonization villages, the amount was fixed (between 25 and 50 kilograms of rice, varying from village to village), but in the new villages the amount of the *djanggolan* is optional, to be considered as a symbol of the people's gratitude toward the village administrators for their tireless efforts. Usually the rice is collected at each *pedukuhan*; part is distributed among the *kamitua* and the various *kebajan* and part given to the *lurah*. Together with the *tjarik* and the various *kebajan*, the *lurah* actually also receives a portion of the *djanggolan* from the *kradjan*, that is to say, the part of the village where he lives. The *lurah* receives the largest portion, and after him come the *tjarik* and the *kamitua*, while the several *kebajan* get the smallest shares. Consequently, the larger the number of village administrators, the smaller each one's share. Aside from *djanggolan*, the *lurah* and the *tjarik* receive directly administrative fees from people who need affidavits or certificates. Communication and good mutual understanding between the *lurah* and the people is accomplished through the *kamitua* and the *kebajan*, whereas the meetings of the members of the village administration attempt to determine the general opinion of the people in the various *pedukuhan* and the smaller sections of the village. The villages usually hold recurrent meetings at the *pedukuhan* level, which is much more efficient than a meeting of the entire village. Although not always all adult members are present (women are usually absent), the important thing about these meetings is that people get the opportunity to meet with one of the administration, be it the *kamitua* or the *lurah*, to discuss the many problems concerning the community. The dominant individuals at these discussions are usually either the older local pioneers, many of whom are already elderly or middle-aged but are still considered prominent even in the new villages, or the younger veterans, who are often active in political parties or other organizations. The structure of the central village leadership, with a *lurah* who is capable of initiating various constructive activities in the village, tends to strengthen the monolithic character of the Javanese pioneer village communities.

In villages with active veterans' organizations, the *lurah* are often compelled to cooperate with the veterans for the implementation of such important and expensive projects as the building of markets and bridges. This means that the *lurah* are compelled to share authority and leadership with individuals outside the village administration. It is no secret that in the general elections of 1955 and 1956 the many votes obtained by several big parties were a result not only of the influence of the *lurah*, the village adminstration, and the *kepala tebang* but also of the influence of veterans. These veteran pioneers were particularly dominant in two new villages, including both veterans of particular army units, and their relatives, as well as the people among whom they lived during the guerrilla war in West Java.[4]

Aside from this, small informal groups also have developed among friends or neighbors and have stimulated "group activities" in the new villages—the organization of *lumbung* (rice storage) and the accumulation of funds for saving, credit, burial aid, and the like—whereas the women have also formed their own associations. Such associations were not initiated by village administrators and rarely include members from an entire *peḍukuhan*. There was also one political party, active in organizing peasants for group activities similar to those already mentioned, but this party has remained small. Another party, however, had made use of a relay system in aiding small groups of spontaneous settlers during their travels from Java to their new destinations: the new settlers were conveyed from a party branch in one city to that in the next in the various towns or cities along their route. Nevertheless such "group activities," with or without the aid of political parties or veterans' organizations, do not alter the general picture of a "Javanese village" as presented above: a *lurah* and his administration who are responsible for the initiation and organization of constructive village-wide activities, and people ready to carry out these plans.

4. Communication with the Supravillage Level

The major Lampung social and territorial unit, the *marga*, with its subdivision the *kampung*, stresses the element of descent. The major

[4] The veterans' organization that, among others, arranges for the resettlement of veterans has its center in the city of Banḍung.

kinship unit, *buai*, a patrilineal clan, is divided into many *suku*, which occupy many *kampung*, although each *kampung* contains several *suku*. The *suku* chiefs (*penjimbang*) with their respective *adat* titles form a council within the *kampung* called *proatin kampung*, whereas at the *marga* level the *suku* chiefs comprise the *proatin marga*. Genealogies clearly indicate which *suku* is the senior and superior and which the junior and subordinate one. The eldest *adat* chief of the senior *suku* acts as *primus inter pares* within the *kampung* or the *marga*. Ceremonies called *naik pepadon* are held as a qualified *adat* chief is raised to a higher titled position, a promotion that may result from the creation of a new *suku* when a new subdivision is separated from the existing unit. Accordingly, a new *suku* chief is inaugurated and a new *adat* title confirmed. In 1928 the Netherlands East Indies government granted the status of *inlandse gemeente* (native community) to the Lampung *marga*. Thus, based on the requirements of the colonial administration, the territorial boundaries of each *marga* and the office of *persirah* (*marga* head) were established. Eventually, even in the villages, the terms *kepala kampung* (*kampung* head) and *kepala suku* (*suku* head), have assumed significance within the governmental system (see Zwaal 1936, Royen 1932).

The communities of resettlers generally were incorporated into the Lampung social system only in the "administrative" sense. Sometimes the group of newcomers simply became subordinate to a local Lampungese *kepala suku*, or else the leader of the resettlers was recognized as a new *suku* head, or, yet again, a large enough group was accepted as a new *kampung*, with its head taken from among the newcomers. Ever since 1928, these various systems have been adopted to incorporate the Javanese settlers who cleared the land within the territory of a *marga*. However, they never became integrated socially into the Lampung *adat* system, in the sense that they obtained places within the kinship system, with its hierarchy of *penjimbang* titles and so forth.

The various *kepala tebang* (chief clearers) who originally led the pioneers to the Kaliredjo area were initially put under the guidance of a Lampung *penjimbang*, a special *marga* representative whose function was to supervise the clearing of the forest and who was thus called *pengawas tebang* (clearing supervisor). Since 1954, however, the pioneer communities have developed into Javanese villages based on the Javanese social system and customs, and consequently relations with the *marga* or the *negeri* have ceased to exist. Kaliredjo, the first pioneer village, which in 1953 had been granted the status of a *kampung* (according to the terminology of the *marga* or *negeri* administration), was originally incorporated into the *marga* Anak Tuha, later into the larger unit of the *negeri* Seputih Barat and the government subdistrict of Padangratu. The three administrative officials, the *pesirah* (*marga* head), the *negeri* head, and the subdistrict officer, lived at quite some distance from each other, all separated by more than twenty kilometers of jungle from Kaliredjo and the other pioneer villages.

The Javanese pioneer villages, which numbered seven by the middle of 1957, had learned to live together in mutual support, independent of the Lampung social system. Controversies among them, which were unavoidable in the process of development, failed to alter the fact that they all pursued a common goal, the establishment of Javanese villages. Thus they considered themselves as a new social unity with a common basis, common norms, common aspirations, and the same "rhythm" of life.

The Lampung *marga* institutions and regulations, although adequate for the Lampung people themselves, did not appeal to the pioneers, both because *marga* ties seemed too loose for Javanese taste and because the Javanese communities were considered only marginal members of the *marga*. For the local pioneers, who had experienced the prewar *marga* regulations with compulsory *marga* labor, conditions had become easier because these duties had been abolished, but the pioneers still had no clear patterns for leadership in their communities.

Both the local pioneers as well as the newcomers from Java still considered the vertical ties with the higher levels, that is, with the *ketjamatan* (subdistrict) administration, a necessary element in the ideal picture of a Javanese village. If on the one hand people stress the autoactivity of the "Javanese village," on the other hand the guidance and aid of a higher administration is also an integral part of the same conception. Proudly the people of Kaliredjo point to the results of the community development programs in their new villages: the roads connecting villages, schools, markets, mosques, and clinics and their rich harvests of rice and soybeans. Nevertheless, in every respect they are also aware of the limitations of the mutual-help system. Most of the roads are still unpaved, and consequently motorized transportation has not yet reached the villages, whereas in the nearby B.R.N. village several years of substantial aid from the government has made possible the construction of paved roads, a big bridge over the Way Sekampung River, schools, and a hospital. The effect of poor transportation upon the prices of farm products has been deeply felt in the new villages. The building of schools, clinics, and mosques alone will not bring about economic development, while markets are useless without good roads. The various *lurah* of the new villages indeed hold occasional meetings, but no regular cooperation exists at that level. A common decision, if it is to be carried out, must become the concern of each village. The lack of a higher authority also became serious when, for example, a Javanese pioneer was killed by a Lampungese in a conflict about land boundaries. The various *lurah* felt that they had no authority to investigate the case, let alone convict the accused, while the police or other government agencies who were considered qualified to interfere were quite some distance away.[5]

In the middle of 1957, a young *tjamat* (subdistrict officer) was assigned to Kaliredjo, and soon afterward the hopes of the pioneers to have a subdistrict of their own became a reality. However, after only a few months the negative aspects of the situation appeared. The various *lurah* of the pioneer villages, who thus far had learned to make decisions and work independently, could be proud of their achievements in having developed their communities without any government aid. However, the *tjamat*, who wanted to act from the beginning as a superior toward his subordinates, suppressed the autoactivity that had developed among the pioneers in the initial period of their existence as village communities. The village heads thus became subordinates who could only look up to their superior, the subdistrict head, and wait passively for orders.

5. The Pattern of Ecologic Adaptation among the Javanese Pioneers

With Sukohardjo on the Way Sekampung in the south as a base, the local pioneers and spontaneous settlers moved in a northerly direction. The hilly environment of the Way Sekampung area gradually changes in the north and northeast to the wide plains of Central Lampung, with rivers flowing northeast into the Way Seputih. On the bank of the Way Waya, one of the tributary rivers in the area that flattens out toward the north, the first village Kaliredjo was set up, followed by other new villages. Fifteen kilometers to the west of this group of pioneer villages a natural boundary exists in the steep Huluwaisemang Mountains, which

[5] One exception was the unit for malaria campaign that already had the pioneer village on its program.

form part of the Bukit Barisan range, the geographical backbone of Sumatra. Northeast of the village area, the highway and the railroad from
Tandjungkarang to Palembang cross the Central Lampung plains. The
soil around Kaliredjo is mainly granitic and andesitic; generally more
fertile and deeper, it is therefore more highly valued by the Lampung
peasant than the dacitic soil of the Central Lampung plains.

Establishing a village in the middle of a forest requires clearing the
forest in order to lay out the dry fields. Although swidden farming is
quite new to the settlers from Java, they have learned quickly from
local pioneers with previous "colonization" experience. Dry rice farming
has its periods of hard labor and its periods of leisure. Clearing the bushes
and slashing the trees with only axes and knives demands about three
months of hard work from approximately May to June; then follows
a relatively easy four weeks, while waiting for the wood to dry, before
burning season starts; a period of hard work starts as the soil is tilled
by means of a digging stick and planted in August, September, or at
the latest in October, before the rainy season begins. Then follows another
short period of leisure before weeding and guarding the fields begins
in January; finally, three months later, in March the busy harvesting
time arrives. The pioneers practicing swidden agriculture are often short
of labor, but they can obtain additional help by various systems of mutual
aid and by making use of the available supply of labor, although experienced clearers are only available for high wages.

Almost every day spontaneous settlers arrive, and it is therefore quite
natural that only a small portion of them will arrive in Lampung at
the right moment in the agricultural cycle to begin cultivation themselves.
The majority are unable to start farming right away, and consequently
during the first months most of the new settlers have to rely on the
money they brought with them; some must sustain themselves even as
long as the first year of their stay. As they usually run out of money
long before then, they are always forced to sell their labor. A relative
or an acquaintance from the same village or area in Java will usually
assist the newcomer during this difficult initial period and will furnish
him with a temporary place to stay.

Many newcomers work for daily wages with or without meals on
other people's land. Working for others may also mean carrying products
or delivering merchandise from one village to another. This kind of work
requires a bicycle, loaded with up to one quintal of goods, which is
pushed by the owner walking beside it. Those with enough capital com-

bine this transport and delivery service with retail trade (*bakulan*). Working as laborers tends to slow the progress of the new settlers, whose plan had been to become independent farmers. It is thus important for a settler to start farming from the very beginning, even if initially he has to work on rented land. The crops thus directly obtained may mean a "saving" of his labor in comparison with the "income" obtained from the labor he has to sell every day as a peasant worker (to the extent that nature, land fertility, and so on are not taken into account). With the first harvest, no matter how small, the settler will be more able to start further pioneering in the forest. It is not hard to get a share of land from a *lurah* in a new village, but if the new settler lacks the necessary funds, he still has to divide his time between farming and working for wages. The extent to which he must use his time as a wage laborer in the less busy periods of farming indicates whether he has been a successful pioneer.

In addition to rice, which is the staple food, the Javanese pioneers also plant other secondary crops. Lately they have discovered that the cultivation of soybeans provides a profitable source of income, as it produces extensive crops within one hundred days. More and more pioneers have recently started the intensive cultivation of soybeans on stationary plots with a minimum of irrigation (*tegalan*). However, a tremendous problem is combating *alang-alang* (wild grass), which grows rapidly once a plot of forest land has been left fallow after a rice crop. Manpower is often limited in the fight against this wild grass, and very often the pioneer has to surrender and leave the land to open up new swiddens in the forest. The adoption of shifting cultivation, with extensive use of land, means a step backward in the consolidation of farming. Several farmers, however, try it, as it is the method followed by the Lampung peasant. According to this method, the peasant clears the jungle, plants his swidden with rice for one or two years, and then plants productive trees or bushes such as coffee or pepper, while *dadap* (*Erythrina lithosperma Mig*) function as shade trees and also keep the *alang-alang* in check.

Let us now consider the extent to which the Javanese pioneers have developed their farming in the course of the years, by comparing agricultural progress in two recent hamlet settlements. In one of the *pedukuhan* (hamlets) that was going through its second planting season in 1957, out of 161 families registered as residents, only 112 had already been allotted land, and had started farming. These families had on the average a planting area of about .96 hectare, a third of them having cultivated .5 hectare and another third 1 hectare. There also were families who had only been able to cultivate .25 hectare, while several had achieved the cultivation of 2 hectares. Of the .96 hectare per family, .66 hectare were planted with rice and .30 hectare with secondary crops like soybeans.

In a *pedukuhan* in its fourth rice planting season in 1957, only 251 out of the 300 registered family heads had received shares of land. (The other 49 had not yet been allotted plots of land, possibly because many of them were only lodging temporarily in the hamlet and intended to settle permanently in other villages.) The records of this second *pedukuhan*, presented in Table 20, reveal that the pioneers have been

Table 20. Landowning pattern at one *pedukuhan*

Per cent of landowning families	Land distributed	Average land per family in hectares
37.5	1 location	1.12 (from .5 to 2.5)
42.5	2 locations	2.02 (from .5 to 4.5)
15	3 locations	2.93 (from 1.5 to 7)
5	4 locations	3.83 (from 2.25 to 5)

able to increase their landholdings in subsequent years. The additional plots of land are rarely located adjacent to the initial property. Quite a number of peasants thus own several plots of land, sometimes located at a considerable distance from each other. In every new area cleared in the *pedukuhan*, each pioneer is allotted a share of approximately one hectare. Usually in shifting cultivation, one family can only clear at one time approximately one hectare of land, or at least this seems to be the general rule adopted by the village heads in distributing forest land to the peasants.

Another problem worthy of investigation is whether the transition from a "soybean economy" (in which money is quickly returned, but the amount is small) to a "coffee economy" (in which the return is slower, as crops are expected only after two years, but the amount of money is larger) can be carried out satisfactorily by every pioneer. In the initial period of coffee cultivation, the need for capital is very urgent, for the workers who weed the coffee groves three times a year must be paid wages and the family must be maintained during the two years before the first crop is harvested.

The Lampung peasant grows his coffee within the shifting cultivation system. He constantly opens new swiddens, which provide him with the necessary rice and food crops, while in his old clearings he cultivates coffee, which eventually gives him a steady crop. Old groves that do not yield well any more are abandoned and left fallow, to be opened again after a period of several years. In contrast to the Lampung method of shifting cultivation, the Javanese method attempts to establish sedentary coffee cultivation and thus needs substantial capital at the beginning. If capital is insufficient, the Javanese pioneer can only rely on his own family as a labor force, and consequently the small size of his coffee grove will keep his standard of living low. Such conditions compel him to labor at all kinds of odd jobs in order to keep going from season to season, or even from day to day; otherwise he must leave the Kaliredjo area to look again for new forest land where he can practice shifting cultivation.

If the problem of limited labor cannot be solved by sufficient initial capital, some of the "first-wave" pioneers have worked out the following system: they not only provide temporary lodging in their houses for newer pioneers but also give out land in their abandoned swiddens on a kind of sharecropping basis. The transient peasant receives an old swidden on the condition that the land be returned after one year, during which time the temporary occupant converts it into a coffee grove. As compensation, the cultivator will receive the first harvest and subsequently part of the coffee crop or sometimes part of the land itself, depending on the terms of the initial agreement. Another advantage in this arrangement is that the temporary occupant will clear the land of wild grass, while the "first-wave" pioneer will be able to leave his farm to seek new fertile primary land in the forest. The village administration does not prohibit the clearing of new land as long as one does not neglect the land he has left behind. The newcomers consider temporary cultivation as only a springboard for further development. Generally they prefer to obtain fertile primary forest rather than secondary land which has, after all, already decreased in fertility. In addition to seeking new land locally, expansion by joining other villages that still have an abundance of forest land is also frequent.

With the purpose of gaining "land for wet rice fields" in the river valleys to the north and northeast, leaders of the various villages themselves often encourage the opening of new land. This drive for expansion in the lower parts of the river valleys to the north and northeast has already become a source of friction and tension among the pioneer villages of Kaliredjo. In addition, chief clearers have organized the clearing of land farther to the north, approaching the area of the Lampung villages.

In 1957 the *negeri* head appealed in vain to the pioneer villages to prevent the further arrival of new settlers and the clearing of new land. As long as there is enough spare land for dry cultivation, the Lampung system of agriculture works quite well, but the Javanese settlers, who have outnumbered the original residents in only seven years, invade the unused portions of the *marga* forests. The government has begun worrying about the future fate of the Lampung peasant, who depends on spare forest land, a reserve that has already been drastically reduced.

The ideal of the Javanese peasants is to develop sedentary wet rice cultivation in the river valleys of the area. Consequently they often express the desire for government aid to build dams and irrigation works. Both the old settlers from the "colonization" period as well as the spontaneous settlers from Java believe that only the government is able to help in setting up irrigation works. In the whole pioneer area, after six years, *sawah* or wet rice fields laid out by the people themselves have developed only in one or two small marshy valleys, and these areas total not more than a few hectares. Usually settlers practice shifting agriculture, with new fields which continuously yield abundant crops. This system, however, requires an abundance of land. The development of sedentary dry cultivation, which is certainly the main problem if resettlement is going to be effective and successful, is not thought by the peasants to be a problem that can be solved with government aid. Intensive sedentary dry cultivation involves new techniques and new attitudes, but the pioneers, never having known a better standard of living, do not seem to feel the need for radical agricultural innovations. From the government the peasants only expect aid for the development of wet rice farming, as previously government aid has only been extended to wet rice farming.

The roads that have been constructed to link the new villages with the old villages and with the town Pringsewu, farther south, as well as the markets that have been built in several villages, show that the settlers also depend on trade to exchange their farm produce for consumer goods from the towns. The majority of the merchants and wholesalers at the markets are not pioneers but people who come from elsewhere.

Many of the merchants and shopkeepers come to the village markets, while many Javanese women from Pringsewu come every market day to sell their merchandise. Many wholesalers, among whom Javanese women are also found, visit the pioneer villages regularly to buy farm produce at the houses of the peasants or along the roads leading to the markets. Although only one or two Chinese have ventured to come to trade in the pioneer villages, quite a bit of Chinese capital seems to be in circulation in the area, as many Indonesian merchants operate with capital borrowed from Chinese in the southern towns.

Although the merchants were doing a great service to the economy of the developing villages, the condition of the roads, which around 1957 did not yet allow motorized traffic, hampered communications with the outside world. Consequently the prices of imported consumer goods were high. In a pioneer village the price of rice right after harvest was 40 *rupiah* per quintal, while in Pringsewu, only fifteen kilometers from the village, the price was already close to 90 *rupiah*.

Not many enterprises or occupations outside of agriculture exist in the pioneer settlements of Kaliredjo. Only a few small workshops make bricks and tiles to serve the constant need for building materials. The owners of these workshops are also farmers who work only part-time at their enterprises, with almost no additional or skilled labor and with very simple equipment. As there exists a great lack of skilled workers among the pioneers themselves, most villagers have to rely on Lampung carpenters to construct their house frames or to make their furniture, and on Lampung millers to process their paddy and coffee beans. As these people often live at quite a distance from the pioneer settlements, the problem of transportation becomes crucial. Similarly, for many other services the pioneers of Kaliredjo often still have to go to quite distant places. The pioneers indeed have not yet reached a more comfortable way of living.

Chapter XII

Situradja: A Village in Highland Priangan[1]

ANDREA WILCOX PALMER

CORNELL UNIVERSITY

1. The Sundanese

The Sundanese, who occupy much of the province of West Java, are the second largest ethnic and linguistic group in Indonesia, numbering approximately ten million in 1961. The high central mountainous area, the Priangan highlands, forms the core territory, with its well-known capital Bandung, a large city of approximately one million inhabitants. The Sundanese language, which has a written literature and its own script (similar to the Javanese script), consists of several dialects that gradually change into Javanese in the areas of Indramaju and Tjirebon to the east of the Priangan highlands. In the northwestern part of West Java the rural population is bilingual, speaking Sundanese and a dialect of Javanese (Banten Javanese), but the urban elite is mainly Sundanese.

This large Indonesian ethnic group has been relatively little described. Most articles and books on Sundanese culture are obsolete, and very little information on the rural population exists, except facts on *adat* law that have been published in several articles in the journal *Indisch Tijdschrift van het Recht* or are included in Soepomo's excellent volume on Sundanese *adat* law (1933; see also Kennedy 1955, II, 513–524).[2]

[1] The author wishes to express her thanks to all in Situradja, who showed every kindness to her and who will never be forgotten. She begs forgiveness for her mistakes. The description here applies to the years 1956 and 1957, unless otherwise noted.

[2] This brief information on the Sundanese is the responsibility of the editor.

2. *Location and Population of Situradja*

The Sundanese village Situradja is located on a hard-surface *kabupaten* (regency) road, about thirty-eight miles northeast of Bandung. It is linked with this big city and also with the regency capital, Sumedang, by frequent bus and *oplet* (station wagon) service. Beginning in 1952, it became a "model village," receiving technical and financial support from the government for purposes of community development. In addition it is the capital of the *ketjamatan* (subdistrict) Situradja.

The boundary of Situradja surrounds a region including high hills, river valleys, fishponds, and fields of rice, corn, peanuts, tubers, and cassava, with neat and pleasing settled areas. In the north, settlements are scattered, but in the south, most of the residential areas have grown together along the regency road to form the *kota* (town) of Situradja, where most of the subdistrict offices are located. By vehicular road the center of the town is from two and one-half to thirteen kilometers distant from the other villages in the subdistrict. Pamulihan, the most isolated northern settlement of Situradja, is six kilometers by arduous footpath. Many villagers have never been there. The town has two foci: the market area, including the market owned by the village government, and most of the sixteen *toko* (shops) of the village; and the *alun-alun*, a central grassy square surrounded by the mosque, the central and local government buildings, and two schools. Other central government offices are scattered through the town. In general, settlements emphasize and expand along roads and paths. Schools, prayer houses, graveyards, holy places of ancestral spirits and shops seem to be almost haphazardly located in various settlements throughout the village.

In 1950, the village population of 6,078 people lived in 1,557 houses. Six years later, in 1956, the 6,779 inhabitants lived in 1,690 houses. In 1956 the density of population per square kilometer was 378 in the subdistrict and 566 in the village. While density of population in relation to total land may be slightly higher in many Javanese areas, density within the residential areas alone is higher in Situradja, perhaps because there are fewer gardens within the residential blocks. Population increase results entirely from the fact that the number of births is more than double the number of deaths. In 1955 there were 106 deaths and 237 births. The health conditions in Situradja are good, although more than half of the deaths were of children under the age of six.

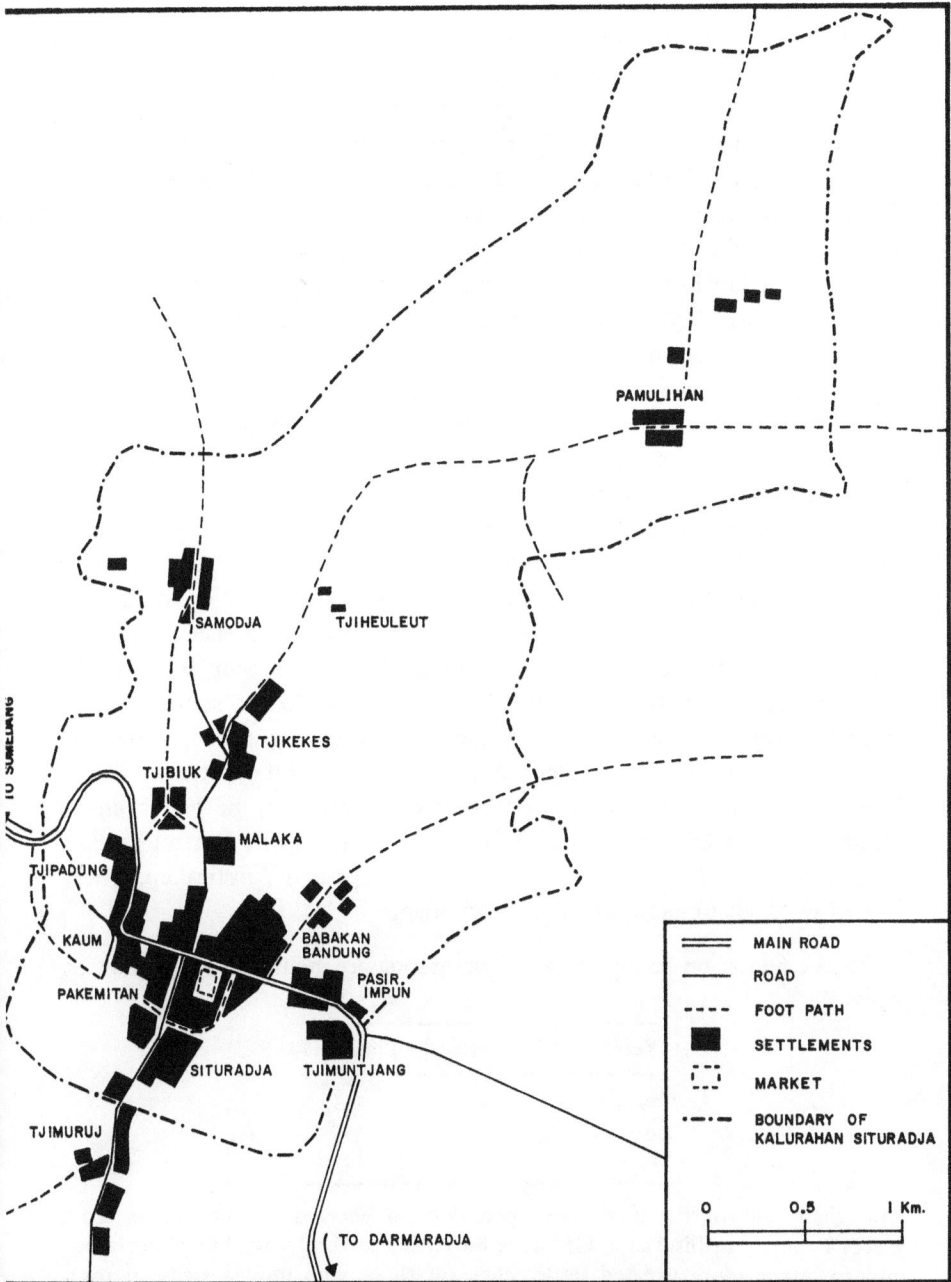

Map XV. Kalurahan Situradja

The people of Situradja, including the central government officials in residence, are Sundanese. The few individuals in Situradja who are of other origin have generally been assimilated or are only part-time residents. In contrast, in 1938 there were so many Chinese in Situradja that it was decided in a village meeting to provide land for a Chinese graveyard. The Chinese left the village during the Indonesian revolution. In 1954, one Chinese family moved to Situradja from Sumedang, in spite of the opposition of local merchants, and rented a store in the market area. The national ban on Chinese trading outside regency capitals, which started in 1959, probably made them return to Sumedang. Many Chinese forced from numerous other villages in West Java after 1959 have managed to continue their trade on the village level, by delegating the management of their village shops to Indonesians or by marrying Indonesian women who will take care of their business in the village.

Although the village population is homogeneous, the villager meets people of other ethnic origin through his geographical mobility. According to village records, emigration exceeds immigration.[3] People frequently leave the village briefly for government work, trade, labor opportunities, higher education, visiting relatives, and excursions for pleasure. A high-status woman is the least mobile within the village, but more likely to have visited outside Situradja than women of lower status. Village specialists such as midwives, circumcisers, mediums, and *réog* clowning entertainers are at times called to other villages. Of 54 family heads interviewed in the town neighborhood of Pakemitan, 34 had been to Bandung, 19 to Djakarta, 17 to Tjirebon, 5 to places in Central or East Java, 1 to Central Sumatra, and 1 as far as Egypt and Amsterdam, where he had worked as chauffeur for a Dutch man.

[3] Some figures on immigration and emigration are included in the following table:

Year	Immigrated	Emigrated
1954	110	143
1955	115	165
1956	112	157

Less than one-fourth of the 110 people who entered in 1954 came from places larger than Situradja. Of these, 80 settled in the "town" neighborhoods and 30 in the more isolated settlements. Of those who moved away in 1954, over one-third were going to larger towns. Much of this movement is temporary, lasting for only a few years.

Outsiders often come to the village. The central government sends officials to Situradja; occasionally visitors from other parts of Indonesia and even from other countries come to see the model village; the air force holds maneuvers, when many officers and men, often of other ethnic groups, live with the people of Situradja for a short time; the army stations a unit in the village; outside entertainment troops present *wajang golèk* (wooden rod puppet shows), *réog* clowning, or *topèng* (mask) dancing; traders, including a few Tjirebon Javanese, carry their wares to the village market or the village household; a soccer team comes to play a game; relatives and former residents visit.

3. Subsistence Economics, Land Ownership, and Occupations

Although Situradja is a "minus area" that does not produce enough rice for its own needs, its economic condition is fairly satisfactory. This is owing to a diversified economy, with a fair emphasis on secondary crops (*palawidja*) and small-scale food industries, and also to the large number of villagers who are employed by the government, who work in village services or trade, or who work on a semipermanent basis in cities as hotel waiters, porters, pedicab drivers, or other unskilled labor. The villagers as a whole are not economically dependent on one crop, on one source of employment, or on one or a few extremely rich landlords, creditors or employers. Those not in government employment are seldom subject to superiors who live outside the village context.

Situradja is reported to have an extent of 1,197 hectares (11.97 square kilometers). In 1940 when the land was last classed for taxation (see Table 21), 1,036.3 hectares were under private ownership (*milik*), and of this, 345.7 were in *sawah* (wet-rice fields), of which approximately 67 hectares can be planted with rice twice a year, and 690.6 were dry land, of which approximately 75 to 100 hectares, largely from classes I, II, and III, were residential. There were 107.985 hectares for grazing in 1940, "given" by the government to the village for that purpose. Then, as now, some was rented to farmers. Statistics are contradictory and incomplete, but the village government probably owns about three or four hectares of communal land including the village square, the land on which stand the village hall, the clinic, the offices of the subdistrict, most of the village schools, and probably the mosque, the village market, the sports field, and about eight hectares of graveyards. Unlike five other villages in the subdistrict, Situradja does not own *tjarik* fields (official fields), to provide income for village officials.

There is no communal, but only private, ownership of agricultural land. Total ownership by any villager is difficult to calculate, since land registration is within village boundaries, while many villagers own land

Table 21. Types of privately owned land and fragmentation of ownership in Situradja in 1940

Type, class, and old tax in *rupiah* per hectare	Extent in hectares	Number of lots	Lots owned by women	Lots owned by absentee owners from:	
				near	far
sawah					
I (9 Rp.)	31.51	183	64	7	8
II (6.70 Rp.)	67.54	423	169	12	11
III (5.10 Rp.)	67.78	330	136	17	7
IV (3.50 Rp.)	109.08	560	203	28	12
V (2.60 Rp.)	46.94	203	82	10	5
VI (1.00 Rp.)	22.85	112	35	3	
Totals	345.70	1,811	689	77	43
dry land					
I (7.50 Rp.)	11.86	189	70	11	14
II (5.70 Rp.)	31.79	555	218	9	12
III (3.80 Rp.)	50.01	497	168	2	8
IV (2.30 Rp.)	101.74	630	179	25	6
V (1.40 Rp.)	145.15	547	159	11	2
VI (.70 Rp.)	334.80	892	269	21	6
VII (.35 Rp.)	15.25	40	5		
Totals	690.60	3,350	1,068	79	48

in other villages and even outside the subdistrict. In 1940, there were 1,444 private owners of land in Situradja. By June 1957 there had been a gain of 719 new owners recorded in the register of landownership, with a loss of 264 owners, making a total of 1,899 owners. In Table 22, 1,863 owners for which data were clear are classified by the place of residence of the owner divided by eight polling districts,[4] and by

[4] Neighborhoods included in eight polling districts are: (I) Pakemitan, Tjipadung, Kaum, part of Malaka-kantor; (II) Situradja; (III) Tjimuntjang; (IV and V) Babakan Bandung; (VI) Malaka, Tjikekes, Tjibiuk; (VII) Samodja, Tjiheuleut; (VIII) Pamulihan.

the amount of land owned as indicated by the 1940 tax rate (see Table 21), making it possible to equate ownership of *sawah* and dry land in various classes. The table indicates the general uniformity of land distribution throughout the village, with the number of landowners equaling about half of the number of registered voters, and the lack of a clear gap betweeen small and large landowners. It also shows that most owners

Table 22. Classification of owners of *milik* land in Situradja by place of residence (polling district) of owners and by amount of land owned in village as indicated by 1940 tax rate

Tax Group	I	II	III	IV & V	VI	VII	VIII	near	far	Total
				Polling district				Other villages		
0– .08	7	7	5	18	7	8	21	3	0	76
.08– .50	102	69	46	121	69	47	107	37	4	602
.51–1.00	61	55	26	70	38	39	72	25	2	388
1.01–2	67	47	15	73	58	53	53	17	4	387
2.01–3	25	25	10	42	14	19	29	6	3	173
3.01–4	18	13	7	22	9	11	11	2	3	96
4.01–5	7	8	1	14	2	6	12	2	1	53
5.01–6	10	4	1	5	3	2	6	1	0	32
6.01–7	3	1	2	4	3	1	2	0	1	17
7.01–8	2	1	0	4	0	0	1	0	0	8
8.01–9	1	0	0	3	1	1	1	0	0	7
9.01–10	0	0	0	1	0	0	0	0	1	2
10.01–15	4	1	3	1	6	0	0	0	0	15
15.01–20	2	1	0	1	0	0	0	0	0	4
20.01 up	1	1	0	1	0	0	0	0	0	3
Total	310	233	116	380	210	187	315	93	19	1863
Voters 1955	642	495	297	859	380	422	602			
Voters 1957	580	487	314	843	402	434	642			

fall in the lower tax brackets. Approximately 26 per cent of the local population own land within the village,[5] while the largest landowners do not live in the outlying settlements. About 1,212 residents (18 per cent of the total population) are recorded as owning *sawah* within Situradja. The percentage of the total landowners is of course higher

[5] Most people own their own houses. In one sample of 54 families in Pakemitan, all owned their own houses, 40 on their own land, 8 on their parents' land, and 6 on land belonging to others.

306

Villages in Indonesia

than 26 per cent, as people from Situradja own more land in adjacent villages than vice versa. Absentee landholdings, however, are not extensive in Situradja and are held mainly by people in surrounding villages. A large proportion of those Situradja villagers who do not own land are young married couples, and they often have the right to use their parents' land, both residential and agricultural. They may work the fields of relatives or others on a sharecropping basis, but renting land is rare.

There is little restriction on the frequent transfer of land. What is known as *mutlak* sale gives the purchaser absolute rights to the land that is now his. *Mutlak* gifts may be distributed to heirs before death, although the legally recorded division may sometimes be much later. In *djual gade* (pawning), the land must be redeemed within a fixed period if it is not to pass into the creditor's permanent possession. In *djual akad* (mortgage), the former owner or his heir may buy the land back at any time he presents the sale price. Land trades may be made in the attempt to get fields closer to home.[6]

Holdings are scattered, and land fragmentation is worse now than in 1940, when the largest owner had twenty-four pieces of land, with a total area of 1.785 hectares dry land and 4.5 hectares *sawah*. The smallest owners had .015 hectare dry land. The average owner held 1.25 *sawah* fields with an extent of .24 hectare and 2.3 pieces of dry land with an extent of .48 hectare.

Capital is in scarce supply in Situradja. The villager usually needs credit for consumption purposes. He can pawn his land in the village or his personal possessions such as gold and jewelry at the government pawn shop in Darmaradja. He can buy on credit in the market, borrow from relatives, or obtain loans in money or rice from personal acquaintances at high rates of interest or from the neighborhood rice cooperatives. Capital is usually invested in land or in the purchase of goods for trading. Middlemen use the most capital. Capital will also be invested in houses, tools of small-scale industry, and animals. For capital expenditure, loans may be made by the bank or the savings and loan cooperative. Capital investment by the purchase of shares, though tried occasionally, has not been successful. Almost all of the large improvements in the village are

[6] In Situradja between September 1952 and 1956 129 *sawah* fields were transferred, 113 by *mutlak* gift or sale, 13 by *akad*, 2 on pawn, and 1 by exchange; while 188 pieces of dry land were transferred, 182 by *mutlak*, 4 by *akad*, 1 on pawn, and 1 by exchange; and 13 unclassified lots were also transferred, 12 *mutlak* and 1 *akad*.

a result of government projects. However they have the nature of public works rather than being investments in new forms of production.

Although there is said to be a shortage of agricultural labor because "the children who used to hoe and care for cows are now going to school and then on to become teachers and take other work," population growth constantly increases the labor supply. The continued existence of underemployment is perhaps indicated by the 58 youths from Situradja who became army applicants when given the opportunity in 1957.

Table 23. Occupational distribution of family heads by polling district in the village of Situradja

Occupation	Polling district							
	I	II	III	IV	V	VI	VII	VIII
Farmers	145	176	113	139	133	168	195	262
Traders	35	15	1	33	15	2		
Traders-farmers	3	7	1	11	10	9	2	7
Coolie labor	37	10	15	6	12	9		
Coolies-farmers	28	30		18	18	1	1	2
Central government								
Officials	13	7	1	4	3			
Police, army	13	3	1	4				
Teachers and school administration	28	14	15	9	6	1		1
Pension	5		5	3	1			
Village government	2	1	3	3	1	2	1	2
Village cooperative	1	1						
Cottage industries and special services	9	4	6	6	8		2	

Table 23, based partly on figures for election registration in the various polling districts and partly on the census, gives an impression of the broad outlines of the distribution of occupations in Situradja, and generally indicates the main source of income of the family. The tremendous role the central government plays in this village is indicated by the number of people receiving their income from it, and this table does not include the 203 children from the subdistrict who in 1958 were on government scholarship at the government junior teacher's school (S.G.B.N.), the army or air force men stationed in Situradja without their families, or other sorts of economic support to individuals or groups. Central government employees are concentrated in the polling districts of the town (districts I, II, IV, V), while village government employees are more evenly distributed. Two village cooperative officials are listed under other occupations. Many individuals combine trading or cottage industry and sometimes, but rarely, government employment with farming activities. In one sample of 54 family heads in Pakemitan, 37 had traded or were now engaging in trade. Among those in Situradja who obtained at least part of their income from cottage industries and services in 1955, there were 11 who made *krupuk* (shrimp chips), 4 who made soy sauce, 15 who fried bean curd, 25 who prepared *ontjom*, and up to 51 who made peanut oil, 20 were making roof tiles, 4 repaired bicycles and other equipment, 5 were blacksmiths, 6 or more were carpenters, 4 did cement work, 6 were tailors, and 3 were launderers.

4. Labor Recruitment and Mutual Aid

Increasingly, labor is paid for with cash wages. There seems to be social pressure against paying labor more than the commonly accepted wage and thus competing for it. Often daily wages include meals, but the monetary return is higher if the meals are omitted. Wages vary with the skill of the worker and the tools he employs. The minimum wage is considered to be 4½ *rupiah* a day without food.[7] In contrast, male and female servants living in the household seldom seem to be paid regular wages. Often—but not always—poor relatives, they are treated as such. They get their keep, perhaps occasional pocket money, new clothes at Lebaran, and the expense of their wedding feast if married from the house.

Hiras labor is done on the request of another without wages other than meals. It is said in the past everybody could request *hiras* labor. Now it is difficult to obtain except from people economically or otherwise dependent. According to a decision of the regent in 1950, and following in a long tradition, the *lurah* (village head) has the right to order a village inhabitant to do *hiras* labor one day a year on his fields or house, giving him only food and "coffee" three times a day. Lesser village officials have similar rights, usually to the labor the *lurah* does not use. If a person can not work himself, he can pay wages for another person to replace him.

[7] A tiller gets 4 *rupiah* a day and food; sawers get 6 to 7 *rupiah* a day plus 1 *rupiah* for the rent of the saw. Carpenters get 12 *rupiah* and three to four meals a day, or 17 *rupiah* without food.

Other labor is done for shares. As with wages, the employers seem to be subject to pressure from other employers against giving too much. In some parts of Java anyone who wishes can participate in the harvest rice-cutting. In Situradja only those who have helped transplant the rice and/or weed it (usually for their meals and one *rupiah* a day) can harvest rice, obtaining usually, one-eleventh of what they cut. This is an example of labor being organized more on an individual basis, less on a communal basis, than elsewhere. Only at the height of the harvest season when the demand exceeds the labor supply will others be invited to participate. Women who pound rice may be given one-to-ten or one-to-twelve parts pounded.

There is sharecropping in Situradja, but the land is often worked by a relative of the owner. The person who is working the land pays the cost of labor and seed. If the owner pays, it is returned to him before crop division. Payments of rice to village officials and to the irrigation supervisor (*tjengteng*) are subtracted before the crop is halved, the usual division. In some cases, the state tax seems to be paid by the landowner, in some cases it seems to be halved. The man who works the land usually decides what the secondary crop will be. If it is peanuts, the owner gets half. If it is tubers, the owner is usually given some, but no formal division is required. The man who halves another's land may feel subject at times to demands for *hiras* labor by the owner, as well as to demands for fruit from his trees and other favors.

Sometimes labor is traded (*liliuran*). For example, a man may go or send his servant to plow another's *sawah* in exchange for later work on his own. Such an exchange, involving a pair of individuals, does not usually seem to be considered an instance of *gotong-rojong*, which generally implies a mass of people participating without thought of immediate return.

Gotong-rojong may be applied to a wide variety of work arrangements. Government authorities, though not always the villager, use the term in discussing free labor by village citizens on village and even occasionally central government projects. To the villager, such work is sometimes considered "forced" and thus not genuine *gotong-rojong*. Seemingly more valued is helping one's friends and neighbors when needed on a nongovernmental, noncorporate, and largely reciprocal basis. For example, men may assist a neighbor in building his house. They are given two meals and a snack and drink each day and the implied promise of a return of housebuilding labor in case of later need. Some people are not eager for such *gotong-rojong* help because it is unskilled labor compared to hired carpenters, it is a bother to feed the workers, and there are many extra people who come "but only sit because there is no work for them to do."

There is little quibble with helping one's neighbors and relatives at times of illness and death and life-cycle feasts. *Gotong-rojong* may include aid in the form of goods and money as well as services. Help given at times of death is unsolicited. At other life-cycle feasts, labor only, and not other contributions, is usually requested, but even so is almost always given willingly. There is an astonishingly vital, efficient, and productive organization of goods and effort: funeral, burial, and the cooking and distribution of food to approximately 800 participants took place within eight hours on the day after the death of the father of the *lurah*. Social status and dyadic relations rather than any corporate structure determine the work each individual does.

5. Ceremonial Feasts and Life-Cycle Customs

A family may hold a ceremonial feast or *hadjat* at a stage in the agricultural cycle, in housebuilding or any other new undertaking, or at one of numerous life-cycle events. Usually the *hadjat* is small and is in many respects similar to the Javanese *slametan*. It includes making certain small food offerings, the burning of incense (*menjan*) after whispering a formula (*djampe*), followed by a call to those present to witness the ceremony and a call on various spiritual beings, including the local "ancestors" and Islamic figures, to fill the requests of the host (*ichral*). The ceremony ends with a prayer in Arabic (*doa*) and the eating of a special cone of rice. The minimum number of participants includes males of the immediate family and a few male witnesses, usually close neighbors.

Certain life-cycle feasts, while always including the small feast just described, are usually elaborated ceremonially and artistically. The nature and extent of this elaboration, the expense for food, ceremony, and entertainment, and the number of people participating in one way or another depend on the event, the social status of the family holding the *hadjat*, and their personal preference. Most events usually involve close to the minimum given (a); some involve ceremonies of some duration in one day and usually under one hundred participants for even a high-status person (b); the most public events involve well over one hundred participants for high-status people and complex ceremonies, taking place in part outside the house, on two or more days (c); while some feasts are rare in Situradja (d). In the following brief outline of life-cycle ceremonies, the presence of variations must be recognized. The usual degree of emphasis placed on the different feasts will be indicated with an a, b, c, or d.

During pregnancy there may be feasts at three months (a, d); five months (a, d); seven months (*tingkeb*, a, b); and nine months (a, d). At seven months the expectant mother may go to the traditional midwife (*paradji*) with a gift to request her help (*sewaka*). Ceremonies during labor and after birth include taking the placenta ("younger sibling") to the river. There is a feast at the time of the dropping of the umbilical cord (a). At forty days after birth (*mahinum*, a, b) a special food of beans is eaten. The relation with the midwife is terminated with hand-washing and asking her pardon (*manjoan leungeun*) and a ceremony with a live chicken for the welfare of the child (*ngahurip*). Girls have their ears pierced. The first haircut (*ngajun*, b) is often combined with *mahinum* but may be held any time. Men cut the hair of the infant and pray for it. *Santri*, villagers of stronger Islamic orientation, invite male guests in to sing the Marhaba.

Circumcision (*sunnat*, c) is rare for girls but universal for boys; usually two or more boys between years four and nine are circumcised together by a male *paradji* after a cold morning bath in the river. An animal (*bela*) is slaughtered at the time of the circumcision of each. Ceremonies for young female relatives as well as the boys at this time may include symbolic tooth filing (*ngagusaran*); bathing in rice water (*mandi kembang*); costuming and public parading of children; showering with rice and money during a song of advice (*sawer*); *manjoan leungeun* and *ngahurip*. The completion of the reading of the Koran (*chatam*, b, d) may be celebrated in combination with circumcision.

At marriage, most ceremonial elaboration occurs when it is a first marriage (c). Some time before, the relatives of the boy ask the girl's parents for her, give money, and arrange the time of the wedding and the money and goods they should contribute (*ngalamar*). The couple goes to request legal permission (*djagrag*). The groom and his family move to the house of the girl, and goods and money are given to her father (*seserahan*). On the night before the wedding the couple may be specially dressed, and there may be *ngahurip* and a long ceremony with the couple during which old women make up betel-chewing packets (*ngeujeuk seureuh*). At all weddings, whether at the mosque or, more rarely, at home, the man and woman accept the marriage contract in front of the subdistrict religious official. It is then signed by the groom and the guardian (*wali*), a male relative of the bride. Money (*mas kawin*) is paid or promised to the bride. Afterward there may be a *sawer* with advice sung to the couple in front of the bride's house. Symbolic ceremonies before coming on to the porch (*emper*) may include the groom taking two hairs from the bride's head, stepping on an egg and small bamboo, having his feet washed by the bride, and stepping over weaving tools. A torch (*harupat kawung*) lit from a dish with burning cotton strands (*palita*) is extinguished with water, and the waterpot (*kendi*) is smashed. Then the bride may enter the center of the house and close the door, after which there is a song dialogue between the couple or their representatives in which the groom requests that the door be opened (*buka pintu*). The couple eats together from one plate and may feed each other during a big feast for the two families (*huap lingkung*). The relatives of the groom leave him and go home. The couple carry food to the boy's parents and other relatives and are given money (*mundjungan*). There may be a secret *hadjat* later (*numbas*). Finally, the parents of the groom have a *hadjat* to receive the bride and her parents (*mulung mantu*).

The numerous feasts marking death include one on the day of burial (*njusur taneuh*, c) and feasts at three days (*tiluna*, b), seven days (*tudjuhna*, b), and forty days (*matang puluh*, b, c). Less important and rarer are feasts at fifty days (*neket*), one hundred days (*natus*), one thousand days (*newu*) and a special yearly feast (*mendak taun*, a). Money is usually given to those present at a death feast so they will say a special prayer for the soul of the deceased (*salawat, kiparat*). The dead person is bathed by relatives, wrapped in cotton and white cloth, prayed over (*disalatkeun*), and buried within a day in the Islamic manner with the village Moslem official, *lĕbe*, officiating. After the corpse is in the grave there is the call to prayer (*adan*). The *lĕbe* sitting on the grave reads the *telekin* if the deceased is not a child. For seven nights after death and often for seven nights before the forty-day feast men gather for a process called *dikir*, which includes numerous repetitions of certain Arabic phrases, especially "There is no God but Allah." Stones used as counters at this time are later placed on the grave. This and the reading of the Koran (*ngadji*) for up to forty nights after death are a "gift" for the deceased. Non-*santri* keep a lamp burning and give offerings at a special place for the deceased for forty days. Then there is a ceremony to open the road to heaven for the soul leaving the house (*mileuleujankeun*) and a final *dikir* with a Sundanese song added about the long road to heaven.

6. Participation in Islam

In Situradja, there are no strong corporate groups based on religious practice. The traditional *hadjat* is based on the nuclear family and mystic exercise on the individual. Islamic worship also is mainly an individual matter. The villagers, with the partial exception of a small Permai Party membership,[8] are Moslems. The taboo on pork is almost universal. Though a fairly high percentage of villagers may fast for at least a few days during the month of fast, in one case of forty men giving *gotong-rojong* aid to tile a roof, only five refused to eat immediately when food was served on a fasting day. Of the obligatory offerings to the poor, no one pays the complete *zakat* but almost everybody subject to *pitrah* pays something, often through the village government.[9] Only two men were listed in the election registration as *hadji* (men who have performed the pilgrimage to Mecca). They came from outside Situradja and do not dress as *hadji* or act as religious leaders. Villagers invest in secular education rather than the *hadj*.

Situradja has one mosque, which as a religious office serves the subdistrict, and twelve or thirteen neighborhood prayer houses (*tadjug*). About 200 to 400 men, including the junior teacher's school pupils, may pray at the mosque on Friday, and many of these come from neighboring villages. The congregations of mosque or prayer house are not important as such. Perhaps about 15 per cent of the villagers perform the five daily prayers. Mosque records list fifteen religious experts outside the *kaum*, all with only moderate influence.

In 1955, nine people were teaching the reading of the Koran to 390 pupils. There are no religious boarding schools (*pasantren*) in the area. Most religious instruction is done by teachers from the Ministry of Religion through the secular schools, where also special observances of Islamic holidays take place. There are no mystic sects in Situradja.

[8] With forty stable votes on the two 1957 ballots.
[9] For the terms *zakat* and *pitrah* see section 10.

7. Kin Groups

There are no large corporate kin groups in Situradja. The *golongan* and the *bondorojot* can not be considered as such: *golongan* sometimes indicates the mass of kin to whom a given individual is related or doubly related (*gulangkep*) and sometimes those kin living in a given locality; the *bondorojot* is the nonunilinear descent line, generally unrestricted, of all people descended from a given ancestor. Various taboos may be placed by an ancestor on his descendants for seven generations (*tjadu*). Supernatural punishment may be visited on descendants for the sins of their ancestors. Natural properties, sacred heirlooms, character traits, powers, and skills generally pass to individuals in the *bondorojot*, although inheritance does not consistently follow one particular unilineal line of descent. Generally items are not properties of the *bondorojot* as a whole. More important than *bondorojot* membership is the relation of the individual with each of his ancestors. This is shown by ceremonial visits to the grave at certain times in the Islamic calendar year and before new undertakings. The spirit of the ancestor may appear to a descendant during dreams and ascetic exercise (*tapa*). Such relations could exist even if the *bondorojot* did not.

For the nuclear family, also, what is most recognized and valued is not the unit but the relations to individuals, whether spouse, parent, child, or sibling. Such relations are considered very close. For example, while a man does *tapa*, a supernatural experience may come to his wife or daughter. Siblings are sometimes believed to have had the same placenta. One should honor and obey those who are older (husband, parent, older sibling) and protect, support, and guide those who are younger (wife, child, younger sibling). In comparison, the idea of maintaining the good reputation of the nuclear family unit as such is not important. Relations between members of the nuclear family become the model for all social interaction, as indicated by the extension of the terms used for these close relatives to other relatives and to unrelated people. Less often, the nuclear family unit becomes the model for social groupings. The high divorce rate (94 divorces to 120 marriages and remarriages in 1956) weakens the nuclear family as a unit.

Ideally the family unit is associated with house and hearth and thus strengthened. Actually, while the household usually consists of members of one nuclear family, it frequently includes other relatives, boarders, or servants. Its actual composition is constantly changing as relatives come to stay after sickness or economic hardship in the city, sons-in-law move in temporarily at marriage, married daughters come home to bear their children or return after divorce, and children of a child or sibling or more distant relative join the household for a period of from days to years—now, in part, to take advantage of Situradja's good schools.

The nuclear family is the unit of the budget, the unit of most decisions about consumption, savings, and investment, and the unit of most production. The *hadjat* is based on the nuclear family unit, even when it is not held by one family. Thus, each nuclear family takes rice and incense to a neighborhood feast. A man can ask pardon from others for his family as a whole.

In the past, the central government emphasized the nuclear family. Today, as in voting for elections and land taxation, the individual is the unit. Similarly, in organizations such as some cooperatives, both men and women may be members and attend meetings. In contrast, while legally all voters may now attend village meetings, in practice it is still only male family heads who do, not women or unmarried men. While the rice contribution to support the members of the village government (*pantjèn*)[10] is based on individual landownership, generally the nuclear family is considered as a unit in assessing contributions in labor and money to village projects.

8. Territorial and Political Organization

The rural Sundanese never seem to have developed strong corporate groups, either extended kin groups or territorially based groups. Territorial units within the Sundanese village today include those superimposed from above, which mainly have administrative functions. Situradja has 21 to 39 *tugu* (neighborhoods), many *lembur*, five *kampung* (wards), and eight polling districts.

The *tugu* (in Indonesian called *rukun tetangga*), was introduced by the Japanese during the war. Its head, the *tugu*, extends invitations to village meetings and requests of the government to the families under him. He helps in taking the census and classing families for contributions to village projects, such as schools. He attends meetings of *tugu* heads, sometimes held instead of full village meetings of all family heads. For

[10] *Pantjèn* is a tax on landowners in rice or its money equivalent to provide the major part of the compensation of the *kalurahan* officials.

his work he is freed from certain village obligations and he receives payment for census taking. The five *kampung* in Situradja are Pamulihan, Malaka (including the neighborhoods of Tjikekes, Tjibiuk, Malaka, Samodja and Tjiheuleut), Situradja (including Situradja, Tjimuntjang, Tjikedok, and Pasir Impun), Babakan Bandung and Pakemitan (including Pakemitan, Tjipadung, and the Kaum around the mosque). Each is headed by a member of the village administration, a *kokolot*, who plays almost no public role in village meetings.

The *lembur* usually includes more than one *tugu*. It usually has a name, although some names date from the time the land was classed for taxation in 1940. It has a territory in residential land. The families of a *lembur* may meet together once a year to hold a *hadjat lembur*. The *lembur* is often associated with a rice storage cooperative. Between 1951 and 1956, nineteen of these (*lumbung patjeklik*) were established in Situradja. In 1956 the smallest cooperative had 11 members, the largest 142. Thus not all residents of a *lembur* become members. *Tugu* heads, or past or present village officials living in the *lembur*, sometimes serve as leaders in organizing the *hadjat lembur* or establishing the cooperatives. The officials of the cooperative may be the most formal expression of any governmental apparatus in the *lembur*. Meetings of either *lembur* or cooperative are rare and informal. For example, plans for next year's *hadjat lembur* may be agreed to in a few minutes at this year's feast.

The unit by which village labor obligations such as road cleaning and night watch are administered is sometimes identical with the ward, sometimes with the *lembur*, and sometimes falls between them. Outside of the town this unit may be a separate settlement. Decisions to build or repair a prayer house or a house for a poor widow may be made at informal meetings.

Perhaps because of the lack of strong corporate groups and the existence of only relatively insignificant small territorial communities in the Priangan, the development within the last century of a strong superimposed village administrative unit (*kalurahan*) was easier than it has been in Central Java. The Priangan *kalurahan* is larger, perhaps because amalgamation of smaller units was easier. It may be more able to support a modern administration on a money basis. Although not autonomous, for its development was largely in response to central government regulations and support, its government, as formalized largely by the Village Regulation of 1906 (Inlandsche Gemeente Ordonantie) and its amendments, effectively assumed more and more functions. In 1925

the Priangan *kalurahan* was more likely than its Javanese counterpart
to have such modern corporate characteristics as a village hall, a rice
granary, a bank, and schools (see Soetardjo Kartohadikoesoemo 1953,
400, 408).

Today in Situradja the functions of the village rice granary have
been taken over by those of smaller neighborhoods. Generally, however,
the recent requirements of security, as well as the increased use of the
village unit by various ministries of the central government, have given
the village increasing corporate strength in relation to its inhabitants.
The central government adds to the economic resources of the village,
backs its official leadership, pushes it in various projects and in the establishment of such semiautonomous organizations as village cooperatives
or the village defense organization (Organisasi Kesedjahteraan Desa or
O.K.D.). For a while the village got special financial and other aid as
an experimental village.

The village's budget—for example, that of 1957 as decided on in
a village meeting on October 3, 1956—gives data in concentrated form
on many of the village's corporate characteristics. Estimated income is
derived largely from village rental properties and village taxing powers,
but the budget does not include the labor—or its substitute—required
of village citizens.[11] Estimated expenditures indicate many government
functions while overlooking others, such as record keeping, the settlement
of inheritance and other disputes, tax collecting, and channeling central
government orders and information to the people.[12]

[11] Estimated income in *rupiah* for 1957 included the following: 200 from
the products of trees on village land; 500 from the sport field (10 per cent
of the O.K.D.'s net profit on its use for O.K.D. purposes); 1,920 from the
rent of houses and offices to individuals and branches of the central government; 5,100 from the rent of schoolrooms to the Ministry of Education;
60 from monthly rent of the village hall by the Bank Rakjat Indonesia;
13,000 from fees paid by traders in the village market; 180 from fees on
marriage, divorce, and remarriage; 30 from a tax on celebrations; 250 from
a tax on slaughtering cattle; 100 from a tax on housebuilding; 400 from
the rent of village roads for heavy transport; 106 interest on money saved
in the Bank Rakjat Indonesia; 1,800 contribution from the village cooperative;
9,700 from enlarging an elementary school with special contributions from
the inhabitants divided by wealth into five classes; 2,040 to support the O.K.D.
drawn from special contributions of the villagers according to four classes
of wealth; and 7,860 remainder from 1956: total receipts, 43,246 *rupiah.*
[12] Estimated expenditures in *rupiah* for 1957 included the following: 450
for paper and other office supplies; 1,625 (12.5 per cent of estimated market

The budget does not include supplementary payments other than the *pantjèn* made to village officials. Most of these are listed in a decision of the *bupati* (regent) of Sumedang in 1950: voluntary gifts of food from family *hadjat;* meat from those who slaughter animals; food or money at the time of the four calendar feasts (*hadjat bulan*); a portion from secondary crops; fees for writing letters of information and permits; money for witnessing land exchanges, loans from the bank and the division of inheritance; 8 per cent of the state tax as a commission for collecting it; and *hiras* labor. Not mentioned in the decision of 1950 were the temporary subsidy the *lurah* (village head) got from the central government and the commission received for approving loans of the village cooperative. The *lurah* receives all of these payments, the clerks most of them, and the other officials less. For the lower officials, some of the fees come directly from the people in return for services and others through the *lurah*. In addition the religious officials derive income from their religious duties as fixed by the Ministry of Religion.

Besides the village officials and the *mandor pasar* (market supervisor), two full-time *djugul* (messengers) are village employees. Usually on call at the village office, they run errands for village officials and from the subdistrict office deliver some of the twenty to forty pieces of mail, including official letters, that villagers get each day. Not provided for in the budget, they receive direct contributions from village inhabitants, such as rice at the time of *pantjèn* payment, and money solicited from central government employees. The *tjengteng* who supervises water distribution in a block of land is paid by the respective landowners. Working

---

income of 13,000) to the *mandor pasar* who collects the fees paid by traders in the village market; 480 for sweepers of the market; 250 for market tickets, writing tools, etc.; 5,000 to build new market buildings; 20,000 to build the school including labor costs; 2,000 to repair other buildings, including labor costs; 1,000 for bridges including labor costs; 2,040 contribution to the O.K.D. to pay one member of the Regu Keamanan (security group) 135 a month and to contribute 35 a month to the O.K.D. guarding a mountain post; 7,124 savings in the Bank Rakjat Indonesia, and 3,277 (10 per cent of total estimated expenses) to meet unknown expenses: total expenditures, 43,246 *rupiah*. The total budget of 56,836 also includes 13,590 *pantjèn* (see note 10). Based on a harvest price of 90 *rupiah* per quintal of rice, the officials received the following annual remuneration: the village head, 5,760 *rupiah;* the two clerks, 1,775 each; the five *kampung* heads, the village police officer, and the village irrigation supervisor, 540 each; the three religious officials, who have duties relating to marriage, divorce, death, and record keeping, 180 each.

under the *ulu-ulu* (overall village irrigation supervisor), he is appointed by the *ulu-ulu* with the agreement of the farmers. He can initiate light maintenance on the irrigation system, but heavier work is arranged through the village.

The *lurah*'s role in the *kalurahan* is supported by his wealth, his education (six years in elementary school), and his extensive and important kin connections. In addition he has been sent to a special course for village government officials. The other village officials are relatively weak in one or more of these respects, although the clerks have had the same level of education. The *lurah* does appoint some of the village officials (*ulu-ulu* and *lěbe*), subject to the approval of the village meeting. Village officials are drawn from the entire area of Situradja, a fact which, if not just a convenient administrative tool, may indicate the *lurah*'s desire to obtain backing from each village section. The *ulu-ulu*, however, lives in the village to the south. Classes of citizenship based on length of residence in Situradja do not really exist, and local leaders, like the *ulu-ulu*, may come from elsewhere. The official powers of the *lurah* are defined by government regulations, and the central government is able to support him in other ways. For example, in village meetings central government officials have spoken in favor of the *lurah* and his activities. The *lurah* has received a temporary financial subsidy from the government, and he wields the power to approve loans given by the bank or the village cooperative.

Day-to-day decisions regarding village affairs, made by the *lurah* alone or in conjunction with the other officials, are unrecorded. More important matters are aired at various types of public meetings, usually taking place in the village hall and recorded in the minutes of the village clerk. Between 1951 and 1956 there was a yearly average of ten meetings, of which six were meetings of the village citizens as a whole. Between 1951 and 1955 most of the other meetings involved the sections of the village development committee (Seksi[2] Panitia Pembangunan Desa), either alone or with *tugu* heads and prominent village inhabitants. No longer functioning during my field work, this committee was set up in connection with the establishment of an experimental village in Situradja; it was composed of smaller subcommittees more or less closely related to various branches of the central government. Financial support for village projects was channeled in part through this organization. For a while, central government officials who were village citizens were actively involved in village affairs. In 1956 most of the smaller meetings involved *tugu* heads, other *tugu* representatives, and prominent people. All meetings included the dissemination of information and announcement of government directives; most involved decision making. Some small meetings were called to implement the decisions of a general village meeting, for example when *tugu* heads and other representatives assigned the population to economic classes for school contributions. Other small groups prepared for a larger assembly, as in early discussions of the annual budget. On certain issues a formal decision by the village meeting was needed; generally the required vote was provided by the unanimous decision of those family heads who were present. Women were invited to attend only one such meeting. The meeting follows a predetermined program; decisions by unanimous voice vote are almost automatic after explanations have been given by local or often by central government officials. A question-and-answer period ends the program, when people may also make suggestions for future consideration. Objections are seldom expressed openly during the meeting; opposition not resolved beforehand may result in the decision's being executed only partially if at all.

9. Education and Artistic Expression

The early expansion of secular education in Sumedang, as indicated in 1930 census data, perhaps explains the role of schoolteachers, especially school heads, in Situradja village government and political life. Prominent speakers in village meetings, they are frequently initiators. From the 1920's they have established, led, and actively participated in various organizations. The major criteria by which the villager ranks the prestige of occupations are the education necessary for the work, the income or wealth associated with it, and the position of the occupation in the official hierarchy. The school head is highly rated on all these counts. He is not moved around like other government employees, and thus he is more likely to be richer than the average, owning land in the village as well as having the security of salary and pension. He is more likely to have kin in the village. Few government officials come to village meetings except to support central government programs, while the school head comes both as a village citizen and as a representative of his school, teachers, and pupils. He also represents the school in other meetings and can even ask pardon for this "family."

The school system plays a predominant role in social, economic, cultural, and even religious life. Education is valued as a means of preparing for government employment, an occupation usually equated with high social status. The high value assigned to education by the villager is indicated by the amount he is willing to pay for education as a parent and, as the budget shows, as a citizen. Children in elementary schools must contribute .5 *rupiah* per month in addition to special charges for school programs. Secondary schools may have large entrance fees and/or monthly tuition. In August 1957, Sumedang became the first regency in West Java, and the third in Indonesia, with compulsory six-year elementary education. Everybody in the regency had to pay ten *sen* (cents) for this program. In the village of Situradja the Ministry of Education was the largest source for employment and provided money for special educational projects, rent, and scholarships as well as salaries.

The Bureau of Mass Education (Djawatan Pendidikan Masjarakat) as well as other ministries have sponsored numerous courses for adults. In general these seem to be temporary affairs, in marked contrast to elementary and secondary education. In July 1957, thirty-three men and women were teaching 1,059 pupils in four six-year elementary schools.[13] On the secondary level, the government junior teacher's school (S.G.B.) in 1955 had ten teachers and 280 pupils from the subdistrict, and in 1958, 436 pupils. The two private junior high schools (S.M.P.) had 240 pupils. One, taught by teachers from the S.G.B. met in the S.G.B. building; its pupils were associated with regular students of the S.G.B. in school programs and scouting activities. The other, taught by teachers from Sumedang, met in an elementary school.

The schools are the most significant social groups associated with artistic expresesion. Today many Sundanese art forms, whether aristocratic, popular, "Islamic," or modern, are practiced mainly or entirely by school children and occasionally by schoolteachers in the schoolroom or in public performances. Examples are the *serimpi* and other dances, old formal songs, the Islamic *pentjak* dance of self-defense, and Sundanese *sandiwara* (plays). Modern Sundanese songs and the arts of other ethnic groups in Indonesia, for example Sumatran dances, as well as Indonesian and English songs, are also learned in the schools. Schools give performances at various times, especially Education Day (Hari Pendidikan) and Promotion Day (Saman). The latter is second only to the August 17 Independence Day celebration in village life as an occasion for recreation and artistic expression.

[13] The Ministry of Education owned two school buildings (10 rooms) and rented five (20 rooms) from the village government.

Popular folk arts, performed outside the school by people from Situradja or nearby villages, include the *angklung* (a bamboo instrument) music of men on night watch, plowing and counting songs, and arts done for commercial gain: the *sawer* song of advice at circumcisions and marriage, forms of song narrative including the *pantun* by a blind singer accompanying himself on the *katjapi*, the hobbyhorse trance dance (*kuda lumping*), and the *réog* (clowning group).[14] The *réog* troupe, a group of related farmers from Babakan Bandung, also does *umbul* (dancing by female impersonators) and *reak* (with drum and *angklung*).

Most art performances and recreation in Situradja are sponsored by individuals holding ceremonial feasts (*réog*, more rarely singers, *pantun*, or *wajang golèk*), by the schools (their own acts or *wajang golèk* from Bandung), by the village (*wajang golèk*, fights of dogs and wild pigs, *ronggeng* or *najub* dancing), by a division of the central government (usually movies), or by a neighborhood (*ronggeng*). Admission to some of these may be charged for public purposes, such as supporting the village defense organization. Private sponsorship for purely commercial purposes is rare, as are unsponsored itinerant entertainers such as *topèng* dancers in the market place.

Three soccer clubs attract large crowds to games, the income sometimes being used for public purposes. Sports are important in the schools, though few interscholastic competitions are held. Badminton, bridge, and chess are played by government employees. When there was and is electricity in Situradja, twelve radios operate, otherwise only five battery operated sets. Soccer games and *wajang golèk* are the favorite programs. Kite fights, ram fights, and greased pole climbing may be held on August 17 as well as other arts and sports.

10. Associational Groups

Since the revolution a number of organizations and branches of national organizations have come into being in the subdistrict of Situradja. Considering the traditional weakness of corporate groups, it is not surprising that this is largely the result of pressure from above, either official or unofficial. People usually join organizations to maintain harmony in lineal or collateral relations, not because they see benefits to be derived for themselves or society from group activity. For example, government

---

[14] A *réog* performance requires four men carrying drums who sing and clown, with an orchestra to accompany them.

employees may join the party of their superiors, sharecroppers that of their landlords. Some organizations have ended almost with the founding meeting; some have little more than a paper existence in subdistrict records, yet they may still be invited to send "representatives" to be members of committees set up by the subdistrict office to work on the August 17 (Independence Day) program or other projects. The life span of an organization and its activities depend on its leaders. The total membership seldom meets or otherwise participates in group activities. Local leaders will be active to attain social goals or for personal gain, but not if their organizational membership or their activity disrupts lineal or collateral relations important to them. Thus the nonexclusive features of group membership are often stressed, and "representatives" of other organizations are invited as guests to meetings. Nonmembers as well as members were to pay the same rate for *hadjat* dishes, rented out by the cooperative of the National Women's Organization (Perwari). The most vital organizations in terms of participation by leaders and members, economic resources, and growth, as evidenced by an expansion of membership, were the various savings and loan cooperatives, the village cooperative, the neighborhood rice granary cooperatives (*lumbung patjeklik*), the cooperative of Perwari, and the cooperative of the union of Indonesian teachers (P.G.R.I.). Providing financial rewards to officials as cooperative employees and much-needed credit to members, these are in little danger of disrupting existing social relations and are highly valued officially.

The following listing includes many, though not all, of the national and local organizations and parties that now have, or at one time had, members in the village of Situradja. Except for farmers' organizations, the center of most national organizations and parties in the subdistrict is in Situradja.

Organizations of government employees include the Union of Indonesian Islamic Teachers (P.G.I.I.), the union of employees of the Ministry of the Interior, and the police union. Most active in Situradja is the Union of Indonesian Teachers; a cooperative, a soccer club, and probably the Situradja teachers union are associated with it. A union of village government employees at one time was making an effort to obtain salaries from the central government.

Women's organizations were generally auxiliaries of parties: Gerwani for the Communist Party (PKI); Muslimat for the Muslim Party (Masjumi); Wanita Demokrat for the Nationalist Party (PNI), or of government employment organizations: Pertiwi for wives of administrative service and village officials; Bajangkari for wives of police. The independent Perwari was the most active. The Communist group Barisan Tani Indonesia (B.T.I.) seemed the only important farmers' organization in the village not organized by the government.

Religious groups, organized mainly through the subdistrict religious office, included a body for care of the mosque, a body for advice on marriage and divorce settlement, and a body for courses in religious knowledge.

Organizations specifically for welfare, the Red Cross and the Social Body of the subdistrict of Situradja, were short-lived. At present much charity is given on an individual basis or through already existing social organizations. *Zakat* and *pitrah,* if not given to the poor directly, may be collected through the mosque, the village government, or the schools. Government employees are asked by their superiors to contribute to flood relief, scouts collect money, movies are shown at the initiative of the army, and lottery tickets are sold. Gifts of food are associated with national holidays, especially August 17, when each neighborhood contributes a decorated litter. The collection and sale of this food is carried out by representatives of women's organizations. Educational projects outside the school system may be sponsored by an already existing organization, such as the kindergarten of Perwari, or by a temporary organization created for that purpose. Parent-teachers associations, one for all the elementary schools in the village and the other for parents of S.G.B.N. pupils, are not active; the functions of the former are filled by "the *lurah* talking at village meetings." Youth organizations are primarily several scout groups, which since 1961 have been reorganized on a national level into a single scout organization. Security organizations include the Regu Keamanan and the O.K.D. The O.K.D., receiving financial support from the village government and other organizations, is an autonomous government-instituted organization.

Political parties in Situradja in 1957 included IPKI, Masjumi, NU, PIR, PKI, PNI, PSI, Parindra, Permai, and Partai Republik. Many parties received votes in the elections of 1955 and 1957, and even within a single polling district there were usually at least two major contenders. The major parties in the elections of 1955 were, in descending order, PNI, IPKI, PKI, and Masjumi. In 1957 they were PKI (more than doubling its 1955 vote), PNI, Gerakan Pilihan Sunda, IPKI, and Masjumi. As recorded by the subdistrict office, there were almost no PKI members in the subdistrict. Yet through the farmer's group B.T.I. and the women's Gerwani, the Communists early organized the farmers in the outlying settlements of *kampung* Malaka (districts VI, VII). The activity of these organizations did not seem great, but the impression made by Sumedang Gerwani leaders coming and sleeping overnight in this *kampung* probably was. A poor farmer from a neighboring village, promised a seat in the regency-level People's Representative Council (D.P.R.), engaged extensively in most effective house-to-house canvassing. In contrast, parties that seemed only concerned with the rather restricted and passive membership of government employees or prominent persons in the town of Situradja, or which for reasons of harmony avoided campaigning, especially in already committed areas, were not successful.

The party fragmentation of the southern "town" settlements contrasts with the homogeneity or polarization of the vote in the north. Vote changes between elections in the latter seem to have been made in larger blocks. Why? In the south there is greater occupational heterogeneity and a greater diversity of ties to superiors both within and outside the village, for example to those in different lines in different ministries. A part of the population is more or less transient, with no kinship relations supporting collateral ties based on temporary common residence. In the north, ties within the settlement, both collateral and lineal, are more important. Votes based on party membership because of a strong ideological commitment and/or on a tie to a committed superior on whom one is dependent are not changed between elections. Thus the votes for true minority parties tended to remain stable between elections. Votes which did change occur when party choice is not too important to the voter. They are based on collateral relations or on lineal relations to a superior who changes his position, as did the *lurah* and some others within the village. Different village officials were affiliated with different parties, and, while relatives, neighbors, and others often seemed to follow their lead, they did not seem to campaign openly or use undue influence in determining the election's outcome.

Chapter XIII

Djagakarsa: A Fruit-producing Village near Djakarta

SOEBOER BOEDHISANTOSO
UNIVERSITY OF INDONESIA

1. Location, Natural Environment, and Settlement Pattern

Djagakarsa, one of the twelve fruit-producing villages in the area of the *ketjamatan* (subdistrict) Pasar Minggu, is located within the boundary of the territory administered by the governor of Djakarta, the capital of Indonesia. It is cut across by a motor road which connects Pasar Minggu town, the center of the subdistrict, and the city of Bogor to the south. At the border of the village territory is the railroad station Letengagung, where daily many electric trains carrying passengers and goods between Djakarta and Bogor stop for short intervals. The villagers have also built and restored parts of existing roadways and trails to connect the various parts of the village with other surrounding ones and with the main road connecting Pasar Minggu and Bogor. The junction of the village road and the main road is used as a market place where, in a row of small shops (*warung*), goods for daily needs are available and where, in the middle of the night, the fruit-producing peasants sell their products to wholesalers.

The village, with a territory of nearly 588 hectares,[1] is divided into

[1] The village territory of 587.141 hectares is comprised of (a) property of the villagers, covering an area of 553.926 hectares, cultivated as fruit gardens and rice fields; (b) property of the village, covering an area of 32.233 hectares, used for construction land and public welfare enterprises; and (c) property of the state, covering an area of .982 hectare, used by a few inhabitants of the village who possess rights for its disposal.

four *kampung*, or wards: Djagakarsa proper, Babakan, Klapa Tiga, and Kandang. The boundaries of these four *kampung* are clearly indicated by dividing roadways, footpaths, ditches, and hedges (see Map XVI).

The villagers have certainly not been indifferent to the opportunities offered them by the red fertile soil, which is continually enriched by sediments carried by a number of little streams and a larger river, the Tjisarua. Nearly all the available arable land has been cultivated as rice fields or fruit gardens. After World War II, many of the rice fields, which previously covered nearly half of the village area, or 250.767 hectares, were turned into fruit gardens. The size of the village's fruit-producing tract, limited in earlier times to 326.454 hectares of land situated somewhat away from water resources, has thus increased considerably. During the period when landlords controlled this area,[2] any clearing of the fruit forests was prohibited. In addition to cultivated land, the village inhabitants also had patches of land for grazing their cattle.[3] Pressed by the need for agricultural land, the villagers have recently divided and cultivated nearly all this pasture land.

With fruit cultivation, most of the peasants are so tied to the land that they feel the need to live in or near their fruit gardens. This is different from the earlier settlement pattern, in which the peasants built their houses on land away from the water, forming compounds called *babakan*. Recently, however, there has also been a tendency to build houses along village roads.

[2] The area around Djakarta was part of the extensive estates found in various areas of Java. Land was sold to private individuals by the Dutch East India Company, and later by the Dutch colonial government, in particular under Governor General H. W. Daendels, in order to raise funds for government expenses. About the history of these estates, usually called *particuliere landerijen*, see J. Faes (1893); about the estates around Djakarta in particular, see W. de Veer (1904). According to the older people in the village of Djagakarsa, the land of this area had been the private property of a certain Tuan Polmak. This name, given to the landlords by the population, was probably derived from the Dutch word *volmacht*, meaning in fact the executive rights of the lands rather than the landlord.

[3] A variety of domestic animals are kept by the villagers as supplementary occupation. These animals are generally considered by their owners as valuable savings, for not only can their energy be used, but also their dung, as fertilizer. There are, then, 125 cows and 161 water buffaloes. The 247 sheep and 88 goats are less highly priced and thus can be easily traded, which makes them very popular as a means of saving. Quite a number of villagers keep poultry, primarily to obtain eggs. In addition, the 7 horses maintained in the village are employed to draw carts.

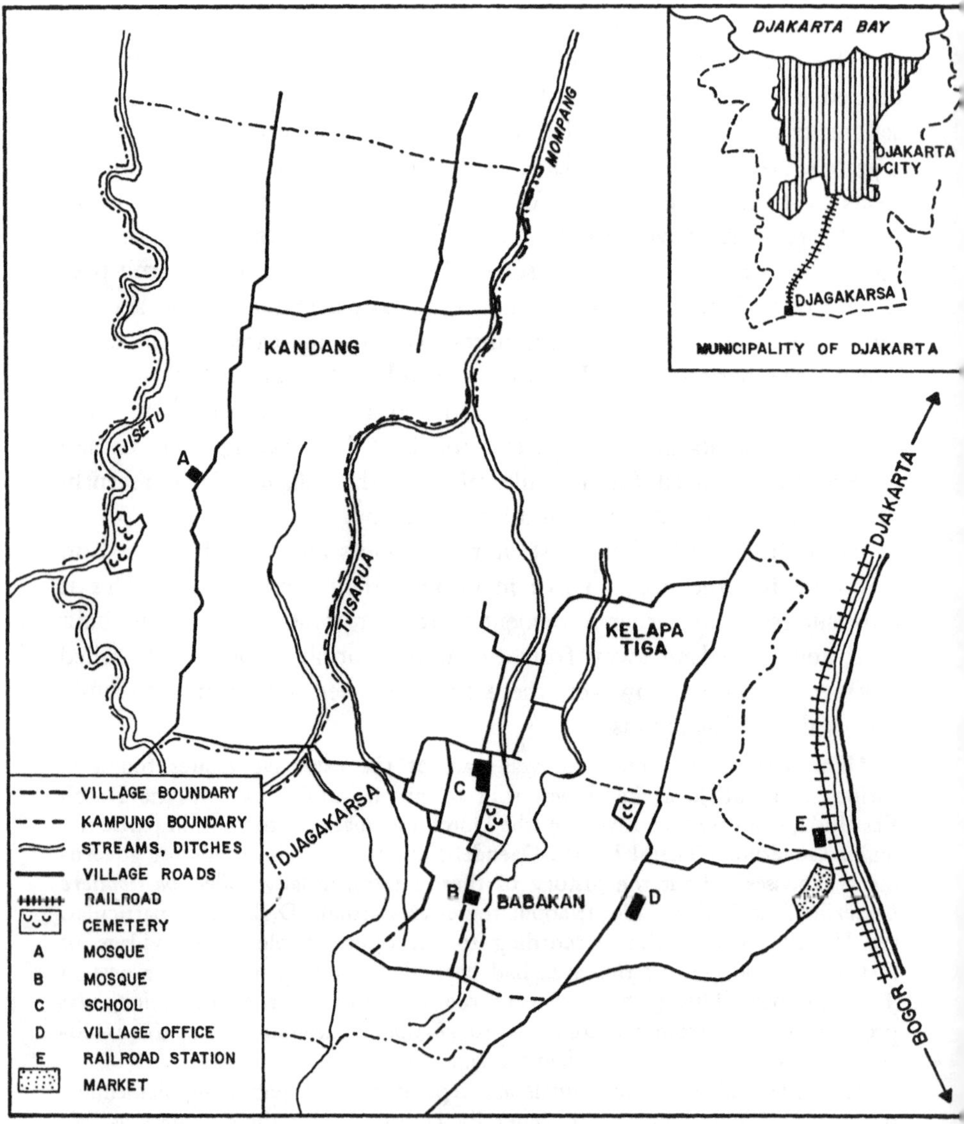

DJAKARTA BAY

DJAKARTA CITY

DJAGAKARSA

MUNICIPALITY OF DJAKARTA

KANDANG

TJISETU

TJISARUA

MOMPANG

KELAPA TIGA

DJAKARTA

DJAGAKARSA

C

B   BABAKAN   D

E

BOGOR

⋯·— VILLAGE BOUNDARY
--- KAMPUNG BOUNDARY
≋ STREAMS, DITCHES
━━ VILLAGE ROADS
╫╫╫ RAILROAD
⌣⌣ CEMETERY
A   MOSQUE
B   MOSQUE
C   SCHOOL
D   VILLAGE OFFICE
E   RAILROAD STATION
▦ MARKET

Map XVI. Djagakarsa

2. *The Population*

No data are available concerning the origins or time of arrival of the first settlers, although some information could be collected from a few older people. According to them, the first people to settle and cultivate the soil were peasants who were skilled in wet rice farming, since the Dutch or Chinese landlords who owned the lands in this area until 1930 offered land only to those who were willing to cultivate it as rice fields. Gardening on the landlords' property, except in small plots near the peasants' dwellings, was hardly possible, as clearings were only allowed for building purposes, once a permit had been purchased. The ability to cultivate land was usually found among people inhabiting inland areas, where mountain slopes and rivers made simple irrigation possible. These first settlers probably came from the Bogor area. Pressed by the need for land and attracted by the irrigation works already established by the landlords around 1830, these inland people gradually came to settle in the village, tilling the soil as tenants who paid their landlords part of the crop as rent.

Until 1870, there were only 17 houses in the village, with an approximate population of fifty to sixty people, whereas in 1930 there were about 120 houses. Based upon this, an estimate could be made of the number of people at that time. In the year 1937, the colonial government started to survey and define property boundaries, since from around that time private lands owned by landlords were distributed to those cultivators who could afford to buy the property rights. From these records it appears that there were about 800 landowners among the village inhabitants. However, it is not easy to estimate the number of inhabitants from the total landowners, since not all landowners were heads of families.

There are no records from the period 1937–1951 that could be used as a source for census figures. In 1952 a preliminary census was taken in which 3,626 inhabitants were registered. Between 1953 and 1957 (3,671 people), the population seems to have remained relatively constant, but in 1960 the number jumped and then increased rapidly until 1961 when, for the first time, a census was taken. Vital statistics concerning births and deaths for 1952 to 1961 are shown in Table 24.[4] The rapid

---

[4] It is very difficult for the village administration to keep records of births and deaths. They often have to devise various incentives to make people report vital statistics to the office, e.g., by selling cloth at reduced prices.

330 *Villages in Indonesia*

Table 24. Population, births, and deaths in Djagakarsa

Year	Number of inhabitants	Births	Deaths
1952	3,626	41	29
1953		65	21
1954		48	
1955		26	
1956		19	7
1957	3,671	36	17
1958		53	13
1959		37	7
1960	4,736	40	44
1961	5,165	52	26

population increase in 1960–1961 seems to have been caused by an influx of people who had to leave the city because of housing difficulties and the pressure of government plans for urban expansion, which has been forcing the urban population to move far out into the country. Thus, as well as centers for fruit production for city consumption, these villages have also become residence areas for people who are employed in the city.

3. Fruit Cultivation

Although at present fruit cultivation is the predominant means of village subsistence, this has been practiced extensively only since World War II. The deterioration of the irrigation system during and subsequent to the Japanese occupation seems to have been one of the reasons for the shift from rice farming to fruit cultivation, while the favorable location of the village in relation to Djakarta has greatly influenced the development of fruit production. In the eyes of the villagers, fruitgrowing requires less effort and is more profitable than rice cultivation. Once planted, the fruit trees need relatively little care, and one has only to wait for the annual picking season. A small fruit garden will also produce a larger yield than the same land planted in rice.

The fruit farmers still work with very simple methods and tools. They use the *tjangkul*, or hoe, to turn the soil; the *blentjong*, a sickle, to weed; and a *linggis*, or crowbar, to till hard and dry soil. For fertilizer, manure or compost is used, and only recently have some of the more wealthy fruit farmers begun to employ modern chemical fertilizers, which are both expensive and difficult to obtain. Seed selection to improve the quality of the crops has been widely practiced.

The fruit gardens of Djagakarsa usually occupy only small pieces of land. As is shown by Table 25, more than half of the property is not larger than half a hectare.

Table 25. Landholding in Djagakarsa

Size of land in hectares	Under ¼	Under ½	Under 1	Under 2	Under 3	Over 3
Number of landholders	303	224	185	103	29	9

The farmers have acquired their property through inheritance or purchase. The inherited pieces are usually too small to provide an adequate source of income. The young farmer thus will often try to increase his holdings, piece by piece, through purchase or other means, until he has acquired several plots of land. These are usually located in several places, often at a considerable distance from one another. The increase of land property for one farmer means a decrease for another. In addition, many people from the city have also started buying land in the village, so that the number of local landholders within the village has become smaller and smaller. The poor villagers who only possess very small pieces of land, and those who have none at all, work for people with larger gardens, while a great number of them work as fruit sellers in the markets or in Djakarta.

As well as the advantages gained from cultivating the land as fruit gardens, there are also certain disadvantages. Since, with the simple methods of farming in Pasar Minggu, the fruit cannot be stored or kept for a long time, there is always an abundance of fruit during the harvest season. With the increase in the supply, the demand will usually drop rapidly, as fruit is not considered essential to the ordinary Indonesian diet. Fruit prices indeed do not vary greatly, except when there is an exceptional rise or drop in the price of rice, the index used by the farmers for establishing fruit prices. The importance of the rice price in the village economy is reflected by the term the villagers use for it, namely *harga bijang*, or *harga induk*, the "mother price."

A fruit farmer of Pasar Minggu never concentrates on one kind of fruit but always plants several kinds of trees, each with a different ripening season, planted on a single piece of land or in separate plots. In this way, he hopes to avoid a huge surplus of one kind of fruit during the harvest season. *Musim patjeklik*, or periods of famine, often suffered by rice farmers, are seldom experienced by fruit farmers cultivating several kinds of fruit.

The most important kinds of fruit cultivated in Djagakarsa are papaya (*Carica papaya*), guava, or *djambu batu* (*Psidium guajava*), rambutan (*Nephelium lappaceum*), durian (*Durio zibethinus*), and *kedondong* (*Spondias dulcis*).

Papaya is a fruit which has only recently become known to the villagers. The tree requires continuous care: the ground has to be turned several times and needs fertilization, which is rather expensive for the less well-to-do farmer. On the other hand, the tree starts bearing fruit when only six months old, and from that time on each tree will yield thirty or forty fruits every season, one being picked every four days throughout four months. On less than a quarter of a hectare a farmer can plant approximately two hundred papaya trees. *Djambu batu* (guava) is a second profitable fruit, since after three years it will bear fruit twice yearly for a period of fifteen years. The plant can be grown from cuttings in a special plot or mixed with other fruit trees. It does not require much care other than extensive fertilization. To speed fruit bearing, the trees may be watered frequently. Each season a tree will yield twenty to forty fruits at each picking for as long as three months. Rambutan trees are grown from seeds or from cuttings and do not need special care. When four or five years old, the tree will bear fruit once a year for a period of fifteen years. Durian trees, grown wild without much care, bear fruit once a year from the time they are ten years old. The crop, however, is easily damaged during the flowering season, and although the price can be high the yield is often small. *Kedondong* trees grow wild and will bear fruit after four years. If well taken care of the *kedondong* will bear fruit throughout the year, each picking giving a yield worth half a crop of a rambutan tree. The fruit, however, does not get the attention it should from the villagers of Djagakarsa.

Beside the trees mentioned above, there are others in which the villagers are less interested, although they will always pick and sell the fruit to supplement their income. These fruits are the *mangga kebembem* (*Magifora odorata*), a type of mango which grows wild in the gardens; the *nangka* (*Artocarpus integrifolia*), a fruit eaten as a vegetable when unripe and as a very tasty fruit when ripe; the *nangka belanda* (*Anoma muricata*), which finds a good market in the fruit-juice factories in the city; the *belimbing*, or carambola (*Averrhoa carambola*); the *manggis*, or mangosteen (*Garcinia mangostana*); the *duku* (*Lansium domesticum*); and the *duwet* (*Eugenia cumini*). Other fruit trees even less popular with the farmers are the banana (*Musa paradisiaca*), which must be cut down after each crop and requires too much space; the *salak* (*Salacca edulis*), cultivated in small numbers since they obscure the view in gardens that have to be guarded; and *sawo* (*Manilhara kauiki*), which are not very well cared for by the villagers, perhaps because the elaborate picking process demands much extra labor and the market price is not very attractive.

4. Daily Life of the Fruit Farmer

The majority of the fruit farmers of Djagakarsa take their own fruit for sale to the local markets, or very often into the city as well, so as to receive a larger profit than when sold to the wholesalers. Consequently they are always busy, sometimes working in the gardens, other times selling their produce at the market or in the city. For those who do not go to the market or to the city to sell their fruits, the day begins rather late: they get up and start work after eight o'clock. Morning activities consist of preparing the ground for new plantings, fertilizing and trimming the trees, and sometimes picking ripe and overripe fruit. These morning activities do not take a long time, for as soon as it gets hot, around eleven o'clock, the farmers go home. They arrange the fruit to be sold or set it to ripen for sale on another day. At about noon they have their first meal of the day: rice and some side dishes prepared by the women. Work is begun again around three o'clock, mainly picking fruit, arranging it in baskets or binding it into bunches, and, if possible, selling it to the village middlemen, who usually do their business in the late afternoon or the middle of the night.

The male members of the household do all the work in the fruit gardens, from preparing the soil, planting and caring for the trees, to picking and preparing the crop for sale. The women restrict themselves to household duties and never take part in the activities connected with fruit planting, not even during the extremely busy rambutan season, when many hands are needed to bind the heaps of fruit into bunches of a certain size.

The farmers who take their own fruit for sale into the city are not able to work in their gardens during the morning, since they do not return home before noon. This does not seriously affect the routine, since the preparation of the soil can be done in stages, whenever the need occurs. The activities of these farmers do not differ very much from those of the *tengkulak* (wholesalers) or middlemen, who sell the crops to the consumers in the city. Activities begin in the dead of night, usually around midnight, when the wholesalers come to the local market where the farmers sell their fruit. When they have done their buying, they leave for the city by the earliest train, around four in the morning, or by bicycle. At the earliest they return to the village around noon. Thus the village seems deserted until midday, when the roads begin to fill with people returning from the city. Farmers and *tengkulak* walk in groups on the village road, each carrying his purchases, such as rice, salted fish, salt, and kerosene. On the way home, prices are discussed, the intermediaries meanwhile sounding out those farmers who are willing to do business with them. For the farmers, this is also an opportunity to find buyers for their crop. Having arrived at home, they eat their midday meal and take a brief nap. Around three o'clock in the afternoon the intermediaries search again in the village for crops to buy. They go home around sunset, have their evening meal, and then try to get some sleep before it is time to sell the crop at the village market or to catch the early morning train to the city. As a rule, Pasar Minggu farmers go to bed early, except on evenings when they are invited to a feast. The younger people, on the other hand, keep late hours, since many of them have religious classes with the local teacher.

For the greater part of the male population in the village, not much time is left for other productive activities after the tiresome daily trips to the city. Nor do the women, although they seem to have more leisure time after their household duties, practice many handicrafts. Only some of them plait mats or make bags of pandan leaves (*Pandanus tectorius Sol.*) for their own use, while some older men make bamboo rope and wooden handles for hoes.

Because fruit farmers earn money consistently throughout the year by selling various fruits with different seasons, the social and ceremonial activities in the community are not restricted to particular periods or months. Festivities celebrating the inauguration of a new house or celebrating transitional events along the life cycle, like circumcisions and weddings, occur throughout the year, with of course the exception of the fasting month, Ramadan.

5. *Transition and Marriage in the Individual's Life Cycle*

To acquire heirs is the greatest hope of a couple starting their married life. This is not only because offspring strengthen a marriage but also because children will inherit the family properties and support their parents in old age. There are many rites and festivities surrounding the birth of a child, especially the first one. One of the important ceremonies is the *kekaba*, performed when a woman is seven months pregnant for the first time.[5] The woman is bathed with water made fragrant with flowers, in order to drive away the evil spirits, and a *slametan* or communal sacred meal is held, attended by the closest neighbors.

A pregnant woman, even if it is her first pregnancy, will continue her household duties until shortly before her delivery. Often, nearing the time of delivery, a woman will return to her parental home to be sure that she will be well cared for. If the woman prefers to stay in her own home, her mother or mother-in-law will come to assist in the household. At the crucial moment the woman will have her mother or mother-in-law and other experienced relatives near her, while a midwife helps her deliver the child. After the birth of the baby there will be a *slametan* ceremony. Neighbors are sent some sacred food, as an announcement of the baby's arrival and as a token of joy. A bigger ceremony, called the *turun tanah* ceremony, is held when the baby is forty days old. During this ceremony the child will touch the ground for the first time and will have its nails cut. Therefore the ceremony is also called *kerik tangan*. If the baby is a girl, she will then be circumcised.

A baby is usually weaned when a year or a year and a half old and occasionally later. If the mother becomes pregnant again, however, weaning may occur at an earlier age. The baby is cared for and reared not only by the mother but usually by all the older members of the family. Before the baby can crawl it is carried about in a sling rather than left alone. It will play with other children of its own age only when it is able to walk. Groups of these little children play in the yard or accompany their older brothers to herd the cattle or to work in the fields.

[5] Nowadays most of the ceremonies celebrating the important events along the life cycle are not rigidly observed, except circumcision and marriage.

Boys are circumcised at school age, six or seven years. In the evening of the day of the circumcision, festivities of various kinds, such as a *hadjat* or an extensive meal and a folk performance, are held. Usually these festivities afford an opportunity for the families involved to receive *paketan* money from the mutual-aid association (see Section 8). Public circumcision ceremonies are sometimes held by the village or the *kampung*, where children of the poorer families may be circumcised without charge.

After circumcision the boys are taught to work in the fruit gardens or at home. Very often they participate in the fruit-raising activities, such as picking and storing the fruit and helping to make arrangements for sale of the produce in the town. Teaching the children to work intensifies the feelings of responsibility toward the family. Girls also share in the responsibilities of the family, even though they do not work in the fruit gardens; they help their mothers with household chores or work in small industries.

Besides the practical upbringing received from their parents, such as work in the fields and gardens or even trading, many children receive education at the six-year elementary school in the village, starting when they are six or seven years of age. Usually only the younger pupils attend school regularly. Consequently, only the lower classes of the elementary school are overcrowded; for them, additional rooms and teachers are needed.[6] The older children, nearing adulthood and feeling responsible for the welfare of the family, leave school in order to help their parents in agriculture, fruit cultivation, and trade. It is not surprising, therefore, that the highest grade of the elementary school does not have more than fourteen pupils, whereas the first grade cannot accommodate all the pupils. The shortage of teachers and the failure of the government to provide writing materials and books are greatly felt. Many village children discontinue their studies because they are unable to buy the required books. Parents are more inclined to buy tools, which are of immediate, practical benefit to the family's livelihood, than expensive books for their children. Religious education is generally considered important, and at an early age children are sent to school to learn to recite the Koran.

A child's responsibility for the welfare of the family seems to contribute to early maturity. Boys start courting at the age of thirteen to

[6] During the school year of 1960–1961, the local elementary school was forced to hold two classes, one in the morning and one in the afternoon, for the first and second grades.

fifteen years. Groups of boys go to festivities or performances to "hunt" for girls, who also attend these occasions. Distance is no obstacle, and young boys go to festivities sometimes quite far from their own village. At these parties the youth become acquainted. The more fortunate young man may accompany the girl home, where they continue their conversation. If the young man is attracted by a girl, he will visit her subsequently. At these visits, which are called *ngglantjong*, the boy is often accompanied by a friend. During *ngglantjong* courting, the young man and the girl are free to talk and tease each other until early in the morning. Sometimes, when it becomes late, the girl will go inside the house but will continue talking from within her room to the boy, who sits or reclines on the bench on the front porch. Very often boys fall asleep on the bench. Such courting will eventually lead to the choice of a marriage partner.

A village girl is considered "ready" for marriage at the age of fifteen to seventeen, whereas for the boy the right age is eighteen to twenty. The boy is usually slightly older, as he needs time to accumulate savings for wedding expenses and for the needs of his new household. Boys as well as girls are free to choose their own partners, and since meeting places are not limited to the village, there are many intervillage marriages.[7] The consent of the respective parents is important, primarily because the parents play an important role in the arrangement of the marriage.

As soon as the young man and the girl have reached an agreement, the young man announces his intention formally to his parents, so that they can ask for the girl's hand. Usually this is only a formality, since the girl's parents ordinarily give their consent. Therefore, the meeting of parents becomes an opportunity to arrange the wedding and to discuss the expenses. At this occasion the young man's representatives traditionally offer a valuable gift (*paningset*) to the girl, and after this she is considered engaged. If the engagement is called off, the girl must return the gift. During the period of the engagement, the young man tries to increase the sum he has already accumulated to pay for his marriage expenses, and if possible he will build a house. As a rule the young man's parents will help him acquire the necessary sum and build the house.

Shortly before the day of the wedding, relatives of the young man

[7] Of the 89 marriages taking place in 1960, 57 were village-exogamous. Of the 67 marriages in 1961, 47 were village-exogamous.

will take the sum constituting the groom's part of the wedding expenses to the bride's home, together with some wedding gifts, unwrapped so as to be clearly visible to the public. The number and variety of gifts and the number of relatives who attend the presentation ceremony is a matter of pride for the families of both bride and bridegroom.

The formal Islamic wedding ceremony will be conducted by the *penghulu* either at his office or at the bride's home. The wedding party is held at the bride's home, where the formal "meeting" between bride and bridegroom takes place, usually followed by a performance of popular folk plays or music to entertain the guests.[8] After the "meeting" ceremony, all the young man's relatives visit, a custom which is called *besanin*.

After the wedding, the young couple will stay in the home of the bride for a few days. Then they are moved to the house of the young man's parents, where a party is given to welcome the bride into the family. If the young man has a house ready, the young couple will soon move into their own house. Although as a rule the young man's parents will provide their son with basic household necessities, it is not unusual for the bride's parents to provide the house and garden. This is especially true when the girl is an only child or the youngest, who is expected to take care of her parents in their old age.

It is considered acceptable for a man to have more than one wife, although not more than 5 per cent of the men in the village practice polygyny. A man with more than one wife must provide as many houses as he has wives, since it would be difficult for the wives to live peacefully in the same house. Polygyny is practiced primarily by the wealthy villagers and the more well-to-do village officials and therefore has become

[8] Folk plays and music in Djagakarsa are performed by groups of entertainers who usually come from other villages. The various forms of entertainment, arranged according to the number of performances held during the years 1960–1961, were as follows:

Year	*wajang*	*lenong*	music	*topeng*	*golek*	Others
1960	33	35		7	4	7
1961	22	14	36	13	2	7

Music is usually performed by a band of *krontjong* players (Malay string music with solo songs), a band of *gambus* players (Arab-influenced string music), and a group of *tandjidor* players.

an indication of a man's wealth. Those who have succeeded in increasing their wealth try as well to gain status in the community by taking a new wife.

Although every newly married couple hopes to acquire heirs who will support them in old age, most of the village people do not want to become a burden for their children. The older people remain active and work in the fields, even when their children meet their needs. Ordinarily the old people are cared for by their unmarried children, with the help of those already married. If all children have married, the parents will live with one of them or ask one of the children to stay in the parental home. Usually the old people prefer to stay with one of their married daughters, and it is therefore sometimes necessary for a man to live with his wife's parents and cultivate their land.

6. *The House*

Usually a nuclear family in Djagakarsa exclusively occupies a single house, although because of the housing shortage there is an increasing tendency for several related families to live together. In 1957, registration showed 963 families occupying 845 houses; in July 1961 the number of families had increased to 979, while in October 1961 (after the national census taking), 1,027 families were living in the same number of houses. The traditional house is built of planks and plaited bamboo, but nowadays there are also many houses built of brick. Basically the houses in the village consist of three main parts: a front porch, a central section, and a back part. The front porch does not have a door. There are only two side walls, against which two wide benches are placed for visitors and family members to sit in the evening. Young men visiting the daughters of the house are also received there. Many people have already replaced one of the benches by a table and set of chairs for visitors. The central section of the house is the most important part. It is separated from the front porch by a wall with a central door flanked by windows. This center section is divided into bedrooms, the *pendaringan* (storeroom) and sometimes a room where the family has its meals. The room adjacent to the front porch is usually reserved for the daughters of the house, so that they can talk freely to the young men on the bench outside. The parents' room is usually next to the daughters' or farther back. The *pendaringan* is a place where people keep their valuables and store their seeds and rice. The back part of the house is used for cooking and storing farming implements and firewood. Sometimes there is a wide bench where the family eats. A special room for the young male members of the family is not considered important. They can sleep wherever they want, either on the front porch bench, in the kitchen or eating place, or, when they have reached maturity, on the bench of their girl's front porch.

7. Family and Household

A married couple is considered a basic family unit (even though they may still be living with parents) since they will form a new nuclear family apart from their family of orientation. Thus the young couple enjoys the same status as their elders. For the man this means that he has not only gained the rights attached to the head of family but also the responsibilities. Heads of nuclear families, who are automatically considered heads of households, have the right to represent their families at important events in the village, such as village meetings and elections for village head. At these elections they have the right to vote as well as to be elected.

A new family will usually set up its home as soon as possible. Ordinarily some of the husband's and wife's relatives move with them into their new home. The older relatives will help the husband to earn his livelihood or help the wife with the household activities, such as preparing food and taking care of the children. Because of housing difficulties and the high cost of building, there is a tendency for the grouping together of more than one nuclear family in a single house. Generally, however, the nuclear families as well as the households are not large, as can be seen from the figures included in Table 26.

Kin groups larger than the nuclear family are called *permili*. The range of this bilateral kin group is not very clear. Often a person is said to be "still related" or "a relative" to show that there is a kin relationship, although it is often very difficult to trace the exact one. Members of the *permili* visit each other and help each other whenever possible. The intensity of this relationship depends in fact upon the distance between their respective homes. Sometimes the paternal relatives tend to be closer, since, as has been mentioned, a family usually settles in the area of the husband's relatives. Close contact and mutual aid between relatives are limited to members of the same generation or those of adjacent generations. It is therefore not surprising that people often do not

Table 26. Sizes of 1,027 households in the four *kampung* of Djagakarsa (source: Register of the Village Cooperation for Consumptive Goods, 1961)

Size of households	Number of households			
	Djagakarsa	Babakan	Klapatiga	Kandang
2	15	26	8	25
3	61	46	32	40
4	66	41	36	53
5	54	51	17	60
6	42	40	21	43
7	50	16	15	36
8	20	24	6	22
9	9	10	8	14
10	6	3	5	3
11	2		1	1
Total	325	257	149	296

know the names of the relatives of their parents' generation or tend to forget the names of grandparents.

8. *Neighborhood,* Kampung, *and Other Associations*

Since houses are scattered all over the village, sometimes rather far apart, those near together have formed *rukun tetangga,* or neighborhood associations, in accordance with government directives, mainly those from the Department of Home Affairs, the Department of Social Affairs, and the Department of Information. In Djagakarsa there are twenty-six neighborhood associations, each led by a member elected by family heads at a meeting of the association's members. The aim of the neighborhood association is to foster the prosperity, increased knowledge, and general welfare of its members. Its activities include, among others, the construction of public works and local roads through collective effort, the organization of the village night watch, and mutual aid in cases of disaster.

The village ward organization (*rukun kampung*) aims to promote cooperation between the inhabitants of the respective *kampung.* The four *rukun kampung* of Djagakarsa, corresponding to the four *kampung* divisions, include the twenty-six neighborhood associations. As in the neighborhood association, the leader of the *rukun kampung* is elected by its members. The leader of the *rukun kampung* assists the head of the *kampung* (*mandor*), performing his duties without pay. The *rukun kampung*, with its wider area and more extensive membership, has greater responsibilities than the *rukun tetangga*. Its activities include, for instance, the repair of irrigation works and village roads and other collective undertakings. In the beginning of 1962, in accordance with directives coming from the Department of Cooperatives, each *kampung* organization set up its own consumers' cooperative to supersede the former village cooperatives. The consumers' cooperative in each *kampung* is expected to facilitate the distribution of foodstuffs and textiles to the village inhabitants. Another recent activity of the *rukun kampung* was the substantially successful organization of literacy campaigns.

The *kampung* neighborhood organization is not only supposed to limit its activities to its immediate *kampung* but also to cooperate in collective undertakings for the development of the whole village. Thus, in addition to the mobilization of laborers, the *rukun kampung* also collects gifts of both material and money for such projects as the construction of roads, village offices, prayer houses, mosques, and schools. Some projects have indeed been successfully completed with this system of community effort; those which are most spontaneously undertaken in this way are the building of mosques and prayer houses. A part of the expenses needed for village buildings was collected by the *rukun kampung* from the inhabitants, while the rest was raised from gifts by well-to-do individuals in the village. Similarly, the six-year elementary school building was completed in 1961, partly by collective effort, partly by government support.

The older forms of mutual aid or *gotong-rojong* in the village have decreased in importance following the shift from rice farming. Small fruit gardens do not need much additional labor outside the family, whereas large gardens usually rely on paid labor.

Mutual aid is also found in the *paketan* system. A group of forty to fifty people, the majority of whom live in a particular *kampung*, form associations for the purpose of contributing money to support feasts given by members at circumcisions, weddings, or other occasions. Besides the regular guests, invited or uninvited, all the members of the *paketan* association are obliged to come. At the feast they offer the host a sum of money; the amount is not fixed, and wealthy members may give thousands of *rupiah*, while the less wealthy give only several hundred or less. All the contributions, however, are carefully registered in the *paketan* book. The money collected by the host, often quite a substantial sum, is only partially used for the feast itself, because these expenses are usually sufficiently covered by the contributions of neighbors and other guests. The *paketan* money is spent to acquire land or cattle, to repair the house, to invest in business, or to buy fancy clothes, furniture, or other expensive things. Another time a different member will give a feast to inaugurate his new house or to celebrate the circumcision of his son or nephew or the marriage of his daughter or niece, and all the members of the *paketan* club must come and contribute money. The first host must contribute exactly the same amount of money that he received at his own feast from the second feast-giver. A member of the association may not give another *paketan* feast until each of the forty to fifty members has had his turn. Thus he is able to receive the large sum of *paketan* money only once every two or three years. Wealthy villagers, however, are often members of more than one *paketan* association, while several are even members of all five of the *paketan* clubs that exist in Djagakarsa. In this way they can give more *paketan* feasts and receive *paketan* money more frequently, although consequently they also must contribute to many more people at many more feasts. Members who contribute only small sums of money and who associate with only one *paketan* organization will receive a relatively small sum of money only once. Members who are in need of money and unable to wait for a later opportunity will give a *paketan* feast by "borrowing" a nephew to be circumcised or a niece to be given away in marriage. The earlier sum a person receives from his *paketan* club is thus money he borrows to be paid back in installments without interest, while a later sum is money he has saved. A member who is the recipient of *paketan* money is also obliged to contribute a part of that money to his organization.

In addition to the *paketan* organizations, there are also "meat-buying" cooperatives organized for the collective buying of a water buffalo, cow, or goats to provide its members with meat for important holidays, such as Idulfitri, the end of the fasting month, and Iduladha, the end of the *hadj* month. Other mutual-aid organizations are "burial organizations," established for relieving the burden of a member whose family has suffered a death. The sum of money collected by burial organizations is usually not very large and is considered as an additional means to help pay funeral expenses, the greater part of which is generally met by spontaneous contributions from neighbors.

9. Social Grouping and Stratification

As has been mentioned above, not all inhabitants derive their income from farming. Fruit farming, producing a crop that has to be converted into money quickly, not only compels the greater part of the farmers to do their own selling but also provides work for nonfarming inhabitants as middlemen between growers and consumers. Based on type of livelihood, the villagers can be divided into three categories: the *tani*, or fruitgrowers; the *tani dagang*, or farmers who sell as well; and the *tengkulak*, or middlemen who are exclusively fruit traders.

Although not all farmers derive their main income from land cultivation, all villagers of the first two categories do call themselves *tani*, since they indeed cultivate some land. Many are compelled to find an additional source of income. The villagers therefore make a distinction between rich and poor farmers. Rich farmers are those who own sufficient land to require labor from outside the family for its cultivation and whose holdings yield produce exceeding household needs. There are only nine of these farmers in the village (as can be seen from Table 25). Employing labor from the village is very profitable for the rich farmers, as it increases the produce of their gardens to an extent not possible with labor from the family alone. It often happens that these rich farmers do not cultivate the lands themselves, and thus can enjoy the produce of their lands without having to do any work. For selling their fruit, they usually know particular wholesalers who come to buy their crops; in addition, they market their crop through the poor farmers who have no initial working capital. The rich farmers have large incomes, which they often invest or use to enlarge their properties and also to gain more prestige in the community. They build themselves large houses, take new wives, and thus have to maintain more than one household. Polygyny, practiced only by the rich farmers and well-to-do village officials, has thus become the main index in measuring a person's wealth. To gain prestige in the community, rich farmers will also try to collect the money to undertake the pilgrimage to Mecca and to become a *hadji*. Although most of the rich farmers are *hadji*, not all *hadji* are rich farmers.[9] Many have been compelled to sell their property to cover the expenses of the pilgrimage and have thus returned poor landless farmers.

Poor farmers are those with small plots of land, the crop of which is barely sufficient to meet their daily needs, or those who do not possess any land at all. These farmers not only need to work their own fields and sell their own crop, but to add to their income they must also sell their services to the rich farmers as paid laborers or as fruit sellers without working capital.

[9] In all there are thirty *hadji* in Djagakarsa.

Farmers who sell in addition to working in their gardens are called *tani dagang*, or trading farmers. They usually own a fairly large plot of land, and to increase their income they try to develop capital through trading. During the seasons with abundant crops they act as fruit sellers, but when the fruit is scarce and the market quiet they work in their own gardens. This group of trading farmers is the second largest group after that of the farmers. It is important that these trading farmers do not get their produce from their own village alone; particularly when the harvest is late, the trading farmers and middlemen go from one place to another to get fruit and often act as retailers for the wholesale fruit dealers in town.

The middlemen (*tengkulak*) are villagers whose main occupation is to sell the farmers' crop to consumers in town. This category therefore includes newcomers or villagers who have no land to cultivate but do have the small working capital sufficient for a fruit business. Most of these intermediaries do not have much money, which indeed is not necessary, since the means of selling the goods is primarily dependent on human energy. Although the fruit is transported to town by electric train or motor vehicle, it has to be carried from the farmers' homes to the station and from the station to be hawked. As a person's strength is limited, he needs only enough money to buy as much as he can carry. A fruit seller with enough capital to buy large quantities at low prices, yet not enough funds to provide storage and prevent rotting, will risk a loss if his purchase cannot be immediately brought to market. There are nevertheless a number of *tengkulak* with sufficient capital to have permanent fruit stands in the city, who buy the crops of other farmers in the village. This, however, means that the fruit seller must stay in the city while leaving his family in the village, and consequently this type of work is not popular. The intermediary, therefore, keeps his working capital at a relatively constant level and, whenever possible, invests any profit in land, houses, or cattle to provide for a subsequent shortage of capital.

Although one can become rich in the fruit trade and emulate the rich farmer, the villagers feel there is no difference between a wealthy fruit seller and an ordinary one. This is mainly because more value is assigned to landownership than to other kinds of property. Also, a fruit seller will always try to gain more and more, and eventually he will leave the village.

Besides the social distinctions between inhabitants involved in fruit cultivation, the village has another group that has recently increased rapidly, those people who work in the city for private enterprise or the government. Although the villagers accept and treat these individuals like other villagers, their different occupations and interests tend to limit any interaction between the two groups.[10]

The social stratification of the community has no influence on the civil rights of the individual. Each family head, regardless of property, wealth, or occupation, has the right to vote at village meetings, to elect or be elected as *lurah* (village head) or other village officers.

10. Political Organization

As has been mentioned before, Djagakarsa is one of the villages located in the subdistrict of Pasar Minggu, *kewedanaan* (district) of Kramat Djati, *wilajah* Djakarta Selatan (the area of South Djakarta). The village is a geographic and political entity with fixed boundaries and executive powers, under the leadership of a *lurah* who is directly responsible to his superior, the *tjamat* (subdistrict head).

The *lurah* is elected by all the family heads who are registered inhabitants of the village. Elections can only be held if there are at least four candidates proposed. The individual elected is then appointed as a civil servant, with the right to receive a salary from the city government of Djakarta. Besides his salary as a civil servant, the *lurah* receives an honorarium for the taxes he collects, and at various occasions he will receive gifts from the villagers. A *lurah*'s duties are not limited to those of a government employee. As the elected leader of his people, he often is consulted in problems arising from conflicts between the members of his community, such as cases concerning inheritance, deception, or household disputes, before referral to the proper authorities. He is generally considered as a father and a leader of his people. The *lurah* also acts as a government information officer, since he is supposed to know the administration's development plans and the measures adopted.

As a government employee the *lurah* is responsible to his superiors, reporting to the subdistrict officer once a month or whenever there is a meeting of the subdistrict. On the other hand, through the village

[10] For example, laborers, whose only source of income is derived from wages received at fixed times, find it impossible to join the *paketan* associations, which compel their members to contribute money whenever there is a feast.

council, which meets at least once a year, he is also responsible to his people. At this meeting the *lurah* not only accounts for his management of village affairs but also puts forward plans for village development, the costs of which must be paid by the village, for the council's approval.

In the daily performance of his duties, especially his administrative duties, the *lurah* is assisted by a clerk, usually referred to as *Pak Ulis* (*ulis* = *tulis*, write). The clerk helps with the administration and often represents the *lurah* at important events. The clerk is appointed by the *lurah*, and he is confirmed by the government. Beside the *lurah*'s clerk, each *kampung* has a head called *mandor*, appointed by the *lurah* and later confirmed by the government. As the *lurah*'s subordinate, the *mandor* has to send in reports and assist the *lurah* within his own *kampung*.

To maintain peace and order in the village, the *lurah* is assisted by four members of the Organisasi Pertahanan Rakjat or village defense organization, men who have had military training and who are supervised by the officers of the military subdistrict of Pasar Minggu. Besides the village defense organization, the police force of the subdistrict may be summoned if the need arises.

In the field of social welfare, the *lurah* is assisted by the heads of the *rukun tetangga* (neighborhood associations) and the *rukun kampung* (village ward). In religious affairs, the *lurah* is assisted by two Moslem religious officials, *amil*, who represent the *penghulu* of the subdistrict. The *amil* handle marriages and divorces, subject to final approval by the *penghulu*. The *amil*, for a fee, are also asked to pray at religious events and during funeral ceremonies.

As village communities acting as suppliers for a large metropolis, Djagakarsa and other villages in the vicinity of Djakarta have certain characteristics. The villagers, the majority of whom are engaged in fruit cultivation and trade, lead an extremely busy day-to-day life, owing to the limited amount of capital in circulation, the very simple methods of fruit cultivation, and the underdeveloped methods of processing and distributing the produce. Consequently, very little time is left for active participation in the social life of the community, and artificial organizations superimposed by the central government, like the *rukun tetangga* or the *rukun kampung*, or energetic village administrators are required to initiate and organize social activities for the benefit of the village as a whole. In this respect the village Djagakarsa has fared quite well.

Chapter XIV

Negeri Taram: A Minangkabau Village Community[1]

HARSJA W. BACHTIAR
UNIVERSITY OF INDONESIA

1. The Minangkabau Village

The purpose of this chapter is to introduce the reader to one of the numerous village communities of West Sumatra, the land of the Minangkabau people. There are many excellent publications about this ethnic group, most of them written in Dutch. There are, for instance, studies that deal with the matrilineal structure of Minangkabau society, frequently described as the embodiment of matriarchy. There are studies that deal with its traditional normative system, made in the interests of the government and the judiciary. There are studies that describe and analyze the peculiar position of Islam, a puritanical religion with patriarchal prescriptions in a matrilineally structured society of devout but grandeur-addicted individuals. There are books and articles reviewing the major historical events, commencing with the development of a seemingly mighty empire in approximately the fourteenth century, running through the internecine wars with various neighboring countries, the

[1] The author wishes to acknowledge his indebtedness to the University of Indonesia and the Military Academy of Law for enabling him to visit *negeri* Taram in October 1962 after a study had been made of the relevant literature. He is also very grateful to Mr. Kaharudin Datuk Rangkajo Basa, Governor of West Sumatra, who not only showed his personal interest in the study but also granted the use of facilities under his disposal. The author also wishes to thank Captain Tarmizi, Lieutenant Sukarlan, and Mr. Parsudi Suparlan for assisting him in collecting necessary data.

Padri war between orthodox religious leaders and traditional local functionaries, the subjugation to Dutch colonial rule, the occupation of the
land by Japanese troops, and the outbreak of the national revolution.
There are publications about its colorful language, its folklore, and its
literature, the last written in Arabic script. There are also a number
of physical anthropological studies giving data on various measurements
and attempting to explain the origin of the people and their relationship
to a number of other ethnic groups.

It is not, of course, the author's intention to list all available publications about the Minangkabau, since detailed lists of the existing publications can be found elsewhere (Joustra 1924, 1936; Kennedy 1955, I,
171–187), but only to indicate the kinds of existing studies in order
to draw the reader's attention to the complexity of Minangkabau society.
Unfortunately no descriptions of actual village communities are available,
except in a few novels.[2] In view of the need for a description of a Minangkabau village community, *negeri* Taram has been selected as a source
of information with the understanding, however, that *negeri* Taram
should not be regarded as a typical Minangkabau village community.
In fact, there is no such thing as a "typical" Minangkabau village community. Each territorially based community known as *negeri* has existed
autonomously for a very long time, in some cases for four or five centuries. The inhabitants of each *negeri* reserved the right to regulate their
own community affairs. They did not recognize any higher authority,
except God, as holding the right to participate in their affairs without
their consent. When Minangkabau had a ruler, he was acknowledged
only as a nominal chief to whom respect and honor but nothing else
were due. It should be admitted, however, that there was a time, probably
in the fifteenth century, when the ruler did have power and when the
inhabitants of each village settlement did recognize his authority and
his right to govern.

Since each village community existed independently, each developed
its own traditions, rules and regulations, and way of life. Until recently,
throughout the four to five centuries of autonomous existence, there was

---

[2] See M. Radjab (1950). L. C. Westenenk wrote an excellent study on
the *negeri* (1915), but it is not a description of an actual village community
as a whole. There is, however, a description of the physical aspects of the
village Singkarak as it existed in the middle of the nineteenth century; the
study is written by A. W. P. Verkerk Pistorius (1869). More recent is a
description by K. A. James (1915).

no authority to impose standard rules and regulations upon all these village communities. The boundaries separating the numerous *negeri* from one another were scrupulously guarded by the villagers. Within the boundaries of each *negeri* the inhabitants were their own masters. Thus, the similarities that are found in the activities of nearly all Minangkabau village communities may result from the common initiation of norms and regulations by, among others, the colonial and later the national government. Thus it is not difficult to understand why no single *negeri* can be regarded as a typical Minangkabau village community; this in itself is a fact which has usually been overlooked in other studies based on Minangkabau data.

Presently the reader will be taken to one of these varied village communities, to *negeri* Taram, in order to become acquainted with an actual Minangkabau village community as it appeared in mid-1962.

2. Natural Environment

Taram is a village situated in the western part of Central Sumatra on a highland plateau between two parallel mountain ranges of the Bukit Barisan, the mountains which run along the western coast of Sumatra. The plateau is actually a basin, filled with volcanic massifs during the diluvial period, located a little more than five hundred meters above sea level. Both the eastern and western mountain ranges are about a thousand meters high; both are covered with a dark green blanket of densely growing trees. The southern part of the extensive plateau is dominated by an impressive dead volcano, Gunung Sago, the summit of which is 2,202 meters high. The northern end of the plateau is not walled in by mountains, thus offering a seemingly endless view toward the northwest.

Wet rice fields, planted or fallow, form a large part of the plateau's surface. The landscape, attractive as it is, is made even more so by some curiously shaped hills, volcanic deposits scattered about without any apparent order. From the distance Taram can be located by a soaring, solitary, rather barren hill called Bukit Gadang, which towers in the middle of the village land. Aside from these scattered hills, the plateau also contains numerous coconut groves. The coconut fruit forms an important part of the inhabitants' diet, being used as one of the essential ingredients in the preparation of food. Among other trees, the plentiful bananas should not be forgotten.

Through the territory of Taram flows the Sinamar River, majestically making its way from the southern slope of Bukit Putus, weaving toward the southeast, on its way receiving water from other streams and brooks, finally to join with the Umbilin River. Eventually the Umbilin River merges with a number of other rivers to form the powerful Kuantan River of Indragiri on the eastern coast of Sumatra.

Another river, more important for irrigation purposes, is the Tjampo, which runs through the jungle to the east of Taram, making its appearance at Kapalo Banda, a dam built to control the water for the rice fields. From this dam, a canal directs part of the water through the village land, thereby dividing the land into two halves. Both the artificial canal and the Tjampo River itself empty into the Sinamar, the former in the southwestern and the latter in the southeastern part of Taram.

The plateau receives a great deal of rain, the annual total averaging 2,444 millimeters. In July, the month with the least rainfall, the plateau still gets about 100 millimeters, while in December the rainfall may be as much as 290 millimeters. There is, then, enough water to enable fruitful agricultural activities, provided that the inhabitants can make proper use of the water, which unfortunately is not always the case. Heavy rainfall frequently causes both the Sinamar and the Tjampo rivers to overflow their low banks, flooding the adjacent areas.

The jungle, east and south of Taram, is the home of apes and monkeys, wild boars, bears, snakes, and tigers. There is also a great variety of birds, large and small. Occasionally tigers still make their presence known by attacking stray domestic animals, particularly goats. The possibility of such attack has occasioned various measures by the villagers to protect their livestock. Once in a while a tiger may still venture to roam near a dwelling site. Among the domestic animals, in addition to sheep and goats, there are cows (*djawi, sapi*), water buffaloes, chickens, and monkeys trained to procure coconuts from tall trees.

3. Communications

Taram is connected with the town of Pajakumbuh, the capital of the regency (*kabupaten*) Limapuluh Koto, by twelve kilometers of partially asphalted road, which, after passing through Taram, joins the village with the main road from Pajakumbuh to Pakan Baru. Pajakumbuh itself, advantageously located with regard to communications, became the site of a Dutch settlement in 1832. Since 1896 the town has been a major market place. On Sundays people from the surrounding areas pour into Pajakumbuh to sell, buy, or merely enjoy the weekly festivities at the market place.

The road connecting Pajakumbuh and Taram is used daily by public autolets and *bendi,* carriages drawn by horses, which carry people and goods to and fro. Bicycles, sometimes pedaled by women in native dress, are also seen on the road, protected from the sun by the trees growing along the sides. Near the town of Pajakumbuh, modern houses made of brick are prevalent, including buildings to be occupied by the Faculty of Agriculture of the University of Andalas. Gradually, as one leaves the town, such houses become scarce and are replaced by traditional native houses, slightly adapted to more modern needs. At last the scenery changes completely, and one finds himself in the midst of rice fields and bushes. Taram is also connected with the centers of surrounding village communities by numerous paths, both wide and narrow, some passable only on foot.

With regard to more modern communications media, a number of villagers own radios, which enables them as well as others to hear what is going on outside their own village. Letters, newspapers, and magazines are delivered through the office of the *tjamat,* the government administrator at Tandjungpati, whose territorial jurisdiction covers *negeri* Taram together with the territories of sixteen other *negeri.* Some villagers who are regular visitors to Pajakumbuh have a mailing address there in order to receive their mail more promptly.

As Taram is off the main road, it is rather isolated in its location. However, there is enough communication with the outside world to prevent Taram from being a community that people would tend to identify as "primitive."

4. The Land

The villagers have their own conception of the limits of their *negeri's* territory. For them, the boundaries were established in olden times by their ancestors and the formulation then transmitted orally to the present-day inhabitants. The oral recounting of Taram's limits enumerates the various boundary marks provided by nature and used by man and at the same time reiterates that whatever exists within these boundaries, even a grain of sand or a blade of grass, is owned only by the members of the village community of Taram as a whole.

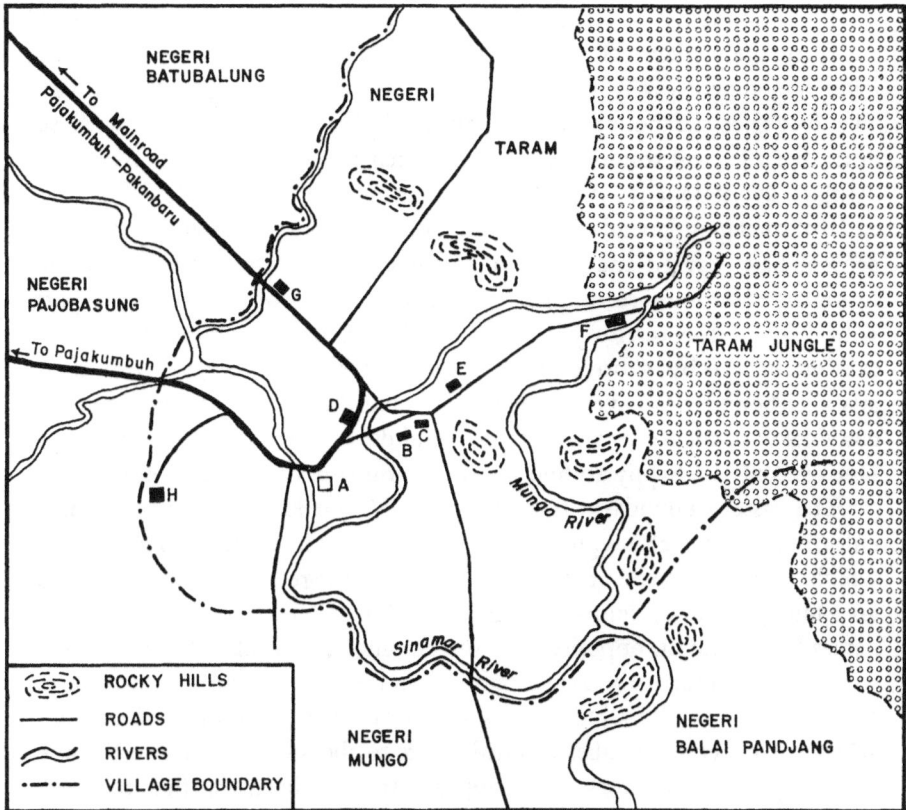

Map XVII. Negeri Taram
A. Market. B. Mosque. C. Sepulcher of Sjech Ibrahim. D. Village council hall (Balai Koto). E. Village council hall (Balai Tangah). F. Site of old village hall (Balai at Kapalo Banda). G. Brick factory. H. Brick factory.

Officially, as stated in government reports, *negeri* Taram is bounded to the north by *negeri* Pilubang; to the west by *negeri* Batubalang, Bukit Limbuku, and Pajobasung; to the south by *negeri* Andalas, Mungo, and Balai Pandjang; and to the east by the residency of Riau. The reader is aware, then, that Taram's eastern boundary thus comprises a segment of the eastern boundary of the residency Sumatra Barat (West Sumatra). This eastern boundary is also part of the eastern limits of what is known as the *alam* Minangkabau, or the land of the Minangkabau people, a fact which allowed *negeri* Taram a special position within the realm of the former Minangkabau kingdom.

The boundaries of *negeri* Taram as recognized by the government are fortunately identical with the boundaries of *negeri* Taram as known from the ancient orally transmitted tradition of the villagers themselves. The fact that the boundaries recognized by the government and those described by local tradition are identical has to be emphasized. Attempts by the government in West Sumatra, during the Dutch colonial period and following independence, to establish an efficient administrative apparatus have caused the creation of some artificial *negeri* through the fusion of two or more original *negeri*, the merger of an existing *negeri* with part of the territory of another *negeri*, or the diminution of an existing *negeri* by subtracting part of its territory. *Negeri* with such artificial boundaries have frequently become the source of endless social conflicts with regard to various rights and duties, either real or imaginary. One can only be happy to find *negeri* Taram free from such conflicts.

The eastern boundary, formed by the Taram jungle, is actually difficult to determine, although official maps do show its location. This jungle, which composes part of the Bukit Barisan range, covers an extensive area uninhabited by human beings. Probably it has been given different names by people on opposite sides of the jungle, each claiming the jungle within his own territory. Any boundary in this area can only be arbitrary. In former times, such jungle area could become the source of conflict whenever different families claimed rights to the same jungle site because their respective ancestors were supposed to have been the first to break a branch, *djolong rantieng dipatah,* thus establishing the rights of their family over the land involved.

Although much of the territory of *negeri* Taram has been cultivated, an extensive part still consists of swamp and jungle. In fact, part of the land that had once been cultivated is presently lying fallow because of the manpower shortage caused by the recent rebellion.

The land creates the primary source of livelihood the territory offers to its inhabitants. The principal crop is rice, for both home consumption and trade. Mainly practiced on wet terraced land, rice cultivation involves at least three kinds of work, namely, the building and maintenance of irrigation canals (*banda*), the cultivation of seedlings on special plots of land (*pasemajan*), and work in the rice fields themselves (*sawah*). The land under use must be irrigated, saturated with water, plowed by water buffaloes or tilled by men, cleared of undesirable plants, walled properly, and planted and tended carefully, particularly during the first days after the transplanting of the young rice seedlings. Not all of the land can be irrigated by water from higher levels. In areas where the water sources are lower than the land to be irrigated, the necessary water is obtained by the use of locally made water wheels (*kintjie*), which scoop the water from the river in bamboo containers and carry it upward to bamboo irrigation pipes, the water wheels being rotated by the power of the river current. There are also a number of water wheels that are used as rice mills.

Aside from rice, the production of coconuts and tobacco, both considered to be of excellent quality, is also very important. The jungle offers the inhabitants various marketable products, including wood for the construction of houses. Rich fishponds, scattered about the *negeri* territory, provide both personal subsistence and a source of income.

Mention should also be made of the existence of two brick industries. Both factories are located apart from any village settlement, but, other than by exploiting local land resources through the use of clay as the principal material for brick production, these industries do not seem to exercise much influence on the life of the villagers.

5. The Community Setting

Negeri Taram does not consist of a compound of dwellings surrounded by rice fields, such as the term "village community" might suggest. On the contrary, within the boundaries of the *negeri* numerous dwelling sites are found, some spread far apart, some situated close to each other. The center of the *negeri* community is formed by a sizable market on one side of the village square, through which the road from Pajakumbuh passes. The roomy market halls are surrounded on both sides by a connected row of two-story wooden stalls, shops, and eating houses (*lapau*). One of the second-floor rooms of these stalls serves as office for the *wali negeri,* the government-recognized administrator of the *negeri.* The office is modest in appearance, with a view of the market on one side and on the other a view of the Sinamar River, its long but narrow steel bridge, and the road from Pajakumbuh. Mondays and Thursdays are market days, when the market (*pasa*) becomes the meeting place for traders and buyers from both the *negeri* itself and the surrounding areas. The market of Taram is one of the leading markets in the Pajakumbuh area.

Across the village square are two other small eating houses. Behind these two wooden structures, somewhat concealed in the shadows of a cluster of sprawling trees, is a broad, placid pool, somewhat like an abandoned stone swimming pool. Here too stand a number of houses in traditional style, each supported by wooden pillars. Between the market and the water pool, perched on a low hill facing the bridge, is the elementary school, with its barren playground in front. Not far from the village square, but out of sight of the market, is a government clinic where first aid can be given. Farther along, in the direction of the main road, there is a police post, standing as if it were unconnected with the daily activities of the community's members.

The village road, pathways, irrigation canals, and gardens look clean and well-tended. The narrow road leading to the dam at the edge of the Taram jungle—a road that can be used by automobiles—passes the two village mosques (*masdjid*) and the ancient wooden village council hall (*balai*), a solitary structure surrounded by vast rice fields across from the soaring mass of volcanic material known as Bukit Gadang. Numerous little coffee houses, only frequented by men, are scattered along the main road and pathways.

Actually there is only one regular mosque in *negeri* Taram. This stone building is rather idyllically situated away from the road in a shadowy spot near a quiet, spacious water pool. Each Friday people gather at the mosque to perform the prescribed prayers. Nearby, closer to the road and thus more noticeable, is another mosque of about the same size, known as Surau nan Tuo, or the "old prayer house." This, indeed, is not a mosque where regular observances are held but a prayer house connected with the sepulcher of the widely known semimythical figure Sjech Ibrahim. The earth at the sepulcher, believed to be the spot of his ascent for his flight to Mecca, is considered by many women to have magical powers for the bearing of children or the promoting of a good harvest. On market days women from neighboring *negeri*, or sometimes also from distant places, come to visit this sacred place in order to pray and to secure a clod of earth from the sepulcher. The prayer house also functions as a resting place for these visitors. The women of *negeri* Taram itself do not seem to believe in the power of Sjech Ibrahim.

If the mosque symbolizes the Islamic religion of the villagers, the *balai* or village council hall represents their traditional culture. The first *balai* was established long ago at Kapalo Banda, the site of the dam at the edge of the jungle. This site is supposed to have been the location of the first village settlement in the territory of *negeri* Taram, but at present no remains of the former settlement exist. The current *balai* has been mentioned. Called Balai Tangah, it consists of a single elongated room with only one entrance, reached by a flight of stone stairs. At the far end of the official meeting room is a platform. There is no furniture of any sort, and when meetings are held the participants take their seats on mats spread on the floor; the sitting arrangement is regulated by tradition. Attached to the wall facing the road is a marble plaque with the inscription: *Balai Tengah, didirikan kembali 10 Juli 1929 oleh Kerapatan Negeri. Tamin Datoe' Tan Simaradjo nan Pandjang, kepala negeri.* ("Balai Tengah, re-built on July 10, 1929, by the Village Council. Tamin Datoe' Tan Simaradjo nan Pandjang, head of the *negeri*.")

There was once a third *balai*, with an elevated stone foundation, known as Balai Koto. It was located on the road connecting the Taram market with the main Pajakumbuh-Pakan Baru road—approximately halfway between the market and Balai Tangah. Both Balai Koto and Balai Tangah were used at the same time, a phenomenon which does not correspond with the general concept that each Minangkabau *negeri* should have one *balai*. At present, however, nothing of the old Balai Koto remains but its foundation; the structure was destroyed during the recent rebellion. While Balai Koto still existed, the village council held meetings concerning judicial cases there. If no agreement could be reached, the participants then moved to Balai Tangah to continue the deliberations, in the hope that a new location would create an environment favorable to agreement.

The greatest number of village buildings, of course, consist of residential houses, still predominantly shaped in accordance with the prescriptions of ancient tradition.

6. The Residential Houses

The traditional residential house in *negeri* Taram is known as *rumah gadang* or *rumah adat*. Each member of the community should have a *rumah gadang* as his official residence, although he may very well live elsewhere. Traditional formal activities, such as weddings and family councils, should only take place in a *rumah gadang* built in accordance with the prescribed rules and regulations.

The traditional family house is a large elongated wooden structure, supported by at least twenty-five bulky towering wooden pillars (*tiang*), although the prescribed number of pillars is actually thirty. The floor is built a man's height above the ground and can be reached by climbing a ladder attached to the house. Very likely in olden times this type of floor was constructed as a precautionary measure against possible attack by wild animals or treacherous enemies. A number of *rumah gadang* have annexes at either end of the structure, with bedroom at one end and kitchen at the other, the latter also serving as entrance to the house. The roof, made of palm-tree fibers (*idjuk*) or more recently of zinc plates, has the shape of a stylized buffalo horn (*gondjong*), with one peak at each end of the house. Frequently a smaller roof of the same shape is attached to the shoulder of the main roof, thus creating four peaked gables.

The floor and walls are made of planks or bamboo matting. The elongated rectangular floor is divided lengthwise into two parts (*labuah*), the back constructed a little higher than the other. Part of the elevated floor is taken up with small sleeping apartments (*bilik*), each enclosed by sheets of wood or other covering. The remaining part of the elevated floor is used to sit on. The lower part of the floor (*tangah rumah*) is nowadays occupied by a set of chairs, one or two tables, and some other European-style furniture. On formal occasions this lower section is cleared by removing the furniture to create space for sitting, and the wooden floor is then covered with plaited mats. During official gatherings, as at the *balai*, everyone sits on these mats in conformity with his recognized position in the community.

In spite of reports by various writers indicating a trend toward the disappearance of the traditional *rumah gadang*, no such trend is apparent in *negeri* Taram. In fact, preparations were being made to build, or rebuild, a number of *rumah gadang* in order to fulfill the needs of a number of families who, for one reason or other, did not possess the required traditional house. The construction of a *rumah gadang* is a tremendous amount of work, considering the size of the solid wooden pillars to be used, the number of planks, and the quantity of palm fibers required. Fortunately the villagers of *negeri* Taram can still obtain the necessary wood from the seemingly boundless Taram jungle nearby, and they still rely on the aid of their fellow villagers in the transportation of the wood and the erection of the new house.

In front of each *rumah gadang*, the often picturesquely decorated rice sheds (*lumbuang*) are placed. These rice sheds consist of a single high chamber held up between four wooden posts erected at such an angle that the square floor of the shed is smaller than its ceiling. The opening is located at the top, immediately below the roof, and can be reached by a tall narrow ladder placed against the opening. According to local tradition, which is still in evidence, each *rumah gadang* should have three rice sheds: one for the storage of rice for daily use, one for the rice kept for formal occasions, and one for rice that is stored for visiting guests. The actual existence of this number of rice sheds for each family house is an index of the wealth of rice in *negeri* Taram.

Since bachelors are not supposed to spend the night at their respective family houses, prayer houses are also used as sleeping places. The *negeri* has twenty-three prayer houses (*surau*), places where religious instruction is given. Formerly, in *negeri* Taram, bachelors who were not religiously inclined and were thus unwilling to spend the night at one of the prayer houses could find sleeping accommodations at one of the secular men's houses (*bandjur*), where instead of reciting the Koran or discussing religious matters the young men could occupy themselves with technological work to fulfill the material needs of the community, usually under the supervisory eye of an elderly man. The *bandjur* was the place where young men were introduced to the traditional norms of the village community and also where more mundane information was exchanged. These *bandjur* houses do not exist any more. The last *bandjur*, known as *bandjur* Katiang, was turned into a dwelling occupied by a regular family unit in 1949.

Not all of the existing residences are *rumah gadang*. Quite a number, some made of stone, are not different from the nontraditional houses in other parts of Indonesia. These houses are built to accommodate those people who cannot find a place at their family's *rumah gadang*, either because it has become too crowded or because the traditional rules forbid them to make their home there. There are, of course, also some houses built for the sake of modern convenience. The community setting, however, is still dominated by the traditional family house.

7. The Population

Although the official census figures obtained in 1961 have not proved very accurate (owing in part to the lack of understanding of the operational definitions of the various concepts used by those collecting the information), we should try to get a notion of the numerical strength of the village population. According to the census figures of March 1961 there were 3,936 inhabitants in the territory of *negeri* Taram. 1,980 of these inhabitants were entered as males and 1,956 as females. Eight months later, in November 1961, the census counted 3,784 inhabitants, 152 individuals fewer than in March 1961. These official figures indicate that only 2,901 were Indonesian citizens, which would imply a large number of noncitizens in *negeri* Taram, while actually there was not a single non-Indonesian citizen registered as an inhabitant of the *negeri*. In spite of these inaccuracies, however, it would not be too far from the truth to state that *negeri* Taram has about four thousand inhabitants.

Perhaps the most important demographic characteristic of *negeri* Taram is its ethnic homogeneity. Except for one or two individuals from Java who came to West Sumatra as forced laborers during the Japanese occupation, all are Minangkabau people, believed to be the descendants of ancestors who had their home in the double *negeri* Pariangan-Padang Pandjang, situated on the southern slope of the 2,892-meter Mt. Merapi.

Local oral tradition relates that in very early times the ancestors of the Taram villagers left their original home, as did the ancestors of many other Minangkabau people, to wander through the dense jungle of the Padang Highlands until they reached the foot of Sago Mountain, where they established a settlement named Tepatan. It is not known when these ancestors reached the foot of Sago Mountain. Nor is it known when some of these people continued to wander through Air Tabit until they came to the Sinamar River at a place now occupied by the market of Taram. This spot on the bank of the Sinamar River, which at this point is broad and sluggish, was still jungle, but it was thought a favorable place to build a small hamlet (*taratak*). Presumably this first settlement was built by a small group of energetic men, perhaps accompanied by a few women. Since a Minangkabau saying describes such work as *mantjantjang malateh, manambang manaruko*, meaning that trees are cut, bushes trimmed, mines exploited, and virgin soil upturned, it may safely be assumed that these ancestors, after having cleared the site to build their dwellings, went out to explore the surrounding jungle area and at this time marked trees with a chopping knife, thus indicating that they had taken possession of the area. Land where the trees had been marked was either cleared for agricultural purposes or left in its natural state in reserve for future descendants.

However, the location of this first settlement on the low-lying bank of the Sinamar River did not prove satisfactory. The river frequently overflowed its banks, destroying the carefully tended gardens of the settlers. In addition to these natural catastrophes, the settlers were also harrassed by their neighbors, the inhabitants of *negeri* Mungo and Andalas. In times of attack the location of the first settlement made the settlers vulnerable, since no natural protection existed to fortify the settlement against enemy raids. Therefore, the first settlers moved to Tjompo, presently known as Kapalo Banda, where at the foot of the eastern mountain range they could build a more tenable settlement at a higher elevation. The new settlement soon grew into a *dusun* called Sawah Tjompo, a name indicating that wet rice fields were already in use. Local tradition also mentions the existence at that time of another *dusun* called Tambang nan Tudjuh. Both village settlements were located within the boundaries of present-day *negeri* Taram, but neither exists today.

As time passed, more people from other areas came to join the village settlement, and the original inhabitants themselves also increased in number. Alien families came to seek the protection of established family heads and were granted land from which to obtain their livelihood. Others established themselves independently by clearing part of the jungle and building their own settlement. A number of villagers from the main settlement also began to expand, clearing some stretches of land for dwellings and others for gardens and rice fields. Although each family group built its own house and cultivated its own piece of land, the settlers were very much aware that they could not live without each other's assistance. Various common needs established strong ties between them, and they then wanted a place where meetings could be held to discuss matters of common interest. Thus the first *balai* or village council hall was built, and with it a *koto* was born, although not yet a *negeri*. The existence of a *balai* in a village settlement is an indication of its permanence, and this village settlement is known as *koto*.

In the distant past a *koto* was usually fortified to protect its inhabitants from possible attack. *Koto* Balai-Balai, for such was the name of *negeri* Taram's first *koto*, was no exception. Four fortifications were built to protect the village settlement, for warfare was still prevalent at the time. The command of each fortification was assigned to a functionary known as *dubalang*, whose position was, and still is, hereditary in accordance with the matrilineal rules of inheritance. The defense of *koto* Balai-Balai was further strengthened by assigning three other individuals to protect the villagers' safety in particular sections of the village territory. The

responsibility for village defense was thus divided among seven functionaries and subsequently among seven semigenealogical groups called *suku*.
The sites of the earlier fortifications are still remembered, and the titles
of these village commanders are still used by their successors. The present
bearer of the honorific Sutan Dua Puluh, one of the *dubalang*, for instance, is a boy thirteen years of age named Basri, a sixth-grade pupil
in the local elementary school.

As the number of inhabitants increased, a political structure had to
be created to regulate and coordinate village affairs. The family heads
organized themselves by dividing the various rights and duties, creating
specialized functionaries, formulating the most essential norms to be adhered to by all villagers, determining the boundaries of the village territory, and satisfying all the requirements necessary for the creation of
a *negeri*.

The prevailing Minangkabau tradition demanded that a *negeri* should
at the very least have the following properties: *batjupak bagantang,
baadat balimbago, bataratak bakapalo koto*, that is, a *negeri* should have
standardized measurements for dry and fluid goods, explicit norms, hamlets and a settlement center. It should also have a *balai*, a mosque for
Friday prayers, a court where cases can be tried, roads and pathways,
and bathing places. A settlement which claimed to be a *negeri* but did
not have its own *balai* was not considered a *negeri;* it was merely a
settlement, perhaps called *dusun*. In the *balai* the voice of the people
was expressed through family heads who not only functioned as spokes-
men but also as rulers. Since Islam was adopted as the religion of the
Minangkabau people approximately at the end of the sixteenth century,
no *negeri* is considered complete without a mosque. Free citizens of a
negeri would not like to use an alien *negeri*'s mosque for their Friday
prayers, except on such occasions when they were in a *negeri* other
than their own.

8. The Norms of the Village Community

The social relations of community members are regulated to a great
extent by ideal patterns that are widely regarded as obligatory and consist
of specific prescriptions for the course of action supposed to be taken
in given situations. Examining both modes of enforcement and sources
of authority, three distinct groups of related prescriptions can be discerned: the traditional *adat*, the Moslem *shari'ah*, and the laws and regulations of the Indonesian state.

The *adat* is comprised of norms developed by the inhabitants of *negeri* Taram in the course of their history; it is regarded as an inherited blueprint of the community. Every new inhabitant of the village community, just born or newly arrived from outside the *negeri* territory, at the very least gradually becomes acquainted with the behavior an individual is expected to follow when dealing with other members of the community in the course of daily life. The *adat* norms are enforced by diffuse pressure from the *negeri* as a whole, and only in extraordinary cases do the acknowledged traditional village functionaries participate in their enforcement.

The *adat* of *negeri* Taram, as has been noted before, is in some regards rather different from the *adat* of other *negeri* where similar local communal sanctions are maintained. But when a *negeri* is examined as part of the larger territorial unit, the *luhak*, all the *negeri* composing a single *luhak* share some characteristics that are then considered the *adat* of that particular *luhak*. Minangkabau society itself is comprised of three *luhak*: *negeri* Taram belongs to *luhak* Limapuluh Koto. The three *luhak*, in turn, have their own *adat;* nevertheless, each also has some characteristics in common when one examines the larger collectivity, the society of the Minangkabau people.

When new social situations arise that are incompatible with the existing *adat*, and the *negeri* community deems it necessary to sanction these new situations, the community institutes new norms to deal with them. In practice, then, these new norms replace the traditional *adat* that actually covers the social situation. At the same time, the traditional norms are still reverently acknowledged as being valid. In their actual behavior, however, the members of the village community agree to follow the newly agreed upon norms rather than the traditional norms. Consequently, for one social situation there may now be two sets of norms, both equally valid. Those who were in the village when the new norms were instituted know that two sets exist. But the next generation usually only knows about the new ones, which are regarded as the *adat* of the community, since it has learned that these particular norms are the proper norms. The old norms are forgotten.

Not many individuals know all the norms that comprise the prevailing *adat* of the *negeri*. Those who do have such knowledge need not necessarily be the top functionaries of the *negeri*. In reality, only three to four persons have paid special attention to the inherited norms. Thus by virtue of this knowledge, these individuals have become known as the *adat* experts of the community. Because such knowledge is acquired through experience, *adat* experts are found among older people. Rather characteristically, in *negeri* Taram the foremost *adat* experts are a religious leader named Landjanun Datuk Maradjo Kajo nan Putih, age forty-seven, a well-educated gentleman who takes part in political activitites beyond the *negeri* boundaries and who maintains a great deal of personal interest in local affairs; and a Communist leader named Pituhan Datuk Paduko Basa, age sixty-two, reputed to be a brilliant and shrewd intellectual. These two *adat* experts may be described as living reference books, to be consulted whenever problems concerning proper *adat* norms arise. They differ in their influence, however, on the basis of their manner of presentation, the form of their assertions, and their personal relations with the other members of the community.

The second set of norms, the *shari'ah* known locally as *sjarak*, unlike the *adat* developed by the people of Taram themselves, has been acquired as part of the heritage received when the Minangkabau adopted Islam. The main components of the *shari'ah* consist of the teachings of the Koran, the traditional prescriptions based on Mohammed's conduct and ideas known as *hadith*, the deduction of legal prescriptions from both the Koran and the *hadith* through analogy known as *kiyas*, and, although less common in *negeri* Taram, the consensus of opinion of religious functionaries known as *ijma*.

The *shari'ah* emphasizes the importance of the individual, as opposed to the *adat*, where the family group or the community as a whole is stressed. However, like the *adat*, the *shari'ah* is composed of prescriptions that define ideal behavior patterns seemingly for all activities of the individuals within the *negeri* community. Therefore, in a particular social situation, the individual may have to choose between the appropriate *adat* or Moslem prescription, a decision not always easy to make. There is a saying, frequently cited though often mistakenly, that describes the relation between *adat* and *shari'ah*, *adat basanda sjarak, sjarak basanda adat*, or, in English, *adat* leans on the *shari'ah* while the *shari'ah* leans on the *adat*. This statement is basically inaccurate, as there are a great many *adat* norms which are very much opposed to the *shari'ah*, and vice versa.

The villagers of *negeri* Taram, being Moslems, feel the need for both the *adat* and the *shari'ah*. In consequence they also recognize the authority of specific functionaries who deal with religious matters. Each of the seven *suku* groups within the village community has its own religious functionaries: a *malim*, a *chatib*, and a *bilal*. The mosque is administered for a period of three years in rotation by the religious officials of one particular *suku* group. Aside from these religious functionaries, *negeri* Taram also maintains a *wali hakim*, the official chief authority of religious affairs. Again, it is characteristic of *negeri* Taram that the previous *wali hakim*, Rusli, was a Communist, considered well versed in religious matters because of his religious training under prominent teachers.

In the course of his upbringing, nearly every villager studies Moslem norms in regular gatherings, which all children are expected to attend, when religious instruction, *mangadji*, is given. Furthermore, the teachings of Islam are inculcated and disseminated during the Friday prayers at the mosque and at the recitation and discussion meetings in the numerous smaller prayer houses. Naturally, just as not all villagers know all the prevailing *adat* norms, not all are familiar with the norms of the *shari'ah*, either.

The third group of prescriptions governing the villagers' lives derives from the Indonesian national government, the highest formal authority in the land, of which the *negeri* forms but a very small part. Consisting of the norms contained in the 1945 Constitution and the laws, ordinances, and regulations issued by the government or its authorized agencies, it also includes other norms developed as the natural consequence of the emergence of the Indonesian nation.[3] A number of these regulations have reached the level of the villagers, who have adopted some while rejecting or simply ignoring others. Some of the adopted rules have been assimilated into the local *adat*, and for a great many people they have become indistinguishable from the traditional *adat* rules. Others are still identified as rules and regulations imposed by the government and thus only adhered to because of the government. Not all norms associated with the Indonesian state have been issued as laws, ordinances, or regulations by the government. Quite a number have been adopted by individual villagers from other outside sources, such as school teachings, publications, radio broadcasts, or activities observed during visits to towns. These individually adopted norms are not supported by any authority but rather by the personal strength of their adherents.

[3] Aside from the ordinance which claims all land without proven ownership to be property of the state (*Ind. Stb.*, 1874, No. 94), there are, among others, the *Nagari-ordonnantie voor Sumatra's Westkust* (*Ind. Stb.*, 1914, No. 774, and 1918, No. 677), *Agrarische Reglement voor Sumatra's Westkust* (*Ind. Stb.*, 1938, No. 490), *Maklumat Residen Sumatra Barat* No. 21, 1946, *Peraturan Komisariat Pemerintah Pusat* No. 81/Kom/U.-1948, and *Instruksi Gubernur Militer Sumatra Tengah* No. 10 GM/ST/49.

9. *The Family Group*

Social activities in *negeri* Taram are strongly related to recognized kinship patterns. It is therefore imperative to pay attention to the structure of the family groups of which the village community is comprised.

The primary constituent of the family group is the marriage bond between a man and his wife, a union established by the act of marriage based on Moslem prescriptions known as *nikah*. The choice of a marriage partner may be made by the individuals concerned, the initiator being the man, the woman, a close relative, or an obliging friend. After the choice has been made, further preparations are regulated by traditional *adat*, which prescribes that the wedding ceremony should be arranged by the relatives of both sides acting as two distinct family groups. The wedding is performed according to the Moslem rites at the ancestral house of the bride's maternal family. The ceremony is usually, but not always, followed by a ceremonial dinner held in accordance with *adat* rules and attended by relatives, friends, and officials. The number of people attending a wedding ceremony depends on the importance attached to the new union. A marriage bond is considered, after all, to be not only a union between two individuals but also one between two family groups, the relatives of the bride and the relatives of the groom.

Customarily, the wife does not leave her ancestral house after her wedding. The husband, however, also remains at his own family's ancestral house, except when he has no such house in *negeri* Taram, or when the wife is permitted and willing to leave her ancestral house, taking her lodging elsewhere with her husband. In the case of a man who has come from outside the *negeri* to settle in Taram, his wife's family may accept the husband as a member of their household. Customarily the husband lives with his own family group (his mother and sisters), and thus he only meets his wife when she brings him his lunch in the field at noon, as the husband is expected to work the plot of land allotted to his wife by her family group.

During the day, the men, regardless of their official position in the village community, usually work in the rice fields, hoeing and plowing the soil, building and repairing the rice-field dams, and tending the irrigation system. After the women have brought them their lunch, neatly arranged to be more appealing, these men continue to work for another two or three hours. Then they return home, usually to their mother's ancestral house, although some may return to their wife's house or to any other place where they have their lodging. Thus a married man, who after his daily work spends some time at his mother's ancestral house taking care of family needs, only joins his wife in the evening. Those who have more than one wife (polygyny is permitted) are supposed to divide their time equally between their wives, paying nightly visits to one wife for a week, to the other wife the following week, and so on, changing their visiting schedule regularly on Fridays. In polygamous marriages, however, the wives' families expect the husband to perform his duties toward each of his wives. In view of the heavy burden this entails, a married man who wishes to take another woman as his wife may resort to the convenient institution of *talak*, the formal repudiation of his wife, which subsequently frees him from any further responsibilities toward the disavowed wife. In such a way a man may consecutively marry quite a number of times.[4] Such marriages, dissolved or maintained, are effective ties that bind the respective family groups together seemingly for eternity. Although the children of these broken marriages are counted as members of the mother's family group, the father's kin also regard them as blood relatives, even though the father has dissolved his union with the mother.

Since the father usually comes to visit his wife and children only in the evening, there is not much opportunity for the nuclear family to be together as an independent unit. It is the mother's brother who looks after the affairs of the household; the eldest man of the eldest generation within the family group is considered to be the master of the house. The matrilocal extended family group thus formed is known as *kaum*. A newly born infant automatically becomes a member of the mother's *kaum* group. The child is raised by his mother, who ordinarily lives in her own mother's ancestral house, the *rumah gadang*. As he grows up, the child becomes aware that while in his family group he should respond to the beck and call of his mother's brother(s), his *mamak*.

[4] The Communist leader Pituhun Datuk Paduko Basa, for instance, has had fourteen wives, although presently he remembers the names of only three. Landjanun Datuk Rangkajo Basa nan Pandjang has four divorced wives, and, of his two other wives, he visits only one. Mardamin Datuk Maradjo Basa nan Putih has had eleven wives; the thirty-three-year-old Djasir Datuk Paduko Maradjo nan Gamuk has already had seven, at present maintaining two of them.

His actual father is considered only a regular guest of the family, a *semando*. Thus his *kaum* group consists of his brothers and sisters, his mother, his mother's brothers, his mother's sisters and their offspring, and his grandmother. If the grandmother has living sisters and brothers, they also may belong to the group, which would then include children of the grandmother's sisters in the maternal line. The grandmother's sisters may have established a separate *kaum* with its own ancestral house and its own parcel of land, which are the primary constituents of a *kaum* group's ancestral property, called *harto pusako*. In order to be able to support his *kaum*, the head, known as *mamak kepalo waris*, is given authority to administer the ancestral property. Properties known as *harto pusako* are regarded as inalienable and should remain so, except in specific circumstances defined by *adat*.

The daughters and sons of a man's sisters are called his *kemanakan*, while he shares the honorable status of *mamak* with his brothers. It may happen, of course, that none of a man's sisters has a living child, a very undesirable situation. In such a case the man has no *kemanakan* and therefore does not act as *mamak* to anyone. To have sisters who bear no daughters is certainly a cause for lament, since it means the disappearance of the *kaum* group as soon as its present members have died. The *kaum* group is then said to be *punah*, or blotted out.

The *adat* invests the *mamak* with the authority to affirm, and if necessary to enforce, the norms to be adhered to by the members of his group or, at least, by his *kemanakan*. The head of the *kaum* group, however, does not act on his own but discusses every important matter with all members of his *kaum*, both men and women. In fact, the elder women may have the most to say in a family discussion when the *kaum* decides on any action to be taken in its behalf. Such a family gathering, held at the ancestral house in accordance with the *adat*, naturally also airs conflicting interests between members of the group when the appropriate *mamak* has been unable to solve the dispute. In the discussion (*mupakat*) there is a search for unanimous agreement (*kato sepakat*), a value held dearly in the social life of the villagers. Conflicts between members of a *kaum* ideally are kept within the group; to bring discord into the open is thought to shame the family group. In unimportant matters, decisions can be made on the basis of common majority rule, if this is sufficient to ensure that the decision will be supported by most members of the group. The *mamak*, as head of his *kaum* group, should therefore be well informed about whatever any member of his *kaum* intends to do or has already done. Because innumerable *kaum* groups form the foundation for the social order in a Minangkabau village, an understanding of the *mamak's* position is essential in obtaining an understanding of the Minangkabau village community itself.

The pattern just described is not without exceptions. There are, as has been mentioned in passing, a number of men who are not native inhabitants of Taram. If they are married, they live with their wives, for they do not have an ancestral house in *negeri* Taram. There are also a number of men who for some time have been living outside *negeri* Taram as government officials, traders, political party functionaries, or in other occupations that require their presence elsewhere. When married men do reside outside the village territory, most often they take their wife and children with them. Consequently the nuclear family group detaches itself physically from its parental *kaum* group and becomes a distinct, relatively independent unit. Upon the return of such a nuclear family group to the village, there has been a tendency to keep the group intact by dwelling together in one house, either with other members of the wife's *kaum* group or separately in a nontraditional house, thus freed from the *adat* norms that regulate behavior in the traditional ancestral house. Elder men who are not the eldest of the eldest generation within their *kaum* group and thus not masters of the household in their ancestral house, may take up permanent residence at their wife's ancestral house, although they are not expected to participate in the family councils of their wife's *kaum* when they are not invited to do so. The presence of a father at the dwelling place of his nuclear family entails the transfer of a number of obligations customarily regarded as part of the duties of his wife's brother. School tuition and other expenses necessary to meet the daily needs of his children are now the responsibility of the father.

In short, as part of the *kaum* group, customarily residing at an ancestral house, a nuclear family tends to be dominated by the interests of the *kaum* group as a whole and is thus not able to exert its identity as a distinct group. On the other hand, the nuclear family may be united in particular situations, such as the transfer of the husband to a place outside the *negeri* territory. Nevertheless, a *mamak* still may have his say in matters relating to his *kemanakan*, his sister's offspring.

10. Penghulu Andiko

Descendants of a maternal ancestor connected with a particular ancestral house (*rumah gadang*) form a *sabuah parui* (out-of-one-womb), a matrilocal extended family that in reality may well be identical with the *kaum* group, though it may also be composed of a number of separate *kaum*. The formal head of such a *sabuah parui* is known as *penghulu andiko*, a person who is entitled to bear the official honorific of the family group. This title, or *galar*, is distinguished from ordinary names by the prefix *datuk*, followed by an impressive name of royal character such as Datuk Temenggung, Datuk Leloangso, Datuk Paduko Maradjo or Datuk Bagindo Simaradjo, the honorific to be placed after the personal name of the *penghulu andiko*. A *penghulu andiko* is referred to, and also addressed, by his title.

The *penghulu andiko* (hence to be referred to as *penghulu*) is the embodiment of the authority and honor of his *anak buah*, the members of the family group whose *galar* he proudly bears. He is therefore a much-respected member of the village community, at least among members of his own family group, who have elected him on the basis of both his hereditary rights and his personal qualifications.

In accordance with the matrilineal rule of inheritance, the *penghulu*-ship falls to the sister's son of the deceased functionary. Upon the death of a *penghulu*, his family group immediately gathers at the ancestral house to select his successor, for as well as the rule of inheritance the family group must also consider the qualifications of the candidate(s). Their own interest is at stake in the selection of a successor, who should be a competent man, willing to serve and lead the group, who can be trusted to defend the group's honor. The first in line may be bypassed with the choice of a man who is not the immediate heir but who, considering his personal qualifications, is rather more acceptable to the group as a whole. After approval by the officials of the larger family group, the *suku*, the successor is publicly announced, which may occur at the funeral ceremony. The new *penghulu* is then given his predecessor's title together with the deceased's formal attire. When a *penghulu* dies and no one can be installed as his successor, pending an acceptable candidate, the title is said to be *dilipat* (wrapped up), a situation that may exist for a considerable time. There are at present quite a number of such unoccupied *penghulu* titles in Taram.[5] Some of the *penghulu* in *negeri* Taram

[5] The title of Datuk Rotih (Bodi) has been *dilipat* for about sixty years, the family group involved now consisting of five members. Both the title of Datuk Damoangso nan Hitam (Bodi) and Datuk Gadang (Bodi) have been unoccupied for about forty years, and the title of Datuk Pangeran nan Kunkun (Bodi) has shared the same fate since about 1946. The view that the position of *penghulu* is eagerly sought after and consequently is

were installed when they were very young. The head of *suku* Piliang Lawas, one of the seven highest *adat* functionaries in the community, is a lean schoolboy who has just left elementary school. Another boy, the son of the head of *suku* Bodi, became *penghulu* at the age of nine upon the death of his maternal uncle.

The village community of *negeri* Taram recognizes the existence of exactly 150 *galar* and thus there should also be 150 *penghulu*, each connected with a specific family group. The number of *galar* is reported to have remained unchanged since 1914, when the Dutch colonial government issued an ordinance that required the registration of the *galar* in each *negeri*, in order to ensure better control of these local functionaries. Following the official registration, the government did not permit the institution of any new *galar*, an order complied with by the villagers. In former times, a *galar* could be divided when one family group split into two separate *sabuah parui*, each with its own *penghulu andiko*. For example, a section of a *sabuah parui* group may have moved to a dwelling site rather distantly located from their ancestral house. Communication with the mother group would then be difficult. In due time the newly separated section might request the right to maintain its own *penghulu*. If the *penghulu* of the ancestral house and the members of the family group as a whole did not have any objection, the request would be brought to the attention of the village leaders for approval and recognition. The request and the candidate nominated by the new family group would be examined not only on the basis of its legal foundation and the candidate's personality but also with regard to the balance of power

---

a cause for fiery conflict does not always accord with reality. It should not be forgotten that a *penghulu*ship not only awards certain rights and honors but duties and responsibilities as well. One person, for instance, refused to be elected *penghulu* because he preferred to be a *bendi* driver, an occupation considered unsuitable for *adat* functionaries, since *bendi* drivers are addressed by their customers in an undignified manner which could only be regarded as an insult to the honor of the family group. Another person refused to succeed the deceased *penghulu* because he speculated on the possibility of acquiring a higher ranked *penghulu*ship, at that time occupied by another maternal uncle whose sister did not have any children to succeed him. The speculator would not have been allowed to occupy the coveted position if he had accepted the lower-ranking *penghulu*ship. In the end the speculation of our ambitious man proved unavailing; before the higher-ranked uncle died, his sister bore a son who was given the *penghulu*ship left by his uncle.

between the various family groups within the community of Taram. In case of approval by the village functionaries, a new *penghulu*ship would be created with the appropriate ceremony. The newly instituted *penghulu* would then be given the right to bear the honorific of the *penghulu* of the parent *sabuah parui* group, to which a further title would be added to distinguish the new from the old. The added designation usually described one of the striking features of the new functionary, and once the new *galar* had been officially recognized this designation could not be changed, the honorific becoming part and parcel of the family group. In this way a functionary of short stature may be known as Datuk Radjo di Radjo nan Pandjang, that is, Datuk Radjo di Radjo the Tall, merely because the first individual holding the title had been a tall man.

It may happen that a *penghulu* of another *negeri* wishes to settle in Taram and become a member of the village community. Before 1914, an alien *penghulu* who joined the village community as a new member was recognized as such. This situation is illustrated by the case of Datuk Radjo nan Sati, who arrived in Taram together with his family from beyond the borders of the *negeri*. Datuk Radjo nan Sati, a member of a group bearing the name of Sumpadang in his *negeri* of origin, requested acceptance as a member of the Taram *suku* with the same name. The *penghulu* of *suku* Sumpadang in Taram complied with the request and, after the heads of the other six *suku* groups declared their approval, the alien *penghulu* was installed as an additional *penghulu* of *suku* Sumpadang in Taram, hence to be known as Datuk Paduko Sati instead of Datuk Radjo nan Sati. However, after 1914 no increase in the number of *penghulu* was allowed by the government, and consequently alien *penghulu* who have come to settle in the community are no longer recognized as *adat* functionaries. Thus, when Dohan, an alien from *negeri* Mungka who settled in *negeri* Taram in 1907, was installed in 1950 as *penghulu* in his *negeri* of origin and given the honorific of Datuk Tumenggung, only his right to bear that honorific was recognized by the *penghulu* of Taram, not the right to participate in the official activities of the Taram *penghulu*.

The family group of a *penghulu* need not only consist of his blood relatives but may also include aliens who have been accepted as members of his family group, or his *pajung*. The *adat* provides for a classification of *kemanakan*, nephews and nieces in the maternal line of a *mamak*, actual or assumed. The *adat* distinguishes the following types:

(1) *kemanakan batali darah*, or sons and daughters of own sisters, those known as "blood relatives" in the maternal line of the *penghulu*; (2) *kemanakan hinggok basatumpu tabang batjakam*, or alien individuals who have been accepted as members of the family group because they want to settle in Taram and live from its land; (3) *kemanakan dagang batapatan galeh basandaran*, or alien individuals who make recurrent visits to Taram to do business and therefore become members of a *penghulu's* family group for local protection; and (4) *kemanakan dibawah lutui*, or descendants of slaves who, although not regarded as slaves any more, are still members of the family group of their former masters. Only *kemanakan batali darah*, the actual "blood relatives," have the right to inherit the position of *penghulu*, although the others are allowed to inherit land.

Because a *penghulu* is considered an official functionary, a public figure, his activities are regulated by a number of publicly known *adat* prescriptions. He is not expected, for instance, to become excited in a meeting, to stamp on the ground, to roll back his sleeves, to climb a tree or to run away, to carry a heavy burden on his head, or to fish in ponds other than his own. All these enumerated activities are considered undignified and not in accordance with the respected position of a *penghulu*. On the other hand, a *penghulu* has the right to represent his family group in the village council or at any other official occasion. He may derive considerable power and influence from such a position.

11. The Suku

It has been stated (see section 9) that each individual is a member of his mother's family group. The fact that, in turn, each family group belongs to a particular *suku* means that from birth each individual is also a member of one of the seven *suku* groups of which the community of *negeri* Taram is comprised. An individual whose mother is a member of *suku* Bodi automatically becomes a member of that group, regardless of his father's *suku* affiliation.

An individual who originates from beyond the borders of the *negeri* and intends to settle in Taram is expected to join one of the seven existing *suku* groups by finding a *mamak*, a family head who is willing to accept the newcomer as a member of his family group. A Minangkabau man, being a member of one of the *suku* in his *negeri* of origin, may report himself to one of the *penghulu* of the *suku* that bears the same name or is believed to be closely related to his original *suku*. If he prefers to join a totally different *suku*, he may do so as long as he finds himself a *mamak*. As soon as the alien has been installed as a member of a particular *suku*, he must observe the rules and regulations of his new affiliation. Furthermore, he acquires the right to live from the properties of his new *suku*, which generally means that he may be allotted a share of *suku* land.

We should realize at this point how artificial and misleading the label "genealogical unit" is if taken literally as a description of the *suku*. We see that aliens are allowed to become members of a *suku* as long as a *penghulu* is willing to accept them into his family group. There is even an actual case of an individual who detached himself from his own *suku* to join another *suku* in the same *negeri*. The ancestors of all *penghulu* of a *suku* may long ago have belonged to the same family group when the *negeri* community was founded. Even this relationship need not exist, for we have also seen that the ancestors of Amat Datuk Paduko Sati, one of the *penghulu* of *suku* Sumpadang in Taram, were not among the founders of the village. Furthermore, the *suku* is not exogamous, since marriages between its members are allowed, as long as bride and groom are not under the jurisdiction of the same *penghulu keampek suku*, one of the four top functionaries of the *suku*. The present head of *suku* Bodi, for example, has had two wives from *suku* Bodi. The first wife's family is subordinate to another of the *penghulu keampek suku* and the second to still another.

Is the *suku* a territorial unit? As it is not really a genealogical unit, neither is it a territorial unit. The members of each *suku* live interspersed with members of other groups at numerous dwelling sites throughout the community's territory. A search for the boundaries dividing the territory of the *negeri* into seven sections, each belonging to one *suku* group, would be fruitless. In early times, each *suku* may have had its own contiguous land, occupied or claimed by its relatively few members. Later, as the groups increased in size, new plots were sought and marked as land owned by members of the respective *suku*, to be cultivated to meet the growing needs of their groups. Today we are met with the results of this process. Patches of land occupied, cultivated, or owned by members of *suku* Bodi are found in the midst of land belonging to members of *suku* Piliang Gadang; other members of this second *suku* may own bits of land surrounded by plots of different groups. Although not all the land within the boundaries of Taram has been cultivated or employed in any other manner, there is no piece of land which does not belong to one of the seven existing *suku*. A *suku* does not have its own territory as such, but its land consists of the sum total of all the scattered plots owned by its members.

12. The Suku *Functionaries*

A number of *suku* functionaries have already been mentioned. Let us consider for a moment the position of these various functionaries within their respective *suku* in order to get a comprehensive picture of the distribution of authority within a *suku*. The discussion will treat the ideal pattern, according to the prevailing *adat* norms; in actual practice there is not much deviation from this pattern.

In *negeri* Taram each *suku* group has its top functionary, designated as *putjuk suku* or *penghulu putjuk*, the highest-ranked individual among all *penghulu* within a *suku* group. During the day, the *putjuk suku*, clad in black pajamalike dress, works as a peasant in the rice fields, looking not unlike the other able-bodied males of the village community. On official occasions, however, his appearance is markedly different, hardly recognizable to those who have seen him up to his knees in mud. Europeans, with their sense of history, would evoke images of Renaissance princes. In his official attire, which comprises part of his family group's ancestral property, the *putjuk suku* is clad in a long-sleeved black blouse lined with brocade, called *badju gadang*, and broad black trousers, black being the color of the *penghulu*. His black costume on such occasions is adorned with the other attributes reserved for the top ranking *penghulu*, such as the *karih* (dagger), *pendiang* (golden belt), *deta karui* (turban), and *tungke* (cane).

While all functionaries—indeed, every member of the *suku*—possess to a greater or lesser extent some authority within the *suku*, the *putjuk suku* occupies the position at the apex of *suku* authority. As chief he expects to be kept informed about any extraordinary activities involving members of his *suku* (the definition of "extraordinary" is a potential source of dispute between the *putjuk suku* and other members). As the person to whom the members have delegated authority, he represents and acts for the *suku* as a whole in dealings with outsiders.

Since the village community is comprised of seven *suku*, there should also be seven *putjuk suku*, but unfortunately the *putjuk suku* from *suku* Pitopang died recently and left no *kemanakan* who could succeed him.

The last person who was head of Pitopang was Saleh Datuk Leloangso nan Tinggi. He died, an elderly man of ninety-three, in 1959. He left three members of his family group, but none could succeed him since they are elderly women who do not have any living children. In such a case, when there is no hope of finding a successor, the title is said to be *dibanam* (buried).[6] Nonetheless, the duties (*beban*) of the previous occupant continue to exist, and these are usually assumed by one of the *penghulu* of his *suku* group.

The *putjuk suku* is not expected to interfere with the affairs of all the members of his *suku* group. In fact, he has no right to deal directly with his *suku* group members if he bypasses their immediate headmen. Within his *suku* group the *putjuk suku* must share his authority with three other functionaries, known respectively as *bendaro*, *panglimo*, and *kadi*, ranked in descending order. Each of these functionaries, known also together or individually as *penghulu keampek suku*, has a number of *penghulu andiko* under his jurisdiction.[7]

As the *putjuk suku* is regarded as chief of his *suku* group, the *bendaro* is considered secretary or treasurer; the *panglimo* as commander with control over means of coercion, and the *kadi* as functionary in religious affairs. In reality not all of the seven *suku* groups have a complete set of *penghulu keampek suku*. Table 27 shows the distribution of functionaries among the seven *suku* of *negeri* Taram.

If one of the *penghulu keampek suku* dies without an heir in accordance with the matrilineal rule of inheritance and succession, the *suku* group concerned incurs the loss of a powerful position in the village council, thereby decreasing its influence in community activities. In the manner described, a *suku* group may gradually lose all its *penghulu keampek suku*, thus forfeiting its right to be represented in the ruling village council of the *negeri*. Such an ill-fated *suku* is then said to be *dipae katiang pandjang* (nailed on the high pillar). Only the ancestral

---

[6] The six remaining *putjuk suku* in *negeri* Taram are: Djasir Datuk Paduko Simaradjo nan Gemuk (Melaju), Ramli Datuk Paduko Sinaro nan Gadang Tanduk (Bodi), Marisan Datuk Temenggung nan Kajo (Piliang Gadang), Masri Datuk Bagindo Simaradjo nan Bakupiah (Piliang Lawas), Djaluk Datuk Paduko Simaradjo nan Gamuk (Simabur), and Djusan Datuk Paduko Simaradjo nan Pandjang (Sumpadang).

[7] The *bendaro* of *suku* Piliang Gadang has sixteen *penghulu andiko* as his subordinates, but, as three of these *penghulu*ships are "wrapped up," this leaves thirteen actual *penghulu andiko*.

lands and no other rights may be inherited by the various *suku* members who are not *kemanakan batali darah* of the deceased *penghulu*.

Mention has been made in section 7 of the *suku* functionary who was responsible in the historic past for the defense of the village community, the functionary known as *dubalang*. The *dubalang* is a subordinate of the *panglimo*. Presently he is important only in traditional ceremonies, where he is easily distinguished from the other functionaries by his reddish costume. The *bendaro* also has a subordinate, known as *manti*, whose function can be compared to that of a constable. The *manti* delivers messages from the *suku* authorities, announces decisions that are to be made public, and arrests those considered to have harmed the group.

Table 27. Distribution of functionaries among the seven *suku* of *negeri* Taram

Name of *suku*	Penghulu keampek suku			
Melaju	*putjuk suku*	*bendaro*	*panglimo*	—
Bodi	*putjuk suku*	*bendaro*	*panglimo*	*kadi*
Piliang Gadang	*putjuk suku*	*bendaro*	*panglimo*	*kadi*
Piliang Lawas	*putjuk suku*	*bendaro*	*panglimo*	—
Simabur	*putjuk suku*	*bendaro*	*panglimo*	*kadi*
Pitopang	—	*bendaro*	*panglimo*	—
Sumpadang	*putjuk suku*	*bendaro*	*panglimo*	—

The *kadi* has jurisdiction over three special functionaries, namely, the *imam*, *chatib*, and *bilal*, all serving the needs of the inhabitants in their adherence to the Moslem faith. The maintenance of the mosque is the responsibility of these religious functionaries; the three *kadi* subordinates of one *suku* serve for three years, subsequently to be replaced in rotation by those of each *suku*. At present, for instance, the maintenance of the mosque and all activities connected with it are held by *imam* Hadji Kian, *chatib* Ramsah, and *bilal* Udin, members of *suku* Melaju. During their period of service the functionaries live at the mosque, where they get their meals and other necessities from its visitors and the *zakat-fitrah* or alms tax, to be paid by the villagers as prescribed by the Moslem *shari'ah* law.

13. The Elite

One of the widespread myths about the Minangkabau, believed both by its people and by those who have studied them, describes their society as democratic. The saying *tagak samo tinggi, duduk samo randah*, that is, "to stand equally high and to sit equally low," is frequently cited as a truthful description of status among the Minangkabau people, particularly among those who live in rural areas such as *negeri* Taram. Isn't it true that the village community is comprised of family groups, each an autonomous unit with regard to economic, social, and political matters? Isn't it true that each family group has elected its own leaders, who are recognized as such by the community as a whole? Isn't it true that all important matters are jointly deliberated upon by the members of the family group concerned, who seek to come to an agreement together as to what action to take? Isn't it also true that the village council consists of heads of the family groups who, because they have been elected by their respective family groups, together truly represent all the inhabitants of the *negeri*?

And yet a closer examination of the village community of *negeri* Taram does not yield a situation which could justly be labeled "democratic." Its inhabitants are, as we know by now, grouped into seven distinct *suku* groups. We also know that newly born individuals automatically become members of their mother's group, and that aliens who have come to settle in the *negeri* are allowed to become members of an existing *suku*, depending on the *suku* affiliation of the individual who is willing to accept them as his *kemanakan*. Although such a situation seems to give every member of the village community an opportunity to voice his opinion, make decisions, and have representation on the village council, the *adat* actually classifies people according to their rights and duties in such a way that distinct social classes have been brought into being. The upper class, or the elite, consists of individuals who have the right to elect a *penghulu* or be elected as such and includes all *penghulu* and their immediate "blood relatives." The other social class, on the whole enjoying fewer rights and less power, consists of the remaining members of the village community, those who are not *kemanakan batali darah*, or the "blood relative" of any *penghulu*. It should be made clear, though, that in Taram the distinction between these social classes does not involve the ownership of land, a situation easily suggested by the word "class." Since Taram still has a surplus of land, the distinction relates to unequal opportunities in the realm of political power and social prestige.

When one counts the number of actual kin of the family groups of each *penghulu*, as distinguished from aliens who have been accepted as members, and adds this total with the number of *penghulu,* one gets the figures shown in Table 28.

These figures add up to 810 individuals, all mentioned by their respective *penghulu* as members of their family groups. If we compare this figure with the census figures from November 1961, showing a total population of 3,784 in *negeri* Taram, we may conclude that roughly three thousand individuals are excluded from the category of *penghulu* and their actual kin. In other words, whereas less than a thousand individuals belong to the elite, about three thousand individuals belong to the class that does not have the right to elect or be elected *penghulu,*

Table 28. Actual kin of *penghulu* by *suku, negeri* Taram

Name of *suku*	Number of members
Piliang Gadang	208
Bodi	151
Sumpadang	148
Pitopang	101
Simabur	100
Piliang Lawas	62
Melaju	40

with all the resultant consequences. The latter class, therefore, is comprised of either *kemanakan* who are not *kemanakan batali darah* of any *penghulu,* as has been indicated, or individuals who reside in *negeri* Taram but do not take part in the community affairs that involve the *adat,* such as a number of seasonal laborers from the two brick workshops. It appears, also, that aliens do not always abide by the *adat* regulations, although a disregard for the *adat* invariably involves the possibility of only limited action.

14. The Wali Negeri

The *wali negeri* is an office imposed upon a *negeri* by the government. To such a person, regarded as the official head of the village community, is delegated some of the administrative authority that, according to the laws of the land, is the right of the government. He thus acts as the representative of the government in the *negeri.* On the other hand, since the *wali negeri* should be nominated and elected by the voting inhabitants of the *negeri* for a term of three years, he is also regarded, especially by the government, as the representative of the *negeri* community. This double and somewhat ambiguous role may become a potent single focus of power in the *negeri* system of government or, to the contrary, an insignificant office without any influence on the affairs of the inhabitants of the community.

The rights and duties of the *wali negeri*, as formulated by the government, are sanctioned by the government, which provides him with a salary as partial compensation for the time and labor expended to perform the work. In reality, since in terms of communication *negeri* Taram is rather distantly located from the centers of government, the *wali negeri* has no actual coercive power to enforce his decisions on his fellow villagers. In fact, when instructions received from the government must be implemented, he has to adapt these instructions as much as possible to the prevailing opinions of the community members with whom he must live. Without any means to enforce his will, he cannot afford to incur the resentment of his fellow community members. Only when the *wali negeri* is also a village functionary by right, on the basis of traditional *adat*, does he actually possess some means for coercion, provided within the prevailing *adat* norms and thus sanctioned by the *negeri* community as a whole. Otherwise, as in the case of the present *wali negeri*, he is forced to seek the approval of the existing traditional *negeri* functionaries who do possess some actual coercive power, accorded to them as elected leaders of their subordinates. The traditional *negeri* functionaries can, therefore, provide the necessary sanctions to enforce the execution of government instructions or projects. Without the approval of the traditional *negeri* functionaries, and in the absence of any actual coercive means, no enterprise can be carried out. And if some individuals, nevertheless, make an attempt to proceed with the rejected proposal, nothing prevents the traditional *negeri* functionaries from creating obstacles to bar any fruitful result from the undertaking.

Although the foregoing description gives the impression that the *wali negeri* effectively is powerless, this is not entirely the case. First of all, as the government's representative he receives information about government regulations. He obtains such useful information in the form of written, mimeographed, or printed documents sent to him by his superiors. Occasionally he may be called to their office to get instructions and comments necessary to clarify the meaning and intent of new directives. In the *negeri*, the *wali negeri* may be said to be the sole repository for practical information about government regulations. He has the power to withhold information that he considers harmful for his own or his group's interests, and he also has the power to provide those individuals or groups whom he favors with particular information that could benefit their interests.

The *wali negeri* also regulates and supervises the distribution of government rations, such as sugar and soap, which gives him control over the distribution of certain imperative goods. Such economic power can, at times, be used to coerce the villagers to act in accordance with the wishes of the *wali negeri*. When his instructions are not carried out, he merely has to withhold government rations from his opponents. This method of coercion naturally would be effective only in periods of economic crisis, when the government provides the primary source of relief and the necessary goods are not available elsewhere.

As the scope and complexity of the villagers' activities have expanded as a result of rapid socioeconomic developments in most of Indonesia, needs are felt that, in turn, require funds to reach fulfillment. The need for capital to finance construction projects and the like provides the *wali negeri* with additional power, since, as head of the *negeri* administration, he is the man who receives government funds for allocation to finance projects to serve the needs of the villagers.

Finally, the *wali negeri* is in a position to select information to be reported to his superiors, thus functioning as the eyes and ears of the government within the community. He is expected to keep the government informed about activities in the *negeri* that would be to its interest. His reports are transmitted in written or oral form to his immediate superiors, who, in turn, submit the relevant portions to higher levels for consideration. It is within the means of the *wali negeri* to submit unfavorable reports about groups or people who, for one reason or other, are not to his liking, or to praise those with whom he has common interests; the former would not come to the attention of the government when candidates are sought to fill vacant offices.

The present *wali negeri*, Marisan, is an intelligent young man of thirty years who has worked outside Taram for some time as a tailor. During the recent local uprising, the P.R.R.I. rebellion, Marisan acquired the reputation of being very harsh, if not cruel, in his actions. He served at that time as leader of a local people's combat group, or O.P.R. unit, part of an organization established to fight the rebels. As *wali negeri* of Taram, his office is at the market place. As an ordinary villager,

Marisan, a member of the Communist party, makes his home with his wife's family (*suku* Melaju). As a member of the *suku* Bodi, he is subordinate to the *putjuk suku* of Bodi.

15. Political Parties

The proclamation of independence of the Republic of Indonesia on August 17, 1945, and the adoption of a democratic system in which popular representation was required as one of the basic principles of the state, brought about the emergence of competing political parties. Various people joined these political organizations to gain representation or, more importantly, to join forces in the struggle for the acquisition of power to be used in the interest of the power-holding parties.

On October 1, 1945, at a meeting attended by local political leaders considered to be the representatives of the inhabitants of West Sumatra, the first native Indonesian resident of West Sumatra, the highest local administrator, was elected. A week afterward, this resident appointed territorial administrators for the eight *luhak* that together comprise the residency of West Sumatra. *Negeri* Taram, as part of *luhak* Limapuluh Koto, came under the jurisdiction of the administration at Pajakumbuh. Previously, the position of resident and *luhak* head had never been held by Indonesians, as both the Dutch colonial government as well as the Japanese occupation forces reserved these powerful positions for themselves. On January 23, 1945, the first *demang*, or territorial administrators next in rank to the *luhak* heads, were appointed. All these offices were regarded as key positions by people concerned with political affairs, not only because of the power and authority connected with these offices but also because of the prestige that went with them. Then there were the other public offices to be considered, such as the office of *wali negeri*. Who would obtain those positions?

Political parties, primarily those with headquarters in the capital of the newly established republic, sought to strengthen their position by recruiting as many members as possible. Soon various political party branches or sections emerged in *negeri* Taram. The most important were the Moslem groups Masjumi and Perti, the Partai Komunis Indonesia (PKI) and the Partai Nasional Indonesia (PNI). The PKI and Perti had already existed during the last two decades of Dutch colonial rule, the Communist party being a few years older than the Moslem one.

There were a few active members of long standing from these two parties in *negeri* Taram, one of them being the highly respected or much-feared Communist, Pituhan Datuk Paduko Basa, mentioned in section 8 as a leading *adat* expert.

On March 17, 1946, the resident of West Sumatra issued an ordinance instructing the establishment of *negeri* councils of representatives (*dewan perwakilan negeri*) and the election of *wali negeri* by popular vote. A *negeri* council of representatives, according to the ordinance, was to consist of representatives from the various social categories in the *negeri* community as defined by the government, of which the *adat* functionaries formed only a single category. On the other hand, the traditional village council (*kerapatan negeri*), consisting of the family heads as formulated by *adat*, continued to exist. In this manner, democracy in its old form and democracy in its new form existed side by side. The first elected *wali negeri* of Taram was Sjamsian Datuk Bagindo Simaradjo nan Bakupiah, head of *suku* Piliang Lawas, showing the confluence of *adat* and government authority in a situation not based on the traditional *adat* normative system. The first elected head of *negeri* Taram, after the proclamation of independence, held office until 1948, when new developments in the struggle between the Dutch and the Indonesians demanded a different kind of *negeri* administrator, a functionary empowered with military authority, the designated military head of the *negeri* (*wakil negeri perang*). It was his task to organize the recruitment of men for the armed forces, the collection of provisions for the fighting guerrilla troops, and the maintenance of communication lines between the various areas.

The local branches of the various political parties took an active part in the selection of leaders who could be depended upon to deal with organizational problems never experienced before. In fact, during the revolutionary war, a number of political parties each had their own armed groups. The Madjelis Islam Tinggi, which later merged with the Masjumi party, maintained its Barisan Sabililah; the Moslem Perti party maintained for its male members the Lasjkar Muslimin Indonesia (Lasjmi) and, for its women, an armed organization named Lasjkar Muslimat; the Communist PKI had its Tentara Merah Indonesia, later renamed Barisan Merah Indonesia, and so on. In view of this, one of the main functions of the political party machines was the recruitment of new members for these various armed organizations, all actively engaged in fighting the Dutch aggressors. These armed organizations disbanded or merged with the national army when the government succeeded in exerting itself as the sole authority empowered with the monopoly of armed warfare.

After the revolution, the local political party branches in *negeri* Taram directed their activities to the acquisition of political power in the *negeri* community, trying particularly to occupy the office of *wali negeri*. The government has prescribed that the head of the *negeri* should be elected by its inhabitants. Only the formal nomination of candidates was made by the political parties, although this is usually one of their major functions. Instead, candidates were picked on the basis of family affiliations and interests other than those of the political parties. In 1950, for instance, Pituhan Datuk Paduko Basa was nominated for the office of *wali negeri* at a meeting attended by all *penghulu* of *suku* Pitopang, the *suku* group of the candidate. The meeting was presided over by the head of *suku* Pitopang, the aged Saleh Datuk Leloangso nan Tinggi. Pituhan happened to be a member of the Communist party and thus, although nominated by his *suku* group, he became the candidate who was thought to represent the PKI. The other candidates, except one person who did not get much support, were also *adat* functionaries, prominent men in their respective *suku* groups and therefore also in the *negeri* community. These individuals were, then Hamzah Datuk Singo nan Bamedjan of *suku* Simabur, Ramli Datuk Radjo Sampono of *suku* Piliang Lawas, Mardamin Datuk Maradjo Basa nan Putih of *suku* Simabur, and Rustam of *suku* Melaju. All were duly nominated by the various political parties at a village meeting held in the traditional *balai* and attended by the adult members of the village community.

Although each political party has its own ideology, which is supposed to distinguish it, in *negeri* Taram ideological concepts do not seem to exert much influence on the activities of the respective party members. The reason for joining a political party is indeed frequently not connected at all with political ideology but rather with more immediate needs, such as the wish to enter a son or daughter in an elementary school established or maintained by the members of a particular party branch, the wish to please the head of the family group who happens to be a member of the political party, the wish to participate in an attractive project sponsored by one of the political parties, or various other personal, nonpolitical reasons.

At present the largest political party in *negeri* Taram is the Perti branch, an organization which claims more than a thousand members, presumably including the children of the adult members since, one should remember, *negeri* Taram has a population of not more than 4,000. Next in size is the nationalist PNI, and the smallest but seemingly best organized party is the Communist PKI, which achieved its present political ascendency in *negeri* Taram because it was the only political party without any member involved in the recent uprising against the central government. The Masjumi party, of course, ceased to exist when the central government banned its existence some years ago.

16. Conclusion

To a certain extent, *negeri* Taram reflects the problems exhibited by Indonesian society as a whole. Basically these problems result from the existence of people who derive their power and influence from traditional norms and established vested interests, political or economical, in opposition to the emergence of people whose increasing power and influence are based on nontraditional factors, not always beneficial to the *negeri* community but possibly more compatible with newly felt needs. There are conflicts of interests, hostile relations, and other such destructive phenomena. But, like the Indonesian nation, the community of *negeri* Taram also manifests hope for a better future and has directed fruitful activities toward its fulfillment.

There are certainly problems, some complicated and others quite simple, which must be dealt with. However, life goes on, and people seem to be able to adjust themselves to their fellow villagers. After all, they must live together: they are part of a single community—the village community of *negeri* Taram; part of a single local society—the Minangkabau of West Sumatra; and part of a single larger, heterogeneous, and dynamic society—the Indonesian nation.

Chapter XV

The Village in Indonesia Today

KOENTJARANINGRAT
UNIVERSITY OF INDONESIA

1. The Variety of Villages in Indonesia

It has been explained in the Preface that the articles presented in this book are primarily intended as sources to obtain impressions on social phenomena in village communities in Indonesia today. A more intensive knowledge of these phenomena, in specific sociocultural settings, will enable us to formulate, with greater accuracy, problems and hypotheses on the social system of village Indonesia in general. The characteristics of the Indonesian village, or *desa*, that will be summarized in the following sections of this final chapter must be considered as only tentative knowledge, the validity of which has to be tested by more sophisticated quantitative methods. The area of Indonesia, with its dominantly rural population and its great diversity of rural cultures and social systems based on a common Malayan and Malayo-Polynesian substratum, forms a favorable *ethnologisch studieveld*,[1] or area of controlled ethnological comparisons.

The latest census (1961) shows that the dominant part of the Indonesian population, that is, 85.4 per cent or approximately 86,700,000 people, is still rural.[2] Over how many village communities those millions of people are distributed we do not know; only a few dubious figures exist concerning the number of villages for Java and Madura for the years 1920 and 1923.[3] An attempt to estimate the average number of

[1] The term *ethnologisch studieveld* was introduced by the Dutch anthropologist J. P. B. de Josselin de Jong (1935).
[2] West Irian is of course not included in these figures.
[3] L. Adam's book on autonomy in Indonesian village communities includes

386

inhabitants of an Indonesian village in general, however, will require an intensive understanding of the various types of Indonesian village communities and of the basic principles that underlie these various types.

There are, of course, several criteria that can be used to develop a typology of Indonesian villages. A very important classification would be a classification based on the two main systems of subsistence economics: sedentary rice cultivation with irrigation and shifting cultivation without irrigation. Village communities based on sedentary rice cultivation are mainly located on Java, Bali, and a large part of Lombok. Outside this central area, sedentary agriculture with irrigation only forms enclaves in several palces in North and West Sumatra, in the coastal areas of Kalimantan, in the areas of Macassar and Menado on Sulawesi, and in several minor places on Nusa Tenggara and Maluku. In the remaining part, however, which means almost 89 per cent of the total area of Indonesia, approximately one-third of the population practices shifting cultivation. The implications of this dichotomy in rural Indonesia have been extensively discussed by C. Geertz in his book on the economic history of rural Indonesia (1963).

Another very important way to classify the large variety of Indonesian village communities is to consider the principles of relationship that underlie their social systems. Such a method of classification has been proposed by *adat* law students, who have suggested two principles of relationship for use in making a typology of village communities in Indonesia: ties of kinship and ties of proximity of residence, thus distinguishing between communities with "genealogical" and those with "territorial" organization. However, although communities based exclusively on genealogical or territorial principles do exist in Indonesia, in reality we only find combinations of both types. Since the several types of village communities which are based on either one or on combinations of both of these principles have been extensively discussed in ter Haar's textbook on *adat* law in Indonesia (1948, 50–56), any further elaboration may be omitted here. In addition to these two principles, however, two other principles of relationship seem to be of equal importance: the ties of common objectives and the ties of relationship that are superimposed from above by a supreme government. Naturally no one-to-one relation-

---

the information that in 1920 Java and Madura had 23,024 villages. Two other figures mentioned in the book are 22,000 and 21,800 for the year 1923 (Adam 1924, 10).

ship exists between the above-mentioned four principles of relationship and four distinct types of village communities. The reality is by far more complex, and an understanding of this complexity will help us to answer the question of ". . . de grenzen van het Indonesische dorp," the limits of the Indonesian village community, which was raised some time ago by various students of rural Indonesia (Boeke 1937).

More intensive observations regarding the processes of development in village communities might be of importance to achieve such an understanding. For this reason, the emergence of new settlements and their institutionalization into village communities in chapter XI on the Javanese resettlers in South Sumatra, as well as the chapters on swidden villages, need our special attention.

The emergence of new settlements in rural Indonesia often takes place as a consequence of separation. The villages Rarak, Soba, and Telang of West Sumbawa, West Timor, and Central Kalimantan, and probably many other swidden villages in Indonesia, have temporary settlements near the clearings and swiddens, where people stay during the busy periods along the agricultural cycle. These temporary settlements may eventually develop into more permanent homesteads or hamlets, usually according to the principles upon which the mother community has based its social system. We might also, however, assume the possible emergence of different types of social systems not necessarily based on genealogical or territorial principles. Geographic, ecologic, and other environmental factors might foster the development of more intensive ties with other settlements than with the mother village, while common objectives between individuals, or motives of efficiency and friendship, might stimulate still different circles of relationship. When the new relationship has institutionalized itself, either conforming to older models or developing new patterns, when the ties with the mother community have become of little significance, and when new symbols of identity—usually a *balai adat* or community building, a sacred house, a mosque, a church, a sacred monument, or a combination of these—have been acquired, the new community is mature enough to separate itself from the mother village.

In this process of development, observers may notice instances where only one of the four previously discussed principles of relationship underlie most fields of village life and activities; on the other hand, more frequently it is possible that two, three, or even all four exist in different fields of social life. The social system of the village community will thus include several interrelated circles of relationship, each of which vary in range. The interrelation of these various circles seems to conform to two kinds of patterns: the concentric pattern and the diverging pattern.

In the concentric pattern, circles of relationship are mutually inclusive and concentrically interrelated. Members of the smaller, inner circles are also members of the larger outer ones. The inner circle includes nearest kinsmen and neighbors with whom people associate on the basis of genealogical and territorial ties; it pertains to daily matters around the household. The next circle includes more extended relations, associates, and friends, similarly assembled on genealogical and territorial principles but also on the basis of common objectives. These relations will concern, for example, agricultural or other productive occupations and related sociocultural activities. This circle is often recognized by the members of a community as a distinct territorial part of the whole, with its own identity and with a specific term or even a name, such as hamlets or hamlet clusters that form territorial wards of a village community. The village Soba on Timor, for example, consists of eleven hamlets, denoted by the specific term *kuan*, each bearing its own name. The village Djagakarsa near Djakarta consits of four wards, denoted by the specific term *kampung*, each also with its own name. In addition, still wider concentric circles may exist, within which people associate with others concerning different fields of village life. At a certain point a general conception of the largest circle is reached; this is the limit of the village community, and all relations with people outside this circle are felt to be relations with outsiders.

In the diverging pattern, on the other hand, various smaller or larger circles of relations are not mutually inclusive but yet are interrelated at several points. Members of one circle are not necessarily members of others. The various circles relate to different fields of village life and may even be based on different principles of relationship. For matters pertaining to the household, people associate within a particular group of close relatives and neighbors, based on genealogical and territorial principles of relationship. For cooperation in the agricultural field, people associate within another circle, which does not necessarily include all the members of the first circle and which may not be based on kinship or territorial ties; still other smaller or wider circles of relationship may exist for different fields of life, based on different principles. Anthropologists have recently observed and described the development of these kinds of village communities. The description of a Coast Lapps community at the Revsbotn Fjord in the province of Finnmark, in northern Norway, gives us a clear picture of this diverging pattern of social relations (Paine 1960), while Geertz's treatment of the village Tihingan in Chapter IX of this book, and of two other Balinese villages in another article (Geertz 1959), shows also the existence of the diverging pattern of social relations in Indonesia. In Tihingan, for matters pertaining to the household and place of residence a villager associates with his fellow *bandjar* members, but, for matters concerning agricultural activities, with the fellow members of his *subak*, who may be quite different people from those belonging to his *bandjar*. Similarly, the title categories or *wangsa* and the politically oriented kin categories or *dadia* form still different separate circles of social relations. Finally, an administrative unit has been superimposed on top of the whole social system of interrelated circles in a noninclusive way. The various mutually independent social circles are usually integrated by a higher identity. In urban communities, where the diverging pattern of social relations usually exists, the integrating force is the higher national identity; in South Balinese villages the recurrent *odalan* ceremonies of the Kahyangan-Tiga temple systems form the integrating mechanism, as all members of the various *bandjar*, *subak*, and other social units who feel themselves affiliated to these central temples cooperate and participate in these ceremonies.

The most important element to determine the limits of the Indonesian village community is thus usually a sense of identity, which is stimulated by some integrating force. Village communities with concentric as well as diverging patterns of relationship based simultaneously on principles of kinship, proximity of living, and common objectives are sometimes integrated both by an identity symbol, in the form of a community house, a sacred center, a temple, a mosque, a church, or combinations of these, and by the social activities centering around these symbols.

In many cases, however, the limits of the village community are determined by the superimposed administrative unit. It usually seems to be a process of several decades or more, however, before the complex systems of interrelated social circles will mold themselves to conform to the limits of the administrative units. In South Bali, for instance, the social system of community life has not yet molded itself into the administrative unit of the *perbekelan;* in Java, however, where the process has been taking place over a much longer period, the village is at the same time a residential unit, a unit of agricultural production, and an *adat* unit, as well as an administrative unit.

In considering the problem of the "limits of the Indonesian village," our attention is drawn to the fact that the size of village communities in general remains within certain limits.[4] Cities that have started to grow will keep growing endlessly, while villages tend to grow only up to a certain point and then always branch to form daughter villages or fall apart into several smaller villages. This universal phenomenon seems to indicate the occurrence of a specific type of relationship within all village communities, namely, that type of relationship that prevails in primary groups and is characterized by spontaneity and great solidarity. This type of relationship forces the community to remain small. Although village communities always split whenever they have reached their limits, the fact remains that village communities still vary in size. Information included in the foregoing chapters shows that Indonesian swidden villages may vary in size from several hundred to a thousand people, with the exception of West Irian, where villages of less than a hundred do exist. Sedentary agricultural villages in Indonesia may vary between seven hundred to sometimes seven thousand inhabitants, although it has to be taken into consideration that the larger villages are often the result of amalgamation by the central government, which began this process early in this century in order to create stronger communities that were supposed to be much more capable of supporting modern democratic administrations (Meijer Ranneft 1919, Legge 1961).

2. Properties of Indonesian Village Communities

Many urban Indonesians tend to think of the Indonesian village as consisting of groups of people who live together in close proximity, forming small societies patterned around kinship that are peaceful, indolent, homogeneous, and resistent to change. The data presented in the thirteen chapters of this book does not always conform to this ideal type, which has been variously designated *societas, Gemeinschaft, société organique,* folk society, and so on.

Kinship, for instance, is one, but by no means the most important, organizing principle. All the chapters in this book, except the one on *negeri* Taram, mention the nuclear family, usually "slightly extended,"[5]

[4] J. H. Boeke has also mentioned this problem in one of his articles (1937, 804).

[5] With this qualification, which is used by Cooley in section 7 of Chapter VI, I intend to designate nuclear families, including dependents—surviving

as the most important kinship-based social unit in the village. The Karo have nonpermanent virilocal extended families as a consequence of the custom of initial virilocal residence after marriage. Among the Minang-kabau of *negeri* Taram, the nuclear family is not always the most important basic kin group, as one finds an extended family of sisters with their respective children, the husbands living "natolocally."[6] The nuclear family, however, does exist, either basically, as many newly married couples take up residence in separate houses,[7] or as a consequence of separation for a large variety of reasons. For the South Balinese, the nuclear family is the basic unit for citizenship in the *adat*, although physically the nuclear families live in close proximity with other nuclear families in walled-up virilocal compounds.

Kindreds are only reported for West Java, South Central Java, West Sumbawa, and Ambon. Concerning Ambon the situation is peculiar, in that the kindred (*familie*) exists within a unilineal setting. I have the suspicion that in this case the Protestant congregation has superimposed upon the individual several Christian ceremonies along the life cycle—baptism, the Christian confirmation ceremony, and the Christian wedding ceremony—and thus the kindred has developed in Ambonese villages in the course of several centuries. In South Central Java there exists an ancestor-oriented occasional bilateral kin group, which is theoretically different from, but in practice often similar to, the kindred. This kin group, which has the sole function of caring for the ancestral graves, becomes ambilineal after the third or fourth generation, in that many members who are not available or who have lost contact with the core do not participate in the activities of the group.

In the areas included in the thirteen chapters, kinship is an important organizing principle in domestic or agricultural activities. Kinship is often also an important determining principle in matters pertaining to political

---

parents, dependent married children with their families, dependent divorced children, and other dependent relatives—who reside in a single household and assist the domestic unit in household activities.

[6] For the meaning of the term "natolocal" see Barnes (1960, 853). Many husbands in Taram, however, do not live natolocally but uxorilocally, although they still have to consider the various obligations toward their mother's ancestral household.

[7] In this case, although physically forming nuclear families, the obligations toward the wife's as well as the mother's ancestral households usually still remain.

status and struggle among the bilateral Macassarese village communities and among all the other unilineal ethnic groups; kinship as a regulating principle in marriage, land tenure, property, and inheritance prevails mainly among the unilineal ethnic groups.

The popular notion that village life is peaceful also does not agree with the information on conflict in the chapters of this book. We have learned how land, status and prestige, differences between generations, and differences between the sexes can be frequent sources of serious friction in little communities in Indonesia, but more elaborate studies still need to be done in order to get an understanding of this matter. The norms and values applied to solve conflicts in village communities have indeed been an important object of study by *adat* law scholars, while particular aspects and forms of conflict, such as witchcraft and sorcery, have been much studied by anthropologists. Still other aspects, however, remain to be investigated. A deeper understanding of the roots and implications of conflict in Indonesian village communities will be of great value for the understanding of the social processes which are taking place in rural Indonesia today.

Village life in Indonesia is also not at all idle and indolent, as has often been assumed by several authors; Boeke once wrote: "The village is not a place for work, but a place for leisure. And leisure is basically the actual life for the Oriental man."[8] We have learned in the chapters on the Javanese resettlement villages in South Sumatra, on Djagakarsa near Djakarta, on Tjelapar in Central Java, on Tihingan in South Bali, on Rarak in West Sumbawa, and on Soba in West Timor that hard work is the requirement for survival in Indonesian villages. Chapter III of this book even includes the information that Timorese villagers highly value a person who can work his swidden successfully with a minimum of aid from outside his nuclear family. The social scientist B. F. Hoselitz suggests that underdeveloped communities need a much better system of incentives to stimulate work, savings for capital formation, and risk-taking for innovation (Hoselitz 1963). Although I fully agree with Hoselitz's opinion, I would like some sharper formulation of the element "work" in his scheme, in particular concerning agricultural village communities in general. No swidden farmer can avoid hard work, and the same is the case with the sedentary farmer. Farming demands hard work

---

[8] "Het dorp is niet de plaats van de arbeid, maar de plaats van de rust. En de rust is toch het eigenlijke leven van de Oosterling" (Boeke 1937, 812).

at particular periods in the agricultural cycle but also has less strenuous times and even periods of leisure. On the other hand, industry requires a different disciplinary system, with a continuous orderly rhythm and effective methods of work. What is needed is not a system of incentives to make the farmer work harder but incentives to make his work more disciplined, orderly, and effective.

The farm unit of the Indonesian small farmer usually consists of members of his "slightly extended" nuclear family or, sometimes, members of his extended family. During busy periods, however, he may request aid from kinsmen, neighbors, or other acquaintances who have fields adjacent to his, on a reciprocal basis, or he may hire additional labor that is paid in kind as well as in money.

The system of reciprocal or mutual aid called *gotong-rojong* seems to exist in most Indonesian village communities. In addition to agricultural activities, it also refers to many other fields of life: activities centering about the household, the preparation for and performance of feasts and ceremonies, and cases of emergency, accident, and death. The types of mutual aid pertaining to these different fields are usually clearly distinguished by the villagers and are sometimes designated by different terms. During my field work in Tjelapar and other neighboring villages some six years ago, I noticed differences in attitude and degree of spontaneity concerning the various types of mutual aid (Koentjaraningrat 1961). When an emergency, accident, or death occurs, neighbors and other members of the village community will gather spontaneously to render aid without much expectation for its return; on the other hand, in agricultural activities people keep careful account of the amount of aid they render. The data on mutual aid in the chapters on Djagakarsa, Situradja, Tjelapar, Rarak, and Soba illustrate some of these points, while the data on Rarak even show how different kinds of mutual aid are used for different stages along the agricultural cycle.

The term *gotong-rojong*, a very popular term in Indonesia today, refers to a complex of institutions that have been adopted by the Indonesian nation as one of the basic properties of its society. In addition to "mutual aid," *gotong-rojong* also means "rendering aid to the community for the common benefit."[9] Similar to the first concept, the second

[9] The *adat* law scholars, following ter Haar, have also made a clear distinction between the two concepts by the terms *wederkerig hulpbetoon* for "mutual aid" and *onderling hulpbetoon* for "rendering aid for the common benefit" (Haar 1950, 121–123).

institution, often also called *kerdja bakti* or *darma bakti,* also seems to have originated in the village community. Many community projects, such as the construction of dams, irrigation works, roads, community buildings, sacred houses, mosques, churches, and schools, have long been completed in Indonesian villages by this type of community effort. Most of the indigenous kingdoms and principalities, and also the various colonial governments that have been in power in Indonesia, have for ages made use of this type of *gotong-rojong* or *kerdja bakti* labor. According to indigenous *adat* regulations, villagers have the obligation to render *kerdja bakti* labor for a certain period, varying between thirty to sixty days, during the year. Thus they may be recruited by the village head for all kinds of community projects and also for routine duties, including services to the village head. In observing the *kerdja bakti* activities in Tjelapar, I also distinguished differences in the villagers' attitudes toward the two kinds of activities. Projects really felt to be useful for the whole community by the majority of the villagers, in contrast to more routine activities, usually have had a much more voluntary and spontaneous character.

Indonesian village communities naturally also know various customary *adat* systems of incentives to intensify *kerdja bakti* labor. Villagers who are under the obligation of *kerdja bakti* are allotted pieces of land and thus are given a respected status in the community. The Dutch colonial government, which also made extensive use of the *kerdja bakti* institution, especially during the "culture system," seems to have increased the importance of land as an incentive for *kerdja bakti* in Java and Madura by specific regulations requiring the peasants to participate in the "culture system" as a means of gaining access to communal land.[10] Also, by a Dutch regulation of 1907, the customary right of villagers to choose their village head was restricted only to those who had participated in *kerdja bakti* services (*Kiesreglement van Staatsblad* 1907. No. 212: 4).

In adopting *gotong-rojong* as an important basic element in the ideal society, the Indonesian government naturally has to make a clear distinction between *gotong-rojong* as a system of mutual aid, with its even more detailed diversity in reference to the various fields of activities in Indonesian village life, and *gotong-rojong* as a system of services for the community, taking into consideration also the differences between participation in village projects generally felt to be of common benefit

[10] See the references cited in Haga's book (1924, 7, 8), i.e., *Eindresumé* (1880, 346) and Bergsma (1896, 64).

and performance of routine obligations. In addition to these two aspects, a third aspect must be clearly distinguished: *gotong-rojong* as a community spirit.

Gotong-rojong as a system of mutual aid seems only to work effectively in small projects requiring work groups not exceeding a maximum of ten to fifteen people, which demand a minimum of specialized skills. The accompanying conventions and etiquette—the obligation to serve the participants a meal in addition to the debt of labor now owed them by the host—make the system very impractical for larger undertakings, which require much more differentiation and specialization of skills. The relationship that underlies the system of mutual aid seems to be based on the principle which Ferdinand Tönnies has called *Wesenwille;* it seems to be closely related to the type of relationship that prevails in primary groups, which are characterized by recurrent face-to-face association and undifferentiated cooperation. We might thus assume the occurrence of systems of mutual aid in villages and little communities not only in rural Africa, Asia, Oceania, and Latin America, or in rural Europe and North America, where primary-group relations still prevail, but even in urban communities, wherever primary-group relations still may exist.

Gotong-rojong as a system of services to the community has proved to be quite successful in various projects of community development in rural Indonesia. This is especially the case where the initiators of the projects are able to persuade and show the village population the importance of the project for the common benefit. Consequently, the villagers are made to feel as if the project has been decided upon on their own initiative, rather than with pressure from above. The project will thus be carried out with great spontaneity. *Kerdja bakti* labor, however, is hardly ever skilled labor.

Gotong-rojong as a community spirit is something different again. It is a sociocultural ethos that underlies the value system, mores, and folkways of a society. In such communities, sacrifice for the common benefit seems to be valued highly, individualism seems to be regarded with disapproval, the rights of the individual are not greatly overemphasized, and the spirit of cooperation forms the basis of social interaction. The spirit of cooperation as a sociocultural ethos does not seem to relate to non-Western societies in the same way as the spirit of individualism relates to urban Western societies, which are based on a modern and extensive market-oriented economic system. Non-Western societies, whether they are urban societies, peasant societies, little communities, or primitive communities, are not always cooperative in spirit and nature. The fact that several little communities and even primitive communities also seem to be characterized by the spirit of individualism has been well illustrated in Chapter VII on the village Muremarēw, in this book, and by Margaret Mead's study on cooperation and competition among thirteen non-Western peoples (Mead 1937). In most village communities in Indonesia, however, an observer will notice the prevalence of the co-operative ethos, and it is this aspect of *gotong-rojong*, rather than the two others, that has been adopted by the Indonesian nation as the most important principle that underlies its national community (Sukarno 1959, 67).[11]

An important manifestation of the *gotong-rojong* ethos in most Indonesian village communities is the institution of *musjawarah*. The concept involves the processes that develop general agreement and consensus in village assemblies, which emerge as the unanimous decision or *mupakat*. This unanimous decision can be reached by a process in which the majority and the minorities approach each other by making the necessary readjustments in their respective viewpoints, or by an integration of the contrasting standpoints into a new conceptual synthesis. *Musjawarah* and *mupakat* thus exclude the possibility that the majority will impose its views on the minorities. *Musjawarah* and *mupakat*, however, imply the existence of personalities who, by virtue of their leadership, are able to bring together the contrasting viewpoints or who have enough imagination to arrive at a synthesis integrating the contrasting viewpoints into a new conception. Chapter VII on the village community Muremarēw, West Irian, illustrates how the lack of a leader with the ability to integrate disagreeing opinions as to how certain activities should be carried out can lead to months of indecision and inactivity on the part of the community. The information on village meetings in a Javanese village included in Chapter X, on the other hand, illustrates how a leading personality who is able to integrate conflicting viewpoints in the community into a new concept, through informal behind-the-scenes operations, can present the general consensus of the community, which at formal meetings creates the starting point for a unanimous decision. This system of conducting village meetings has long been noted in various Indonesian village communities by Dutch *adat* law scholars,[12] since the solution of conflicts in Indonesian *adat* law usually seems to be based on the principle

[11] See also Sukarno's *Lahirnja Pantjasila* (1947, 23).

[12] Notice especially the following references: Vollenhoven (1917) and Haga (1924, 27-34, 112-118).

that the two contrasting viewpoints should be reconciled rather than the idea that the one should overrule the other. The *adat* law scholars have thus also associated the institution of *musjawarah* in Indonesian village communities with a *commune trek*, or a communal characteristic, which seems to prevail in the *adat* law system of Indonesia (Holleman 1935).

3. *Social Stratification and Village Administration*

The information in the previous chapters on social stratification in the various village communities contradicts the popular image that the Indonesian village is homogeneous in nature. *Adat* law scholars have indeed placed the rural population of Java and Madura in three social categories based on the criterion of landownership: (1) the villagers who own agricultural land as well as a compound for a house and who are thus supposed to occupy the highest social status in the village community; (2) the villagers who do not own agricultural land but only a compound for a house, who are accordingly supposed to occupy the next lower social status; and (3) the lowest social level consisting of the landless villagers who own neither agricultural land nor a compound for a house and who thus work for wages in other people's compounds (Vollenhoven 1906–1933, I, 524–526). Despite the fact that such categorization and other similar ones may be useful for various purposes, a special study of social stratification on the village level is also necessary for a deeper understanding of the Indonesian village community. Such a special study, including the analysis of occupational evaluation and patterns of association (see Barber 1957), has, as far as I know, never been conducted in Indonesian village communities. The data included in the previous chapters, however, give us the impression of the existence of at least four patterns of social stratification.

The first pattern is based on the principle of seniority of kin groups or families. Those kin groups or families who are the descendants of the first settlers of the village enjoy the highest status and prestige. We have seen how in the village Kutagamber of the Karo, the patrilineal descendants of original settlers form the highest social level or *bangsa taneh*. We have also seen in the Timorese village Soba that the patrilineal descendants of the original settlers, the *kuatuaf*, also form the upper social level in the community. Similarly the highly respected *orang asali* of the Ambonese villages are patrilineal descendants of the original settlers;

the highest social level in the village Muremarēw of West Irian is occupied by the senior clan Soromadja; while in many villages of Central and East Java the upper social level is the *wong baku* or "standard people,"[13] the descendants of the original settlers.

A second pattern is based on identifying a social category within the village community with other social categories, groups, or occupations, either within or outside the village, that are the center of orientation and are regarded very highly by the villagers. Sometimes the notion of the social category, group, or occupation is of a vague, abstract, or symbolic nature. Chapter X on the South Central Javanese village Tjelapar, for example, includes information on a powerful and respected social class called *kénṭol*, whose members regard themselves to be descendants of an alien settler considered to be of noble origin. A local mythology connects this alien noble ancestor with the ruling dynasty of an ancient Javanese kingdom. A village upper class has thus identified itself through a complex of mythology, sacred heirlooms, genealogies, and other symbols with a nobility that is supposed to exist at a higher, supravillage level. The same principle can be observed in Macassarese villages. The most respected social levels of the village Bontoramba near Macassar, for example, consist of those families who can identify themselves through kinship or other relations with the princely family of the principality of Goa, or secondarily with the family of the *adat* head of Borongloë. Even rural Balinese social stratification, which superficially seems to be of a quite different nature, is in fact also based on this second pattern. Villagers who belong to the highest social levels are those who can identify themselves through their *triwangsa* titles with occupations or status, either real or symbolic, that are highly valued in the society: priests, members of the nobility, and civil servants.

The third pattern of social stratification seems to be based on occupations and positions within the village. The village upper class simply consists of those people who occupy functionally or traditionally the leading positions in the village. In the Minangkabau village *negeri* Taram, for example, the various *penghulu andiko, penghulu putjuk suku,* and their direct relatives form the village elite; while in Sundanese villages, illustrated by Situradja in this book, the members of the village adminis-

---

[13] According to *adat* law scholars, at several places in Java the *wong baku* do not play an important role in the political and economic life of the village (see Berg 1901, 89). As explained in Chapter X, the *wong baku* of Tjelapar are unimportant in comparison with the *kénṭol*.

tration, the local Islamic religious leaders, and their relatives form the village upper class.

The fourth pattern of social stratification seems to be based on generational differences. Although teknonymy is a frequent element in systems of kinship terminology in many Indonesian languages, only in several societies is the custom very extensively used. In these societies the village population seems to be divided into age levels consisting of individuals who are addressed or referred to by a childhood name, individuals who are addressed or referred to by the epithet "father of so-and-so," and individuals who are addressed or referred to by the epithet "grandfather of so-and-so." We have seen this custom illustrated for West Sumbawa and South Bali in Chapters II and IX.

Many systems of social stratification in Indonesian village communities are, of course, based on combinations of these criteria, or the various patterns may exist independently side by side. The villagers of Tihingan of South Bali, for example, classify themselves according to the *wangsa* system and, apart from that, also according to the seniority of generations. They thus pay respect to persons who bear a high *triwangsa* title and also to people of great age. Within the main system of social stratification, Indonesian villagers may also distinguish more detailed stratifications based on other, more usual criteria of stratification: political power and influence, individual quality, and wealth.

The criterion of landownership as a basis for social stratification, especially on Java and Madura, seems to be, in my opinion, a relatively recent development, stimulated by the Dutch colonial government. Land has indeed always been a valuable and highly desired possession. As mentioned in Section 2 of this chapter, it has long been used by village communities as an incentive to stimulate service work. Villagers who were assigned the heavy burdens of *corvée* labor and services for the community, namely the *kuli* or *gogol*, were allotted pieces of land for usufruct during their period of service. The Dutch government increased the status of people who participated in *corvée* labor by regulations that limited certain rights—the right to elect or be elected village head, the right of access to communal land, etc.—only to the *kuli*. The *corvée* laborers became a respected class, enjoying certain exclusive rights of which landownership was the most obvious one. Thus a landowner also became a respected man.

Patterns of social stratification in Indonesia are closely related to systems of village administration. In the previous chapters and in the extensive literature on the subject we may notice the large variety of systems of village administration throughout Indonesia. The many forms, however, may be boiled down to only three patterns: (1) a village administration centered about a council; (2) a village administration based on dual leadership; and (3) a village administration based on single leadership.

The first pattern is noticeable, for instance, in *negeri* Taram and other Minangkabau villages, where the council of the *penghulu putjuk suku* forms the central decision-making authority. Similarly, in Tihingan and other South Balinese villages exists the council of the five *klian bandjar;* and in Ambonese villages a council called *Badan Saniri Negeri.* These councils represent the most dominant kin groups in the community, respectively the *suku* in Taram, the *dadia* in Tihingan, and the *mata rumah* of Allang. Information from other parts of Indonesia indicates that similar village councils may represent the most respected kin groups of the community—the senior kin groups or descendants of the original settlers—or may represent all the existing sections of the community. Membership in these councils is based on election by the groups represented and also on a consensual basis by a meeting of the total community. The members of these councils speak for their own respective groups and make decisions entirely by unanimous agreement. Supervision by an additional council of elders, restriction by the public opinion in the community, and the right of the villagers to petition the higher authorities gives the system a democratic character. The members of the village councils, however, are highly respected and their status is supported by various symbols of authority, such as sacred heirlooms and seats. In the execution of their daily tasks, the village leaders are always assisted by a number of other village officials.

The second pattern, that of dual leadership, is illustrated by the team of two leaders of Rarak on West Sumbawa, consisting of the *kepala kampung,* whose realm covers the civil *adat* affairs, and the *lebè,* whose realm covers Islamic and religious matters; and by the team of two leaders of Soba on Timor, consisting of the *amnais ko'u,* who takes care of the intervillage relations, and the *amnais ana',* who has to manage the internal affairs of the village. Some information on this pattern of dual leadership is included in older reports on Kuantan (Schwartz 1893), Kampar Kiri (O'Brien 1906–1907, 939–978), Karo and Pakpak (Ypes 1907, 358) of North and East Sumatra, and on East Sulawesi (Goedhart 1908). In East Indonesia also this *adat* system of village administration seems to have been in existence, but it was abolished by the Dutch (see

Roo van Alderwerelt 1906, 271). In the system with two village heads, neither is subordinate to the other; in fact they perform complementary functions, and symbolically they are often considered to be siblings. The two headmen are usually recruited from the two most important senior kin groups of the villages, usually by election but sometimes based on inheritance. They are also assisted by a staff of village officials.

The third pattern, that of single leadership, prevails in West Java, Central and East Java, and Madura. In these areas the village head was formerly elected by the *wong baku*, villagers considered to be the descendants of the original settlers and the founders of the village; after 1906, when the Dutch issued an ordinance regulating the local village community (Inlandsche Gemeente Ordonantie), they were elected by villagers who had participated in *kerdja bakti corvée* labor; and, after World War II, by all adult members of the community. In villages of South Central Java like Tjelapar, however, membership in a powerful village elite, the *kéntol*, is still an important determining factor for candidacy as village head. Generally, however, the village administration in Java also has a democratic character, as the village head is usually supervised by a council of elders and restricted by public opinion and by the right of the villagers to petition higher authorities. As in all the other systems, the village heads of Java are assisted by a staff of village officials, in West Java usually only four to five people, but in Central and East Java usually up to ten or fifteen.

The Dutch colonial government superimposed, on these various systems, their own administrative system consisting of a village headman whose main function was to collect taxes, organize *corvée* labor, keep records of the census, and relay information and regulations from the central government to the village population. In the Minangkabau villages of the Pajakumbuh, a functionary called *wali negeri* has been superimposed upon the *penghulu putjuk suku* council; while in South Balinese villages, the *perbekelan* administrative unit is superimposed upon the network of *subak, bandjar*, and other social units. In Timorese villages with the system of dual leadership, a third headman, the *temukung*, is added to the two *adat* headmen, *amnais ko'u* and *amnais ana'*. In Ma'anjan villages, the functions formerly vested in a single individual, the *pembakal*, were divided between two positions: the functions connected with the central government bureaucracy were taken over by an individual retaining the older title *pembakal*, while functions involving the traditional legal aspects of village leadership were relegated to a separate position carrying the title *pangulu*. In Javanese villages with the system of single leadership, the *adat* headman is assigned to perform the additional functions of the central government bureaucracy. In many villages of Indonesia with a single leader, however, the Dutch government has appointed another functionary in addition to the *adat* headman. In many villages of West Irian, for instance, a village official or *korano* is appointed next to the *adat* headman or *ondowafi*. In many areas the superimposed government system does not conform to the local *adat* system and is still considered as an alien institution. Various conflicts have their roots in this situation. In other areas, however, the government and the *adat* system have developed into a much more integrated system.

4. Relations with the Supravillage World

Most Indonesian village communities have been dominated by a supreme government, the majority from the period of the indigenous kingdoms onward, many others from the subsequent periods of colonial domination, and others from relatively recent periods of direct colonial administration. Consequently, hardly any isolated, primitive, autonomous self-sufficient communities, unaware of the existence of higher levels, exist. To most Indonesian village communities we may apply Redfield's concept of the peasant community, as most of these villages are inhabited by "rural people in old civilizations, . . . who control and cultivate their land for subsistence and as a part of a traditional way of life and who look to and are influenced by gentry or townspeople whose way of life is like theirs but in a more civilized form" (Redfield 1956, 20).

Although most villagers in Indonesia are aware of the existence of a higher tradition, of higher levels of authority, of a higher colonial government, and of a higher national government, this does not necessarily mean that they also have an extensive perception, knowledge, and understanding of the world beyond the village. Information on this subject included in the foregoing chapters indeed illustrates the often very low degree of sophistication of the villagers on matters pertaining to the supravillage world, as did an investigation conducted by the Indonesian sociologist Selosoemardjan in 1962, in a sample of villages in North Sumatra, West, Central and East Java, and Sumbawa concerning the perception, knowledge, and understanding of the peasants about selected national concepts and issues.[14]

---

[14] The results of this study are not published.

The peasants' range of relationships with individuals or groups beyond the village must be considered apart from the extent of their awareness and the range of their perceptions concerning the world beyond the village. This aspect does not necessarily have to be consistent with the first two. By the nature of his existence, a peasant has an awareness of the world beyond his village; he may even know a great deal about that world, although his circle of relations may be very limited. A second peasant, however, aware of the existence of a world beyond his village, may not know very much about it, despite the fact that he may have extensive contacts with people or groups in that world, for a number of different reasons. In my opinion, it seems worthwhile to distinguish between the three aspects mentioned and to pay particular attention to the third one. A convenient concept for the analysis of the various ranges in social relations seems to be Barnes's one of "social fields" (1954), which gives the student the opportunity to observe carefully how different people in a community move in different "fields" or circles of social relationships, under different circumstances, at different periods. A majority of Indonesian peasants probably find most of their social relations in the agricultural field. This circle of relations includes their closest relatives, neighbors of the same hamlets, acquaintances from other hamlets who have agricultural land adjacent to their own, residents of other hamlets who share membership in the same *subak* organization, landlords whose land they work on a sharecropping basis or whose land they rent, and agricultural laborers from distant villages who come to work for wages during particular times of the year. Some of these peasants, although not all of them, are oriented toward trade. In addition to their kinsmen, neighbors, friends, and acquaintances within the villages, these peasants include within their circle of relations buyers and sellers from other villages, wholesalers from the towns, and many other people who come to the markets on recurrent market days. Several among those peasants may still be oriented toward another wider social field, which involves relatives or friends in distant towns, cities, or even other islands, who attract them to these places to work on a semipermanent or on a temporary basis, as recurrent or seasonal migrants, while a more intensive analysis may make the observer aware of the existence of still other social fields, each of which he can describe minutely as to the nature, frequency, quality, and range of the relationship. Comparisons with other communities may lead to generalizations about the sociopsychological nature of the relationship in the various social fields and subsequently to the construction of types of social fields which might be used in cross-cultural analysis.

Loyalties toward certain persons, groups, or causes are usually determined by the interest the peasant has in these persons, groups, or concepts, which is in turn determined by the "social fields" in which the peasant customarily associates and toward which he is oriented. The range of his knowledge and perception is of minor importance in relation to loyalties. Naturally, as his most important social field is restricted to his village and its surroundings, his interests are similarly determined; consequently his loyalties are mainly focused on local persons, groups, or causes, although other peasants in his community who may be oriented toward other social fields may have different loyalties. The anthropologist G. W. Skinner and several other specialists on Indonesia who have discussed the interplay between *Local, Ethnic, and National Loyalties in Village Indonesia* (1959) have also concluded that in a selection of five Indonesian villages the primary sense of loyalty of most villagers is to local groups and causes. On the other hand, ethnic loyalties very often originate from urban centers, where members of different ethnic groups have to face each other in a competitive struggle for existence and power. The conflict between ethnic and local loyalties in the village does not seem to be very significant. The interplay between local and national loyalties in village communities, however, is of basic importance. The villagers' sense of national loyalties can actually be considered as an extension of their local loyalties, in that they usually take interest in national concepts and ideas only as far as these concepts and ideas have penetrated into the village and have been related to local persons or groups. It might even be a good thing to keep the interest of Indonesian villagers oriented toward local goals, thus keeping better educated villagers from moving away from the village, which would prevent the village from losing its best people. The villagers' knowledge and perception of the wider world, however, must be improved constantly. The organizers of community development thus have to take into consideration the sharp distinction between the awareness, the perception, the relations, and the loyalties of the Indonesian villager in reference to the world beyond the village and in reference to the Indonesian nation.

Bibliography

The following abbreviations for periodicals have been used:

AA   *American Anthropologist*
BKI   *Bijdragen tot de Taal-, Land- en Volkenkunde van Neder-*
          landsch-Indië
IAE   *Internationales Archiv für Ethnographie*
ITR   *Indisch Tijdschrift van het Recht*
JAI   *Journal of the Royal Anthropological Institute of Great*
          Britain and Ireland
JIAEA   *Journal of the Indian Archipelago and Eastern Asia*
JRASMB   *Journal of the Royal Asiatic Society, Malayan Branch*
JRASSB   *Journal of the Royal Asiatic Society, Straits Branch*
KS   *Koloniale Studiën*
KT   *Koloniaal Tijdschrift*
MKAWAL   *Mededeelingen der Koninklijke Akademie van Wetenschappen,*
          Afdeeling Letterkunde
MNZ   *Mededeelingen van wege het Nederlandsche Zendelinggenoot-*
          schap
TBG   *Tijdschrift voor Indische Taal-, Land- en Volkenkunde, uitge-*
          geven door het (Koninklijk) Bataviaasch Genootschap van
          Kunsten en Wetenschappen
TNAG   *Tijdschrift van het (Koninklijk) Nederlandsch Aardrijkskun-*
          dig Genootschap
TNI   *Tijdschrift voor Nederlandsch Indië*
VBG   *Verhandelingen van het (Koninklijk) Bataviaasch Genoot-*
          schap van Kunsten en Wetenschappen
VKAWAL   *Verhandelingen der Koninklijke Akademie van Wetenschappen,*
          Afdeeling Letterkunde
VKI   *Verhandelingen van het Koninklijk Instituut voor de Taal-,*
          Land- en Volkenkunde (van Nederlandsch-Indië)

Aboetari
  1932   *De Verhouding van de Koloniale tot de Theoretische Eco-*
          nomie. Thesis, Nederlandsche Handelshoogeschool te Rotter-
          dam. Rotterdam, F. Bosman.

408   *Bibliography*

Adam, L.
1924   *De Autonomie van het Indonesisch Dorp.* Thesis, Leiden.
          Amersfoort, S. W. Melchior.

Adriani, N.
1932   *Verzamelde Geschriften.* 3 v. Haarlem, De Erven F. Bohn
          N. V.

Adriani, N., and A. C. Kruyt
1912–1914 *De Bare'e-sprekende Toradjas van Midden-Celebes.* 3 v. Batavia,
          Landsdrukkerij.

Albertis, L. M. d'
1881   *New Guinea: What I Did and What I Saw.* 2 v. Boston,
          Houghton Mifflin.

Anonymous
1892   "Het Landschap Amarassi." *Tijdschrift voor het Binnenlandsch
          Bestuur,* VII, 201–227.

Arndt, P.
1929–1931 "Die Religion der Nad'a." *Anthropos,* XXIV, 817–861; XXVI,
          353–405, 697–739.

1931   *Die Religion auf Ostflores, Adonare, und Solor.* Wien-Mödling,
          Mechitharisten Buchdruckerei.

1932   *Mythologie, Religion, und Magie im Sikagebiet (Östl. Mittel-
          Flores).* Ende, Arnoldus.

1936–1937 "Déva, das Höchste Wesen der Ngadha." *Anthropos,* XXXI,
          894–909; XXXII, 195–209, 347–377.

1939   "Dua Nggae, das Höchste Wesen im Ligo-Gebiet (Mittel-
          Flores)." *Annali Lateranensi,* III, 141–210.

1951   *Religion auf Ostflores, Adonare, und Solor.* Wien-Mödling,
          St. Gabriel.

1952   "Zur Religion der Dongo auf Sumbawa." *Anthropos,* XLVII,
          483–500.

Bachtiar, Harsja W.
1963   "Beberapa Angka Mengenai Penduduk." *Penduduk Irian Barat.*
          Edited by Koentjaraningrat and Harsja W. Bachtiar. Djakarta,
          Penerbitan Universitas, pp. 95–110.

Bachtiar Rifai
1958   *Bentuk Milik Tanah dan Tingkat Kemakmuran: Penjelidikan
          Pedesaan Didaerah Pati, Djawa-Tengah.* Dissertation, University
          of Indonesia [mimeographed manuscript]. Bogor.

Bangert, C.
1860   "Verslag der Reis in de Binnenwaarts Gelegene Streken van
          Doessoen Ilir." *TBG,* IX, 134–218.

Barber, B.

1957 *Social Stratification: A Comparative Analysis of Structure and Process.* New York, Harcourt Brace.

Barnes, J. A.

1954 "Class and Committees in a Norwegian Island Parish." *Human Relations,* VII, 39–58.

1960 "Marriage and Residential Continuity." *AA,* LXII, 850–866.

Bastian, A.

1884–1894 *Indonesien; oder, die Inseln des Malayischen Archipel.* 5 v. Berlin, F. Dümmers.

Bastin, J.

1954 "Raffles' Ideas on the Land Rent System in Java and the Mackenzie Land Tenure Commission." *VKI,* XIV. The Hague, M. Nijhoff.

Befu, H., and L. Plotnicov

1962 "Types of Corporate Unilineal Descent Groups." *AA,* LXIV, 313–327.

Benedict, R.

1947 *Patterns of Culture.* New York, Mentor.

Berg, L. W. C. van den

1892 "De Afwijkingen van het Mohammedaansche Familie en Erfrecht op Java en Madoera." *BKI,* XLI, 454–512.

1897 "De Afwijkingen van het Mohammedaansche Vermogensrecht op Java en Madoera." *BKI,* XLVII, 83–182.

1901 "Het Inlandsche Gemeentewezen op Java en Madoera." *BKI,* LII, 1–140.

Bergsma, W. B.

1896 *Eindrésumé van het Onderzoek naar de Rechten van den Inlander op den Grond op Java en Madoera.* Part III. Batavia, Landsdrukkerij.

Bertling, C. T.

1936 "Huwverbod op Grond van Verwantschapsposities in Middel-Java." *ITR,* CXLIII, 119–134.

Bink, G. L.

1897 "Drie Maanden aan de Humboldts-baai." *TBG,* XXXIX, 143–211.

1902 "Lijst van Woorden, Opgetekend uit den Mond der Karau-Jotafa, bewoners der Humboldts-baai." *TBG,* XLV, 59–90.

Boechari

1963 "A Preliminary Note on the Study of the Old-Javanese Civil Administration." *Madjalah Ilmu-ilmu Sastra Indonesia,* I, 122–133.

Boeke, J. H.

1910   *Tropische-Koloniale Staathuishoudkunde: Het Probleem.* Dissertation, Leiden and Amsterdam.

1930   *Dualistische Economie.* Lecture, Leiden. Leiden, S. C. Van Doersburgh.

1937   "De Grenzen van het Indonesisch Dorp." *TNAG*, LIV, 797–819.

1938   "Keuze en Opleiding van den Candidaat-Indisch Ambtenaar. Verslag van de Algemeene Vergadering V.v.A.B.–B.N.I." *KT*, XXVII, 219–261.

1952   *Dorpsherstel.* Lecture, Leiden. Haarlem, H. D. Tjeenk Willink.

1953   *Economics and Economic Policy of Dual Societies, as Exemplified by Indonesia.* Haarlem, H. D. Tjeenk Willink.

Boetzelaer van Asperen en Dubbeldam, C. W. T., Baron van

1941   "De Geschiedenis van de Maleische Bijbel-vertaling in Nederlandsch-Indië." *BKI*, C, 27–48.

1949   "Albertus Christian Kruyt." *BKI*, CV, 143–146.

Boomgaard, S. R.

1926   *De Rechtstoestand van de Getrouwde Vrouw Volgens het Adatrecht van Nederlandsch Indië.* The Hague, Avondpostdrukkerij.

Bromley, M.

1960   "A Preliminary Report on Law Among the Grand Valley Dani of Netherlands New Guinea." *Nieuw Guinea Studien*, IV, 235–259.

Bruner, E. M.

1961   "Urbanization and Ethnic Identity in North Sumatra." *AA*, LXIII, 508–521.

Bruyn, J. V. de

1958   *Anthropological Research in Netherlands New Guinea Since 1950.* (Reprint from *Oceania*, XXIX, 1958.) The Oceania Monograph, X. Sydney, University of Sydney.

Buddingh, S. A.

1859–1861 *Neêrlands Oost-Indië, Reizen.* 3 v. Rotterdam, N. Wijt.

Bühler, A.

1942   "The Ikat Technique." *Ciba Review*, 44, 1586–1596.

Burton, R.

1855   "Cannibalism Among the Battas." *JIAEA*, IX, 358.

Camerling, E.

1928   *Ueber Ahnenkult in Hinterindien und auf den Grossen Sunda Inseln.* Rotterdam, Nijgh & Ditmar.

Capelle, M. C.
1951   *Dr. Alb. C. Kruyt, Pionier van Poso.* The Hague, J. N. Voorhoeve.

Chabot, H. T.
1950   *Verwantschap, Stand en Sexe in Zuid-Celebes.* Groningen, J. B. Wolters.

Chys, J. A. van der
1872   "Koepang Omstreeks 1750." *TBG*, XVIII, 209–227.

Colijn, H.
1907   *Kolonisatie in Nederlandsch Oost-Indië.* . . . Weltevreden, A. M. van Belkum.

Conklin, H. C.
1961   "The Study of Shifting Cultivation." *Current Anthropology*, II, 27–61.

Cooley, F. L.
1962   *Ambonese Adat: A General Description.* New Haven, Yale University Southeast Asia Studies.
1962a   "Ambonese Kin Groups." *Ethnology*, I, 102–112.

Cortesão, A.
1944   *The Suma Oriental of Tomé Pires: An Account of the East, from the Red Sea to Japan, Written in Malacca and India in 1512–1515, and the Book of Françisco Rodrigues.* 2 v. London, Hakluyt Society.

Covarrubias, M.
1938   *Island of Bali.* New York, Knopf.

Cunningham, C. E.
1958   *The Postwar Migration of the Toba-Bataks to East Sumatra.* New Haven, Yale University Southeast Asia Studies.
1964   "Order in the Atoni House." *BKI*, CXX, 34–68.
1965   "Borrowing of Atoni Children: An Aspect of Mediation." *Proceedings of the American Ethnological Society, 1964*, M. E. Spiro, editor pp. 21–37. Seattle, University of Washington Press.
1965a   "Order and Change in an Atoni Diarchy." *Southwestern Journal of Anthropology*, XXI, 359–382.
1967   "Recruitment to Atoni Descent Groups." *Anthropological Quarterly*, January (forthcoming).

Dam, W. P. van
1937   *Inlandsche Gemeente en Indonesisch Dorp.* Thesis, Leiden. Wageningen, H. Veenman.

Deacon, A. B.
1925   "The Kakihan Society of Ceram and New Guinea Initiation Cults." *Folklore*, XXXVI, 332–361.

Dewey, A. G.
1962   *Peasant Marketing in Java.* New York, Free Press of Glencoe.

Djojodigoeno, M. M. M., and R. Tirtawinata
1940   *Het Adatprivaatrecht van Middel-Java.* Soekamiskin, Dept. van Justitie.

Djoko Santoso, Ali Wardhana
1957   "Beberapa Segi Transmigrasi Spontan di Indonesia." *Ekonomi dan Keuangan Indonesia,* X, 98–115.

Does, L. P. van der
1948   "Sociaal Onderzoek in Indonesië." *Mens en Maatschappij,* XXIII, 257–279.

Dormeier, J. J.
1947   "Banggaisch Adatrecht." *VKI,* VI. The Hague, M. Nijhoff.

Downs, R. E.
1956   *The Religion of the Bare'e-Speaking Toradja of Central Celebes.* Thesis, Leiden. The Hague, Exelsior.

Drabbe, P.
1940   *Het Leven van den Tanémbarees: Ethnografische studie over het Tanémbareesche Volk.* Leiden, E. J. Brill.

Du Bois, C.
1944   *The People of Alor: A Social-psychological Study of an East Indian Island.* Minneapolis, University of Minnesota Press.

Durkheim, E., and M. Mauss
1901–1902   "De quelques formes primitives de classification: Contribution à l'étude des représentations collectives." *L'Année Sociologique,* VI, 1–72.

Duyvendak, J. P.
1926   *Het Kakean-genootschap van Seran.* Thesis, Leiden. Almelo, W. Hilarius.

Eechoud, J. P. K. van
1962   "Etnografie van de Kaowerawédj (Centraal Nieuw-Guinea)." *VKI,* XXXVII.

Eindrésumé
1876   *Van het Onderzoek naar de Rechten van den Inlander op den Grond op Java en Madoera.* Part I. Batavia, Ernst.

1880   *Van het Onderzoek naar de Rechten van den Inlander op den Grond op Java en Madoera.* Part II. Batavia, Ernst.

Elbert, J.
1911–1912   *Die Sunda-Expedition des Vereins für Geographie und Statistik zu Frankfurt am Main.* 2 v. Frankfurt am Main, H. Minjon.

Elmberg, J. E.
1955   "Field Notes on the Mejbrat People in the Ajamaru District of the Bird's Head (Vogelkop), Western New Guinea." *Ethnos*, XX, 3–102.

Engelhard, C. F.
1923   *Het Onderzoek naar de Geestesgesteldheid met Behulp van Platen, Toegepast bij den Javaan; Mededeelingen uit het Doorgangshuis voor Inlandsche Krankzinnigen te Soerakarta.* Thesis, Utrecht. Leiden, E. IJdo.

Faes, J.
1893   *Geschiedenis Particulier Landbezit op West Java.* Batavia, Ogilvie.

Firth, R.
1936   *We, the Tikopia: A Sociological Study of Kinship in Primitive Polynesia.* New York, American Book.
1946   *Malay Fishermen: Their Peasant Economy.* London, K. Paul, Trench, Trubner.

Fischer, H. T.
1936   "Het Asymmetrisch Cross-cousin-huwelijk in Nederlandsch Indië." *TBG*, LXXVI, 359–372.
1948–1949 "In Memoriam Dr. Alb. C. Kruyt." *Indonesië*, II, 481–485.

Fokkens, F.
1903   *Eindrésumé van het Onderzoek naar de Verplichte Diensten der Inlandsche Bevolking op Java en Madoera.* 3 v. The Hague, Ter Algemeene Landsdrukkerij.

Forbes, H. O.
1884   "On the Ethnology of Timor-Laut." *JAI*, XIII, 8–31.
1884a   "On Some of the Tribes of the Island of Timor," *JAI*, XIII, 402–430.
1885   *A Naturalist's Wanderings in the Eastern Archipelago: A Narrative of Travel and Exploration From 1878–1883.* New York, Harper.

Freedman, M.
1958   *Lineage Organization in Southeastern China.* London, Athlone.

Freeman, J. D.
1961   "On the Concept of the Kindred." *JAI*, XCI, 192–220.

Friedericy, H. J.
1933   "De Standen bij de Boegineezen en Makassaren." *BKI*, XC, 447–602.

Friedmann
1871   "Der Anthropophagismus der Battaer auf Sumatras Westküste." *Zeitschrift für Ethnologie*, III, 313–325.

Funke, F. W.
1958–1961   *Orang Abung, Volkstum Süd-Sumatras im Wandel.* 2 v. Leiden, E. J. Brill.
1959   *Dämmerungen über Indonesien: Streifzüge Durch Sumatra, Java, Bali, und Celebes.* Bremen, C. Schünemann.

Furnivall, J. S.
1944   *Netherlands India: A Study of Plural Economy.* Cambridge, University Press.

Geertz, C.
1956   "Religious Belief and Economic Behavior in a Central Javanese Town: Some Preliminary Considerations." *Economic Development and Cultural Change,* IV, 134–158.
1957   "Ethos, World-View, and the Analysis of Sacred Symbols." *Antioch Review,* XVII, 421–437.
1957a   "Ritual and Social Change: A Javanese Example." *AA,* LIX, 32–54.
1959   "Form and Variation in Balinese Village Structure." *AA,* LXI, 991–1012.
1959–1960   "The Javanese Kijaji: The Changing Role of a Cultural Broker." *Comparative Studies in Society and History,* II, 228–249
1960   *The Religion of Java.* Glencoe, Ill., Free Press.
1961   "Book review: Bali, Studies in Life, Thought, and Ritual." *BKI,* CXVII, 498–502.
1963   *Agricultural Involution: The Process of Ecological Change in Indonesia.* Berkeley, University of California Press.

Geertz, H.
1961   *The Javanese Family: A Study of Kinship and Socialization.* New York, Free Press of Glencoe.

Geise, N. J. C.
1952   *Badujs en Moslims in Lebak Parahiang Zuid-Banten.* Thesis, Leiden. Leiden, De Jong.

Gelderen, J. van
1927   *Voorlezingen over Tropisch-Koloniale Staathuishoudkunde.* Haarlem, H. D. Tjeenk Willink.

Geurtjens, H.
1921   "De Letterkunde van een Primitief Volk." *De Beiaard,* VI, 401–420.
1926   "Spraakleer der Marindineesche Taal." *VBG,* LXVIII. The Hague, M. Nijhoff; Batavia, Albrecht.
1928   "Associatiebegrippen bij de Marindieezen." *Mensch en Maatschappij,* IV, 233–255.

1933   "Marindineesch-Nederlandsch Woordenboek." *VBG*, LXXI. Bandung, A. C. Nix.

Goedhart, O. H.
1908   "Drie Landschappen in Celebes (Banggai, Boengkoe, en Mori)." *TBG*, L, 442–548.

Goethals, P. R.
1959   "Task Groups and Marriage in Western Sumbawa. Intermediate Societies, Social Mobility, and Communication." *Proceedings of the American Ethnological Society*, Verne Ray, editor, pp. 45–59. Seattle, University of Washington Press.
1960   *Kindred and Community in Upland West Sumbawa*. [Unpublished manuscript.]
1961   *Aspects of Local Government in a Sumbawan Village (Eastern Indonesia)*. Ithaca, N.Y., Cornell University Southeast Asia Program, Modern Indonesia Project Monograph Series.

Gonggrijp, G.
1919   "Koloniale en Theoretische Economie." *KT*, VIII, 1446–1461.

Goslings, B. M.
1938   *De Wajang op Java en op Bali in het Verleden en het Heden*. Amsterdam, J. M. Meulenhoff.

Graafland, N.
1867–1869 *De Minahasa: Haar Verleden en haar Tegenwoordige Toestand (Eene Bijdrage tot de Land- en Volkenkunde)*. 2 v. Rotterdam, M. Wijt.

Grabowsky, F.
1888   "Ueber Weniger Bekannte Opfergebräuche bei den Oloh Ngadju in Borneo." *IAE*, I, 130–134.
1889   "Der Tod, das Begräbnis, das Tiwah oder Todtenfest und Ideën über das Jenseits bei den Dajaken." *IAE*, II, 177–204.
1889a   "Ueber Äusserungen Geistigen Lebens bei den Olo Ngadju in Süd-Ost Borneo." *BKI*, XXXVIII, 144–152.
1892   "Die Theogenie der Dajaken auf Borneo." *IAE*, V, 116–133.

Groeneveldt, W. P.
1960   *Historical Notes on Indonesia & Malaya Compiled from Chinese Sources*. Djakarta, C. V. Bharata. (This work was originally published in 1880 in *VBG*, XXXIX, 1–144.)

Haar, B. ter
1915   *Het Adatproces der Inlanders*. Amsterdam, A. H. Kruyt.
1929   "Aankondiging. De Ontdekking van het Adatrecht door Mr. C. van Vollenhoven . . . ." *ITR*, CXXIX, 241–242.

1937   *Het Adatprivaatrecht van Nederlandsch-Indië in Wetenschap, Practijk, en Onderwijs.* Lecture . . . Groningen. Batavia, J. B. Wolters.

1941   "De Betekenis van de Tegenstelling Participerend-Kritisch Denken en de Rechtspraak naar Adatrecht." *MKAWAL,* new series, IV, 567–590.

1948   *Adat Law in Indonesia.* Translated from the Dutch and edited with an introduction by E. A. Hoebel and A. A. Schiller. New York, Institute of Pacific Relations.

1950   *Beginselen en Stelsel van het Adatrecht.* Groningen and Djakarta, J. B. Wolters.

Haga, B. J.

1924   *Indonesische en Indische Democratie.* Thesis, Leiden. The Hague, Handelsdrukkerij "De Ster."

1928   "Erkenning van Hoogere Inlandsche Verbanden." *KS,* XII, 344–372.

Hagen, B.

1892   *Beiträge zur Kenntniss der Battareligion.* Batavia, W. Bunning.

Harthoorn, S. E.

1857   "Iets over den Javaanschen Mohammedaan en den Javaanschen Christen." *MNZ,* I, 183–212.

Hasselt, J. L. van

1885   "The Object and Results of a Dutch Expedition into the Interior of Sumatra in the Years 1877, 1878, and 1879." *JRASSB,* XV, 39–59.

1889   "Eenige Aanteekeningen Aangaande de Bewoners der N. Westkust van Nieuw Guinea, Meer Bepaaldelijk den Stam der Noefooreezen." *TBG,* XXXII, 261–272.

Hazairin

1936   *De Redjang; de Volksordening, het Verwantschaps-, Huwelijks- en Erfrecht.* Bandung, A. C. Nix.

Hazeu, G. A. J.

1897   *Bijdrage tot de Kennis van het Javaansche Tooneel.* Leiden.

Heeckeren, C. W. van

1901   *Beschouwingen over het voor Chineezen op Java Geldende Recht.* Semarang and Soerabaja, G. C. T. van Dorp.

H[ekmeyer], F. C.

1909   "Het Rechtsleven bij de Minangkabausche Maleiers door Mr. G. D. Willinck." *De Indische Gids,* XXXI, 989–992.

Held, G. J.

1947   *Papoea's van Waropen.* Leiden, E. J. Brill.

1953   "Applied Anthropology in Government: The Netherlands." *Anthropology Today*, edited by A. L. Kroeber, pp. 866–879. Chicago, University of Chicago Press.

Heyting, H. G.

1938   "De Les van Wortelvast Gĕdongtatakan (Javanen-Kolonisatie)." *De Indische Gids*, LX, 1106–1117.

Hidding, K. A. H.

1929   *Nji Pohatji Sangjang Sri.* Thesis, Leiden. Leiden, M. Dubbeldeman.

1931   "De Beteekenis van de Kekajon." *TBG*, LXXI, 623–662.

1935   *Gebruiken en Godsdienst der Soendaneezen.* Batavia, G. Kolff.

Higgins, B.

1954   "Economic Development of Underdeveloped Areas: Past and Present." *Ekonomi dan Keuangan Indonesia*, VII, 778–799.

1955   "The 'Dualistic Theory' of Underdeveloped Areas." *Ekonomi dan Keuangan Indonesia*, VIII, 58–78. (Reprinted in *Economic Development and Cultural Change*, IV, 1955, 99–115.)

Hoëvell, W. R., Baron van

1849   "De Uitbreiding van het Hooger Onderwijs in de Oostersche Talen aan de Nederlandsche Akademiën." *TNI*, XI, 2, 68–78.

Hoeven, J. van der

1950   *Verslag van een Mislukte Toernee naar de Mamberamo, 2–16 December.* [Mimeographed report.]

Hogbin, H. Ian, and C. H. Wedgwood

1953   "Local Grouping in Melanesia." *Oceania*, XXIII, 241–276; XXIV, 58–76.

Holleman, F. D.

1923   *Het Adatgrondenrecht van Ambon en de Oeliasers.* Delft, Molukken Instituut.

1935   *De Commune Trek in het Indonesisch Rechtsleven.* Lecture, Groningen and Batavia, J. B. Wolters.

1938   "Het Adatprivaatrecht van Nederlands-Indië in Wetenschap, Praktijk en Onderwijs. Rede door Mr. B. ter Haar Bzn. op 28 October 1937." *ITR*, CXLVII, 428–440.

Hoselitz, B. F.

1963   "Role of Incentives in Industrialization." *Economic Weekly*, XV, 1237–1242.

Hoven, W.

1927   *De Pasĕmah en Haar Verwantschaps-, Huwelijks- en Erfrecht.* Wageningen, H. Veenman.

418 *Bibliography*

Hupe, C.
1846   "Korte Verhandeling over de Godsdienst, Zeden, enz. der Dajakkers." *TNI*, VIII, 3, 127–172, 245–280.

Inggris
1921   "Volksgewoonten in Bagelen." *Djawa*, I, 89–91.

Ismaël, J. E.
1960   "Keadaan Penduduk di Duapuluhtiga Desa di Djawa." *Ekonomi*, II, 197–223.

James, K. A.
1915   "De Nagari Kota Gedang." *Tijdschrift voor het Binnenlandsch Bestuur*, XLIX, 185–195

Jay, R. R.
1956   "Local Government in Rural Central Java." *Far Eastern Quarterly*, XV, 215–227.

Jensen, A. E.
1948   *Die Drei Ströme: Züge aus dem Geistigen und Religiösen Leben der Wemale, einem Primitiv-Volk in den Molukken.* Ergebnisse der Frobenius-Expedition 1937–1938 in die Molukken und nach Holländisch Neu-Guinea, vol. 2. Leipzig, Otto Harrassowitz.

Jensen, A. E., and H. Niggemeyer
1939   *Hainuwele: Volkserzählungen von der Molukken-Insel Ceram.* Ergebnisse der Frobenius-Expedition 1937–1938 in die Molukken und nach Holländisch Neu-Guinea, vol. 1. Frankfurt am Main, Vittorio Klostermann.

Josselin de Jong, J. P. B. de
1929   "De Oorsprong van den Goddelijken Bedrieger." *MKAWAL*, LXVIII, B, 1–29

1935   *De Maleische Archipel als Ethnologisch Studieveld.* Leiden, J. Ginsberg.

1948   *Customary Law, A Confusing Fiction.* Amsterdam, Indisch Instituut.

Josselin de Jong, P. E. de
1951   *Minangkabau and Negri Sembilan: Sociopolitical Structure in Indonesia.* Thesis, Leiden, E. IJdo.

Joustra, M.
1924   *Overzicht der Litteratuur Betreffende Minangkabau.* Amsterdam, Minangkabau Instituut.

1926   *Batakspiegel.* Leiden, Bataksch Instituut.

1936   *Overzicht der Litteratuur Betreffende Minangkabau 1929–1936.* Amsterdam, Minangkabau Instituut.

Bibliography

419

Kähler, H.

1960 *Ethnographische und Linguistische Studien über die Orang Darat, Orang Akit, Orang Laut, und Orang Utan im Riau-Archipel und auf den Inseln an der Ostküste von Sumatra.* 2 v. Berlin, D. Reimer.

Kampto Utomo

1957 *Masjarakat Transmigran Spontan Didaerah W. Sekampung (Lampung).* Djakarta, Penerbitan Universitas.

1958 "Daerah Metro, Lampung, Sumatra Selatan: Transmigrasi Pertanian Dengan Pola Persawahan." (Lembaran Kerdja diutjapkan pada Kongres Ilmu Pengetahuan Nasional I, Malang).

Karstel, H. R.

1956 *Toernee Rapport naar Enige Agathis Complexen in het Mamberamo Gebied van 16 November–18 December, 1956.* [Mimeographed report.]

Kat Angelino, A. D. A. de

1931 *Staatkundig Beleid en Bestuurszorg in Nederlandsch-Indië.* 3 v. The Hague, M. Nijhoff. (Cf. abridged English edition, *Colonial Policy*, 2 v., Amsterdam and Chicago.

Kaudern, W.

1925–1944 *Ethnographical Studies in Celebes.* 6 v. The Hague, M. Nijhoff.

Kennedy, R.

1955 *Bibliography of Indonesian Peoples and Cultures.* Revised edition edited by T. W. Maretzki and H. T. Fischer. 2 v. New Haven, Human Relations Area Files.

Kindern, T. H. der

1892 "Levensbericht van Dr. G. A. Wilken." *BKI,* XLI, 139–156.

Kits van Heyningen, A.

1925 *Westersche Intellectproeven en Primitieve Psyche.* Thesis, Leiden. Leiden, E. IJdo.

Koentjaraningrat

1958 "Perbandingan Faham 'Rechtskring' dan Faham 'Culture Area.'" *Padjadjaran, Madjalah Ilmu Hukum dan Pengetahuan Masjarakat,* I, 2, 35–42.

1961 *Some Social-Anthropological Observations on Gotong Rojong Practices in Two Villages of Central Java.* Ithaca, Cornell University, Modern Indonesia Project Monograph Series.

1964 "Additional Information on the Kénthol of South Central Java." *Madjalah Ilmu-Ilmu Sastra Indonesia,* II, 17–24.

Koes Sardjono

1947 *De Botjah-Angon (Herdersjongen) in de Javaanse Cultuur.* Leiden. [Mimeographed manuscript.]

Korn, V. E.

1924   *Het Adatrecht van Bali*. The Hague, M. Nijhoff.

1933   *De Dorpsrepubliek Tnganan Pagringsingan*. Santpoort, C. A.
           Mees.

Krieger, M.

1899   *Neu Guinea*. Mit Beiträge von A. von Danckelman, F. von
           Luschan v.a. Berlin, Bibliothek der Länderkunde, 5–6.

Kruyt, A. C.

1906   *Het Animisme in den Indischen Archipel*. The Hague, M.
           Nijhoff.

1918–1920 "Measa, eene Bijdrage tot het Dynamisme der Bare'e-spre-
           kende Toradja's en Enkele Omwonende Volken." *BKI*, LXXIV,
           233–260; LXXV, 36–133; LXXVI, 1–116.

1921   "Verslag van eene Reis over het Eiland Soemba." *TNAG*,
           XXXVIII, 513–553.

1921a   "Verlag van een Reis door Timor." *TNAG*, XXXVIII, 769–807.

1921b   "De Roteneezen." *TBG*, LX, 266–344.

1922   "De Soembaneezen." *BKI*, LXXVIII, 466–608.

1923   "De Timoreezen." *BKI*, LXXIX, 347–490.

1923a   "De Mentawaiers." *TBG*, LXII, 1–188.

1923b   "Koopen in Midden Celebes." *MKAWAL*, LVI, Series B, 149–
           178.

1924   "Een Bezoek aan de Mentawei-eilanden." *TNAG*, XLI, 19–49.

1930   "De To Wana op Oost-Celebes." *TBG*, LXX, 397–627.

1937   "Het Leggen van een Knoop in Indonesië." *MKAWAL*,
           LXXXIV, Series B, 147–166.

1938   *De West-Toradjas op Midden Celebes*. (*VKAWAL*, Nieuwe
           Reeks, XL.) 4 v. Amsterdam, Noord-hollandsche Uitgevers-
           Maatschappij.

Kuperus, G.

1936   *Het Cultuurlandschap van West-Soembawa*. Groningen and Ba-
           tavia, J. B. Wolters.

1937   "Tot Welken Adatrechtskring Dient West-Soembawa Gere-
           kend te Worden?" *KT*, XXVI, 605–611.

Leach, E. R.

1951   "The Structural Implications of Matrilateral Cross-cousin Mar-
           riage." *JAI*, LXXXI, 23–55.

Leeden, A. C. van der

1956   *Hoofdtrekken der Sociale Struktuur in het Westelijke Binnen-
           land van Sarmi*. Leiden, E. IJdo.

Leeden, C. van der
1952   *Het Aspect van Landbouwkolonisatie in het Bevolkingsprobleem van Java.* Thesis, Leiden. The Hague, Excelsiors Foto.

Legge, J. D.
1961   *Central Authority and Regional Autonomy in Indonesia: A Study in Local Administration, 1950–1960.* Ithaca, Cornell University Press.

Le Roux, C. C. F. M.
1926   "Expeditie naar het Nassau-Gebergte in Centraal Noord Nieuw Guinee." *TBG*, LXVI, 447–513.
1928   "De Elcano's Tocht door den Timor-archipel met Magelhães' Schip 'Victoria.' " *Feestbundel Uitgegeven door het Koninklijk Bataviaasch Genootschap van Kunsten en Wetenschappen bij Gelegenheid van zijn 150 Jarig Bestaan,* II, pp. 1–99. Weltevreden, G. Kolff.
1935   "De Exploratie." *Nieuw Guinea,* I, 18–154. Amsterdam, J. H. de Bussy.

Leur, J. C. van
1932   "De Opleiding der Indische Bestuursambtenaren." *KT*, XXI, 577–585.

Lobach, L. A. L. M.
1951   *Streekbeschrijving Landschap Amarasi Timor en Eilanden.* Kantor Perantjang Tata Bumi. Bogor [unpublished]. The Indonesian translation *Rentjana Daerah Wilajah Amarasi (Timor)*, Bogor, 1954 [unpublished], is complete but has numerous typographical errors.

Loeb, E. M.
1928   "Mentawei Social Organization." *AA*, XXX, 408–433.
1929   "Mentawei Religious Cult." *University of California Publications in American Archaeology and Ethnology*, XXV, 185–247.
1929a   "Mentawei Myths." *BKI*, LXXXV, 66–244.
1933   "Die Soziale Organization Indonesiens und Ozeaniens." *Anthropos*, XXVIII, 649–662.
1933–1934 "Patrilineal and Matrilineal Organization in Sumatra: The Batak and the Minangkabau." *AA*, XXXV, 16–50; XXXVI, 26–56.

Logemann, J. H. A.
1938   "Om de Taak van den Rechter." *ITR*, CXLVIII, 27–42.

Maass, A.
1910–1912 *Durch Zentral-Sumatra.* 2 v. Berlin, Wilhelm Süsserott.

Maclaine Pont, H.
1924   "Javaansche Architectuur." *Djawa*, IV, 44–73.

Madjelis Permusjawaratan Rakjat Sementara, Republik Indonesia

1961   *Ringkasan Ketetapan Madjelis Permusjawaratan Rakat Sementara, Republik Indonesia.* Djakarta, Departemen Penerangan.

Malinowski, B.

1948   *Magic, Science and Religion, and Other Essays.* Garden City, N. Y., Doubleday.

Mallinckrodt, J.

1927   "De Stamindeeling van de Maanjan-Sioeng-Dajaks, der Zuider- en Ooster-Afdeeling van Borneo." *BKI*, LXXXIII, 552–573.

1928   *Het Adatrecht van Borneo.* 2 v. Leiden, M. Dubbeldeman.

Marsden, W.

1783   *The History of Sumatra: Containing an Account of the Government, Laws, Customs, and Manners of the Native Inhabitants.* London, Thomas Payne.

1838   *A Brief Memoir of the Life and Writings of the Late William Marsden, Written by Himself* . . . . London, J. L. Lox.

Mayer, L. T.

1893   "Vier Javaansche Legenden Uit de Residentie Madioen." *BKI*, XLII, 41–70.

1894   *De Javaan, als Mensch en als Lid van het Javaansche Huisgezin.* Batavia and Solo, Albrecht & Rusche.

1894a   *Javaansche Legenden en Sagen.* Batavia and Solo; Albrecht & Rusche.

1894b   *Javaansch-Hollandsche Samenspraken.* Batavia.

1897   *Een Blik in het Javaansche Volksleven.* 2 v. Leiden, E. J. Brill.

1898   *De Javaan als Landbouwer en Veefokker.* Batavia, Albrecht.

1918   *De Javaan als Doekoen. Een Ethnographische Bijdrage.* Weltevreden.

Mead, M. (editor)

1937   *Cooperation and Competition among Primitive Peoples.* New York and London, McGraw-Hill.

Meerwaldt, J. H.

1892   "Wijzen de Tegenwoordige Zeden en Gewoonten der Bataks nog Sporen aan van een Oorspronkelijk Matriarchaat?" *BKI*, XLI, 197–207.

Meijer Ranneft, J. W.

1919   "Grondslagen en Voorwaarden voor de Hervorming van de Desa." *KS*, III, 1–42.

Middelkoop, P.

1949   "Een Studie van het Timoreesche Doodenritueel." *VBG*, LXXVI. Bandung, A. C. Nix.

1950   "Proeve van een Timorese Grammatica." *BKI*, CVI, 375–517.
1958   "Adat-marriage for Christians on the Island of Timur." *Madjalah untuk Ilmu Bahasa, Ilmu Bumi dan Kebudajaan Indonesia,* LXXXVI, 538–557.

Moore, F. W. (editor)
1961   *Readings in Cross-Cultural Methodology.* New Haven, Human Relations Area File Press.

Moszkowski, M.
1911   "Die Völkerstämme am Mamberamo in Holländsch-Neuguinea und auf den Vorgelargerten Inseln." *Zeitschrift für Ethnologie,* XLIII, 315–346.

Murdock, G. P.
1949   *Social Structure.* New York, Macmillan.
1960   "Cognatic Forms of Social Organization." *Social Structure in South East Asia,* pp. 1–14. G. P. Murdock editor. New York, Wenner-Gren Foundation (Viking Fund Publications in Anthropology, XXIX).

Nat, J.
1929   *De Studie van de Oostersche Talen in Nederland in de 18e en 19e Eeuw.* Amsterdam and Purmerend, J. Manusses.

Needham, R.
1954   "A Penan Mourning-Usage." *BKI*, CX, 263–267.
1954a   "Reference to the Dead Among the Penan." *Man,* LIV, 10.
1954b   "The Systems of Teknonyms and Death-names of the Penan." *Southwestern Journal of Anthropology,* X, 416–431.
1955   "A Note on Some Murut Kinship Terms." *JRASMB,* XXVIII, 159–162.
1956   "A Note on Kinship and Marriage on Pantara." *BKI*, CXII, 285–290.
1957   "Circulating Connubium in Eastern Sumba: A Literary Analysis." *BKI*, CXIII, 168–178.
1957a   "Kodi Fables." *BKI*, CXIII, 361–379.
1958   "A Structural Analysis of Purum Society." *AA,* LX, 75–101.
1960   "Jātaka, Pañcatantra, and Kodi Fables." *BKI*, CXVI, 232–262.

Nicolspeyer, M. M.
1940   *De Sociale Structuur van een Aloreesche Bevolkingsgroep.* Thesis, Leiden. Rijswijk, V. A. Kramers.

Niemann, G. K.
1870   "Bijdrage tot de Kennis van den Godsdienst der Bataks." *TNI*, 3rd series, IV, 1, 288–307.

Nieuwenhuis, A. W.

1898   "La récente expédition scientifique dans l'île de Bornéo." *TBG.* XL, 508–541.

1900   *In Centraal Borneo.* 2 v. Leiden, E. J. Brill.

1904–1907 *Quer Durch Borneo.* 2 v. Leiden, E. J. Brill.

1913   "Die Veranlagung der Malaiischen Völker der Ost-Indischen Archipels, Erläutert an Ihren Industriellen Erzeugnissen." *IAE,* XXI, supplement.

Nieuwenhuyzen, T.

1932   *Sasaksch Adatrecht.* Leiden, E. J. Brill.

Nooteboom, C.

1940   *Oost-Soemba: Een Volkenkundige Studie.* The Hague, M. Nijhoff.

O'Brien, J. L.

1906–1907 "Rapport Omtrent de Tegenwoordige Politieke en Economische Verhoudingen en Toestanden in de Kampar-Kiri-Landen." *TNAG,* XXIII, 939–995; XXIV, 57–62.

Oosterwal, G.

1959   "The Position of the Bachelor in the Upper Tor Territory." *AA,* LXVI, 829–838.

1961   *People of the Tor; A Cultural-Anthropological Study on the Tribes of the Tor Territory, Northern Netherlands New-Guinea.* Assen, Royal van Gorcum.

1963   "A Cargo Cult in the Mamberamo Area." *Ethnology,* II, 1–14.

Ormeling, F. J.

1956   *The Timor Problem.* Groningen and Djakarta, J. B. Wolters.

Ossenbruggen, F. D. E. van

1911   "Eigenaardige Gebruiken bij Pokkenepidemieën in den Indischen Archipel." *BKI,* LXV, 53–87.

1911a   *Mr. G. D. Willinck Over Wijlen Professor Dr. G. A. Wilken.* The Hague, G. C. T. van Dorp.

1916   "Het Primitieve Denken, Zooals dit zich Uit Voornamelijk in Pokkengebruiken op Java en Elders." *BKI,* LXXI, 1–370.

1918   "De Oorsprong van het Javaansche Begrip, Montja-pat, in Verband met Primitieve Classificaties." *MKAWAL,* series V, III, 6–44.

1926   "Het Magisch Denken van den Inlander." *De Indische Gids,* XLVIII, 289–303.

1935   "Het Oeconomisch-magisch Element in Tobasche Verwantschapsverhoudingen." *MKAWAL,* LXXX, series B, 63–125.

Paine, R.

1960   "Emergence of the Village as a Social Unit in a Coast Lappish Fjord." *AA,* LXII, 1005–1017.

Palmier, L. H.
1960   *Social Status and Power in Java.* London, Athlone (London School of Economics: Monographs on Social Anthropology, no. 20).

Pelzer, K.
1945   *Pioneer Settlement in the Asiatic Tropics; Studies in Land Utilization and Agricultural Colonization in Southeastern Asia.* New York, American Geographical Society.

Pigeaud, T.
1927   "Alexander, Sakènḍèr en Sénapati." *Djawa*, VII, 321–361.
1938   *Javaanse Volksvertoningen, Bijdragen tot de Beschrijving van Land en Volk.* Batavia, Volkslectuur.
1949–1950 "Bibliografie in Indonesië," *Indonesië*, III, 124–129.

Pijnappel Gz., J.
1859   *De Koninklijke Akademie te Delft, Als Inrigting tot Opleiding voor Indische Ambtenaren* . . . . Amsterdam, F. Muller.
1863   *Drie Stellingen over de Opleiding der Indische Ambtenaren.* The Hague, M. Nijhoff.
1868   *De Rijksinstelling van Onderwijs in Indische Taal-, Land-, en Volkenkunde te Leiden en de Hoogeschool.* The Hague, M. Nijhoff.

Poel, A. van der
1846   "Oorsprong van den Naam Bagelen en het Aldaar Gevestigd Geslacht der Kentols." *TNI*, VIII, 3, 173–180.

Poensen, C.
1864–1865 "Een en Ander Over de Godsdienstigen Toestand van den Javaan." *MNZ*, VIII, 214–263; IX, 161–204.
1870   "Iets over Javaansche Naamgeving en Eigennamen." *MNZ*, XIV, 304–321.
1873   "De Wajang." *MNZ*, XVI, 59–116, 204–222, 233–280, 353–367; XVII, 138–164.
1875   "Javaansche Woningen en Erven." *MNZ*, XIX, 101–146.
1876–1877 "Iets over de Kleeding der Javanen." *MNZ*, XX, 257–299, 377–420; XXI, 1–21.

Poerbatjaraka, R. Ng.
1938   "De Geheime Leer van Soenan Bonang (Soeloek Woedjil). Inleiding, Tekst, Vertaling en Toelichting." *Djawa*, XVIII, 145–181.

Pospisil, L.
1958   *Kapauku Papuans and Their Law.* New Haven, Dept. of Anthropology, Yale University.
1958a   "Social Change and Primitive Law: Consequences of a Papuan Legal Case." *AA*, LX, 832–837.

Pranahadikoesoema, S.
1939   "De Kéntol der Desa Kréndétan." *Djawa*, XIX, 153–160.
Radjab, M.
1950   *Semasa Ketjil Dikampung (1913–1928)*. Djakarta, Balai Pustaka.
Raka, I. Gusti Gde
1955   *Monografi Pulau Bali*. Djakarta, Pusat Djawatan Pertanian Rakjat.
Rassers, W. H.
1922   *De Pandji-roman*. Thesis, Leiden. Antwerp, D. de Vos-Van Kleef.
1925   "Over de Zin van het Javaansche Drama." *BKI*, LXXXI, 311–381.
1926   "Çiwa en Boeddha in den Indischen Archipel." *Gedenkschrift uitgegeven ter gelegenheid van het 75-jarig bestaan van het Koninklijk Instituut voor de Taal-, Land- en Volkenkunde van Nederlandsch-Indië*, pp. 222–253. The Hague, M. Nijhoff.
1931   "Over den Oorsprong van het Javaansche Tooneel." *BKI*, LXXXVIII, 317–450.
1940   "On the Javanese Kris." *BKI*, XCIX, 501–582.
Redfield, R.
1956   *Peasant Society and Culture*. Chicago, University of Chicago Press.
Riedel, J. G. F.
1886   *De Sluik- en Kroesharige Rassen Tusschen Selebes en Papua*. The Hague, M. Nijhoff.
Röder, J.
1940   "Die Leo-Frobenius-Expedition, I." *Ethnologische Anzeiger*, LIV, 306–318.
1948   *Alahatala: Die Religion der Inlandstämme Mittelcerams*. Bamberg, Meisenbach.
Roo van Alderwerelt, J. de
1906   "Historische Aanteekeningen over Soemba." *TBG*, XLVIII, 185–316.
Rosenberg, C. B. H. von
1878   *Der Malayische Archipel* . . . . Leipzig, G. Weigel.
Rouffaer, G. P.
1907   "Alb. C. Kruyt. Het Animisme in de Indischen Archipel . . . ." *TNAG*, XXIV, 266–271.
Royen, J. W. van
1927   *De Palembangsche Marga en Haar Grond- en Waterrechten*. Leiden, G. L. van den Berg.
1932   "De Verdwijning der Lampoengsche Margas. 1855–1913." *KT*, XXI, 171–200.

Sadli, M.

1957   "Some Reflections on Prof. Boeke's Theory of Dualistic Economies." *Ekonomi dan Keuangan Indonesia,* X, 363–383.

Salim, Emil, Sjarief Samsudin, Isbodjroini Suwarno, Retno Astuti

1959   *Kehidupan Desa di Indonesia. Suatu Case Study daripada 23 Desa di Djawa.* Dajakarta, Lembaga Penjelidikan Ekonomi dan Masjarakat, Fakultas Ekonomi, Universitas Indonesia, No. 12A [mimeographed].

Sarasin, F. and P.

1905   *Reisen in Celebes. Ausgeführt in den Jahren 1893–1896 und 1902–1903.* 2 v. Wiesbaden, C. W. Kreidel.

Sarkar, H. B.

1934   *Indian Influences on the Literature of Java and Bali.* Calcutta, Greater India Society.

Sastra Amidjaja

1924   "Het Bouwen van Javaansche Huizen." *Djawa,* IV, 105–113.

Schadee, M. C.

1903–1908 "Bijdrage tot de Kennis van den Godsdienst der Dajaks van Landak en Tajan." *BKI,* LV, 321–344; LVI, 532–547; LVIII, 489–513; LIX, 207–228, 616–647; LX, 101–127.

Schärer, H.

1946   *Die Gottesidee der Ngadju Dajak in Süd-Borneo.* Leiden, E. J. Brill.

Scheltema, A. M. P. A.

1923   *Ontleding van het Inlandsch Landbouwbedrijf.* Batavia, Dept. van Landbouw; pp. 1–176. (Mededeelingen van de Afdeeling Landbouw, no. 6.)

1931   *Deelbouw in Nederlandsch-Indië.* Wageningen, H. Veenman.

Schilfgaarde, P. van

1925   "De Psyche van den Javaan." *Djawa,* V, 86–130.

Schmidt, W.

1910   *Grundlinien einer Vergleichung der Religionen und Mythologien der Austronesischen Völker.* Denkschriften der Kaiserlichen Akademie der Wissenschaften in Wien, LIII. Vienna, Alfred Hölden.

1929   "Der Pandji-Roman und die Austronesische Mythologien." *Feestbundel van het Koninklijk Bataviaasch Genootschap van Kunsten en Wetenschappen. Bij Gelegenheid van zijn 150 Jarig Bestaan, 1778–1928,* pp. 353–369. Weltevreden, G. Kolff.

Schrieke, B. J. O.

1921   "Some Remarks on Circumcision in Dutch-India." *TBG,* LX, 376–507.

428   *Bibliography*

1929   *The Effect of Western Influence on Native Civilisations in the Malay Archipelago.* Batavia, G. Kolff.

1957   *Indonesian Sociological Studies: Selected Writings.* 2 v. The Hague and Bandung, W. van Hoeve.

Schrieke, J. J.
1921   *De Lagere Inlandsche Rechtsgemeenschappen in Nederlandsch Indië.* Weltevreden, Commissie voor de Volkslectuur.

Schröder, E. E. W. G.
1917   *Nias: Ethnographische, Geographische en Historische Aanteekeningen en Studiën,* 2 v. Leiden, E. J. Brill.

Schwaner, C. A. L. M.
1853–1854 *Borneo: Beschrijving van het Stroomgebied van den Barito en Reizen Langs Eenige Voorname Rivieren van het Z. O. Gedeelte van dat Eiland . . . .* 2. v. Amsterdam, P. N. van Kampen.

Schwartz, H. J. E. F.
1893   "Nota over den Politieken en Economischen Toestand van het Landschap Kwantan." *TBG,* XXXVI, 325–342.

Selosoemardjan
1962   *Pembangunan Masjarakat di Desa.* Djakarta, Lembaga Penjelidikan Ekonomi dan Masjarakat, Universitas Indonesia.

1962a   *Social Changes in Jogjakarta.* Ithaca, Cornell University Press.

1963   *The Dynamics of Community Development in Rural Central and West Java: A Comparative Report.* Ithaca, Cornell University, Modern Indonesia Project.

Sirks, M. J.
1915   *Indisch Natuuronderzoek.* Thesis, Utrecht. Amsterdam, Koloniaal Instituut.

Skinner, G. W. (editor)
1959   *Local, Ethnic, and National Loyalties in Village Indonesia: A Symposium.* New Haven, Yale University Southeast Asia Studies.

Slamet, I. E.
1963   *Pokok2 Pembangunan Masjarakat Desa (Sebuah Pandangan Anthropologi Budaja).* Djakarta, Bhratara.

Snouck Hurgronje, C.
1888–1889 *Mekka.* 2 v. The Hague, M. Nijhoff.

1893–1894 *De Atjèhers.* 2 v. Batavia, Landsdrukkerij. (Translated into English 1906: *The Achehnese,* 2 v., Leiden, E. J. Brill.)

1903   *Het Gajoland en Zijne Bewoners.* Batavia, Landsdrukkerij.

1924   "De Opleiding van Ambtenaren voor den Administratieven Dienst in Nederlandsch-Indië." *Verspreide Geschriften,* IV, 2, pp. 51–76. Bonn and Leipzig, K. Schroeder.

Soebroto
1925   *Indonesische Sawah-Verpanding.* Thesis, Leiden. The Hague.
Soedjito Sastrodihardjo
1959   *A Sectarian Group in Java, with Reference to a Midland
          Village: A Study in the Sociology of Religion.* London. [Un-
          published M.A. thesis.]
Soekanto
1933   *Het Gewas in Indonesië Religieus-Adatrechtelijk Beschouwd.*
          Leiden, M. Dubbeldeman.
Soekasno
1941   "Credietverhoudingen op een Langpongs Kolonisatie Terrein."
          Volkscredietwezen, XXIX, 463–496.
Soenarjo Dipodiningrat
1954   *Proces Demokratiseering dan Otonimiseering Pemerintahan di
          Daerah Istimewa Jocjakarta.* Jogjakarta.
Soepomo, R.
1933   *Het Adat Privaatrecht van West-Java.* Soekamiskin, Dept. van
          Justitie.
Soetardjo Kartohadikoesoemo
1953   *Desa.* Jogjakarta.
Stöhr, W.
1959   *Das Totenritual der Dajak.* Cologne, E. J. Brill. (*Ethnologica,*
          I.)
Stoppelaar, J. W. de
1927   *Blambangansch Adatrecht.* Wageningen, H. Veenman.
Stutterheim, W. F.
1925   *Rāma-Legenden und Rāma-Reliefs in Indonesien.* 2 v. Munich,
          G. Müller.
Sukarno
1947   *Lahirnja Pantjasila.* Djakarta, P. T. Grafica.
1959   *Manifesto Politik Republik Indonesia, 17 Agustus 1959.* Djakarta,
          Penerbitan Chusus Departemen Penerangan R. I., 76.
Sundermann, H.
1899   "Die 'olon Maanjan' und die Missionsarbeit unter denselben."
          Allgemeine Missionszeitschrift, XXVI, 464–478, 531–536.
Tamboen, P.
1952   *Adat-Istiadat Karo.* Djakarta, Balai Pustaka.
Teffer, M.
1860   "Eene Bijzondere Soort van Afgoderij op Boâno." *MNZ,* IV,
          77–83.
The Liang Gie
1958   *Pemerintahan Daerah di Indonesia.* Djakarta, Djambatan.

430   *Bibliography*

Thenu, A., and J. M. Kröschell

1958   *Verslag van een Mamberamo-toernee, 14 Maart–29 April, 1958.* [Mimeographed report.]

Thomas, W. L. and A. M. Pikelis, ed.

1953   *International Directory of Anthropological Institutions.* New York, Wenner-Gren Foundation.

Tjan Tjoe Siem

1941   "Javaansche Kaartspelen: Bijdragen tot de Beschrijving van Land en Volk." *VBG,* LXXV, 1.

Toorn, J. L. van der

1881   "Aanteekeningen uit het Familieleven bij den Maleier in de Padangsche Bovenlanden." *TBG,* XXVI, 205–233, 514–528.

1890   "Het Animisme bij den Minangkabauer der Padangsche Bovenlanden." *BKI,* XXXIX, 48–104.

Tylor, E. B.

1899   "Remarks on Totemism, with Especial Reference to Some Modern Theories Respecting It." *JAI,* XXVIII, 138–148.

Ukur, F.

1960   *Tuaiannja Sungguh Banjak.* Bandjarmasin, Geredja Kalimantan Evangelis.

Veer, W. de

1904   *Particuliere Landerijen en de Openbare Veiligheid in de Residentie Batavia.* Batavia, Javasche Boekhandel.

Vergouwen, J. C.

1933   *Het Rechtsleven der Toba-Bataks.* The Hague, M. Nijhoff.

Verheijen, J. A. J.

1951   *Het Hoogste Wezen bij de Manggaraiers.* Wien-Mödling, St. Gabriel.

Verkerk Pistorius, A. W. P.

1869   "Het Maleische Dorp." *TNI,* 3rd series, III, 2, 97–119.

Verstappen, H. T.

1956   *Dasar Fisiografis dari Transmigrasi di Sumatra Selatan.* Djakarta, Balai Geografi (Djawatan Topografi A. D., Publ. 6).

Veth, P. J.

1881–1892 *Midden Sumatra. Reizen en Onderzoekingen der Sumatra-expeditie Uitgerust door het Aardrijkskundig Genootschap, 1877–1879, Beschreven door de Leden der Expeditie, onder Toezicht van P. J. Veth.,* 4 v. Leiden, E. J. Brill.

Vierkandt, A.

1898   *Natürvölker und Kulturvölker.*

1907   "Die Anfänge der Religion und Zauberei." *Globus,* XCII, 21–25, 61–65.

Vollenhoven, C. van

1909   *Miskenningen van het Adatrecht, Vier Voordrachten aan de Nederlandsch-Indische Bestuursacademie.* Leiden, E. J. Brill.

1906–1933 *Het Adatrecht van Nederlandsch-Indië.* 3 v. Leiden, E. J. Brill.

1917   *Het Onbaatzuchtige in Recht en Staat.* Rectorale Oratie . . . der Leidsche Universiteit. Leiden.

1919   *De Indonesiër en Zijn Grond.* Leiden, E. J. Brill.

1928   *De Ontdekking van het Adatrecht.* Leiden, E. J. Brill.

1933   "Taalfamilies en Rechtsfamilies." *Het Adatrecht van Nederlandsch-Indië,* III: pp. 569–576. Leiden, E. J. Brill.

Vroklage, B. A. G.

1936   *Die Sozialen Verhältnisse Indonesiens: Eine Kulturgeschichtliche Untersuchung.* vol. 1: *Borneo, Celebes, und Molukken.* Munich, Aschendorff.

1949   *Primitieve Mentaliteit en Zondebesef bij de Beloenezen en Enige Andere Volken.* Roermond, J. J. Romen.

Wallace, A. R.

1869   *Malay Archipelago, the Land of the Orang-Utan and the Bird of Paradise: A Narrative of Travel with Studies of Man and Nature.* 2 v. London, Macmillan Colonial Library.

Warneck, J.

1909   *Die Religion der Batak: Ein Paradigma für die Animistischen Religionen des Indischen Archipels.* Leipzig, J. C. Hinrichs.

Wechel, P. te

1915   "Erinnerungen aus den Ost- und West-Dusun-Ländern (Borneo)." *IAE,* XXII, 1–24, 43–58, 93–129.

Wellenstein, E. P.

1930   "Een en Ander over 'Dualistische Economie.' " *KS,* XIV, 115–134.

Wertheim, W. F.

1951–1952 "De Stad in Indonesië." *Indonesië,* V, 24–40.

Westenberg, C. J.

1892   "Aanteekeningen omtrent de Godsdienstige Begrippen der Karo-Batak." *BKI,* XLI, 208–253.

Westenenk, L. C.

1915   *De Minangkabausche Nagari.* Batavia, Papyrus.

Widjojo Nitisastro

1956   *Some Data on the Population of Djabres, a Village in Central Java.* Djakarta, Lembaga Penjelidikan Ekonomi dan Masjarakat, Universitas Indonesia.

Widjojo Nitisastro and J. E. Ismaël
1959   *The Government, Economy, and Taxes of a Central Javanese Village.* Ithaca, New York, Cornell University Modern Indonesia Project Monograph Series.

Wilken, G. A.
1873   "Het Landbezit in de Minahasa. Bijdrage tot de Kennis van het Landbezit in den Indischen Archipel." *MNZ,* XVII, 107–137.
1875   "Iets over Naamgeving en Eigennamen bij de Alfoeren van de Minahasa." *TBG,* XXII, 363–389.
1875a   "Bijdrage tot de Kennis der Alfoeren van het Eiland Boeroe." *VBG,* XXXVIII. Batavia, Bruining & Wijt.
1880   "Over de Primitieve Vormen van het Huwelijk en den Oorsprong van het Gezin." Chapters I–III. *De Indische Gids,* II, 2, 601–664, 1177–1205.
1881   "Over de Primitieve Vormen van het Huwelijk en den Oorsprong van het Gezin." Chapter IV. *De Indische Gids,* III, 2, 232–288.
1883   "Over de Verwantschap en het Huwelijks- en Erfrecht bij de Volken van het Maleische Ras." *De Indische Gids,* V, 1, 656–764.
1883a   *Over de Verwantschap en het Huwelijks- en Erfrecht bij de Volken van den Indischen Archipel.* Beschouwd uit het Oogpunt van de Nieuwere Leerstellingen op het Gebied der Maatschappelijke Ontwikkelingsgeschiedenis. Leiden, E. J. Brill.
1884   "Het Animisme bij de Volken van den Indischen Archipel." Chapters I–IV. *De Indische Gids,* VI, 1, 925–1000; 2, 19–100.
1885   "Het Animisme bij de Volken van den Indischen Archipel." Chapters V–VI. *De Indische Gids,* VII, 13–58, 191–142.
1885a   "De Besnijdenis bij de Volken van den Indischen Archipel." *BKI,* XXXIV, 165–206.
1886   "Plechtigheden en Gebruiken bij Verlovingen en Huwelijken bij de Volken van de Indischen Archipel." Chapters I–III. *BKI,* XXXV, 140–219.
1886a   "Het Tellen bij Nachten bij den Volken van het Maleisch-Polynesische Ras." *BKI,* XXXV, 378–392.
1887   "Iets over de Papoewas van de Geelvinksbaai. Opmerkingen naar Aanleiding van Uhle's 'Holz und Bambus-geraethe aus Nord West Neu Guinea.' " *BKI,* XXXVI, 605–640.
1888   "Oostersche en Westersche Rechtsbegrippen." *BKI,* XXXVII, 121–140.
1888a   "De Verbreiding van het Matriarchaat op Sumatra." *BKI,* XXXVII, 163–215.

1888b   "Iets over de Mutilatie der Tanden bij de Volken van den Indischen Archipel. Opmerkingen naar Aanleiding van Uhle's 'Ueber die Ethnologische Bedeutung der Malaiischen Zahnfeilung.' " *BKI*, XXXVII, 472–504.

1888c   "Het Pandrecht bij de Volken van den Indischen Archipel." *BKI*, XXXVII, 555–609.

1889   "De Couvade bij de Volken van den Indischen Archipel." *BKI*, XXXVIII, 250–265.

1889a   "Plechtigheden en Gebruiken bij Verlovingen en Huwelijken bij de Volken van den Indischen Archipel." Chapters IV–V. *BKI*, XXXVIII, 380–462.

1889b   "Iets over Schedelvereering bij de Volken van den Indischen Archipel." *BKI*, XXXVIII, 89–129.

1890   "Huwelijken Tusschen Bloedverwanten." *De Gids*, LIV, 2, 478–521.

1891   "Over het Huwelijks- en Erfrecht bij de Volken van Zuid-Sumatra." *BKI*, XL, 149–235.

1891a   "Verkrachting in Kinderhuwelijk." *De Verspreide Geschriften van Prof. G. A. Wilken*, I, pp. 611–628. Semarang and Soerabaja, The Hague, van Dorp.

1891b   "Eene Nieuwe Theorie over den Oorsprong der Offers." *De Gids*, LV, 3, 534–572.

1912   *De Verspreide Geschriften*. Collected by F. D. E. van Ossenbruggen. 4 v. The Hague, van Dorp.

1926   *Opstellen over Adatrecht*. Edited by F. D. E. van Ossenbruggen. Semarang, van Dorp.

Wilken, P. N.
1863   "Bijdragen tot de Kennis van de Zeden en Gewoonten der Alfoeren in de Minahassa." *MNZ*, VII, 117–264, 289–332, 371–391.

Willer, T. J.
1846   *Verzameling van Battaksche Wetten en Instellingen te Mandheling en Pertibie, Gevolgd door een Overzigt van Land en Volk in die Streken*. Batavia and The Hague, M. Nijhoff.

1849   "The Battas of Mandheling and Pertibi." *JIAEA*, III, 366–378.

1858   *Het Eiland Boeroe: Zijne Exploitatie en Halfoersche Instellingen*. Amsterdam, F. Muller.

Willinck, G. D.
1909   *Het Rechtsleven bij de Minangkabau Maleiërs*. Leiden, E. J. Brill.

Wink, P.
1924   "De Bronnen van Marsden's Adatbeschrijving van Sumatra." *BKI*, LXXX, 1–10.

Wirz, P.

1924 "Anthropologische und Ethnologische Ergebnisse der Central Neu-Guinea Expedition 1921–1922." *Nova Guinea.*

1925 *Im Herzen von Neu-Guinea. Tagebuch einer Reise ins Innere von Hollandisch Neu-Guinea.* Zurich.

1926 "Die Krankenbehandlung bei den Dajak des Siang-Landes." *TBG,* LXVI, 240–258.

1928–1929 "Het Oude Nias." *Nederlandsch-Indië Oud en Nieuw,* XIII, 163–174, 197–207.

1929 *Bei Liebenswürdigen Wilden in Neuguinea.* Stuttgart.

1929a *Nias, Die Inzel der Götzen.* Zurich, G. Füssli.

1929–1930 "Het Eiland Sabiroet en zijn Bewoners." *Nederlandsch-Indië Oud en Nieuw,* XIV, 131–139, 187–192, 209–215, 241–248, 337–348, 387–397.

1931 "Die Totemistischen und Sozialen Systeme in Holländisch Neuguinea." *TBG,* LXXI, 30–106.

1950 "Der Ersatz für die Kopfjägerei und die Trophäen-imitation. Unter besonderer Berücksichtigung der vom Verfasser auf Neuguinea und Sabirut (Mentawei) gesammelten Objekte." *Beiträge zur Gesellungs- und Völkerwissenschaft R. Thurnwald gewidmet,* pp. 411–434. Berlin, Mann.

Wouden, F. A. E. van

1935 *Sociale Structuurtypen in de Groote Oost.* Leiden, J. Ginsberg.

1956 "Locale Groepen en Dubbele Afstamming in Kodi, West Sumba." *BKI,* CXII, 204–246.

Ypes, W. K. H.

1907 "Nota Omtrent Singkel en de Pak-Pak Landen." *TBG,* XLIX, 355–642.

Zollinger, H.

1850 "Verslag van een Reis naar Bima en Soembawa, en naar Eenige Plaatsen op Celebes, Salayer, en Floris Gedurende de Maanden Mei tot December 1847." *VBG,* XXIII. Batavia, Lange.

Zwaal, J. van de

1936 *Inlandsch Gemeentewezen in Zuid-Sumatra en Javanentransmigratie.* Dissertation, Utrecht. Wageningen, H. Veenman.

Index

www.ingramcontent.com/pod-product-compliance
Lightning Source LLC
Chambersburg PA
CBHW030633270326
41929CB00007B/58